Paris, *Moi*, and the Gang

A Memoir...of Sorts

∽

Frances Gendlin

Summertime Publications
Paris • Scottsdale

Summertime Publications Inc.
7502 E. Berridge Lane, Scottsdale, AZ 85250, USA
www.summertimepublications.com
email: summertime.publications@gmail.com

Library of Congress Control Number: 2009902576
ISBN: 0-9823698-0-8
EAN13: 9780982369807

Any factual information concerning Paris was current as of January, 2009. Laws change, restaurants and shops come and go as quickly and often as the tourists, and the unexpected occurs—unexpectedly. Thus, the author and publisher bear no responsibility for any such changes, for the sometimes unhelpful service, or even the occasional bad meal. Yes—even in Paris. As the French say, "*C'est la vie!*" That's life.

Frontispiece photo by Andrea Valerio

Printed in the United States of America

To Judith and Gerry
my Freds

Note

SOMETIMES, A SIMPLE REMARK CAN RESULT in a book. For me, it was when I was sitting on the terrace of Perry's—long a favorite bar of San Franciscans—having a glass of champagne with my friend and agent Fred Hill, I freezing in the damp incoming fog, and he smoking and encouraging his dog Pancho to sit still. I remarked (not too kindly, I think now) that in Paris we could have been cozily inside with both the dreaded cigarettes and the adorable dog, and *voilà*, he suggested a new book. My real life in Paris. Paris, day by day. Although looking for a new project of one sort or another, I thought, *Hmm, this could be tricky.* But what I said was, "Yes, why not?"

So, I began to reflect on this particular middle-aged, American, twice-divorced travel writer living on her own in one of the world's great cities, obviously content in some ways but still having to keep a lifelong restlessness at bay. "You dwell too much," one of my friends sometimes tells me, and usually she's right. But this time, I kept on. In my mind I relived the previous year—in what many in my rather diverse group are convinced is the last civilized city in the world. How had that year unfolded for us all, people who are so different but who at least have a commonality of loving this American-Parisian way of life? And for me, honestly, how had my life been each day in that year when I was writing my most recent city guide—*Culture Shock! Paris*?

During the following couple of years, when I was trying to pay more attention to reality than I usually do—being a rather distracted sort—I listened to anecdotes from expat friends outside my immediate crowd, as well. And I borrowed (so to speak) some of their stories—those that had something to show. So, although most of the events herein happened in some way or another, the truth is that they didn't all happen to me or to my little gang, although they certainly could have. And I realized that it would be extremely politic not to use real names and to turn us all—cleverly, I hope—into fictionalized characters. So, whether this book finally is a guide or a memoir with a little bit of fudging thrown in or even something other, I can no longer positively say. But I'm not certain it matters, for I've come to think that life is life, no matter how it's told. It's just that Paris every day really does seem somehow to make it better, no matter the differences in the lives being led, and that is what I hope to convey in this book.

Frances Gendlin
Paris, November 2008

rue Servandoni

The Saga Unfolds

GOD KNOWS I'M NOT THE FIRST American to write about falling under the spell of Paris or about coming here to live. But sticking to fact, neither was Ernest Hemingway, who spent some time in Paris in his youth and wrote about it later, or even Gertrude Stein, who stayed and dissected Parisian life until the end of her days. Nor, despite current hagiography, were they the most famous—although so much is made of their sojourns here, of moveable feasts and lost generations and literary salons. No, honors in all these categories must go to Benjamin Franklin, bespectacled and wise, who in 1776 conquered *le tout Paris,* and whose own memoir shows him to have taken Paris to his heart as fully as its citizens took him to theirs.

Strange as it may seem, I think often of Franklin as I walk with my grocery bags and *baguette* down rue de l'Ancienne Comedie, passing Procope, the oldest café in the city, where he is known to have dined. Sometimes—if my bags are not weighing me down—I even go out of my way to pass by, just to peer in. The restaurant no longer resembles that ancient café, of course, but it amuses me as I look in to imagine where Ben might have sat, who his companions might have been, and what political deals they might have been hatching there on behalf of the newly formed United States.

Moi, I rarely eat at Procope. It primarily serves tourists now, and I find myself, these days, considering Miss Stein's words that "America is my country and Paris is my home town and it is as it has come to be." For me, as well, this might (or might not) turn out to be true. Yet, about six weeks ago, toward the end of blustery November—just before taking off on my annual trip to the States—I did take some visitors to Procope, which I save for

American history buffs or for a Sunday if my regular hangouts are closed. Or even, as was the case with this rather nervous little-traveled couple, if someone Stateside asks me to meet a relative who has arrived in Paris, and I simply cannot come up with another place that I am sure would suit. These folks—who had never been outside of America before—were the nephew and wife of my old friend Lenore in Chicago, where I had long lived. I was happy to oblige her, but she now owes me a favor, big time.

Yet, I can't say that I minded Procope that night. I ordered a dozen large oysters, and feeling greedy, later I downed a half-dozen more. The couple, though, tittering at the thought of garlicky snails or even *foie gras*, both took the *coq au vin*, ignoring my caution that it really would be cock not chicken, as it would be at home. Try the duck breast and order it *rosé* (rare inside), I suggested. *Magret de canard* is so good. *Mais non*, so I just shrugged and smiled (weakly) when later they seemed to flinch. What else could I do? But while we were eating and drinking a wine the *serveur* suggested, I trotted out some Franklin stories, and we were all generally content.

When he arrived in Paris that fateful year, Franklin's fame had preceded him across the Atlantic. He was compared to Socrates and Newton, and cheered by the people as he walked through the streets. Hardly the simple Poor Richard character he had created, Franklin used his wits and even that endearing supposed simplicity to his advantage. Thus, comporting himself carefully, he succeeded in the mission given to him by the Continental Congress—to forge an alliance with France against George III. It wasn't that Louis XVI favored revolution, as the events in France a decade later fatally proved. He just hated the English and King George.

What surprised my captive audience more than the strongly flavored *coq* was that Franklin—whose manly appetites were also quite well known—found some pleasant diversions here.

Paris was *très sophistiquée*, even then. To the dismay of John
Adams, also on the American delegation—and who wrote of
Franklin's *"discipation"*—Franklin was enjoying himself, especially
at fashionable Parisian *soirées*. "Somebody, it seems," he wrote to
his step-niece, "gave out that I lov'd Ladies; and then every body
presented me their Ladies (or the Ladies presented themselves)
to be *embrac'd*, that is, to have their Necks kiss'd.... 'Tis a delightful
People to live with."

My companions seemed impressed by this lore, which gratified
me, I must admit. "How do you know all this about Paris, Fran?"
they asked—apparently not having done any advance homework
about me with Lenore. I am a travel writer, after all. This means,
to be blunt, that after decades of "day jobs" in publishing offices
here and there, I have finally found a way to get paid for doing what
suits me best: landing myself temporarily in different cultures and
pondering about peripatetic lives (including my own, I suppose).
It also means reading everything in sight, keeping meticulous
records and checking off lists, talking to everyone around, and
exploring neighborhood after neighborhood on foot, figuring
them out. Yes, this suits me just fine.

But what should I have told those young visitors as I curved
my knife around the rim of the oyster shell, loosening the little
lovely and slipping it into my mouth? That my editors had asked
me to prepare a completely new guide to living in Paris? And that
I was going to spend a year once again focusing on Paris life? I
could have left it at that, and probably should have. But it's hard
for me to let things go. To keep myself from spilling out the events
that brought me here. Not to impose with what it is about us
both—this city and me—that seems to be leading me to attempt
a steady life in one place, when I have never succeeded in this
before.

"Oh, I just read everything I can about Americans here," I
started out, managing then to contain myself somewhat. And it

was essentially true. For in my fascination with this particular city's odd magnetism, how it seems to pull people in and then hold on, I think of others over the centuries—and not just Miss Gertrude—who have also been drawn in. But there's more.

Many of the details I know about Americans in Paris are owing to my closest friend, Caroline, whom I met through a historian friend in New York, just after moving here. Caroline, a historian herself, is researching her own book about Americans who had lived in Paris, and she often tells me what she has learned. Occasionally she even calls while I'm back in the States on my regular Christmastime visit to tell me something delicious she has just unearthed (figuratively, of course). I love it. Sometimes I think that—although Caroline is gray of hair, stout of frame, and wears a paisley kerchief, not a veil—she is Scheherazade, destined to keep me hooked for 1001 nights. For her part, Caroline is pleased to have someone to reflect on what life was like then in Paris, whenever "then" happened to be. Yet, as much as we also find Paris delightful, we know that no city is the same as it was two hundred years ago, either in aspect or attitude. Paris today is not the Paris that Franklin knew.

Nor, in fact, is Paris today the city of La Stein or Hem. Although their legends soldier on, Stein arrived more than a century ago— only two years after Queen Victoria died—and Hemingway not long after: just after the Great War, before ballpoint pens, FM radios, Band-Aids, and even beer in cans. And when they came, they came…by ship. So, it is our Paris today, much different than theirs yet in some ways the same, that Caroline and I relish comparing—two middle-aged expats straddling the millennia, Americans who may be different but in some ways much the same as they.

Frankly, as I told Caroline when we first met, my saga—such as it is—had never included any artsy dream of living in Paris. "Don't become too attached to place," the writer Saul Bellow once instructed me (firmly). We lived on the same Chicago street at the time. His comment to a neighbor, much younger than he, was as much a caution for himself, I think now, while walking together and I was griping to him about the relentless wind. But was he right? If I couldn't use place as an anchor, what would it take to feel—once and for all—that I belonged? What would stop that yearning for something I couldn't even identify back then? And I wondered, in a burst of the inconsistency that has accompanied me all my life, where would I look? One had to start somewhere. And clearly, for me, the answer was Rome. I had long wanted to go to Rome. And when I did get there, Rome stole my heart.

It was not difficult when I was just thirty to become infatuated with Rome. Uncertainties of a failing marriage and in the future raising two children on my own could be postponed. That time I first trod the ground of the Caesars, it was like running away from home, and in the Seventies that was just so daring. When I returned, Lenore and others of the wives in that Chicago neighborhood quietly asked me how I had found such courage. But I had needed to get my bearings, and how better, I asked myself, than to get a passport, hire a babysitter, stock the pantry, and inform my husband that I was going to Rome for ten days. Alone.

"Wives don't vacation without their husbands," he said, with some truth. "Women's lib" was just coming in. (And I was on my way out.) But I had an excuse. I had been studying Italian for years.

A few days later I was free. I was overcome: by the brilliant Mediterranean sky, by pasta served under white cloth umbrellas at outdoor cafés, by cobblestone streets, and by the color of ochre, which I had never noticed before. I was in love: with ancient history coexisting with modern life, and with a people who embodied the best of both, or so I thought. With freedom and adventure, although at the time I wasn't aware of having become so infected. And so, misunderstanding myself and the point of it all, I vowed that one day I would live in Rome.

One thing I didn't tell Lenore's nephew at dinner, no matter how much the wine might have been loosening my tongue, was what has prompted me to write about life in Paris, instead of Rome—for sagas start at a point and tend to evolve. It was that the one thing I seem not to have dwelled on when young was about getting older and being on one's own. I had never even thought about survival, and then, one day, suddenly, the question of how best to spend the rest of my life popped up. (And now I can't remember thinking about anything else.) How much time did I have left to make good on those old promises? What about freedom and adventure, after all?   Just what could I still do? And where?

Actually, my life had never been ho-hum. In the later decades of a publishing career—after my daughter and son had gone on to their adult lives—I had decamped on my own several times for some job that beckoned: editor of this, director of that. With them came the exquisite moments, unexpected, unrehearsed. Dancing with a Banana Republic guerilla (cute, if a tad serious) at an international meeting of publishers. Being kissed by a bigwig-ski in the KGB (an evil guy, I was later informed, but an okay kisser) while on an American delegation talking with Soviet publishers. Falling head over heels for a European cabinet minister at an international meeting—until I learned he was known for head-over-heeling women all the time. Or getting my Secret Service clearance so I could fly on planes and interview presidential hopefuls (all of whom lost). Such interludes touched my soul, like once on a summery night in Stockholm when I boarded a tiny plane with other American journalists and flew to Lapland, the land of the midnight sun, saw daylight and reindeer at three o'clock in the morning, and then sleepily flew right back.

And although I had been single from about the moment the sexual revolution came in until the day that AIDS put an end to all that, I was rarely alone. Some relationships stayed awhile, but others came and went in the blink of an eye. "Do men ever tell you that you intimidate them?" a few asked on the first and last date, and I would realize that I had already overstepped the bounds. (But what's so good about small talk?) And, finally, a second marriage, which didn't last near as long as had been hoped. Yet, memory is peppered with moments grasped, and the more they occurred—or the more I brought them about—the less I could do without. "Calm down, kid, you're just restless," Bellow also cautioned me (again firmly) on one of those walks. "The cutoff date for all this is when you get to be thirty-five."

But having reached an age that well exceeded that cutoff date, where was I? It was time to take stock. This I do quite well, which is not to say I learn from experience. And this is what I came to: As a mother of grown-up children—one married, one not—I wasn't needed very often, although email and the phone kept us in close touch. I had given up my jobs in publishing to open an editorial business of my own—rewarding but with no promise of anything new. I noticed that I was beginning to talk about the weather a lot, a sure sign of something I didn't want to face. I had put on more weight than I'd taken off, although at that moment I was on an encouraging downswing. And like most of my single female friends, I was eating more lunches out and reading more books at home in the evening than I cared to admit. Life the next week, easy as it might be, would likely be no different from any other. And that last fact, impatient and restless as I still was, made me crabbier than I could stand. Sometimes, I looked at a line by the poet Yeats taped above my computer screen: *Too long a sacrifice can make a stone of the heart.* So, I startled myself and everyone else by overturning it all to make good on that old vow, figuring that, surely, the world needed another guide to Rome. Fortunately, a publisher agreed.

Rome in the early Nineties seemed just the same: the warm, infinite sky, the medieval streets, the pasta at outdoor cafés, the pastels, past and present side by side. And there I was, once again. "How wonderful," I said aloud, stowing suitcases under the bed in my fifth-floor walkup with the only partially obstructed view of the Coliseum. *How splendid*, I thought while plugging in my computer and arranging my documents (neatly) on the desk. *It's exactly as I remember it.* I could feel love coming on once again. And I was almost right. In essence, Rome then was much the same as it had been two decades before. The problem was that I was not.

Not old by any stretch, no longer could I tell myself I was in extremely late youth. I remembered an Italian neighbor in Chicago kissing his fingers in delicious appreciation of me years before, exclaiming "*Che bella!* A woman of forty!" But suddenly on the other side of fifty, I was still above medium height, not overweight but knowing that eternal vigilance was my fate, given my small-boned frame. Covering the few grey strands in my rather mousy light-brown hair, when it was streaked I looked better in the pastels of spring, for they brought out the blue in my eyes. But when I got too lazy to go to the salon, I reverted to winter colors of black, red, and white. But what else had changed by the time I got to Rome? Just me, altogether, I suppose.

After a short time I tired of waiting by ancient ruins for a bus that seemed never to come. I got frustrated that shops closed in the afternoon, when I had worked all morning and was ready to roll. I wanted pharmacies to be open on Sunday and restrooms to be, well, somewhere in the vicinity of clean. I wanted peanut butter and Marshmallow Fluff sandwiches from time to time. And I wanted my American friends not to bitch endlessly about life in Rome.

What I found was that the sensible low-heeled loafers I now wore were solidly cemented into middle age. Cranky middle age, even in Rome. I wanted people being interviewed to greet me in the realm of "on time." I wanted electricity during rainstorms. But perhaps most of all, I did not want to learn about the wives of all those delectable men who eyed me and said they were available for anything I wished. Was that too much to ask?

This is not to say that Rome wasn't satisfying the two years I maneuvered the cobblestones, working on my book, looking around, talking it up, wondering if this could be "it." After all, the pasta was still delicious, the sky still vivid, and the flirtatious men—married or not—kept my confidence burner on high. And later, if infatuation had diminished, I realized—even knowing it was inevitably to end—that Rome and I could still be friends. So, when my publisher suggested a book about Paris, I took my suitcases out from under the bed.

In just a few blocks of Paris' 6th *arrondissement* where I next perched myself to write about living in Paris and then—surprising even to me—stayed on for the following book, as well, there are hundreds of shops that stay open all day. *"C'est normal,"* the French would say, for the area is known for its hordes of tourists wandering about, carrying their city maps and tissue-stuffed shopping bags. These tourists also hog the tables at the cafés on boulevard St-Germain-des-Prés—people-watching and perhaps even hoping for inspiration from the aura of Jean-Paul Sartre or Simone de Beauvoir, who are still known as the neighborhood's most famous *habitués.*

But hundreds of Americans also live here in this friendly neighborhood, this *quartier*, co-existing peaceably with our Parisian neighbors. We frequent the post office, the markets and supermarkets, the pharmacies—some even on Sunday—the stationery stores, and others that cater to a residential population. I suppose that if we are identifiable at all, it is that we look like locals—although probably not to those French neighbors—carrying our grocery bags, moving with a sense of purpose as we hurry about. Yet, sometimes, tourists stop us and ask for directions, or perhaps we ask someone peering uneasily at a city map if we might help. First, they are surprised that we are American, then that we know our way around. This makes me feel rather smug, I'm sorry to say. "Yes, I'm American, but I live here," I respond, acting as though it were the most normal thing in the world. And as though this was forever for me, although I am never so sure of forever as others might think. And I ask them where they're from and wish them a good time. Caroline teases me about my chatting with those English-speakers on the street on the flimsiest of pretexts. I prefer to call it research.

Even the Chicagoans last fall, who were picking at their *coq*, said with some wistfulness, I think, "You're so lucky to live here." So, I smiled and said something true but not very deep. "Oh yes, it's totally great," is what came out. But what I was thinking was *Luck? What does luck have to do with it?* But I didn't say that, for I did know what they really meant. Wine has that mellowing effect on me. Champagne makes me giggle.

But did they stop there? Did they let it go? No, questions kept coming about my daily life, what I do with my days, and whether I have friends. And again, understanding that they were both curious and slightly envious, I answered as best as I could without snapping, *How could you have life without friends?* Or, *I'm a travel writer. Get it?* I mean, I might have been impatient at how clueless they were, but wistfulness is something I well know.

Yet, in addition to tourists, I also run into my real American friends on the street, and if so, it usually becomes an occasion to pause for more than those three minutes at some nearby café to hash over events, even if we've seen each other only a day or two before. Some of my friends have lived here full time for decades; some, like Jack and Jennifer, come every summer. These two are younger, and others are older, but age doesn't matter here. I've met my friends in various ways, as one does people anywhere.

Of course, we all have our particular reasons for having come to Paris and others, perhaps, for staying, different as they might be, although being entranced by Paris seems to be the common thread. By now I know the sagas of everyone in my group.

This is the gang. Findlay the charming old curmudgeon, who with his wife, Alice, came sixty years ago to work for the Reconstruction of Europe and who never looked back. My professorish buddy Caroline, who is researching her book. Margot the well-known sculptor—moody and sometimes irascible but always with something to say—who's so in demand we only see her in spurts. Edie, who came from Sacramento to study French cuisine after graduating from college some twenty years ago and then opened her own cooking school. Richard the wealthy early-widower, who about three years ago decided to start over and has, or sort of. Sandra the pianist, who has remained in Paris (so far) since divorcing my old publishing colleague Jean-Pierre, and who—aside from her teenagers—is obsessed with her ratty little dog. So very French. (J-P himself, my best French friend.) Paul and Klaus the settled gay couple, both formerly in the ballet world, whom I have known since I was a teenager in Chicago, elderly gentlemen who will stay here until they die. Ida of the Foreign Service, who doesn't give me the time of day. *Et moi*, here simply because, whatever it's doing, Paris is managing to keep me from having to push on.

What surprised me most when first meeting these *américains* was that their daily lives seemed almost ordinary. Yet, after a time, I realized that they weren't, that they were every day rich. Without exception and in their own different styles, they were all taking advantage of what *la ville lumière* put forth. No matter how they approached it—and no lives were similar—they were living *la belle vie,* American style. *Quelle surprise.* A life that was the same but different? This must, certainly, finally, be the answer I was searching for, I was sure. And so, just at that point being done with Rome—its pastas, its sky, and its men—I picked myself up to give Paris a serious try.

So, at least right now, the daily ponderings reflect a different aspect of the saga. Do I have all the right documents so the French won't kick me out? (And can I find them?) How guilty should I feel about visiting my kids in the States so rarely? (They haven't complained. What does this mean?) If prodded, could the adorable, silver-haired *restaurateur* over in rue Guisarde a few streets away talk about anything other than *cassoulet?* (I'm once again ready for some masculine company. Could he be it?) Will I ever write that "one true sentence" that Hemingway said should be the goal of every writer? (And if so, will it make me big bucks?) Can I avoid making an ass of my American self in front of the French today? And again, just what about *monsieur Cassoulet?*

So, home it is, in a way that sometimes meets that lifelong yearning. But it's not just plain, take-it-for-granted home, for Paris is never plain in any sense, which even Lenore's nephew, I think, at least did have some inkling of. Only a clod would not be conscious of loving one thing or two things about this city on any given day of the year. "Oh God…I'll never leave Paris again, I promise, if you'll let me just get there this once more," Katherine Anne Porter wrote. And even Findlay the curmudgeon says that he feels the same about Paris as the day he arrived some sixty years ago.

So, I'm with Findlay on this, and perhaps with Porter, too, although she does seem rather extreme, if you ask me. Yet, years ago, I also came across the words of Oliver Wendell Holmes, that "Good Americans, when they die, go to Paris." And given my nature and my history and all things considered, I decided not to wait that long.

Daily Life Close Up

S O, HERE, FOR THOSE TOURISTS WHO ask, is the truth about my life in Paris. The first part of the day may seem little different than it would be anywhere else—the practically ordinary part. I get up, do a few rather lackadaisical stretches while watching the weather forecast on TV, put on my jeans, and make a cup of Twining's Earl Grey tea. I take the *International Herald Tribune* from my mailbox, glance at the headlines, and put it aside for bedtime. Then I check the email. I look for messages from my kids, knowing that if there are none it's because they're busy, with no crises to report. Others might be from my publisher, London cousins, or Stateside family and friends. And there are usually notices of meetings of Democrats Abroad or the book club, reminders of readings at the English-language bookshops or American Library, and even events at the American synagogue, which, being officially optimistic, kindly keeps me on its list. The special fares of American Airlines sometimes give me a *frisson* of longing, but they get deleted along with the jokes.

When I have a work project, such as the new one for this coming year, I work for several hours at my desk, trying to unearth something no other guidebook has, writing up my comments about some place that I (desperately) hope I'm the first to find. Crossing out others that have gone into the ether—and that I must be the last to know. I'm totally absorbed, making notes and creating lists of points to verify. Adding sites to my Internet "favorites" list. I am, however, interrupted from time to time by the ringing of the phone. Everyone knows I'm at home in the morning, so that's when the phone most rings. I do my best to keep calls short. *Allô?* I answer quickly, giving my best French accent a try. Some people

answer *Allô-oui?* but I always think they're asking "Halloween?" so
I just say *allô* and leave it at that. That's French enough.

With plans for the afternoon set, I toss down an Oreo or
two, put my sunglasses on, and throw a bottle of Evian in my
purse along with my little lined notebook. And thus organized
I head out into (ta-dah!) Paris, France. Now this is the not-so-
ordinary part. First in my mind is to check out some area where
something Parisianly new is going on: a shopping *passage* that's
been beautifully restored, a formerly shabby *quartier* that is now
trendier than thou, a museum that has gloriously reopened after
years of painstaking restoration. Often I'll stop in afterward at a
café that is trying to make it by serving only oysters (and wine), or
another where one of those sidewalk tourists might have gushed
that they just found the best *saumon fumé.* I taste and sample, make
notes, take business cards, and I case out those neighborhoods,
none of which—no matter what will eventually be written—
measures up to my own.

But even without a work trek, there's always something
going on to take in close to home. I cruise the *marché* if I'm out
of fruit, seeing what's colorfully in season—or has disappeared
before I thought to buy more. I notice people browsing the shop
windows and, of course not wanting to miss anything they might
have come upon, do likewise. I might try to drag Caroline to a
film we've been waiting for, and then we'll splurge on a glass of
champagne at one of our cafés, although lately we've switched to
the cheaper Badoit. Or late mornings I might take the bus over
to the American Library to pick up some book I've put on hold.
And if I have cleverly made sure to run into my old pals Klaus
and Paul there, they always suggest lunching and then that I join
them—stopping in afterward at a gallery or walking through a
park that's suddenly in bloom. If Sandy—the canniest shopper
around—is available (between men), we might search rue de
Rennes (cheap) or rue St-Honoré (not) for *promotions*, exulting

when we've snapped up a bargain. I go to the *gymnase* less often than I should, and I don't swim enough, but that's nothing new.

And in the evenings—and this is a fact—I am rarely home with books and my discontent. Instead, I am most likely dining in a bistro with Caroline or widower Richard or visitors from the States, going to a reading, some cultural event or meeting or a *cocktail*, attending with Edie a free concert in an ancient church or something offbeat she has chanced on in a public square, or even (having spruced myself up a bit) just nonchalantly passing by the door of the silver-haired *restaurateur*, in order to chat him up before his tables get too full.

So, life has become *la vie*. Yet, some mornings I wake up bursting out of my skin with the anticipation of what I'll come across in Paris that day. For a person who has always been on the lookout, I haven't yet found anyplace better to be.

It is said that every generation discovers Paris anew, and perhaps it's true. If, knowing each other so well by now, my friends and I no longer talk about our reasons for having chosen Paris, we do talk a great deal (incessantly) about the city, for its fascination is always present in our minds. I refuse to consider this as taking stock, because—with the excuse of the new writing assignment soon officially to start—this is what I do. We try to come up with just what it is about Paris, possibly just one overall thing among the many, that has us hooked. And for each of us it is different, and that is why life here—at least so far—has not yet gotten in my way.

Gertrude Stein, who—even according to her own contemporaries—explained on and on, opens her book *Paris France* by saying: "Paris, France is exciting and peaceful." While this, at least in my opinion, may not be the best sentence ever written, it is certainly true as far as it goes. But even Miss S. Herself had no more of an answer to the question "why" than any of us today—and if she came close, it was too late for her.

"What is the answer?" the dying Gertrude is rumored to have asked her companion Alice B. Toklas (who may have started the rumor herself). But the weeping Miss A.B.T. couldn't respond.

"Then, what is the question?" Miss Stein the self-styled genius asked, perhaps her last words. (That genius who said, "Think of the Bible and Homer, think of Shakespeare and think of me.") But let's be fair. I mean, as I begin to plot out a new guide to living here, maybe I should be looking for the right questions and not answers, which have always eluded me, to say the least. And the first one, I suppose, would be where to start.

"My life really doesn't have much to do with the Louvre or boat rides on the Seine," I went on, while eating my oysters at Procope on that chilly night, "although it is comforting that they are here at the ready." But what I didn't say (and in my life, there have always been things I didn't say and later wished I had) is that in Paris whatever I want on any given day, well, it could be waiting somewhere out there for me to find. Or that once in a while, I might have a fleeting, grateful moment of being a step ahead of the day before.

This I do know, though, that even if I may still be on the prowl for that particular sense of belonging that has always confounded me—in Paris I seem to be more myself than ever, for better or for worse. Oh, France has its problems, to be sure, but I am an American here, and those problems are not really mine. Overall, I'm not so cranky anymore.

Certainly, not every day is life in the Elysian Fields, despite the famous Champs-Elysées that bears that name. But mostly, my friends and I remark on the usual frustrations of city life: dog stuff on the sidewalk, buses that are canceled for yet another *manifestation* (protest marches, often referred to as *les manifs*), the mistaken weather forecasts given by Météo France that make me want to march in protest myself or, being American, to sue. Or occasionally we might be ill treated by someone, perhaps a *fonctionaire* who could have given an inch on something important to us but didn't. Since this kind of thing happens anywhere, we are generally more amused than annoyed—usually after the fact. But here, instead of complaining we laugh, often at ourselves for having gotten it all wrong, as my old friend Paul says, whatever it was, on a particular day. And certainly, life itself brings its moments to whine about, no matter where one chooses to be, although here those moments are rarely routine.

I've known Paul and Klaus since I was a teenager in Chicago, introduced by my mother's cousin, a rather major-minor composer, I think. He had taken me to see Paul conduct the ballet and then for a late supper at Klaus and Paul's North Side apartment. Klaus made spaghetti and Paul showed me how to twirl it properly with my fork (which raised me a notch in Roman eyes later on, I'm happy to say). Somehow, they took to me, becoming something closer to family than friends. That they still sometimes take an avuncular tone with me, I find touching and sweet. Coincidence or not, I seem to have followed after them to Rome—where they lived for a while—and then to Paris. It looks like they're here for good, although occasionally we joke about "where we're going next."

Once, on an occasion when I had uneasily brought up the question of Paris and permanence, Paul used his fingers to tick off a list. "Let's work on why our friends, no matter their particularities, are so satisfied here," he said. "One. Partly it's because they're open to everything new, and there's something to notice about the city every day. Two. They've adapted to the Parisian pace. Three. They understand, certainly on most days, that the French do things the French way, not theirs, and they don't blame anyone else for life's difficulties."

"That's four," Klaus interrupted. "Paul, you've combined three and four."

"Right you are," Paul said, wagging all four fingers at Klaus. "So, last and without a number. Perhaps most important is that I think they're all people who can learn something when differing cultural assumptions collide head on."

"As they *soooo* often do," Klaus intoned and rolled his eyes. Paul and I burst out laughing, amused as much by Klaus's tone of voice as by the truth of what he was saying. Klaus has a way of saying things like no one else. But Paul has a way of saying things, too, and I know he's usually right.

In terms of language, not all Anglophones here speak French well, but just about everyone can order in a restaurant, buy toothpaste at the *pharmacie*, and renew the monthly pass for the *métro*. Richard, the widower from California, however, can barely ask at the *marché* if the melons are ripe. But so what; he doesn't care if he ever says a word in French. Edie, on the other hand, speaks so fluently that the suppliers to her cooking school assume she is French, although probably from the south, or the north, or *en tout cas*, not from here. Some of us who speak decent Foreign French do indeed have strong American accents, and I have to admit it is slightly bothersome when the butcher responds to my questions in English. "*Non,* meesis, the cheeken he is feenneesh-ed," believe me, is not better than my French.

But as Americans, of course, we speak English. In our café ramblings, we talk about films, a new bistro that's *de mourir* (to die for), a museum exhibit that's opened, about our families Stateside (with snapshots, sometimes), or a book we're ready to pass on. These days, of course, we harp on American politics (and I hope not to say more about that). But Findlay is rooted in the old days, Caroline tells me history, Richard talks about wine and finance, and Edie waxes on about *haricots verts* or *sauce béchamel*. Sandy talks about French music or the kids or her hound, and occasionally about some man she is seeing (which to me is like the rich flaunting their wealth before the poor). And I? Whatever I am being intense about on a particular day, my friends indulge me.

For the most part they're used to me, despite Caroline's always patient admonitions that I "dwell" too much.

Like the French, though, none of us talk much about money, at least we didn't use to. Now we do, though, since inflation is high and the dollar has plunged, and everything in euros is costing *américains* more, at least those of us whose income comes from the States. (This, unfortunately, counts as talking about politics.) But it looks to me that, although none of our group lives high on the hog anymore—not even Richard, who could if he were so inclined—we're all, at least for the moment, making do. Caroline is ever more careful about her *centimes*, relying mostly on a pension from her old school. And Paul and Klaus, giving a nod to all the royalty in exile here by calling themselves the "two oldest queens in Paris," while in no sense poor, have cleverly constructed for themselves a life rich in culture and their idea of gastronomy—which doesn't always meld with mine—while keeping within their budget, sometimes to Klaus's dismay. *Moi?* I brought enough dollars over a few years ago so that it isn't worrisome yet—although the time is fast coming. But it wouldn't really matter much anyway, since I've never made a right decision about men or money in my life.

In the past, some Americans here were truly on the edge, such as Henry Miller, who cadged drinks and food, waiting for checks to arrive from his wife at home, all the while being consoled by Anaïs Nin. But qualifications for residence these days are fairly restrictive, and in fact, the French government does have a dilemma it must deal with regarding just whom it lets in and for how long. So, when I start my book in January, I must be sure to write this clearly right away: No one should expect to come today (legally) to hide out in a musty garret and exist on forty euros a day, eating stale *baguettes* and drinking cheap wine, while changing the course of philosophy.

Few people write like Henry Miller, of course, but most *américains* here, like people anywhere, have a daily occupation. Some, like Caroline and me, research and write as we have always done. This includes Findlay, who seems to have been writing magazine articles about Paris "in the old days" for probably fifty years. Artists like Margot will wield their chisels and brushes until they crack, and others may indulge some hobby, like Richard, whose passion, aside from increasing his wealth, is French wine. Part-timers like Jack and Jennifer, who come from New York every summer, may work on their normal projects, take a cooking course like Edie's, study French, or even volunteer at one of the English-language churches in order to meet people here.

At the American synagogue, the few times I've stirred myself to go, it seems that almost always it is the husband who is French and the wife American. Sometimes, she works, too, but often, as Sandra did when she married my publishing friend Jean-Pierre and gave up dreams of Carnegie Hall, she has given up her own career. Not all these marriages last, cultural differences being what they are. Other problems, naturally, are those of families anywhere, as I can attest with Sandy and J-P's divorce, knowing all about the (misguided) beginning and being in at the (tedious) end. Yet their children—teenagers Henriette and Victor—are totally bilingual, and being French, they seem better educated and more polite than their counterparts in America.

Hemingway, too, was here with a young family (which he ditched after a while), and his attempts to explain Paris go along these lines: "It was a fine place to be quite young in and it is a necessary part of a man's education. We all loved it once and we lie if we say we didn't. But she is like a mistress who does not grow old and she has other lovers now. She was old to start with but we did not know it then. We thought she was just older than we were, and that was attractive then. So, when we did not love her any more we held it against her. But that was wrong because she is always the same age and she always has new lovers."

Well, that was fine for Hemingway. But I look at my friends and think they wouldn't agree. And most of them are no longer exactly young. In fact, Findlay and Alice are well into the *troisième age*, although you might not know it from the lives they lead. When I asked Alice about it, she just said, "Paris keeps us on our toes, corns and all. What more could we want?"

It took me some time to meet people in Paris, as it would in any large city. I didn't find them standing around, looking lost. Being me, I never gave up. For me, *c'est normal,* as the French keep saying when remarking on something not normal at all—for no one (in their right mind) would call me shy. I interviewed people for the book I was working on then. I joined groups. I bought a *maillot de bain* that claimed to minimize my hips, and did water aerobics with the neighborhood women in the public pool. I even ventured to the American synagogue, and with my new friend Caroline to the American Church (where Jack and Jenny are now regulars). But Klaus and Paul I already knew, as well as Sandy through J-P. As to the rest, I met them through the others. And *voilà,* here I seem to be.

As to the French, there's no Welcome Wagon here. Yet with some effort and more luck, I've made several French friends and a dozen acquaintances, who may—or may not—sometime in my lifetime move up. Caroline and I shake our heads at newspaper articles that gripe about an offensive experience some American had with a Parisian, always offered as an example of conveying something deep about the French. Certainly, times have changed since Thomas Jefferson lived here (just after Ben) and wrote that, "The French seem to love [America] more than they do any other nation on earth…" but we do not, on a daily level, see any particular signs of anti-Americanism, also *très compliqué*. And that chicken guy who speaks to me in what he thinks is English is really being friendly, that's clear. And I do like it that he waves to me as I pass by his shop. And he likes it that I buy his "cheekens," I'm sure.

Ben Franklin, tired and beset by problems common then to being in one's eighties, including gout and kidney stones, went back to America, despite pleas of his Parisian friends to remain. He was tired and just wanted to be home. Findlay and Alice refuse to think about it, for Paris for them *is* home. "Old age is a moveable target," Findlay often insists gruffly but then adds with a small smile, "You only hit it when something goes wrong."

"I'm sure Franklin thought twice before going back," Caroline said when we were having a *bon voyage* drink, before I left for my winter visit to the States. We were sitting upstairs at the Café de la Mairie with our glasses of champagne. "Given how much the ladies here loved him. And what about Paris herself being a woman, too, sophisticated, still sensual? Ready to enjoy experiences as they come along?"

"Like us," I giggled (the champagne having its effect), but then turned a little serious. "You know, I think I'm about ready to rack up another one. I can feel it coming on. Maybe when I get back from New York."

Caroline nodded and said as she sometimes does, "Yes, I can see that." But she didn't explain what she meant, and I didn't ask. I mean, why ask if you don't want to hear the answer?

Caroline, who exudes contentment with her life, made her decision to stay some years back and has obtained the ten-year *carte de résident*, to which I am not yet entitled. But her calm approach to life rubs off on me (or so I hope). At least right now, I can't imagine feeling so adventurous and comfortable at the same time anywhere else, which I guess (reluctantly) is what La Gertrude must have meant, *n'est-ce pas*? And my apartment does come with a six-year lease.

So, later as we stood up to leave—having dissected my dinner with the Chicagoans and gone over, for the third time, the itinerary for my trip, and having reminded Caroline of my American cell phone number—I realized how much I couldn't wait to get away, anticipating the entire trip. Seeing my daughter in Toronto and my son's new house, assuring my editor (over our regular sushi lunch) that, of course, every deadline would be met, hearing publishing gossip from friends in New York, and eating totally American barbeque ribs that taste like they should, with tangy sauce that drips down your arm. But at the same time, I was already excited about coming back to Paris, starting my new book, being back with the gang, and that delicious moment in January of arriving in this improbably welcoming city that had been waiting for my return.

"So much for living in the moment," Caroline said with a laugh when I told her. "But I always can't wait to get back, too."

That life can be so good here for so many people of differing ages, backgrounds, and expectations totally belies those old myths about Paris as being solely for romance or for the young. These are just as misguided as the ideas about "lovely" April in Paris when, in my opinion, it is usually cold in April and it seems always to rain. Yet I know that, even when the weather is *mauvais* and I will be in some far neighborhood with my notepad and city map, I will just have to look out from under my sodden umbrella to take in the city's message. Paris seems to offer something, something not always definable, that beckons on any day of the year and in any season. Hemingway must surely have thought so, too, for in *The Sun Also Rises* his character Brett Ashley expresses her opinion: "I was a fool to go away," she said. "One's an ass to leave Paris." This always gives me pause for thought.

January in the Rain

A T LEAST HOPING TO BE HONEST about this real-life year, I have to come clean: a friend I haven't mentioned is Napoleon, yet it was he who first took me in hand in Paris. I hardly knew anyone then, and someone had to do it. So, weary as I am on this first day of the rest of my life, after the overnight flight back from New York, and bulky as I feel with a coat, purse, and carry-on bag crammed into the back of an overheated cab on the way home from the airport, I can still feel only gratitude. *Merci bien, Monsieur N.* for helping me to get my bearings here. It isn't that I'm particularly attracted to short tough guys (at least I don't think so), but I'm sure it was the little emperor himself who, on some other cloudy morning, played around with his city, dividing it into numbered *arrondissements,* of which now there are twenty. Thus, since his catafalque at golden-domed Les Invalides is in the 7th and Paris is number 75 in the *départements*, if I wanted to thank him again, I'd send my note to 75007. Actually, it would help pass the time if I could send him an email on my Blackberry from the cab, as we crawl on this drab January morning, waiting for the inbound rush-hour traffic clog to give an inch. Instead, I just email Caroline to tell her that I'm in the cab on my way home.

Immediately, I get a response. "Welcome home, sweetie. Rain today." Well, at least I am forewarned. For the moment, though, I just give myself over to the wait and continue—as I had been doing those last weeks in the States—to let thoughts about Paris just roll in. I'm so ready to begin my new book, to begin the research, to know that taking stock about life here has an official purpose, at least for one year. I've got another year to try and get it right, whatever it is.

Napoleon and his seductive Josephine started married life in her house in rue Chantereine, which shortly became rue de la Victoire, now in the 9th *arrondissement*. (*Moi?* I would not have let my dog bite him on our wedding night, but that's another story.) Changes of street names are rare, but any sidewalk may suddenly bear a pole topped by a blue plaque, such as the one in the 6th that created Place Sartre-Beauvoir. If I am right, this existential honor stretches along the crosswalk from Place St-Germain-des-Prés to the traffic island where the boulevard and rue de Rennes meet. *Ne me fais pas rire*. Don't make me laugh. What is now Place de la Concorde was, for a while, Place de la Révolution, sporting a much-used guillotine. *La veuve*, the guillotine was called, for it made widows of so many wives.

When Napoleon became first consul, he and Josephine moved to the Left Bank, south of the Seine, into the Palais du Luxembourg, now the French Sénat. And another reason he comes to mind today is that the charming Luxembourg Gardens are just across rue de Vaugirard from my apartment in rue Servandoni, and I think of them as my backyard. In clement weather I often take a book and join the Parisians who sit craning their necks toward the sun, claiming for myself one of the ubiquitous green metal chairs and pursing my lips at people who have stolen a second one for their feet. In any case, I like stories about *Monsieur N.,* perhaps because I am someone who understands about moving a lot and even about exile, I sometimes think. Or perhaps I just like men who, at least for a time, command their own continent.

I've never lived across the street from a palace before, and it tickles me no end that I now do. What I know, so far: it was built four hundred years ago by Marie de Médicis, wife to Henri IV. Then, during the Revolution, it became a prison, and it was here that Thomas Paine—who in his revolutionary zeal had become a French citizen and a member of the *Convention*—almost lost his head. He had voted to spare the life of Louis XVI, saying, "It is not by the death of one king that you rid yourself of all kings." Robespierre said *non!* and soon *Peine, Amériquain* seemed for a time on his way to *la veuve*.

As I am wiping with my glove the steamed-up window of the cab, the Luxembourg comes into view. I am startled to see clearly the back of a jogger who is entering the large open gate. His stance reminds me of a man I once knew (rather well) when I was working in San Francisco. One of those computer geniuses that made it big on an idea and then sold it for *beaucoup* bucks just before that idea became passé, he and I—well, rack him up as one of those brief notches on my belt. It wasn't just the huge gold ring he wore, with the family crest. On what I already knew would be our last dinner together, he waved his hand right in front of my face.

"My family can be traced back to 1215," he said, pleased with himself.

"Twelve fifteen?" I said sweetly, wishing I had brought *Cosmo* with its six-step plan for spotting Mr. Right. "That's pretty close to noon." I ran into him a few times after that, and once in London we actually fell into bed again, which was nice but went nowhere. That's all. I wonder (sort of) whatever happened to him. And does he ever (sort of) wonder that about me?

Now, though, with its windshield wipers starting to clack, the cab has almost within its sights rue Servandoni, one of the charming streets of the world. I am almost consumed by the anticipation and relief of home. I have firmly in mind my agenda for the next few days, for on the plane I made a list. (I am good at this.) Caroline by now will be waiting for my call. And even if she weren't, I would only draw back the curtains and turn up the heat before calling to arrange what we refer to as our "catch-up dinner," rehashing every detail we've already gone over several times by phone or email. And after opening the suitcases and at least taking out the American goodies I have brought back, pretending

I am unpacking, I will reach Klaus and Paul, who will be relieved to know I am safely home.

Then, umbrella in hand and my reusable grocery bag on shoulder, I will swing around the *quartier* to lay in some staples, but primarily to discover whatever has had the audacity to change while I was gone. I will, of course, tell myself that I am refreshing my mind about Paris, reminding myself of what I know and what I don't. But after I am satisfied that all is well and that I am in charge of my life, I'll give myself over to a *sieste*, so I can eat dinner with Caroline without dropping my face into the *foie gras*. A call to Alice (not to husband Findlay, who notices nothing) will fill me in on what's new in rue Guisarde, including, I hope, the restaurant of *M. Cassoulet*. And I'll no doubt just leave a message for Sandy, who is available only if there is no man in sight, suggesting an outing to shop the January sales.

A FEW PARIS FACTS

Oldest Street: rue St-Jacques, N/S axis, in Roman times called the Cardo

Longest Street: rue de Vaugirard, 4.4 km (2.7 miles)

Shortest Street: rue des Degrés (2nd), 5.7 meters

Highest Point: 40, rue du Télégraphe (19th), 148.48 meters

Highest Structure: Eiffel Tower, 312.27 meters (without antennae)

Largest Arrondissement: 15th, 588 hectares

Smallest Arrondissement: 2nd, 99.2 hectares

Oldest House: 51, rue Montmorency (3rd), built in 1407 for Prof. Nicolas Flamel of the Sorbonne

Oldest Church: St-Germain-des-Près, built around 550 AD, chapel to the right of the entrance and some chancel columns are original; bell tower from the 10th century

Trees: 184,000 intra muros (excluding 300,000 in the Bois de Boulogne and Bois de Vincennes)

Oldest Trees: Two robiniers dating from 1601, Square René Viviani and the Jardin des Plantes (5th)

Transport: Métro: 14 lines, more than 300 stations. Buses: 59 routes. Tramway: 3 lines.

Taxis: 15,300 ~~(none when it rains)~~

Bicycles for Public Use: 20,000, with 1,000+ docking stations

Free WiFi: 260 municipal areas and 400 WiFi posts—gardens, town halls, museums, and libraries

And then there's Edie, whose cooking school is on the Right Bank at Place St-Honoré, and who's generally available for lunch before her *démonstrations* begin. She's a picnic kind of luncher, preferring on sunny days to sit in the Tuileries gardens, bundled up, eating *sandwichs* and the acidic Boskoop apples she has insisted I like. Edie is just so different, always so serious. Her talk is about food, of course, and of restaurants that have been remodeled or closed, which this year I'll pay great attention to, of course. She sometimes suggests offbeat concerts coming up, for she knows I'm always up for the strange. Unfortunately, she is not one for gossip, nor does she seem interested in the subject of men—or women, for that matter. But I like her despite these obvious failings. Before we part, she usually comments about how she could have made a better sandwich than the ones we picked up. Often, I wish she had.

Edie is in her early fifties, quite robust of build but always well put-together, carrying herself with panache. She wears bright colors, shocking red lipstick, and bows in her brown hair that is streaked various shades of blonde. Being dramatic suits her in a way it would not do for me, perhaps because I am too craven to give it a whirl. Maybe I should give it a try, though, for despite her girth, I've seen men's heads turn—including widower Richard's—when she walks by. In fact, had Edie accepted his advances, which she most decidedly did not, I think Richard would have been the happiest man on either bank of the Seine.

When I take the No. 95 bus to lunch with Edie on the Right Bank, I like to imagine the olden days there. Like the French, I am entranced by the past, while never wanting it to come back. Royalty lived in the Louvre (where I get off the bus), and members of the Court were ensconced nearby. Diplomats stayed in hotels. Supplicants hovered. Sycophants jockeyed. Suppliers curried favor. And commerce burgeoned amid the bordellos, markets, and clothing stalls. What a mess. Finally, Louis XIV removed the whole kit and caboodle to Versailles, where he could keep an eye on it all.

Yet, those businesses that had clustered themselves near the Louvre back then still serve the current elite. No doubt the old Hotel Meurice on rue de Rivoli and the equally venerable Ritz, its neighbor in Place Vendôme, will be used by those in power in this century, whoever they are at any given time.

"When I dream of an afterlife in heaven, the action always takes place at the Paris Ritz," said Ernest Hemingway, who at times was a regular at the hotel's bar. Not I. Once, when I went there to meet Richard after his swim in Ritz's *très chic* pool—where he never has to attempt a word of French—the security guard wouldn't let me in. Okay, so I was a bit bedraggled from the rain, but did he have to ask me so cruelly just what business I had at the Ritz? Ultimately, after invoking the name of the *américain* down in the *piscine*, I got in. And Richard (who thought the story amusing) comforted me (who didn't) by ordering us tea and pastries right in the lobby of the hotel.

When Benjamin Franklin was wooing the ladies of the patrician village on the Right Bank called Passy, now an upscale *quartier* in the 16th *arrondissement*, he was mingling with the descendants of the aristocrats who had a century before moved westward with the Court. Before I found my nest in rue Servandoni, I briefly considered the 16th, but it's too quiet and sedate for someone who needs bustle at all times. I find it *mortel* (deadly), especially in summer, when shutters are closed and the residents retreat to their country homes. Or when the Americans have taken their children back to visit their families, as they do.

When she was married to J-P, Sandy and the kids used to disappear back to the States each summer. Now that her teenagers can travel by themselves, however, her comings and goings seem less predictable. Then again, so does she. I shouldn't be too hard on Sandra, for she has become a single woman in the most romantic city in the world. But so am I, and as I once ranted at Caroline, "Where's Benjamin Franklin when I need him?"

But perhaps my friend Findlay is wrong, and the good old days were really two hundred years ago when Franklin and his Masonic brother John Paul Jones, who also lived here, wowed the ladies (while doing whatever it was they had been commissioned to do). Abigail Adams, taken with Jones, described him like this: "He is of small stature, well proportioned, soft in his speech, easy in his address, polite in his manner, vastly civil, understands all the etiquette of a lady's toilette as perfectly as he does the mast, sails, and rigging of his ship…" I'm convinced. Add Paul—as he was called—to my list. (We will pay no attention to Abigail's husband, John, who called Jones "leprous with vanity.")

And so even today, sluggish as I am, I make a mental note about a point I must write clearly and for all time: In the absence of these good men (although "good" may not be the right word), it is, at least, as hard for middle-aged women to meet single, appropriate men in Paris as it is anywhere else. The notion of coming to France and finding an aristocratic Frenchman and being swept away to his *Architectural Digest* country home overlooking the hills of Provence, with the colorful pottery in the kitchen and the wicker furniture on the landscaped *terrasse*—where everything smells of basil and mint and where ripe tomatoes are warming in the sun in their charming basket, and he brings you a glass of wine produced at his family's château—well, those fantasies should be discarded before any *valises* are packed. French men are married. They have liaisons. They do not notice anyone over the age of thirty-nine. They are self-absorbed. In other words, they are like men anywhere.

But it is true that in Paris we never give up hope. Let us remember *cher* Captain Jones, who either did or did not really say, "I have not yet begun to fight." If we cannot focus on the comfort of true love, we can go for the thunderbolt of romance. So, *moi,*

I review the men I've known in geographical terms. Roman men are great sweet-talkers but are famous for the *sveltina* (quickie), probably because their mothers have *pasta al pesto* waiting for them at home. Brits apologize and say they could have done better, no matter what. Israelis, hot sands of the desert, seem to chase anything female that moves. And after thirty years of American men, I seem to be in a pause. Could this be why I am still now in Paris, since as yet I have no personal experience with French men? This deserves some thought. But for now, unable to garner the attentions of Ben or Cap'n Jones, I will this winter energize myself and give adorable, silver-haired *monsieur* the *restaurateur* a chance. First, though, I must find out his name.

Franklin aside, the only people I know who live in the 16th are Paul and Klaus. They are much in my mind this morning, for when I'm with them, somehow, that lifelong angst takes a half-step back. Especially when I visit them at their home, making that trek to the 16th. Their large *belle époque* apartment, an oasis of familial peace, is just on the inner edge, on avenue Marceau, a few streets from the famous Champs-Elysées. I think the area must remind them of when they were with the ballet—Klaus a lead dancer and Paul with his baton—and it speaks to them of glamour and sophistication.

Rumor has it that Rudolph Nureyev found the apartment for his pal Klaus, for he and Paul could never otherwise afford to live so well. Old and substantial (like my friends), the flat has been enhanced by the memorabilia of their lives. The living room has floor-to-ceiling windows, tapestry drapes, decorative moldings above, and faded (but clean) silk-lined walls serving as background to framed photographs of the two of them at various ballets over the years. A gilt-edged mirror above the sculpted fireplace might once have reflected *la belle vie* but now is almost hidden by medals and ribbons awarded them. The two bedrooms are equally turned out. The kitchen is nicely equipped, which matters little for it's

HISTORY IN PLAIN SIGHT

About 2,200 years ago, a band of Gauls called the Parisii came down from the hills above the Seine and settled the island now known as the Île de la Cité. For about 200 years they plied a river trade from this strategic vantage point, but by 52 BC, the Romans had defeated them and named their new colony Lutetia. Slowly they expanded to the south. North of the river was a marsh—*a marais*—and the trendy twenty-first-century area there is still called the Marais.

Some 9,000 people lived in Lutetia, by 212 AD renamed Paris after those early Parisii, whom the Romans had displaced. The Romans lasted in Gaul until the fifth century, themselves retreating with the rise of Christianity and the advance of the Barbarians, notably Clovis the Merovingian who converted to Roman Christianity and who set Francia on its course for the next thousand years.

Some ancient ruins still exist from Roman times—in the crypt in front of the Cathedral of Notre Dame and in the Latin Quarter, as well. And all around Paris, on your strolls you can see historical names: on street signs, the names of métro stations, and on plaques on buildings, saying who had lived there or what event had happened nearby, all serving to remind Parisians who they are and how their beautiful city came to be.

rarely used, and there are separate rooms for the toilet and the porcelain bath. As to Nureyev, there's a picture (in a polished silver frame) of Klaus and Rudi, as Klaus refers to him, on the large piano that dominates the living room and which is always kept in tune. When I am there, as I no doubt will be in the next week or so, Paul likes to play my old favorites while Klaus puts his arm around me and we sing.

The boys, as they call themselves, may find the Right Bank convenient, but they do not spend much time there, after all. They have their routines. Paul gets up early, does his *toilette* and dresses quietly, so he told me when I was settling in here, although Klaus, with a raised eyebrow, begged to differ. He lets himself out of the apartment, picks up the paper, and walks one flight down the broad marble stairs. Once out on the avenue, he heads to the café where he is an *habitué* to drink his *café serré* (extra strong) with a *croissant*. The *patron* of the café once saw Paul conduct at the Opéra Garnier and so is respectful, as people here are to artists, especially those of *un certain âge*.

It takes Paul about an hour to read the paper, sitting over just one coffee, perhaps two. Most mornings, toward 10:00 a.m. he takes the bus across to the Left Bank. He usually finds a seat. If not, someone invariably rises politely so the elderly gentleman can sit. Ever gracious, Paul indicates his appreciation of the kindness, perhaps with a dramatic little tone of surprise. I've seen this myself. *"Oh! Merci, monsieur."* A little pause. *"C'est très gentil."* He gets off in the 7th *arrondissement*, just at the corner of the American Library in Paris, where he spends the rest of the morning reading the current American periodicals and browsing the newly acquired books.

By noon, when Klaus turns up, he is impeccably dressed. Now in winter he will be sporting a camelhair coat and rich leather gloves, perhaps with a jaunty fedora and a silk *foulard* turned gently at the neck. The two make a striking pair. They love the library, that outpost of American culture, and Klaus swears that one day he will learn to use its computer so he can check his email—"once I figure out what it is," he says with a perplexed laugh. Paul and I are not holding our breaths. Klaus does not have a practical bone in his body.

Had they listened to me, which they didn't (and who could blame them?), the boys would be living on the Left Bank in the 7th, for it reeks of tradition and grace. I mean, it's just like them. Yet, they do lunch there from time to time, the only Americans I know ever to be invited into the private enclaves of the highly placed. (Except for Sandy, who somehow kept a few friends there after splitting from the aristocratic Jean-Pierre.) As to the boys, *le déjeuner* is often *chez* old, dear friends—the words *grande dame* and *monsieur le ministre* come to mind—and it touches me that they are so revered.

But if they have no fixed *rendez-vous*, Paul and Klaus generally lunch in the Latin Quarter, near the Sorbonne. It amuses them, this bohemian area of the 5th *arrondissement,* to see the students and young tourists with backpacks crowding the narrow streets and frequenting the lively inexpensive eateries that, as I have finally come to terms with, they themselves have no intention of trying.

In fact, I know already that, in terms of a lunch in the 5th, for me this coming week there will be no escape. Yet, I'm so eager to be back in the swing that I don't even mind. I suppose La Fontaine de St-Victor demonstrates that anything is available in Paris, and as a travel writer with a new project this should, *en principe,* interest me. A dining room on the *première étage* (one floor up from the ground-floor *rez-de-chaussée*) of the Social Security building, it caters to pensioners, offering inexpensive lunches seven days a week. In fact, when I'm along, I can be the youngest person there, which both relieves me and makes me squirm. "Darling," Klaus reminds me sometimes, if I've expressed boredom with what the boys call their club, "it's good value for the money." Then it is Paul's turn to raise an eyebrow, for it is he who—quite rightly—controls the purse strings in their *ménage.*

"Don't you ever want to try one of the little eateries in the neighborhood?" I asked when I'd just signed the contract to start on this year's new project. Begged, actually. "I've got a year of trying new places ahead."

"Oh no, *le déjeuner* is not to be sneezed at," Klaus answered, and while I was trying not to smile, he went on. "We would never just take a chance with our lunches. Besides, it's crucial for *le foie* not to inflict it with greasy food." Having taken on the attitudes of the French, the condition of the liver is never too far from his mind.

But I can occasionally wheedle them over to my *quartier,* to the 6th, west of the border at boulevard St-Michel. Here they can greet their friends—the writers, publishers, and intellectuals—those students from the Latin Quarter grown up, perhaps. Ancient churches may open onto lovely squares just as in other parts of town, but more important for me than for the boys, I'm sure, is that the cinemas, restaurants, and boutiques provide something interesting every week—necessary for someone with the attention span of a flea.

"Good enough for your book?" Paul shouted at me in late November, shortly before I left for the States. He pushed me on in a bracing wind, as we were scurrying toward noisy boulevard St-Germain. I could see he wasn't happy—despite his cashmere scarf and gloves—in the dampish cold. The three of us had just finished the fixed-price lunch at that Belgian brasserie on rue Racine (Bouillon Racine), where along with my *waterzoi* (a chicken stew kind of thing) I had for some unknown reason ordered a pink beer that tasted like berries.

"Sure," I said. "A beautiful old brasserie that serves berry beer? Why not? You know," I went on, pointing at the electronics store we were passing, "I love this neighborhood. They sell the most modern electronics here at La Fnac, but just a few streets away at the market, the *marchand* still ladles fresh olives out of the jug in the *marché,* and he always stops to ask me how I am."

"And American to the core," smiled Paul, from behind his scarf, "you always tell him too much, don't you?"

"I really do try not to," I laughed, for how could I deny something so true? "But he still makes me feel like a small town girl."

"Not that you ever were one," said Klaus, clearly remembering that teenage girl that I once was.

But finally, it's time for all these reveries to be put aside and for today to take over. I'm home. The curtains are open, although with the fitful rain there's not much light coming in. The heat is coming up, and I can hear the radiators adjusting themselves. My large suitcase and carry-on bag are in the bedroom, unopened. And just as I head for the phone, it rings.

"You beat me to it," I answer, skipping the greeting, for who else knows that I am home?

Caroline laughs. "How about if I reserve for seven o'clock at La Cigale Recamier? A soufflé might be a good welcome home."

A soufflé! What better way to start my life? "Perfect," I say, and I mean it.

"Would you like me to ask the guys? Or do you think they'd want you all to themselves?"

Or the other way around, more like it. "Thanks," I say. "That's nice. But I'll probably have lunch with them, tomorrow. I'll call them later."

Caroline, I think as I as hang up my coat, has also taken Klaus and Paul to her heart. Filled with kindly energy, she puts together a luncheon every six weeks or so, inviting various members of the gang. Last winter one of her knees kept giving her fits, so her January lunch was simple, *pas grande chose*, not a big deal, she said. Nonetheless, Richard, who lives on Place Dauphine on Île de la Cité, trudged over in a driving rain and arrived looking like a drowned dog—he dried his socks with Caroline's blow dryer. The guys bused over on the No. 82 from the library with their book bag, and Alice—hugging the walls and overhangs and wearing a rain poncho that must have been thirty years old—walked the few blocks alone, for Findlay is adamant about not "doing lunch." What he means, I've come to realize, is that he doesn't take to Richard, which is *ridicule*, for Richard is truly *sympa* (nice). I wished Findlay had come, though, for I do love his reminiscences of Paris, no matter which old days he's on at the time.

"But this year," Caroline tells me in the early evening when I am at least semi-awake, doing all I can to keep my eyes open, "in addition to the regulars, Sandra can come, but not until late. And," she goes on, which is good, because I'm too tired to talk about what's already on my mind—how to start organizing for my new book—"Mitzi is bringing some American woman new to town." That's fine with me. I like Mitzi, although I see her only at book club or occasionally at the American synagogue on the occasions that something in my life (and not always guilt) has prompted me to go.

Caroline's apartment is convenient for the gang. She lives in rue de Tournon, a few streets from me. Shrewd as she is, she furnished it almost entirely from the *marché aux puces*, the huge flea market on the city's northern edge. Now she spends her mornings writing at her Louis XVI-style desk by her large front window. She waves at me if I pass by, knowing I'll look up. In summer, with the window open, she calls down, "*Bonjour,* sweetie!" She is older than I—about half a generation, she says—but who cares, for we tend to laugh at the same things. Some definitely wouldn't be funny to anyone else, the kind of stuff where we just roll our eyes and bust a gut.

Next door to Caroline's flat is where John Paul Jones lived and then died in 1792. Caroline thinks that having had Jones as a neighbor is a "hoot and a half." I like it when she says things like that.

"I'm totally envious about Jones living next door," I admit to the group when the luncheon is finally on, a few weeks after my return, when I have settled myself into a work routine, and Caroline has found a day when everyone can come. It is cold, having snow flurried the day before, but the day is bright, which I have definitely willed it to be. Everyone is there by this time, except Sandy, who should arrive in time for dessert. So, along with Caroline and me, it's the guys, Richard, Alice alone, and Mitzi with the new woman, whose name I promptly forget. I spend the lunch wishing someone would call her by name. I did get that she is in Paris with a husband on two-year assignment at UNESCO, but my mind just at that point was straying toward the buffet.

One of Caroline's mottos is "Heat, don't cook." So, on this luncheon day she has walked up rue de Seine to Gerard Mulot, a *traiteur* (caterer, take-out), and we are eating a vegetable *quiche* she has reheated, along with slices of smoked salmon with *crème fraiche* and *blinis*, a salad of *mache* and beets. Alice has brought the *baguettes* and cheeses (that Findlay, no doubt, selected) and *clémentines* and lychees (lychees?) for later. I obeyed the instructions to bring coconut *sorbet* and chocolate *éclairs* from Picard, the chain that sells frozen foods—*les surgelés*. And wine maven Richard, of course, has brought a few bottles of Bordeaux, which we are drinking along with the Italian San Pellegrino fizzy water that Caroline recently switched to, now that she is paying attention to sodium (for this week, anyway) and has discovered it has less than the French Badoit.

"Yeah, I don't think it's fair that no historic American lived on my street," I go on.

"We just haven't found that out yet," says Caroline, reasonably. "Someone will turn up."

"But tell us more about Jones," Mitzi says, and Caroline is pleased to oblige.

Then she starts to tell everyone more lore about Jones, and we all listen intently, even *Mrs. New Woman*. "The French adored him," Caroline says. "Standing ovations and all that. He was sent here to regulate the disposition of captured ships, but in 1784 he went off to be a vice admiral in the Russian fleet. Didn't work out too well. So he came back here and moved right into this street. Can you imagine—he died three years later, only forty-five years old." She looks at me with a glint in her eye. "And later, Fran's friend Napoleon said about him, 'If he had lived, France would have had an Admiral.'"

Yet, Franklin and Jefferson, too, were gone by the time Jones died, and the new American Minister Gouverneur Morris refused Jones a fitting funeral. So, outraged Parisians gave him the sendoff he deserved. Only after another 150 years were his remains transported in honor back to the United States.

In fact, Caroline tells us, Morris may have been a patriot during the American Revolution, but here he favored the king, conniving with him, advising him on escape (not too well, obviously). It was by sharing the mistress of Talleyrand that he got secret information to the king. Caroline provides a James Madison quote: Morris had, she reads from her ever-present notebook, a "fondness for saying things and advancing doctrines that no one else would."

Fortunately, by the time Tom Paine, still a prisoner in the Luxembourg, was to meet *la veuve*, the French had thrown Morris out (in diplomatic terms, had him "recalled"), for he had done nothing to save Paine's head. Just then, though, James Monroe appeared, and Tom got sprung. Monroe wrote to Paine that "To the welfare of Thomas Paine, the Americans are not, nor can they be indifferent." As Klaus says, when Caroline has put her notebook down and reverted to hostess mode, and when we have finally killed the quiche, downed Richard's wine, and are digging into the cheese and fruit, "You see, the Gouv was not one of us." I think I know what he means.

So, the only things left to say are that Mitzi talks about the upcoming bar mitzvah of her son in the summer and about the kosher luncheon out in the Bois de Boulogne. She insists despite my fervent but polite demurral that she will invite me. *I don't even know your son,* I think. *You're scraping the bottom of the barrel with me.* Actually, I suppose I'll go. The synagogue and the park will be two Paris hits for the price of one.

And about Sandy, she breezes in just in time for coffee, scoops up the rest of the coconut *sorbet* and the last *éclair*, and interrupts the conversation with an account of what she has been doing and why she is late. With other people, this would make me crazed, for it seems to me that people who inconvenience you by being late then insist on boring you with the tedious details of just why they have kept you waiting. But this day having downed a few glasses of Richard's Bordeaux, I am tolerant.

"I had an appointment at the Embassy," she says, even while spooning the *sorbet* into her mouth. "They've asked me to play the piano at some function or other in May. Some kind of American evening. But I am definitely on the comeback trail." She turns to me. "Fran, let's shop."

But I realize that we're no longer on the first day I'm home, that I'm way ahead of myself, and that I should go back again to my return to Paris on that drizzly winter morning. Starting again, as we know, is my wont.

I knew better than to call when I might wake up Klaus, and Paul isn't home most mornings. So, early afternoon of my arrival home, after making my inspection of the *quartier* and before my own *sieste,* I left a message on the boys' *répondeur.*

Paul called back almost before I hung up the phone, asking if I'd be free for lunch the following day. Hearing his tone of voice, I knew there was a story in the wind. He suggested thoughtfully that we meet at Le Palanquin, a Vietnamese place a few streets from me in rue Princesse, saving me from their "club."

So, the next day, feeling almost sane, having had a ten-hour sleep of the dead after sharing a *carafe* of the house red with Caroline, beating to death the details of my trip, and listening groggily to the state of her research, I took myself on a sunnier day up to rue Princesse and the Vietnamese. After kisses back and forth with Paul and Klaus, I handed over a bulky sack of American-style oils and unguents and lotions and potions that they had asked for during their Christmas call to me in New York.

After we said hello to the waiter, who shook all our hands (as happens to good customers), and we settled ourselves in, we quickly ordered the *menu midi*, the *prix-fixe* lunch of appetizer, main course, rice, and tea. Then we got down to it. Klaus wanted to hear all about my kids (I showed him photos), and Paul asked about my work schedule for the year. I said I would start by getting as much up-to-date info as I could at City Hall, l'Hôtel de Ville. I found out about the glittering Christmas parties, but how beastly tired they already were of the rain and cold. And there was gossip, otherwise known as news. And then the story began. Paul started to describe the latest Embassy *soirée*—in honor of some American congressman, here on a junket, it seems—and Klaus embellished in delicious detail. Who doesn't want to experience a gala, even second hand? Paul and Klaus, as they should be, are on the American Embassy's social list, and when an engraved invitation arrives from Uncle Sam, they trot out their *smokings*, always ready to gussy themselves up.

The gala was held, as galas are, or so I'm told, at the ambassador's residence. Constructed in 1839 by the Baroness Pontalba—a New Orleans-born *señorita* who lived to be eighty, despite having been riddled with bullets by her father-in-law— the lovely old building on rue du Faubourg-St-Honoré was already sizeable even before the Rothschild family in the 1870s added more wings. After the Nazis used it as their Officer's Club, the Rothschilds moved on. And since 1948, the residence has belonged to America—to you and me, in effect, although neither of us can get in. Luckily, from time to time, Paul and Klaus can.

Over the years, I've been told of many *soirées*, the decorations, the verdant lawn and flowers, the *gaffe* made by some American— including the guest of honor—in English a *faux pas*. This time, some congressman apparently called the wife of a French cabinet minister "honey," and Klaus, a great mimic, imitated her expression of frozen disbelief. *"Incroyable!"* he crowed. I suspect the *crétin* just hadn't caught her name. I know how that is. But he could have and should have addressed her as *madame*. There are people I've known here for years, many of whom I still call by their last names. Even my good friend Jean-Pierre and I formally *nous nous vouvoyons*, never venturing into the familiar *tu*.

But how far does this have to go? Once at the library I browsed through a volume of love letters from Simone de Beauvoir, that steady companion of Sartre, to the American writer Nelson Algren. I noticed that, having shared his bed and whatever else, she still wrote to him, *"Je vous aime."* And *"Vous êtes mon amour."* Perhaps it was some existentialist affection or she was old-fashioned (in this one respect), but if you can't *tutoyer* your lover, just who is there left? And what about Sartre, *après tout,* whom she said was warm in all respects except in bed?

In fact, the Vietnamese was not the first restaurant I graced upon my return. That first day home, during my neighborhood "research," I wound up at Sushi House in rue Dauphine, where I could get a quick lunch and where I am known. The waiter was pleased to see me back, shook my hand, and as I settled myself in, asked with a smile, *"Comme d'habitude, madame, avec Coca Light?"*

"Bien sûr, merci," I replied, also with a smile. Of course, thank you, I wanted what I usually ordered, even if at that moment it had slipped my mind what that might be. After the miso soup and cabbage salad, the waiter brought me *shakedon* (a bowl of rice topped with slices of raw salmon) and a Diet Coke, which I certainly would have ordered had I taken a look at *la carte*. So, I'm predictable even to the waiters in rue Dauphine.

Later, shouldering my laden grocery bag and trying to shield myself, at least somewhat, from the rain with my umbrella, I must have looked a sight. Yet, I took a chance and followed the route home that led me first past Procope and then along the row of restaurants through rue Guisarde, where I would make sure that nothing untoward had happened to my adorable, silver-haired prey while I was away. If one has a project, one might as well get started on it, is the way I look at things. Seeing the restaurant full, however, and Himself nowhere in sight, I started to turn away, to head home to suitcases and mess and then to that nap.

Just at that moment, however, the restaurant door opened and, this is the truth, out walked that man I had seen jogging earlier in the day. And it actually was John, the fellow I had known years ago in San Francisco. Crested ring and all. And with a woman, not young or pretty, not even well dressed. *Must be a wife,* I thought, *and not a new one, at that.*

"John!" I said, hoping I didn't look as worn out as I felt. "What on earth are you doing here?"

"Fran!" he exclaimed, more surprised than I, of course. "We've just moved here," he said and then briefly introduced the wife, whose name he said was Rose. She smiled but said nothing, which was all right with me. "We bought an apartment over in rue de Grenelle. We love it. We've been wanting to do this for a long time. Now tell us about you!"

I've been living here for years," I said, having not missed all those sentences that started with the cosmic "we." "Near the Luxembourg," I added.

"That's where we jog every morning," he said, but I said nothing about having seen him earlier in the day. "It's so great to see you," he went on enthusiastically, as though we had been friends all this time. "We'll have to get together. We want to hear everything and to catch up on your kids. They must be grown up by now." So, we exchanged cards, email addresses, and all. By now I wanted desperately to go home (to check the mirror to see how I looked).

"You look like life is treating you well," he said, as though reading my mind. So, now I remembered that he was a nice man, a bit boring, but just one on the list of those who weren't for me. "We're going back to San Francisco to clear out our house," he said. "So, we'll call you when we're back. And you can tell us everything that you're doing."

Well, every dog and his brother turn up in Paris at one time or another. It wouldn't hurt to be cordial. "I'll look forward to that," I said. And maybe I meant it, tired or not.

THOMAS JEFFERSON QUOTE

"A walk about Paris will provide lessons in history, beauty, and in the point of Life."

But winding up my Vietnamese lunch with Klaus and Paul that next day, I could see that both men were ready to leave. They needed some down time before heading out for the evening—a play at the Théâtre de l'Odéon with some visiting performer friends and then a supper across the square at the fish restaurant La Méditerranée. But first a "lie down" with their library books. That day their long-handled needlepoint bag contained two new books about Paris (which I made a note to put on hold), another "explaining the true story" of the Nazi Rudolph Hess (which I did not), and one of those celebrity biographies they tend to favor.

As it was still a nice afternoon, more cool than cold, we strolled around the side streets toward the No. 63 bus, taking the long way around. Klaus remarked on unusual sights, and in advance of the January sales we window shopped, what the French call *lèche vitrines* (licking the store windows). Klaus, especially, notices everything beautiful *en route*. *"La daily promenade,"* as he calls it, is a feature of most of our expat lives.

As we took our leave, Klaus said to me, "Darling, I hesitate to bring this up…"

"But?" I asked.

"Okay, it's this. Paul and I have seen you through two marriages and several other men. But now that this year is starting and you've got a fresh book to write, wouldn't you like to find a new prince instead of hanging around so much with two old queens? Isn't it time?"

"Oh, Klaus!" said Paul, aghast.

"No, it's okay, I know what he means," I said. And as I often am, I was touched by their concern for me. "And I love you for always having me in your sights."

"Good girl," Klaus said and kissed me fervently on both cheeks, adding a hug to show that he was sorry if he had offended me. "Just mull it over. But when you choose your Prince Charming, don't you dare ditch your old uncles completely. Then I'd be sorry I ever said a thing."

So, now we are caught up. Winter is moving slowly along, and January has given over to February, as it must. My desk is neatly stacked with brochures from my first visits to l'Hôtel de Ville and the Tourist Office, and other papers are waiting to be filed according to chapter headings. I have scotch-taped above my desk my yearlong Plan of Attack, with a column next to each entry, so I can check off things as I go. (Every new checkmark spurs me on.) My notebook is filled with ideas I'd no doubt otherwise forget. Schedules for initial explorations around town. Restaurants to try or try again. Museums to check out. I am absorbed and distracted. I've already been over to Notre Dame, and after walking around inside and looking up at the Rose Window, I went out to look down at the crypt with the Roman ruins (bleached-out rocks, if you ask me). As I suspected, there was nothing new that would make me change what I had been thinking to write. Then, being so close to the Île-St-Louis—and despite the cold and damp—I stopped in at Berthillon and rewarded myself with a dish of *caramel beurre salé* ice cream—caramel made with salted butter—that for that week, at least, was my all-time favorite. Sandy and I shopped, and she bought but I didn't. So, daily life continues, and I suppose it must be according to some choice or other I have made. Napoleon, as we know, had no choice in the end, having thought that he would be exiled to live out his days at some English country manor, accorded the honors a fallen emperor should. Well, one thing I do know is that anyone can misjudge a situation every now and then.

Evenings may be closer to home, but they are not often alone with my books. "Do save us two seats, please, my dear," Paul says one afternoon when I have called him to tell him of an author's evening at the Village Voice, the English-language bookshop in the *quartier*. Caroline and I have already decided to go. So, a tiny umbrella folded in my purse, I walk over early, climb the stairs to the little mezzanine, and I save the seats, rather mischievously, one on either side of me. Sitting between Klaus and Paul, who whisper across me, is—as Caroline says—a "screech."

The boys arrive, wearing more clothes than I could possibly imagine. "It doesn't

THE SEINE

The magnificent river Seine rises north of Dijon in western France, before curving through Paris and around its two central islands, the Ile St-Louis and Île de la Cité. Upon exiting it heads north again, emptying into the English Channel at Le Havre.

For centuries the river has determined the character of Paris. The Right Bank, to the north of the river—which in medieval times was conducive to the unloading of ships and merchandise—has since then been identified as the commercial and financial focus of the city. Aristocrats lived close to the Palais du Louvre, and services for them flourished nearby. The more relaxed Left Bank was known for its intellectuals and artists; the first University of Paris, known as La Sorbonne, was founded in 1257, and the Collège de France in 1530.

Today these historic distinctions remain in the lore of Parisians, but times have changed. Parisians live in every inch of space they can afford, and former commercial neighborhoods on the Right Bank may show window boxes with geraniums above the banks and other enterprises. Areas that were shuttered at night have been revitalized, becoming trendy for Parisians and tourists alike. But across any of Paris' thirty-seven bridges over the Seine, the Left Bank still remains the romantic heart of the capital. Here are the lively Latin Quarter and the upscale St-Germain, the famous cafés and jazz clubs, art galleries, and of course both the Sorbonne (now Université de Paris V) and the Collège de France, still going strong.

do to take a chill," says Klaus, no doubt seeing my look. He unwinds a beautiful multicolored scarf from his neck and removes his fedora. Paul also takes off his coat and lays it carefully across the back of his chair. Underneath, he has on at least two sweaters, the top one with a zip. He sits down and pats my knee, and then he turns toward the front, waiting for the talk to begin.

This time the reading is from a new historical mystery novel by an American who is visiting Paris (a tax write-off, I'm sure). The upstairs is packed. There are a few women I know from book club and other people I recognize from evenings here or at the library. Some people sit on the stairs (blocking any escape). We all wave and smile. The introduction by Odile Hellier the proprietor is charming as always, and the reading and the writer's comments are interesting for a while. But they go on too long. There is little air. I try to pay attention. I fail. Soon I feel totally trapped and also guilty, since the evening was my idea. The question period seems endless. People never stop bringing up the writer's artistic motivation, the repression of the main character (a Roman *consul* who lived here in the first century), the use of mystical imagery and onomatopoeias, and stuff like that. Some people even hold the book in their laps, with passages highlighted in yellow and dozens of little Post-its sticking out of the sides. It's a *policier*, for heaven's sakes, set in Lutetia, or not. I try not to crawl out of my skin.

Later, after downing the *verre amical* (friendly glass of wine) Odile offers her guests, the four of us head over to the Café Mabillon on boulevard St-Germain. Once seated, we decide to share a plate of smoked salmon with *toasts*, Caroline orders champagne ("Budget be damned," she says), and Paul takes a *déca*—caffeinated coffee would keep him awake. Klaus prefers the French version of fresh lemonade, the *citron pressé*, which he says is a *digestif*. And without my saying a word, he orders Badoit for me. "You only have one liver, darling," he admonishes me, as though I were still that young girl with the spaghetti dangling off her fork. "Trust it."

And while I am being taken in hand, Paul says to me, "Your fidgeting was evident again tonight, my dear." Then he adds with a smile, "Do try to restrain yourself."

"Caroline," Klaus says, and we all turn to him, "would you like to go antiquing this weekend? Paul says we have enough in the coffers to do the *puces*. And you, darling, will you come, too?"

Would I say no to the flea market, especially since I am in the mode to re-explore every inch of Paris? It isn't that I love the flea market for myself. In fact, I rarely buy anything there, for I have learned that once you are hooked on the *puces,* it never ends. Caroline, though, remains sensible, and Paul keeps Klaus in line, but there's always a little something one could use, *n'est-ce pas?* It's just that, like tonight, whether or not the activity is one I care for, I'm generally glad I went. I mean, despite Paul's admonition, my fidgeting through life has actually diminished a great deal.

Chez Findlay and Alice

IN WHAT PASSES FOR APPROACHING SPRING, the warming but still soggy days of Paris are brightened by big news. Findlay has been invited to speak at the Embassy next month on "Paris After World War II." I am waiting at the bus shelter for the No. 87 one late morning when Alice calls me on my *mobile* to inform me that I am coming to dinner tonight at 7:30 to celebrate. This is just so Paris. I love it. Spontaneous, inclusive. Just come. A decade ago, when I was starting to write my first book about Paris, I could only imagine being a "regular" at the home of Americans who had lived here, well, forever and who were "known." It took some time after my friend Jean-Pierre—that ritzy French publisher who was then married to Sandy—introduced us for the Lovells to invite me to dine. In that way, they have taken on some of the attributes of the French. Guard your privacy. Hold a little back. Don't volunteer. Keep the Yanks guessing. Not like me, whose son used to advise before I traveled anywhere new, "Please, just don't tell everyone everything." But *petit à petit,* I have become that "regular," and it's just as I imagined that decade ago.

Alice tells me that Caroline is coming, too, as if I didn't know. So, on the bus heading for Paris' newest museum on Quai Branly, I call her to suggest walking over together later, beating her to the punch. Actually, it makes sense since we live close to each other, but we both also know it's better to climb the ninety-five steps to the Lovells' fifth-floor apartment with someone to distract you—starting at the third level—from the pain in the calves and the shortness of breath. So, in the early evening and with our umbrellas open under a soft enveloping mist, we meet.

We've only spoken once today, so we have a lot to chew over. First, we discuss why Ida might be coming to dinner, which is what Alice told Caroline but not me. I mention that I have drafted some introductory pages about my own saga and daily life in general for Americans, and I ask her to take a look. She says to email her the pages tomorrow. I tell her about the long line at the stunning new Musée du Quai Branly, and how after checking it out, I walked over to the Sancerre and ate a huge omelet for lunch. Caroline then starts to talk about William Short, the American in charge here between Jefferson and "the Gouv." But suddenly I interrupt, because when we are passing the restaurant of the adorable spring wonder (who is not near enough to the window to see me pretending not to look), I am reminded to tell Caroline that I have had an email from San Francisco John, saying how delighted he was to see me and that he had told his wife, Rose, all about me. And all this takes us as far as the door to the Lovells' building in rue Guisarde. "I wonder how much of that 'all' he really told her," Caroline says with a wink as we stop at the door, and we laugh.

After we've entered the *digicode* onto the keypad at the outside door, we enter and announce ourselves on the *interphone*. When the inner door unlatches, we press one of the *minuteries* to turn on the stairwell lights, and we start our climb.

"You know, you seem pretty frisky, these days," Caroline says, as we are midway up the narrow, winding staircase. "You're usually complaining about the climb by now."

"Yes…I guess…I'm in a pretty…good mood," I answer (trying not to show that I am beginning to pant). I attempt to go on. "Life…these…days…is…picking…" and then I quit, for by now my breath is truly short and I need it for the climb. Besides, there's something I'm not telling Caroline, and I am consumed by guilt.

Caroline can't press me for more, I'm glad to say, for having reached the last flights up to the Lovells' apartment, even she is mute. Findlay, who might well have pushed eighty, and Alice, maybe a bit younger, are the oldest of the gang. Yet, they still navigate these steps at least once a day, to their favorite *marché*, perhaps to the doctor or to a bookshop, to an exhibit that has just opened, or just for what Alice calls "our Jeffersonian outing" to take in the spirit of the *quartier*. There's often a little surprise (with Alice calling everyone right after, and Findlay's voice correcting from afar). Later they may dine at le Mâchon d'Henri, their favorite bistro in "the Guisarde"—as Alice calls it—although, basically, she prefers to cook. And as we all do, they look for the latest American movies—in *version originale* with French subtitles—at the cinemas nearby at Odéon.

It's true that everyone in Paris expects to climb some stairs, if not five flights—no matter your age. Many of the *hôtels particuliers* that have been converted into apartments, one to a floor, have broad curving staircases and shallow steps. Some less elegant buildings—like the Lovells'—may have narrow stairwells and rickety risers. But many old buildings in the *centre ville* have installed tiny elevators with just room enough for a couple of people and a mutt.

After Sandy's divorce, she used the settlement she received from J-P to buy the first-floor apartment in a centuries-old building over on boulevard Raspail. Or so we think, for Sandy seems to have learned at least something from being married to J-P and doesn't mention money. (For the French, talking about sex is in, but money is out.) Once, having climbed together the purple-carpeted marble stairs to her apartment, I asked why we couldn't have just taken the lift, which was clearly in sight. "Oh, the owner before me refused to pay his portion of the elevator's installation," she said blithely. "So the *ascenseur* does not stop on my floor." Although she could certainly chip in, she hasn't, probably because she only has one flight to climb. But not all buildings have lifts (mine doesn't), and some of these ancient buildings are the most charming. The Lovells' is not among them. But I love their apartment once I'm inside.

Whenever I am in anyone else's flat, I wonder if I would want to live there. How would I find life in that place? It isn't that I don't love my rental apartment in rue Servandoni, for I do. Strategically placed between the imposing church at Place St-Sulpice and the Luxembourg Gardens, narrow, medieval rue Servandoni is one of the most nostalgia-producing streets I've ever seen. Dogs are often splashing around in the fountain on the square well into the autumn—before the water is turned off for the winter—as I cut across toward my cobblestone street, and I'm sure it puzzles Parisians to see some weird woman schlepping her grocery bags and laughing out loud all by herself.

In my building, I climb two flights, just thirty-four steps. *Pas mal.* Not bad, at all. My apartment is what is known as *deux pièces*—two large rooms, plus a commodious entryway, a decent kitchen, and bath. I've got ample room for my desk and bookcases in the light-filled entryway, and in the *séjour,* the dining table that sits just under one of the three tall windows, a large hutch, and a sofa-bed for when one visitor stays. The easy chair is comfortable enough for a nap. And the TV swivels, so I can catch the (mistaken) weather reports from anyplace in the room. The bedroom, which is also spacious and fits another chair to nap in, plus a footstool, looks over a flowery court. In the States I, no doubt, would have complained, but in Paris, at least, size really doesn't count.

Agences immobilières post in their windows notices of available apartments, but pay no attention. The good apartments have all been rented before you've seen the ad. What you have to do is hound the agencies daily, wheedling and generally humiliating yourself, until they crack. That's what I did. I still can't slink past the agency window without turning my head away in shame.

Talk of apartments features strongly in the conversation of all my friends—just as do new restaurants and the semi-annual sales. No matter how you like your apartment, no matter that you've just eaten a splendid meal, no matter if your closet is full. One week, at the height (or depths) of the news about Iraq— and although the French talk about politics the way Americans talk about sports—Paris talked mostly about the thousands of empty apartments around town that the municipality had been keeping off the market and was now being forced to sell. Could these apartments be had cheap? Even Jean-Pierre, who is forever cutting out articles from newspapers and having his secretary fax them to me, said I should buy one right away, but it wasn't in the cards—especially since the dollar was by then already heading into the tank. Many people rent, including the Lovells, who have been living in this same apartment for forty years.

Once Bostonians, the Lovells have been in Paris since Findlay came to work for the Economic Cooperation Administration, otherwise known as the Marshall Plan. His job was to coordinate the more than 150 vessels that were crossing the Atlantic on any given day. Most ECA men were bachelors, thrilled to be in Gay Paree. But Findlay brought his wife and two infant boys. "And after just one visit to the *marché*," Alice once told me, "I knew Findlay would never leave."

First the family lived in the 8th, in an airy flat by the Park Monceau. The area was just as exclusive then as it is now. In those days, when the dollar was high and the franc was rock bottom, life was easy for Americans paid in Yankee bucks. The French, with nothing to buy and no money to buy it, however, called it "the second occupation of France." (And now that it's the other way around, with the dollar so low and American bucks in peril, don't they ask where those American tourists have gone?)

Findlay, it turns out, will speak in the embassy building that houses the American Consulate in rue St-Florentin, just off Place de la Concorde. It was here that Findlay worked and hung out, so it is especially poignant that he will return to the upper floors that he knew so well, but where the public—even he—can no longer get in. In the Fifties, everyone around was American, and as Findlay says somewhat wistfully, "I knew them all."

Some years later, with the Marshall plan winding down and the kids out of the house, Alice moved them here, to what is now the totally trendy, restaurant-filled rue Guisarde. Findlay, in one of his frequent reminiscences, told me once about how when they found this apartment, there was no heat other than a coal-burning fireplace in the main room. Warmth did not make it up to their mezzanine. Tenants went into the hall to a cold-water pipe for their water and to a communal toilet discreetly tucked into an alcove on the stairs. And this was in the mid-Sixties, mind you, not 1925. The Lovells' was the first apartment with hot water, a flush toilet, and radiators. The other apartments have also finally become, in Findlay's terms, "gentrified." I love this point of view. How this shabby building with its tricky, paint-peeling stairs qualifies as gentrification is beyond me.

Still, forty years in a rent-controlled apartment! Some people do have luck. In addition, the young *propriétaire* looks kindly upon these geezers who tell stories of when his grandparents were in charge. And he does little favors when he can. Here the Lovells have created an American-style home—with an eat-in kitchen and a refrigerator-freezer, a bookcase-lined living room with deep couches and easy chairs, bright windows shaded by venetian blinds, and that old fireplace that still sometimes smokes. Two bedrooms are on the mezzanine. Off the kitchen is Findlay's "nerve center"—a curtained alcove holding his computer stuff, stacks of musty papers, and faded clippings taped to the walls. This is where, after the Marshall Plan was over, he wrote several popular books about the aftermath of World War II in France. Alice calls it the "Strange-Lovell Room" and stays out. At her own desk under the window, she edits all his work. And then the American subsidiary of Jean-Pierre's publishing house puts it out.

"Don't you get nosebleeds up here?" I once gasped to Alice as she greeted me at the door. It was the first time I had been invited, and I hadn't yet learned to camouflage the panting.

Alice just laughed and waited for me to catch my breath. "No nosebleeds and no extra pounds, either. Just think of the glorious ride we've had. We may have saved the world, but we never saved a *sou*. And give up a rent-controlled apartment that we've had for forty years? I'll keep climbing these stairs until they lead me up to the Pearly Gates."

Of course, I was not here—actually, still a kid in Chicago—in those particular "old days" when, according to Findlay, rue Guisarde and other streets nearby were the domain of transvestites, prostitutes, and drug dealers. There was even a topless hairdresser, where the staff, half nude, gave good haircuts cheap. That was the real neighborhood, Findlay grumbles. The real Paris is gone. Totally spoiled—*pourri*. Although I love Findlay's stories and Caroline and I continually dissect times past, we don't grasp how every generation in Paris seems to regret something they have known and think they have lost. Especially when it doesn't sound so good to us.

Take Georges Haussmann (please). Even after 160 years, some still carry on about him as an "Alsatian Attila," while others—who also seem to think it was yesterday—contend he saved Paris, fulfilling the wish of Napoleon III for the beauty of Paris to rival ancient Rome. So, the Attilas claim Haussmann razed traditional neighborhoods, displacing the poor to eastern slums, and he slashed wide boulevards through old *quartiers,* just so the military could suppress uprisings of the masses. And didn't individualism suffer? Actually, no one says that any of this isn't true.

The other camp, however, reminds these "sentimental antiquarians" that before Haussmann, Paris was a mess (and I am not one for mess). Some twenty thousand people had died of cholera in 1848. TB was rampant. Streets were running sewers and the city stank. Fresh water was rare. The central city was a labyrinth of dark, filthy streets with a fetid tenement directly in front of the Louvre.

Clearly, I am with the genius bloc. I mean, just how did the city end up? Those slashed-through *grands boulevards* were lovely to stroll. Hospitals and schools were built. Five thousand acres of parks showed Parisians the sun. More apartment buildings were constructed than torn down. Aqueducts provided clean water, and four hundred miles of sewers kept streets clean. Gas mains fueled fifteen thousand street lamps. And despite the carping of the Attilas, about half of the buildings in the *centre ville* still date back at least to Louis XVI.

The Embassy invitation to Findlay, I suddenly realize as I walk into the living room, has come from Ida, who has ensconced herself in the most comfortable chair. So, this is why she's here. A rather dour, fortytish beanpole who is spending her life in the Foreign Service, Ida is assigned to the Embassy here, where she coordinates public events. I think her oldest sister went to school with Alice's youngest brother or something like that. Alice and Ida have become close. Don't ask me why. In my view, Ida, never married, always looks as though her life were somebody else's fault. Yet, sometimes, she gets us invitations to Embassy events. Tonight she has invitations for Caroline and me, and she thrusts at us a stack for other people we know.

Ida tends to talk in pronouncements, which sometimes makes me crazed, regardless of what she says. Last fall, for example, at another of these dinners *chez* Findlay and Alice, she said to no one in particular (not even directly to me), "Fran should get a dog."

"A dog!" I exclaimed, appalled. Everyone laughed, except me. I can't think of anything I'd want less, except maybe a turtle. "Why on earth would I want a dog?"

"Yes, Fran should get a dog," she said again and finally looked at me. "You don't have a man. So, a dog would make you feel more settled."

"I feel settled enough," I said (snapped, actually). "Thank you very much." I mean, the boys taking me in hand is one thing, but Ida is another. What is it about me, anyway? And is this when my silver-haired project came to mind?

"So, sweetie, what's going on with you and Ida?" Caroline asked that night on the way home.

"And just what right does she have to try and figure out my life? I have enough trouble without her."

"What is it that Klaus says?" Caroline asked. "Something about life being the only fulltime job?" After this, we let the subject drop. Caroline has not brought it up again, and neither have I.

This evening, however, Ida seems to be under control. Alice goes into the kitchen while Findlay fusses out the glasses and pours us all some wine. It is always the same, a Brouilly in an unlabeled bottle. Because it is served slightly chilled, some people think of Brouilly as a summer wine, but because he likes it and gets a bargain price, Findlay buys it by the case all year round from a grizzled *commerçant* whom he has cultivated for decades. This burly man shoulders the cases up the ninety-five steps, as he says, as a favor to *Monsieur Loh-velle,* who no longer can do it himself. (Although he does when he has to. God help us if Findlay runs out of wine.)

Findlay passes around a plate of *foie gras* and little pieces of toast. "Have some," he instructs. "It's from old Hubert at the *marché* in rue Cler. This, dear ladies," he says, brandishing a piece of toast he has spread high with the creamy, rich *foie gras*, "is why I came to Paris almost sixty years ago." He laughs. "And why I hope death takes me before Hubert. Dig in, *mes belles*, dig in." Thinking only briefly of the cholesterol-loaded lunch I ate at the Sancerre, I help myself. I am sitting by one of the large bookcases, and I cast an eye over the books nearby. They are about the history of Paris, as, of course, they would be. And they are arranged chronologically. This has to be the work of Alice, I know.

Findlay wipes his mouth and starts right in. "People today only remember De Gaulle," he says. "But it was the Communist Party after the war that controlled the workers, and it almost took over. In 1948 they crippled the city with strikes. Think of it! The gas and electric workers went out, no water supply, and the trains didn't go. No *métro*, bus conductors, garbage collectors, or street cleaners. Unbelievable! We almost froze!"

"Tiens, tiens," exclaims Caroline. "What happened?"

Findlay is clearly pleased to have the floor. "It wasn't pretty, I'll say that. The minister of the interior, Moch—jailed by Petain and then big in the Resistance—accused the workers of being dupes of the Soviets, which they were, of course, and he called out the troops. When the Commies…"

"Don't call them Commies," Alice calls from the kitchen. "And dinner is on. Come to table!"

"Right," says Findlay, as we all stand up. We take our glasses with us.

As we stand to walk into the warm, steamy kitchen, I venture a question that's been on my mind. "By the way, Findlay, did you ever meet Gertrude Stein when you were young?"

"That old windbag? No. Why would I have wanted to?"

"Oh, I don't know," I say, for I'm not really sure why I asked. "Listen, could I borrow a couple of your Paris history books? Ones you're not using for your speech?"

Findlay only nods, points me to a chair, and goes on with his thought. "So," he says, "recovery was underway, and the Communists couldn't keep the masses in line. Even their propaganda—straight from Russia—fell apart. But for a while, they had the people in their grasp. By Jove, they almost won!"

"The Communists had a point," pronounces Ida in her way. She sits down across from Caroline and me. Findlay and Alice sit at the ends. "What about that bombing of McDonald's down in Millau, years ago, and all the complaints about globalization?'

"Nineteen forty-nine all over again!" Findlay brandishes a new bottle of Brouilly he is about to open. "The wine industry went berserk about Coca-Cola expanding their exports into France. The Communists kept talking about the *coca-colonization* of France!" He uncorks the bottle and begins to pour. "But the wine keeps flowing, at least *chez* Lovell. *Voilà*."

"Well, perhaps they were right," says Caroline, nudging me under the table. I happen to like *Coca Light*. Findlay just snorts and downs his wine. He stands to serve the dinner. He walks around the table to place Alice's plate in front of her, and he bends down to kiss her hair. I notice that his face is flushed, perhaps from the wine, perhaps from the heat in the kitchen.

"Have some of this bread," Findlay says, passing a basket around. "It's from the *boulangerie* that won the *Prix de la Baguette* this year." (Of course, it is. Would *M. Loh-Velle* serve anything less?) I take a chunky piece

THE STICK OF LIFE

France consumes more than 30 million *baguettes* each day, meaning that 10 billion of these long crunchy loaves are baked annually. A Parisian knows which baker in the *quartier* makes the best *baguettes* and when. If you've never broken off the top of a *baguette* still warm from the oven and munched on it on the way home from the *boulangerie*, then you've got a treat in store.

Surprisingly, there is a lot of difference in a product that may—by law—be called a *baguette* if it is made only with flour, yeast, water, and salt. So much, in fact, that in 1993 *Le Grand Prix de la Baguette* was created to judge annually the best *baguette* in the city. No prepared mixes or machines may be used, and baking must be on the premises. In fact, an establishment may be called a *boulangerie* only if those criteria are met.

A good *baguette* should have a golden hard crust, that when biting into it will have a flaky crunch. The cream-colored, fluffy inside should be dotted with irregular, fairly large air holes. Overall, the *baguette* should feel crisp and slightly chewy and have a definite flavor that some people describe as "nutty."

The *baguette* starts its day as a *tartine*, sliced lengthwise and spread with butter or *confiture*. At lunch, a shorter or half *baguette* may be split lengthwise for a sandwich. And at dinner (bought after the afternoon's baking) it is in a bread basket, cut horizontally into rounds. *Baguettes* don't last long; if you can't eat a whole one in one day, ask the baker for a *demi baguette*, and you'll get half.

of the *baguette* (stick), sure it will be worthy of its best-*baguette*-of-the-year prize. In the French manner, I put the bread on the tablecloth, next to my plate.

Alice, whose specialty is one-dish meals, has made a *navarin d'agneau*, a springtime dish all around France. Tonight the baby lamb is in a casserole with peas, tiny turnips, onions, carrots, and those little new potatoes that could make me cry for joy. It is April, after all (the month of my birthday), and Alice has bought what's in season at her favorite *marché* in rue Mabillon. In the fall, obliging *marchands* save the best wild mushrooms for her, and she prepares *fricassée de champignons sauvages* and different kinds of game, including a stew of wild rabbit (that seems to me mostly bones), which, while working on my plate, I can usually hide some under the rice. Nonetheless, neither Caroline nor I spend much time cooking, so we are pleased when Alice asks us to come, especially when it's cold and she has had a big meat pot simmering all day on the stove.

"I've got a new recipe that may not be worth a woof," she might say, using an expression she says was popular in the Sixties. "But come over and give it a try."

Fortunately, even tourists can watch what they eat in Paris (not that they do) and still eat well. Indeed, in any restaurant you may inquire politely how a dish is prepared before you choose. If you ask for something to be prepared without an ingredient that gives you hives, however, the *serveur* may agree, but he might also suggest you order something else, as the integrity of the dish could be compromised. Pay attention. Order something else.

Alice, for a while, stopped serving beef, what with all the "hoo-ha" (as she called it) over *la vache folle* (mad cow disease). Many *français* swore off beef for a while, but others didn't, and frankly, I couldn't make up my mind. I put off deciding until the scare was off of the news.

"I don't think anyone wants to hear about politics," Alice says. "I think they want to hear about the American bachelors heading for the bordellos, about the Folies Bergères, about the party atmosphere after the years under the Nazis, about the gay time we had then."

"You tell them, then," Findlay growls. "That doesn't interest me."

"It certainly interested you then," Alice laughs. She looks at Ida, who is attempting a smile. "Lunchtime it was martinis with the journalists at the Hotel Crillon, and after work the cocktail hour at the Ritz. I always knew where to find him."

Of course, life changes. And not just for Findlay. As to the Haussmann debate, for me cholera would not have been the good old days. Could there be a more beautiful city than Paris? And would widower Richard love the Île de la Cité if there were a single rat in sight?

But about fifty years ago, Paris needed to tidy up those eastern slums, and doing so, left the Baron in the dust. And didn't the French complain? *Mais oui.* Massive projects—under both right-wing President Georges Pompidou and then Socialist François Mitterand—revived the city, but gave both sides reason to gripe. It goes without saying that the denizens of the affected *quartiers* complained about the loss of the old neighborhood atmosphere. Whatever that was. If, as Paul has reminded me from time to time, you don't accept that the French resist change with all their might, you'll never understand *la France.*

For Parisians, life would be unthinkable without daily contact with the past, no matter how comfortable their modern life. And is globalization so bad, aside from being inevitable? I may only use *les toilettes* at *McDo*, but Jean-Pierre's son Victor drags him there for lunch occasionally (Henriette—thin as a teenage rail—refuses to go), and J-P claims he likes the fries.

Caroline shakes her head to Findlay's offer of wine. She pours herself some Perrier and turns to Findlay. "Did you ever hear of that American guy in the 1920s?" She rummages in the tote bag that seemingly never leaves her side and produces the famous notebook. "His rich wife got mad at him and went to the Ritz restaurant to cut off her husband's tab. Oh, here it is. Listen to what the *maître-d'hôtel* said: '*Monsieur* will continue to be…welcome at the Ritz, where I shall be honored, in the future, if he would consider himself my guest.'" Caroline shakes her head. "Fancy anyone at the Ritz saying that, these days."

"Ah, the Ritz!" Findlay says, wiping his mouth and eyeing the cheese on the sideboard. No doubt he took the No. 4 *métro* this morning down to his favorite *fromager* (Boursault) in the 14th. Findlay will go to the end of the line if he has to for good cheese. I eye the platter myself, but know that when offered, I will say I'm just too full for both cheese and dessert. This is only partly true. Actually, I'm now feeling guilty about that omelet (filled with ham and cheese and potatoes) I wolfed down at lunch. And I do know enough not to skip Alice's homemade dessert.

"I think it was around 1956," Findlay remembers, "when Hemingway turned up sometimes at cocktail hour, which was still going strong. Well, the porter comes into the bar one evening, takes '*Monsieur Em-in-veh*' aside and asks him to remove the trunks he had stored there back in 1927. Lucky for him, he did. He found all the notes from when he had lived in Paris in the Twenties, and they became *A Moveable Feast*."

"We don't have a real cocktail hour anymore at the Embassy," says Ida, in her declarative way. I can't figure out whether she thinks that's good or bad. She passes her plate to Alice to clear. She hasn't finished what she had been served, something Parisians find rude. Take small servings and ask for seconds, if you like, but leave nothing on your plate. Luckily, we're Americans here, and we understand each other. I wink at Alice and then spear a small slice of lamb from Ida's plate as it goes by. Findlay doesn't notice, but Alice beams with pleasure, and Caroline just rolls her eyes.

Findlay stands, and in an unusual show of domesticity, he takes the dinner plates from Alice, coming back with the cheese *plateau* and a bowl of fresh fruit. After he has distributed little plates to us all, he points to each cheese and describes it lovingly as he asks everyone which they want. There is a Mont d'Or, which is a winter cheese and sometimes heated and spooned onto a round of *baguette* (which I would not have passed up in a million years). There's a chèvre wrapped in a chestnut leaf, an aromatic Livarot, a blue-holed Roquefort, and an aged, crumbly Gouda, which comes from the Netherlands, but so what? Too bad I'm being noble, tonight. (I do love Livarot, though, despite Klaus saying that its smell—I'm sure he meant "aroma"— reminded him of his old

THE KING OF CHEESE

The delights of Roquefort may first have been remarked on by the Roman Pliny the Elder in 79 AD. But for the French it matters more that by the eighth century, it was noted as Emperor Charlemagne's favorite cheese. The subject of Roquefort has entranced the French ever since, and official laws have ensured that the refining processes that guarantee the precious flavor and enchanting texture will never be lost.

In general, a cheese may be called *Roquefort* only if it is made from the raw milk of red Lacaune ewes, and indeed, a true Roquefort always has a red sheep on the package label. The milk may be produced only in seven *departements,* and the ripening (at least four months) must take place in the caves of Mont Combalou at Roquefort-sur-Soulzon (Department of Aveyron). The monopoly for this ripening was first awarded to Roquefort in 1411, and it is in force today. The *penicillium roqueforti* mold—made from hard bread—must be prepared from chemical-free sources from these natural caves. And last, the conditioning and packaging of the three million cheeses produced annually also must take place in the Roquefort commune.

What is so special about Roquefort? This is a question to be asked only if you haven't tasted it. It may well be the greatest blue cheese in the world (the English Stilton and the Italian Gorgonzola, made from cow's milk, might dispute this). Although the color and texture may vary a bit according to the producer, basically Roquefort is a soft, damp, crumbly cheese with an ivory or slightly creamy color. Rich and spicy, it melts in the mouth, leaving an aftertaste of salt and of the prized blue mold seen in the holes. People generally eat Roquefort after a flavorful main course, often accompanied by a muscat or sweet sauterne.

ballet shoes.) But I do help myself to the pear that Findlay recommends and a few grapes, and later to a respectable slice of a deliciously homemade *tarte tatin* (an upside-down apple cake kind of thing). Not being a coffee drinker, I also pass on the *expresso* that Findlay makes himself. I just sip my wine, wishing Alice wouldn't smoke; yet, it is her house, so what can you do?

By now it is getting late, and just as I am thinking of leaving, Caroline kicks me under the table. We both stand. Ida announces her intention to help clear up, so Caroline and I thank Alice and Findlay profusely, and also Ida for the invitations (at least Caroline does). I pick out two books from Findlay's library, and then, having put on our coats, we head down the stairs, ready to rehash the evening as we go.

We walk down slowly, for going down is harder on Caroline's knee than going up. Suddenly, I remember something I recently noted on a scouting tour, and I ask whether, despite the late hour, she would be willing to take a detour on the way home. "I want to show you something I've discovered in rue du Four."

"*Bien sûr,*" Caroline agrees, for of course she is always up for one of Paris' *petites surprises*. Ready to exit the building, we push the *porte* button to unlatch the door, and we go out into rue Guisarde. The air has that pleasing after-rain damp. We have started our gab, disposing quickly of my piggishness with the lamb, Findlay's drinking, Ida (whom I refuse to admit was almost friendly tonight), and that last flight of stairs on the way up. Just before we reach the corner of rue des Canettes, I take a sidelong peek and lo! Himself is at the door of his restaurant, showing two customers out. I smile and give a little (intimate and suggestive) wave of the fingers. He blows me a kiss. Caroline and I walk on.

"He blew you a kiss!" Caroline says with some astonishment.

"Yes, I know," I say modestly.

"Is there something you haven't told me?" she asks suspiciously.

"When there's something I'm not telling you, I'll let you know."

Although we both laugh at this and Caroline doesn't press me further, I am not being exactly honest. But I am not ready to come clean, not even with her. The truth is that my spring project is making my blood stir again, and I'm sure this is why Caroline thinks I am in such a good humor

During the winter, I managed to pass often through rue Guisarde, hoping it looked like sort of a normal thing to do. Sometimes *monsieur* was not in sight, sometimes we just smiled and nodded while I walked on—if I was laden with groceries— but sometimes I stopped for a moment to chat. This is where real progress was made, and I don't think I'm imagining this. Himself moved from saying *Bonjour, madame* to *Bonjour, chère madame* to (by mid-March, I think it was) *Bonjour, ma chère*. Myself kept up with this, of course, escalating my own greetings from *monsieur* to *cher monsieur* to *cher ami*. Hello, dear friend. Believe me, in France, this is hot stuff. But I still didn't know his name.

So, last week as I entered "the Guisarde," I saw *M. Cassoulet* affixing his new spring menu to the front window glass. Calling on all my American brazenness, this time I barely even said hello. (Could I really be so nervous at my age?) I moved right in for the kill.

"*Bonjour,*" I called out and smiled one of my sweetest smiles. "Do you realize that I've known you for two years, *cher ami,* and I don't even know your name?"

"*Joël,*" he smiled back, not having let go of my hand from the handshake that the French so like. He pronounced his name, of course, not like the American Joel, but like the French *Zho-elle*.

"*Moi, je suis Fran-ces,*" I said clearly, so he'd get it. I even explained, so he wouldn't forget. "*C'est comme la France avec une s.*"

"*Frahn-zess,*" he said. And then we (he having relinquished my hand) stood and talked a while, about the dearth of Americans in Paris with the dollar sinking evermore, about the new little oyster café near Mabillon, and something about the city's produce market in the suburb at Rungis that I barely heard, since my mind had wandered toward other possibilities with him. So, now we not only know each other's first names, we're having real conversations, and better yet, we are on blowing-kisses terms. Next on my agenda is his marital status. Luckily, my apartment has a six-year lease.

So, with Caroline this late evening, I guiltily change the subject to one I'd been meaning to bring up, anyway. "I saw that woman who came with Mitzi to your lunch," I say. "I wanted to say hello, but I would have been too embarrassed to tell her I couldn't remember her name."

"Anna. Anna something-or-other," laughs Caroline. "I ran into Mitzi on rue des Ecoles a few days ago, and she says that Anna is making all the usual American mistakes. Listen to this. She went to the *caisse* at the supermarket, and she hadn't weighed her bananas on the scale, so there was no price sticker to scan. The cashier mumbled something that Anna, who is studying French, couldn't understand. The line behind her was getting longer, and she didn't know what to do!"

"*Oh, là là,*" I say. "Didn't anyone there tell her to run back and weigh the bananas?"

"Anna thought the cashier was pointing out a brown spot on one banana, so she dashed to get a different bunch, but she didn't weigh that, either! Eventually, Mitzi says, the cashier got up herself and went to weigh the fruit and came back and showed Anna how to put the sticker on."

"Lord, she must have been mortified," I commiserate, remembering some embarrassing mistakes of my own. "Why don't you ask her to come to the cinema with us late one afternoon?" I say, knowing that Caroline might actually get around to doing that, whereas we both know I never would.

We cross over rue du Four and walk a few steps toward rue de Rennes, when I grab Caroline's arm, saying, "*Voilà!*" I point out to Caroline a beautiful old iron gate that is latched across the recessed entrance to a store, one we've no doubt passed by hundreds of times. The design of the entire gate is an intricate lacework of cogs and wheels and needles and scissors and other implements for sewing, and words at the top spell out "Singer Manufacturing Company."

"Lovely!" exclaims Caroline. "And to think I never noticed it." We stand, just looking, pleased with ourselves. Then Caroline says, "The Singers lived in Paris, of course. I've seen their daughter Winaretta's mansion on avenue Georges-Mandel. So, this probably was a sewing machine store once upon a time."

I nod, for that's what I had thought, too. "Yes, and no Parisian would destroy such a lovely gate. Isn't that just so typical?" Caroline nods, and so I go on. "And Winaretta," I say with some envy (no matter that she's dead), "wasn't she the one who had that *mariage de convenance* with the gay Prince de Polignac?"

Caroline nods and says, "Yes, so she was also a princess." We both sigh.

"Okay, let's go home," I say. "I should know better than to keep up with Findlay and the wine." So, we turn back up rue Bonaparte and walk quietly, each with our own thoughts. Everything about Paris seems so interesting to me. I hope it keeps up.

"Speaking of marriages," Caroline finally starts as we get to Place St-Sulpice where she will peel off, "did you know that it might not have been Hemingway who named the book *A Moveable Feast?*" She doesn't wait for my answer, and frankly, I had none, anyway. "I read somewhere that he had killed himself before the book was published, so his widow chose the title." She smiles a little and shakes her head. "I wish I could remember where."

"It'll be in your notebook somewhere," I say. "But why didn't you say something at dinner about that? Findlay might have known."

"And interrupt his grand moment?" Caroline asks, with surprise. "I'd never do that." I shouldn't even have asked. "Now," she goes on, "what about your moment? Your birthday is in ten days, *n'est-ce pas?*"

Relieved that I don't have to maneuver the conversation around to this myself, I say, "*Exactement.* And yours is the week after. So, what do you want to do this year?"

"How about going to Claude Sainlouis, just the two of us?"

"Only if I can order dessert," I say, already tasting their *mousse au chocolat*, which I think is the best I've tasted (so far). On the other hand, if I'm going to get into real fighting shape for this perhaps totally imaginary relationship with Joël, I better start a *régime*.

"Done," Caroline says agreeably. "If it's you, it's bound to be the *mousse*. Well, another pound or two won't hurt."

Our birthdays settled, Caroline says "*Bonne nuit,* sweetie," as I turn toward rue Servandoni, and she heads over to rue de Tournon. "*A très bientôt.*"

I waggle my fingers at her, much as I had done just minutes before, and I walk the few more steps into my quiet street, thinking about the evening in general and the Paris talk, someone's marital status, and finally about skipping the *entrée* (first course) at Claude Sainlouis, so I'll still have room for dessert. That will be the start of my diet, big time.

As I walk down the street, I look around in an ordinary gesture of caution, and again just before I enter my building. But I feel secure that even this late there will be no problem, unlike my worries when walking down empty streets in New York. Paris is generally safe in these upscale *quartiers*.

"*Mais, Frahn,*" J-P once cautioned me, when I had been telling him of an accordion concert Edie had dragged me to in the Latin Quarter near where she lives, and how I had walked home alone. "*Faites attention. La France* is changing, too fast for some, too slowly for others. Many young unemployed people are angry, and the government doesn't know what to do about it. *Non, chérie,* the *quartiers* in the *centre ville* may be safe, as you've written, but France has a problem it must deal with. And although it pains me to say, this *mondialisation*, what you call globalization, doesn't help."

Safely in my apartment, though, I immediately run a bath. My philosophy of life (the part that doesn't have to do with the merits of Super Glue) is that most things will unfold, although sometimes you have to help them along. As to the rest, you should think about them in a hot bath. So, once immersed in the hot water, I go over the evening again in my mind, including— several times—the possible meaning of that blown kiss (real kiss but imaginary relationship or real kiss and real relationship, or what?), but finally wear the subject out. Well, I think as I finally crawl into bed, Findlay and Alice may have stayed here for the *foie gras* and the wine, and I can certainly understand that. But for me, all told and with the ninety-five steps conquered, tonight *chez eux* was one of those evenings of my middle-aged dreams.

Moi in May

TONIGHT IS FINDLAY'S SPEECH. AND I know already that this is going to be one of those Paris kind of days that had begun to elude me back in the States. I have it all well in hand, despite the fact that I am jumpy as a flea. I will write (or try to) until just before lunchtime, I will dress carefully and get myself ready, and then I will head over to rue Guisarde, where Joël has invited me to join him for an early lunch. Yes, we are finally at a new stage. And it was his idea—and not something I maneuvered—one day when I was passing by, when he mentioned that his chef was creating some dishes for summer and perhaps I would like to come one afternoon and try them with him. *"Volontiers,"* I said, playing it sort of cool. (I hope.) And *voilà,* here we are. Yet, when I can drag myself away from fantasies, I am also looking forward to the rest of the afternoon, for on the way to the American Embassy I will make what is a fairly regular bookstore prowl. So, to take my mind off the lunch, I will think about books, especially mine.

It isn't that I think of myself as a member of the neatness police. It's just that the English-language bookshops usually carry my *Culture Shock!* guides, and when I happen to be near any of them, I go in to check out the stock. My books should be clearly visible on the shelf. If they aren't, *voilà,* I make it so. If there are several copies, they should be together. If they aren't, I make it so. They should be in the middle of the shelf, not at the end. If possible, they should be displayed front cover showing, not spine. And seeing no copies at all, of course, I ask at the desk if the books are on order. By now the clerks recognize me, and I them. So, if they are thinking *"Ce que'elle est maniaque,"* all they say to me is, "But of course, madame. *Bien sûr.*"

In rue de l'Odéon, just a few blocks over toward St-Germain, was once the most famous English-language bookshop of all. (Like Findlay, I am becoming good at waxing nostalgic about things I myself have never known.) In 1919 Sylvia Beach the American "vestal virgin," as she was sometimes called, opened Shakespeare and Company in the heart of the *quartier de l'Odéon*. Everyone helped, including poet Ezra Pound, who hammered up the shelves.

Beach started a lending library for people who couldn't afford to buy books, and she loaned money to people who could afford nothing at all. Hemingway even had his mail sent there. And in 1920 Beach courageously published *Ulysses*, when it was banned both in England and the US of A. Mr. Joyce, as Beach called him, was indebted to her for that—until he left her for another publisher. Yet, in those days, Shakespeare and Company in the village of "Odéonia" was America's Parisian home. "Stratford-on-Odéon" lasted until World War II, when the Nazis shut it down.

Gert herself and the mustachioed Alice were friends of Sylvia Beach, at least until she published *Ulysses* and Miss Snit went into a jealous huff, resigning from the lending library's rolls. "Joyce is a third-rate Irish politician," she said. "The greatest living writer of the age is Gertrude Stein."

Since that stands by itself and I do not have to comment, I will only add that La Stein also didn't much like Ezra Pound. "A village explainer," she called him, adding "excellent if you were a village, but if you were not, not."

But was it not Hemingway himself who, in August of 1944, came on his jeep into rue de l'Odéon, roaring out, "Sylvia! Sylvia?" After the embrace and—as legend would have it—disposing of snipers on the roof, Hemingway zoomed off, as he said, "to liberate the cellar of the Ritz." Beach never reopened the shop. Instead, she gave the name to a bookshop in rue de la Bûcherie, which, even after fifty years, still is going strong. It's run now by the aged proprietor's daughter Sylvia (of course), who, as Klaus would say, "understands."

Today is one of those deliciously sunny days that are turning up regularly now. Given that I hope my lunch will last well into the afternoon (ever the optimist), I won't have time to go to the Red Wheelbarrow over in the Marais. So, I'll just take the No. 95 past the Louvre and start at Brentano's on avenue de l'Opéra. Then I'll stroll down the arcade on the rue du Rivoli, passing the tourist shops and currency exchanges, dropping in at Galignani, the oldest shop on the continent to carry books in English. Last, I'll make a foray to W.H. Smith, the Paris outpost of the ubiquitous British chain. In my own *quartier* there's the Village Voice, of course, where I may twitch through readings but can go into a trance when browsing the books. Today, though, it's not on my route.

Some Americans here have cars, especially if they have children to schlep around. Sandy has an old Renault, but when she's not with kids, she uses the *métro* or bus, for which I'm glad, because I'm sick of hearing about how there's never any place to park, true or not. I take the *métro,* too, of course, when I want to save time, but when I'm not in a hurry, I prefer the bus. I love being able to check everything out on the bus route (while sitting down, for a change), as the bus chugs along. Its pace suits me, although sometimes you get a driver who's a *cow-boy* and then you really have to hold on. You can see a bus coming, and even if you aren't planted exactly at the stop, the driver invariably opens the door. *"Merci, monsieur. C'est très gentil,"* I say, something else I've learned from Paul.

And then the cabs. I rarely take a cab when I'm alone. Sometimes, Caroline and I share one if we are heading someplace far, if it's too hot (or cold), if it's raining, if we're feeling lazy, or if there's a *manif,* and signs at the bus stop say the bus we want is not running. What am I saying? You can't get a taxi when it rains. You can wait on line with the others at a taxi stand and get drenched, or just take the *métro* and be done with it.

Parisians boast of their transport system, except, of course, for their own *métro* or bus line, which is without doubt the worst: the least frequent and the most crowded. And I, having waited for buses in some other cities I could name (and have), love the public transport here, except for the bus that passes close to my own corner, which is the least frequent and most crowded in town.

Now, it is mid-morning, and I have tried, as I do each day— with varying degrees of success—to write Hemingway's "one true sentence" at my command post: my spacious desk with the computer, printer, file folders, and the Plan of Attack taped above the desk, actually with a few items checked off. And there's a large mug of Earl Grey tea (no Oreos, these days) all at reach. But for now, I wonder how sincere a sentence in a guidebook has to be? So, I give up and call Caroline. We agree to meet at the Embassy, as I will first go alone on my bookstore trek. "Let's come home together afterward," I suggest. "There's a lot to catch up on." Although this is clearly rubbish, I have decided to come clean.

Just after I hang up with Caroline, the phone rings. I'm glad it's Jean-Pierre, but he's speaking in French, and so I shift the language part of my brain. I could ask him to speak in English, but I'm too stubborn.

"*Bonjour, Frahn, c'est Jhee-Pay,*" says J-P. He suggests going over to the Embassy together. J-P, newly appointed *PDG (président directeur général)* of an old family publishing house—anyone would recognize his last name—has been publishing Findlay for years, so of course, he will attend. He could have his driver swing by around 5:30 p.m., although J-P says *dix-sept heures trente*. You have to get used to the twenty-four-hour clock. Otherwise, how would you know when a film begins—at *16, 18, ou 20h*?

THE TWO HORSES OF FRANCE

The Germans have the VW Beetle, and the Americans love the Ford Mustang, but for the French it's the funny little Citroën 2CV, called *le deux chevaux*. The two horses. This two-horsepower car first appeared in 1948 and, with updates, stayed popular until its demise 42 years later, in 1990.

Simple and rugged, the 2CV was designed in the 1930s, when 70 percent of the workforce was in agriculture. With a vehicle that used only three liters of gas to travel 100 km, farmers would be able to haul goods over fields or rough roads. The *très petite voiture* (very small car) was ready for manufacture by 1939, but when the Nazis marched in, Citroën hid the plans.

After the war, the 2CV—derided by journalists as a "sardine can"—was an immediate hit. A flat-twin air-cooled engine powered the dual H-frame chassis with its steel shell, flap-up windows, and a detachable fabric sunroof. There were a four-wheel independent suspension, front-wheel drive, four-speed transmission, and inboard front brakes—but no coolant, radiator, or water pump, no distributor, and—except for the brakes—no hydraulic parts. It may not have been the fastest car on the road, but it was safe, and with all sections replaceable, easy to repair. Soon there was a three-year waiting list, then five.

But the decades moved on, and the beloved 2CV just couldn't compete on Europe's new superhighways. So, you might still see some 2CV on the streets, and many of those are generally well-taken care of, as a treasured possession should be. More often, though, they're seen in car clubs and rallies, still revered by the French.

I have known J-P since I was in publishing in New York, where our paths often crossed. So, I knew him first, not Sandy. It's good that in the divorce I didn't have to choose. I tend to like Sandy, except when I think she's being unfair to J-P, or when she lets her dog, Julien, do his stuff on the sidewalk. It's just that I could never have given up J-P. In any case, for this afternoon I decline J-P's kind offer, but, slightly embarrassed, I mention neither my lunch in rue Guisarde nor my bookstore prowl.

Frankly, it's easier to get used to the way the time is displayed than the date. I tell Americans that they shouldn't be surprised to see a date written as 18/09/08, meaning September 18, 2008. The day comes first, then the month, and then the year. It might have been different had Ezra Pound had his way, however, for all records would have started again after the appearance of *Ulysses*. Thus, 1psU—*post scriptum Ulysses*—would have replaced the year 1921.

Just before I close up shop for the day, I check the *méteo* on the Internet one last time, although I have already decided what to wear. Since the forecast calls for sun and I will be walking a fair distance, I wear thigh-high sheer stockings with adorable lacy tops, a short black skirt, and matching silk shirt, with my favorite pale blue cashmere jacket, one that brings out the blue in my eyes. (I'm pulling out all the stops today.) Everything fits just fine, now that I have actually lost a few kilos. My flat shoes look casual but smart (I think). My streaked hair isn't frizzy, owing to a miraculous lack of humidity, and my makeup, for once, is doing for me what it should. And, even the new pink sunglasses I bought in a reckless fit have been wiped clean. I close the door behind me, walk down my thirty-four steps, and I am on my way. I will be about five minutes late, just right.

Late or not, when I get to the restaurant, having checked the entire look in a store window at the corner of rue des Canettes, the place seems closed up tight. In an instant, my heart sinks. But then, through the glass door, I see commotion toward the back, and so I knock on the door. Loudly, firmly, but in a sweet feminine manner. Almost immediately, Joël is at the door, welcoming me in. I can see that all the tables are set for lunch, and there is one table at the back that has fresh flowers on it, a bottle of Chateldon (classier even than San Pellegrino), and a bottle of red wine, already opened. This is getting good.

Here is what I learn at lunch (somewhat in this order), telling myself I must remember every minute, despite drinking two glasses of a lunchy kind of red wine Joël says is a Chinon from the Loire. Cold asparagus wrapped in marinated salmon topped by sprigs of dill, plus thin wedges of melon to the side, will be a good summer appetizer. Joël is separated from his wife.

(I will believe this until I have evidence to the contrary.) *Salade de poulet* with bits of walnuts, avocado, and a slightly spicy teriyaki-type dressing should be a refreshing cold course, as is a hearty salad with cold *haricots verts* (green beans) topped with sliced *foie gras* and tossed with a balsamicky vinaigrette. We devour both. He doesn't have much chance to read but has a collection of cookbooks from all over the world, for he does like reading about exotic cuisines. A hot main course (which we share, for I am unused to all this culinary excitement) is *saumon à l'unilateral*, pan-poached lightly from the bottom up, with warm potato salad and caramelized endive. He has two children, now grown and with families of their own, living in Montbeliard, his own hometown. He does not see them as often as he would like. *Oeufs à la neige* for a summer dessert—with its fluffy meringue and *crème anglaise*—happens already to be on my A-list. He doesn't have a favorite bookstore (one point off), but he loves to explore Paris, especially around the boat basin near the Bastille (point regained). Neither of us drinks coffee, and he says, *"Nous sommes faits pour nous entendre,"* which I must look up, but which I hope means that we're fated to understand each other. And, oh yes, he thinks I have lovely eyes.

Best of all, I learn that not only is he sweetly silver-haired, he is genuinely nice. Why had I been nervous? It isn't, after all, as though we had just met. Had I not made sure I was in rue Guisarde all those months?

Our pleasant, flirty lunch is interrupted several times by customers wanting to chat and by one crisis in the kitchen that only the *patron* could solve. So, we don't wind up until around *14h*, when, well fed, wined, and complimented, I know I must push on. As I stand up, enthusiastically saying, *"Merci mille fois"* for the lunch, I am wondering how to move on to the next step (whatever it might be). But Himself does it first. *"Frahn-zess,"* he says. "Next week I will be getting a shipment of new wines, including an interesting Menetou-Salon. Perhaps you would like to taste it with me?"

Suddenly, I have one of my million-dollar ideas. *"Volontiers,"* I respond (since it worked so well the first time). "But generally, I don't drink wine at lunch. Today was an exception, since I'm not working this afternoon. So, why don't you come over to my place when you're finished here one evening, and we can taste it there?" I do, of course, remember having been told when researching my first guide to Paris that if a single woman invites a man to her home, her intentions are clear. I wait for his answer.

There is only the smallest of pauses, and then a broad smile. *"Quelle bonne idée,"* he says. And it's done. After that, we take our leave, and he shuts the glass door behind me. I am once again standing in rue Guisarde. Well, well, well.

I stand for a moment to clear my head, and then I turn to start the walk over to rue de Rennes to catch the No. 95, which will let me off across the street from Brentano's. I begin, of course, the first mental replay of the entire lunch. Then, despite my mind being totally elsewhere, I hear a voice behind me call, "Fran!" I turn. It's John, the one from San Francisco, and he has in his hands two large bags from Mulot, the same *traiteur* Caroline uses for her luncheons.

"Oh, so you're finally back," I say. Perhaps it's just my excellent frame of mind, but I realize that I am pleased to see him. Even if this is the wine speaking, I am also gratified, once again, that it is a blue blazer day. We fall into step and walk together to Place St-Sulpice, then toward rue de Rennes.

"Yeah, it took longer than we thought to sell the house and to divvy a lot of furniture among the kids. But we got it done. And to treat ourselves we went spring skiing in Aspen for a couple of weeks. But now we're back. We're going to eat dinner on these goodies from Mulot."

"Listen, John," I say, as we are reaching rue de Rennes where I peel off. "Would you and Rose like to come over for a glass of champagne next week or the week after?"

"I'll ask her," he says. "And we'll call you." He walks on toward rue de Grenelle while I make a beeline for the bus stop, as I see the No. 95 coming up the street.

It turns out on inspection that all three shops have my Paris book correctly aligned on their shelves. At Smith's, the last stop, I buy a couple of books. Since I'm too early to show up at the Embassy, I window shop back along rue de Rivioli, deciding there's nothing to take notes about, and finally wind up at Angelina's stylish *salon de thé*. I can leaf through my new books—a biography of Napoleon's son, another of Mary McCarthy, who long lived in Paris (although she didn't always like it so very much), and the new Zagat's guide to Paris restaurants, in English.

Angelina's may be known for its *chocolat chaud,* but today all I want is a cup of tea. Looking around, I wonder whether those women sitting with their own pots of tea feel as smug as I do. Not a chance. I muse a bit about *Zho-elle* and our upcoming *rendez-vous*. (I must be prepared. I will make a list.) But I also wonder who will be at the speech tonight, perhaps someone else new to meet? Yes, as Caroline said, I am feeling pretty frisky, after all.

As I near the Embassy later on, I see my widower friend, Richard, rounding the corner. With him is his friend Max Freifeld, whom I know slightly and who never qualified as "someone new," even when he was. (Richard has always called the guy Freifeld, so the rest of us do, too.) Their hair is damp, so they must be coming directly from the Ritz pool. I first met Freifeld at a party at Richard's shortly after he moved here. They went to the same California college forty years ago, and they love to rehash the old days, when they were part of the radical left. "Solidarity!" they greet each other now, which makes me crazed. At the party, Richard, who is a capitalist *par excellence* and who could buy and sell any of us in our little group, bellowed along with Freifeld, "You Can't Scare Me, I'm Stickin' to the Union" along with other left-wing songs. This, from someone who never misses a Rotary luncheon at La Coupole in Montparnasse?

Freifeld, an aging hippie who has lived in Paris for some thirty years, is married to a French radio *personage* (a classical music announcer, or so I'm told) who works in the evenings. I've never met her. In any case, Freifeld always seems to me rather glum. Tonight, though, he smiles and says he is pleased to see me again. I hope they behave themselves when Findlay lets loose about the Red Scare.

We show our passports and invitations, go through the metal detector, and walk up the ornate staircase to the second floor. A young Embassy employee guides us through what can only be called an antechamber, an enormous pastel-colored room with an extremely high ceiling. Painted cherubs smile down at us, and mirrors reflect their images, and us. It is slightly intimidating in its brilliance, I have to say. (Perhaps I should have come with J-P the *PDG,* after all.) As we enter the main *salle,* I see that chairs have been set up in rows, a small dais and *micro* rigged in front, and a table with refreshments—covered and closed for the moment— over against the wall. Our young American shepherd seems slightly condescending in a way no young French person would be (unless he had found an embassy job, perhaps). He would learn a thing or two if he stayed to hear Findlay speak.

The first person I see is Sandra, seated at a gleaming Steinway tucked into a corner, a concert grand, and she is playing softly some old familiar American tunes. Petite as she is, she looks stunning in the graceful black gown we bought together on sale on that late-January shopping excursion, and she also looks relaxed, for a change. What with her kids and trips out of town, I haven't seen her in a while. I walk over to the piano. I wave and she smiles. A man I don't know is standing by her side, young, tall, and blond, and it is clear he is there for her, not the music. (I hope today's lack of envy keeps up.) But Klaus and Paul are also there, and they are listening with sweet far-away expressions on their faces as Sandy plays. I remember when my mother used to play old phonograph records of the songs of Bing Crosby, Perry Como, and even the Andrew Sisters, who entertained troops during World War II. So, even though Sandy generally plays classical French music, I know from what she told me that the songs she'll play tonight are appropriate to the evening. Now, she is playing *"Darling, je vous aime beaucoup. Je ne sais pas what to do,"* a song, I think, from the 1930s. I go over to the piano and quietly kiss the cheeks of my friends. "I wish we could sing," Klaus whispers to me. "I know all these songs."

Our group stakes off one side. With Klaus and Paul behind me, I head over to where Richard and Freifeld have settled themselves next to Caroline. The Lovells' young landlord is here, which is strange, for I've never heard him say a word of *l'anglais*. Ida is dithering by an inner set of doors, ushering dignitaries, shaking hands. J-P hasn't yet arrived. I wonder what he'll think when he sees Sandy. (I did not tell him she'd be here. Nor did I tell Sandy about J-P. Stupid, I am not.)

Edie, who works late, won't be coming. (I must tell her about the caramelized endive.) And nor will the sculptor Margot, who said she had to go to her bronzer. For me, that would have meant a tanning salon, but for Margot it had to do with some big commission she has received. Too bad, for I only glimpsed her once in the winter, at a crowded *vernissage* (gallery opening) that I went to with the boys, and although we waved, we didn't have a chance to talk, she being surrounded by people who looked like they'd fit in those artist-in-a-garret films. And who else? Jack and Jennifer won't arrive in Paris for another month or more. So, I think that's all. Odile Hellier, the owner of the Village Voice bookshop, comes to join our crew. I hope she's doing better financially than did Sylvia Beach. With the dollar so low and books being sold on the Internet, suddenly I'm concerned, but, of course, I'd never ask. The French never pry.

Alice, wearing a dress and high heels terrifically out of fashion, is sitting in front of the *micro*. From the side, I think she looks rather thin. I hope there's nothing wrong. Findlay always takes center stage, and somehow we tend to let him. But it is Alice who is the mainstay, and we all know it. Findlay does, too, for although he doesn't give her public credit, he is always attentive and affectionate, in his way.

Tonight, Alice is flanked by two almost-middle-aged men, sons Howard and Marc, who have come down from Brittany for the gala event. They are *propriétaires* of a spa directly on the English Channel, *la Manche*. They offer their clients *thalassothérapie*, a seawater cure that the French flock to in droves. I'm always telling Caroline that we should go (the sons having offered us a discount), saying it would be good for her tricky knee. But discount or not, it's not cheap, that's for sure. "The dollar will go back up," she says to me when I suggest such a trip, "and then you just watch my steam."

While waiting, we talk about where to go to dinner afterward and how many will come. It looks like we will be about seven. What's inexpensive nearby? And where might we get in without having booked in advance? "There's a new Japanese noodle bar in rue St-Anne, I've heard about," I suggest, picturing those checkmarks that are beginning to accumulate on my Plan of Attack. Why not get it out of the way tonight? "Is that too far to walk?"

Klaus is immediately indignant. "Count us out!" he exclaims. It had totally slipped my mind that the boys will only eat French food. "I didn't come to Paris to eat Tex-Mex," Klaus goes on, as though he hadn't said that exact phrase any time someone mentions Japanese or Chinese food.

Fortunately, Klaus is liberal in what he thinks of as French. Any island, isthmus, or tropical colony that belonged to France, even for the blink of an eye, counts. In addition to bistros truly French, we could also go Vietnamese, of course, which we often do. But I suspect we'll take the *métro* up to Etoile and walk toward rue Poncelet to eat Algerian couscous, which they like better than Moroccan. Couscous is inexpensive and is often really good. If the English once could claim that the sun never set on their Empire, I think the French might have said that there was always a utensil heading toward the mouth of someone French.

Once, Friefeld (through Richard) asked me to a lecture about the decline of Yiddish, at some Jewish cultural center over near the Bastille. After the talk by the (distinctly unappealing) French linguist, he informed me coldly that he refused to speak English because it was the language of *impérialisme*. This from a citizen of a country that once owned great parts of America, had colonies around the world, and still has *départements et territoires d'Outremer* (overseas)—lumping them together by calling them *les Dom-Tom*? It seems to me that the problem with English for *le professeur* was that America won. Of course, the concern the French have with *mondialisation* is that America's (*inférieure*) culture has truly implanted itself as insidiously as the French had feared. Yet, none of this is the fault of the English language, which—with its elasticity and rich use of idioms—I happen to like.

I do understand how much the French revere their beautiful language, and I hate myself for mangling it when I do. (Even more than the French pity me.) Perhaps more than any other people, the French truly love words. How many languages have one word for a city bus (*autobus*), another for a bus that runs into the country (*car*), and a third for those huge buses that takes foreign tourists around (*autocar*)? But let's not get carried away with admiration, here. Who but the French would say "four-twenty-ten-nine," just to say "ninety-nine"? Not their French-speaking neighbors, to be sure. The Belgians say *"nonante neuf"* and leave it at that.

The audience starts to hush, the doors are closed, and the ambassador comes to the *micro* to welcome us all. His well-dressed wife is standing next to him, smiling. Delighted to see so many old faces here. (Just what does he mean by that?) France and America after World War II. People like Mr. Lovell to document special relationship. Back to days when America was born. Silas Deane, just prior to Declaration of Independence. Negotiated secretly for arms. Cooperation of Louis XVI. "If he's going so far back," Caroline whispers to me, "shouldn't he start with the Native Americans that French traders dragged here to put on display?" Ssh. Have a good time. Refreshments afterward. Do stay. Must go. Bye bye. Friendly wave. We all smile. We all clap. The dignitaries disappear. The young Embassy employee tags along behind. The talk begins.

Just as Findlay begins to speak, Jean-Pierre slips into the seat directly behind me and pats my shoulder in greeting. I had seen him approaching in one of the mirrors. *Elegantissime!* Perhaps in his mid-fifties by now, tall and thin, somehow his totally white hair makes him look younger. He has a rather large nose, but it only adds to his dramatic look of class. (I do not agree with Sandy that it is bulbous.) He is wearing the uniform of Paris executives, the dark suit with the little pin stripe, the light-colored shirt with faint stripes, the gleaming tie. His heavy gold cufflinks, however, a birthday *cadeau* from *Grandpère,* are not what everyone wears.

I'm crazy about J-P. I tell him so occasionally, and he smiles and says only, *"Moi aussi."* It's his reserved French way. He's crazy about me, too. About fifteen years ago in New York—after having served on several publishing committees and panels together—we spent several evenings together, which I think now could have gone either way. But without saying anything explicit—at least I don't remember anything—we drifted into being true friends. When I was miserable in my second marriage, I talked to him. When he was frantic in his first, he called me transatlantic, sometimes waking me up. That was okay with me, then.

Nothing serious could have been in the cards between J-P and me. He's not much younger than I, but when I met him I was in my older-man stage. (This obviously has never happened to Sandy.) His family is part of the *gratin*—upper crust—and mine crept out of Prague in the nick of time. He stays out late to "*pahr-tee,*" and I won't. (Once when I invited him on a Sunday morning outing to the organic market on boulevard Raspail, he sounded perplexed. *"Le dimanche matin?"* he asked. *"Mais, chérie*, there is no morning on Sundays.") He smokes smelly Havanas, which he gets from La Civette, the shop that has been serving his family for centuries. *Et voilà.* Once, I asked him directly if he would please introduce me to one of his nifty publishing friends, but *non,* he shook his head. It was for my own benefit, of course, he said, for they were all *arrivistes."* I should be concerned about whether someone is self-made or *nouveau riche*? *Ne me fais pas rire.* (I mean, isn't *riche* the operative word here?) Well, in some ways, he's just as dense as most of the other men I've known.

Findlay is in his glory, and rightly so. As he arranges his papers and begins to speak, he looks around, nodding to at least half the people in the room. Alice reports to me later that he had assumed most of them were dead. I prepare myself for the Commies but, as always, Findlay is a surprise.

"I suppose I should talk about the hardships in Paris in those years after the war," he starts, "when food was rationed and when Soviet propaganda posed a real threat. But what is more interesting, at least to this reporter," Findlay gives what passes for a snort of modesty, "is understanding that the Paris that came out of the war and the Paris of today are two different cities. Just as life before jets and computers was unlike our life now. And the fact that France has emerged as the fourth largest economy in the world is in great part owing to the generosity of the Marshall Plan.

"Before the war, 70 percent of the workforce was in agriculture. Less than half the population lived in towns. And the cities themselves, if not medieval, were still mired in the nineteenth century, with antiquated industries based on handwork and elbow grease. This included Paris, for little had been improved since those famous—or infamous—Haussmannian improvements."

"Bastard," an elderly man cries out, and everyone laughs. "Nice to see you, Milt," Findlay says sharply. "So, you're still with us, are you?" Everyone laughs again. Findlay continues.

"The terrible wartime destruction required France to overhaul its entire infrastructure. Factories were refitted and new ones constructed, and to make it all work, the bombed-out railroad system was rebuilt. There was a shortage of workers, and all available materials went toward industrialization, not to the people, who sacrificed in order to rebuild. Yet, what took place ultimately was no less than a revolution, although not the one the Communists envisioned.

"First came the economist Jean Monnet, who developed '*Le Plan*' for French government and business cooperation. This, along with the open hand of the Marshall Plan, pushed France forward. As to the city, I remember later when President Pompidou said that Paris had to 'marry its century,' and that is just what he and others made it do."

I can't help it. My mind wanders off. I look around the exquisite room and manage not to shout, *Look where I am! Look at me, now!* I put my notebook in my lap, and I allow myself to feel the intense appreciation that envelops me from time to time. How could I express this? Is there something concrete to do? Write a paean to Paris? (How much can one person write about a city?) Send flowers to Napoleon at Invalides? Light a candle in the church at St-Sulpice?

"What would I do with all my stuff?" I asked Caroline, a few years ago—when I was here researching my second Paris book—we were talking about whether this could be a permanent move for me. Or not. Caroline herself took early retirement from her university in Wisconsin about fifteen years ago, and for her it was like coming home. When she was a baby, her divorced mother decided to live in Paris, and when the Nazis loomed, they stayed in Lucerne, until they managed to get back to the States. Caroline's perfect French makes me pea green—as does the fact that the merchants in the neighborhood don't look at her as though she came from a different planet when she speaks in French.

"I gave everything except some mementos to my children," she said. I brought over a few pictures in my valise, and I had some things sent. But everything else I bought over here."

But choosing what to toss was beyond my ken. Family nick-knacks, the desk my mother's cousin (the one who introduced me to Klaus and Paul) gave me, old framed photos of ancestors I never knew, the silver doodads that were handed down (and that my kids refuse to take off my hands). I kept them all, and now they're here in rue Servandoni with me, some still in cartons, out of sight. Caroline and Alice helped me unpack, listening to the stories of my family's old days, and drinking champagne that I had uncorked. I turn my attention back to Findlay, who seems to be winding up. I realize I've missed much of what he said, and I wish my mind hadn't wandered, but it did. At least I hadn't fallen asleep, the way good old Milt seems to have done. "Today in France," Findlay is saying, "agriculture accounts for only about 5 percent of the workforce, industry 28 percent, and the service sector about 67 percent. And more than 80 percent of the French live in towns. But what we are seeing now is an increasing uniformity of lifestyles and a level of consumerism that would have been impossible before the War. Paris became so central to French production that a few decades ago the government acted to decentralize industry. Yet, Paris remains *kilomètre zéro*, and it holds fast both to power and to the hearts of the French.

"My family and I arrived here more than a half century ago, and as I've no doubt said before, I feel about Paris the same as the day I arrived. I'm grateful to have participated in what was no less than the transformation of an ancient society into a modern wonder, and that its exquisite capital has been so good to me, in return. And last," Findlay smiles as he gathers up his papers and gestures toward the refreshment table, "let us not forget the important question posed by Charles de Gaulle: 'How can you govern, in peacetime, a people with 265 different kinds of cheese?'"

FURTHER READING (PART I)*

Beevor, Antony & Cooper, Artemis: *Paris After the Liberation: 1944-1949*. London, Penguin Books, 1995.

Cole, Robert: *A Traveller's History of Paris*. Brooklyn, NY, Interlink Books, 1994.

Gildea, Robert: *France Since 1945*. Oxford, Oxford University Press, 1996.

Karnow, Stanley: *Paris in the Fifties*. New York, Times Books, 1997.

Lennon, Peter: *Foreign Correspondent: Paris in the Sixties*. London, Picador, 1994.

Walter, Gérard, translated by Tony White: *Paris Under the Occupation*. New York, The Orion Press, 1960.

*All books available at the American Library in Paris, 10, rue du Général Camou, 75007 Paris.

The audience is enthusiastic in its applause. Alice is beaming, and Findlay looks sheepishly pleased. Immediately, a crowd of the silver-haired and bald floats up toward the front to surround them. It's old home week. As for me, I'm already looking forward to what I know will be a dinner *chez* Lovell in the next day or so, for us all to relive the evening's events and its triumph.

"And just who do you think wrote those last sentences?" I whisper to Caroline as we get up. "Unqualified gratitude is not Findlay's style."

"Do you need to ask? Well, he may not give her credit, but he knows what she does for him. Sixty years is a long time to be together."

"That reminds me," I say. "Do you think she's looking thin?"

"Un peu," Caroline says. "I asked her about it, but the doctor claims that except for her smoking so much, she's fine."

"Good. Well, let's go see what our generous ambassador has set out for treats," I suggest. We head for the wall where the refreshments are now uncovered and waiting for us.

"Frahn," calls J-P, coming up behind me. We kiss each other on both cheeks. "I'm so sorry I cannot stay. My brother Antoine has asked me to meet him at the Clos des Gourmets for dinner this evening, and I could not decline. I really must go. But we must talk soon, yes, *chérie?"* I express my disappointment (without so much as a hint as to how much I love the Clos des Gourmets) and we kiss again. He turns away, moving gracefully toward the door. He stops to talk with Sandy, who is back at the piano, shrugs and shakes his head, and then moves on to chat with a few distinguished-looking men on his way to the door. It does not escape me that, once again, he has not introduced me around.

And his brother Antoine? Only slightly older than J-P, he couldn't be more different—dignified, formal, married to one of those cold women Americans would claim are rude. (Actually, I'd use the word "frigid," if looking at Antoine is any indication.) I've met her only a couple of times, for she seems always away, taking one cure or another. Antoine, who is some high-up-something-or-other in the Ministry of Foreign Affairs, is often on his own, and perhaps this evening with J-P is one of those nights. I let J-P off the hook for rushing away. But just who were those guys at the door? And whatever it was that Sandy said to him, I do not want to know (at least not enough to ask).

Odile Hellier, having paid her respects to the Lovells, waves to us as she leaves, with the Lovells' young landlord following her out the door. I suspect J-P will take a cab, having sent his own driver home, or perhaps his brother's chauffeur is waiting for him down below. Odile and the landlord will no doubt take the bus.

Kissing as a greeting among friends is one of the pleasures of French life. The French really can kiss. If each person arriving at a dinner party of eight—mostly family and some friends—kisses all the others on both cheeks, it means 112 *bisous* just when the evening has begun. The kiss at the end of the evening is just the same. Both cheeks, two fast but sincere kisses. All told, there will have been 224 kisses during the evening. No wonder I love life here. But this kind of kissing is an art: Place your cheek lightly, lightly against the cheek of the other person and make the sound of a kiss, with just the merest side of your mouth in contact. Do not turn your head directly toward the cheek and plant the kiss firmly on it with a smack. This is simply a greeting, not a wake-up call. On the other hand, it is a real kiss and not something just mouthed into the air.

The rest of our little group moves determinedly toward the refreshments, which have been uncovered by the young man, who has slipped back into the room. I hope he heard Findlay speak. He stands behind a table of libations—white and red wine and chilled Perrier—and starts to pour. After we have our drinks in hand, we each pick up a paper plate and one of the red, white, and blue napkins that are neatly stacked (or perhaps they're *bleu, blanc, rouge*, in homage to the French). We start our inspection. There's a platter of cheeses, another plate of smoked meat in little rolls, and bowls of guacamole and chips. On each end of the table, there is a *pain surprise*, a large round loaf of bread that when the top is removed shows itself to be full of small, triangular, neatly trimmed sandwiches of various sorts. And dominating the middle, there is a replica of the Eiffel Tower covered in gold foil, with huge strawberries attached to it by skewers, probably the tackiest thing I've ever seen in France.

Plates in hand, we nosh. The sandwiches are cucumber, smoked salmon, and some unidentifiable meat. We all load up on everything, except sort-of-kosher Freifeld, who passes on the meat. Caroline thinks the meat is duck, but who would make a sandwich out of duck? Anyway, it's good. And the strawberries are sweeter than I would have thought. I remove two more picks from the Eiffel Tower and put them on my plate. We all agree this has been a splendid occasion and that Findlay well deserves all the attention. We balance our paper plates and plastic glasses, we sip our wine, and we look around at the others. I notice that the women are wearing low-heeled shoes, all except Alice across the room, who has now sat down.

Eventually, the crowd begins to thin, and we start to talk about dinner. It's time to decide. Caroline speaks up first. "The truth is I'm no longer hungry," she admits. "The ambassador puts on too good a spread. I think I'll just go back across the river."

"Oh, good! I'll go with you," I say quickly, relieved, for I, too, have eaten enough. The smoked salmon sandwiches were tasty, and perhaps I overdid. I'm not exactly full, but I'm no longer hungry enough to go out to eat. And if I go with Caroline, maybe I can persuade her to stop for an *eau minérale* at one of the sidewalk cafés in our neighborhood for a while. It's warm enough tonight to sit outside under the overhead heaters, and by now it's staying light past *21h*. In full summer it stays light until almost *23h*. Of course, that means in dead winter it is dark by *17h*, but when I get back home from my December away, the days are slowly reviving, once again.

Suddenly, the dinner is off. The boys say they had a large lunch and think they will just stroll up toward the opera, perhaps to have a light supper at one of their haunts, a restaurant that they claim caters to aging gays. "Graying gardens," Paul has described the place to me, which is about a ten-minute walk from Concorde, or so they say, having never invited me to go along. "Oh, darling, I call it *le Moribond*," Klaus said once. "You wouldn't like it, not at all."

Now, though, Paul stops me as they leave and suggests lunch tomorrow in the Latin Quarter. This I know means eating upstairs at their "club" in the 5th, which seems to me another graying gardens, but all I do is accept with pleasure. "Good," says Klaus. "We can stay there a long time and talk and talk. They never rush us." I kiss both my friends and agree to meet them outside the door of the building exactly at *13h*.

Richard, after consultation with Freifeld, says they will take the *métro* to the Marais, so they can eat in one of the Middle Eastern felafel eateries he likes. Afterward, Freifeld will walk home, just past Place de la Bastille, and Richard will walk south to the river and back to Place Dauphine. "I'm still hungry," Freifeld says with sort of a whine, but it is true that he didn't gorge as much as the rest of us. I'm tempted because I love the Marais—what could be livelier than a *quartier* dominated by Jews and gays and falafel—but the truth is I'm ready to spill the beans to Caroline. Having waited so long, I can hardly contain myself.

Richard and Freifeld are just behind us as Caroline and I put on our coats, and I can hear Richard say, "I've been meaning to ask you, Max-eroo. Did you see the notice in the alumni newsletter of the reunion in July of the Fair Play for Cuba Committee? I'm seriously thinking of going." It's a good thing they're on their own tonight. I do not have patience for this.

Caroline and I send a salute toward Findlay and Alice, and the sons wave to us but do not leave their parents' sides. So, we walk down the impressive staircase, through all the security devices, out the turnstile, and at the corner turn right toward Place de la Concorde. We arrive at the bus stop. Caroline is eyeing my W.H. Smith bag, and I can see she is perishing with curiosity. I'll let her read the McCarthy biography before I do.

When we are seated on the No. 84, we go over the evening, and I remember to tell her about running into John again on rue Guisarde. The good stuff can wait. I suggest she go with me sometime to check out the Japanese eatery in rue Ste-Anne. And then, showing her a brochure I had picked up at Brentano's, I ask if she'll come with me tomorrow night to a klezmer concert in the downstairs *sous-sol* of an Eastern European delicatessen behind the department store BHV (pronounced *Bay Ahsh Vay*).

"Everybody should hear klezmer music, once," I tell her.

"Sure, I'm game," she says. "And what about Edie? Sounds like her cup of tea."

"No, tomorrow's still a week night. Her cooking demonstration will run too late."

I hand over the McCarthy book, and she stuffs it into that huge tote bag of hers, which seems always to have room for something more. (Contributing, I'm medically sure, to the problems with her knee.) We chat until the bus deposits us on rue du Four, and we walk down rue Bonaparte, turning toward the Café de la Mairie, kitty-corner on Place St-Sulpice across from the *mairie* (the administrative town hall for our *arrondissement*). We sit down and each order a San Pellegrino, and the waiter, who knows us, brings us a plate of olives, just to be kind.

"Okay, sweetie," says Caroline. "I've waited long enough. Could you please tell me just what it is that we're catching up on this evening?"

So, I spit it all out, everything I hadn't told her, about my silver-haired *restaurateur*, about my passing by at strategic intervals, about the escalation in greetings, about his name being Joël, about his saying he is separated from his wife, about our lunch today, about the thigh-high stockings with adorable lacy tops, and I confess about the evening to come *chez moi*.

"I knew it!" she exults. "I knew it! Look, you've lost weight. Your makeup is good. You're wearing your lucky blue blazer.

You're less skeptical than usual. And don't think I didn't see your new sunglasses when you came in. Well, you said you were ready for a new project, and now there's one in sight. I have every confidence in you."

With nothing more to say on this subject (meaning I restrain myself) and eating our free olives, we fuss a bit about the low dollar but talk more about a new *crème* (Eluage by Avène) that is supposed to firm up one's neck. And then, as usual, we kiss our kisses, and I cut across the square to rue Servandoni, while Caroline moves on to rue de Tournon. Alone, I do wax on in my mind in a bubble bath, and I decide to buy the new *crème*. Then I sleep just fine.

Although this next morning I am up early and starting to work, I keep looking at the clock. I wait until a decent hour—that is exactly one minute after nine—to call Sandra. She is awake and it sounds as though she's alone. "Your playing was great last night," I say. "It really added to the evening. And you looked terrific in the dress."

"Thanks," she says. "But if you're calling to find out who he was, there's nothing to tell. He works over at the ministry in Antoine's department, and I met him some time ago through the family. That's all."

"That's all?"

"Well, almost," she laughs. "And now, if you don't mind, I'm going to make myself a cup of coffee." We hang up with vows to get together soon, although I know it's not in the cards until the June sales or she is once again between men. I am glad I managed to keep my mouth shut, and that I will, at least until I have something to tell.

Since the week's forecast predicts more sunny days, after I finish at my desk I walk slowly over to the Latin Quarter for my lunch with the boys. I take the long way, through the always lively Place de la Contrescarpe, where I haven't been in several years. I note that it's still full of kids, students at the Sorbonne or the Collège de France. And I stop in at a few new shops near the famous market street rue Mouffetard. My mouth is almost watering as I move on.

I arrive exactly at *13h* at the building where the boys' "club" is hidden upstairs. It is pleasant to wait outside the doors for the boys to arrive from the library. I am in a fine state of mind. I like Klaus's idea of having time to talk, for I think it's right of me, even at this early stage, to mention that there may possibly be a new man in my life. I am following their instructions, after all. Klaus, I know, will get all in a twitter, and Paul will pat my hand and tell me something wise, whether to be careful or to take it slowly or something that is certainly apt but not at all in my nature.

But I never get to say a word about Joël, or about anything else, for that matter, because as soon as we are seated in the boys' regular corner, and as soon as we have ordered the two-course *menu* of the *entrée* and fish of the day, Paul says something that totally lays me out.

"My dear," he says, "do you recall a warm autumn night in Chicago years ago when we were all walking down the street with Alberto Moravia, that time he had come from Italy for a writers' conference?"

"I'll never forget it," I nod. "Moravia and I were strolling together ahead of you and Klaus, and he intoned to me in that serious way that he had, "*Sono nel inverno della vita,*" and you told me later that he had been saying that for at least twenty years! I really laughed at that. But why? What makes you bring him up today?"

"Well, perhaps Moravia wasn't actually in the winter of his life at that time, as he claimed, but Klaus and I are now." He pauses and looks at Klaus.

Suddenly, my heart stops. I can't breathe. I think I will faint. Something awful is happening, I just know it. "Who's dying?"

I ask, and I can feel myself starting to cry, middle-aged maturity nowhere in sight. "Just tell me. Don't make me wait."

"Oh, little darling, we're not dying," Klaus says and reaches over to hug me. "But we are old, and we have to think about where we should spend our remaining time. And so, when we go to Rome this summer, we're going to think about whether we don't want to live again where it's warmer and where it doesn't rain so much."

At first all I can hear is that they're not dying, so I can catch my breath. To recover even more, I take a piece of *baguette* from the basket, break off a bit of the crust and put it in my mouth. I hold out my glass to Klaus for him to pour some of the Badoit that has been put on the table. But then it hits me what they are actually saying. I realize why they wanted to talk and talk at this lunch. And I realize, too, finally, why they are so busy trying to get me interested in men other than themselves.

"But you belong here. Paris suits you," I accuse them, knowing that I am not looking at this from their point of view. I suppose this isn't gracious, but I can't hold back.

"That's all true," Paul says, patiently. "It's just a thought. Now, my dear, pull yourself together and eat your lunch."

Later, feeling more unsettled than usual, I think I'd rather curl up with Napoleon's son than submit myself and Caroline to the klezmers. I could also read the newspaper—although the current financial news from the States would not help, I'm sure. So, I call Caroline, and after telling her about the boys (and Sandy), she insists I go. "It was your idea, after all. And it will be a hoot."

About the boys, she says, "First of all, they hate the rain and the cold. They've been suffering all winter, in case you hadn't noticed. And second, Rome isn't that far away. My goodness, just don't worry about it. You're dwelling again."

So, all that being true, I agree to go. Caroline tells me to meet her at the bus stop on rue du Four. It's not the same bus stop as the night before, although it's on the same block, for not all buses running on the same street stop at the same place. I suppose it's to avoid congestion, but sometimes it's difficult for me, when I'm playing the odds, thinking to take whichever bus arrives first, and I have to dash.

It's not a long ride on the No. 70 to the BHV, so we are early enough to get good seats. The klezmer music is interesting, and the bass saxophonist is seriously cute. Caroline was right that I should come. During the opening pieces I realize, though, that I had surely been aware of the boys not liking the cold, but that it had never occurred to me just how much. But after just a few pieces, Caroline nudges me, and whispering, we agree that our need for klezmer has been met. We will leave at the *entr'acte*. As we go out, we see Mitzi and Anna, neither of whom, it turns out, has been able to convince her husband to come.

"How's the transition coming along, Anna?" I ask, making sure to use her name.

"Oh, you heard about my fruit crisis?" She nods. "Well, things are getting a bit easier. At least I learn from my mistakes."

"Tell her about your own fruit *gaffe*," Caroline nudges me.

I smile, pretending I had forgotten, but one never forgets. "The first summer I was here, I went to the *marché biologique* to get some produce, and I asked whether they used *préservatifs*, thinking I was talking about preservatives."

"You, too?" Anna rolls her eyes. "I've heard that a lot of newcomers ask whether they put condoms on the fruit. But that makes me feel better," she says.

"Yes, me, too," I say, only a tiny bit miffed at having been classified with the rest of the world, although I understand that particular mistake is almost a standard joke. Couldn't I have come up with an example sort of charmingly unique?

"I think just maybe I'm beginning to get the hang of things here...." Anna starts to go on.

"Don't be too sure," Mitzi interrupts. "Just when you think you're in control, the Parisians let you know in some way that you're not. You just have to laugh it off and chalk it up to experience."

With a sudden pang, I am reminded of Paul's list of qualities an American must have in order to adapt to life here. Perhaps I could just ask innocently if there is such a list about Rome. (Being snide sometimes works.) I could tell him of two more: you have to be able to laugh at yourself when you look like an idiot—at least after the fact—and you should only make each mistake once.

"By the way, Fran," Mitzi says, just as the bell rings and they are about to go back down the stairs, "I'm going to mail the invitations to the bar mitzvah soon," and I smile and nod, thinking *What on earth am I going to get for a kid I don't even know?* Adding insult to injury, she then says, "I'll call you, maybe we can have lunch." Although picturing a lunch with nothing but bar mitzvah talk, I nod again, of course. And after kisses all around and Mitzi making more noise about getting together soon, she and Anna head back inside.

"We never have asked Anna to go to the cinema with us," I say, remembering that we had talked of doing just that.

"I asked her once," Caroline says. "But she couldn't come that day. And then we didn't go. In fact, we haven't been to a film in quite a while. I'll look in *Pariscope* and see what's on this week."

On the way home, even though it is getting late, Caroline and I decide to stop for a drink at the Café Deux Magots. It's filled with locals by now, the tourists having relinquished their spots. Caroline convinces me that we should be drinking champagne, and for a change, I am not at all averse. The bubbly and the lights illuminating the ancient church across the street have their effect. Thinking of the dollar and her purse, I say I will treat. "You got me out of my funk," I say. "You were right."

"Do you know the expression *la vie familiale?*" she asks me, changing the subject.

"The way the French include family in everything they do? Why?"

"Well, running into Mitzi like that reminded me. Isn't that what our group is, in our American way?"

"Family? I suppose so," I say, thinking again of Klaus and Paul. But I don't bring them up, not wanting to ruin my mellow mood. "So, you're saying that's why I felt so content during Findlay's talk?"

"No," Caroline laughs. "It was the blue blazer."

"Yeah," I smile. "But do you think we'll ever get tired of dissecting the wonders of Paris and our lives here?"

"Depends on how long we live," Caroline says. "But that's definitely my last thought for tonight."

"Good. I'm for that. Now, how about another glass of champagne?" Caroline, of course, does not demur, and she signals the waiter by raising her empty glass.

It is past *23h* when we start to walk home in the delicious spring air. As we stroll on our regular route down rue Bonaparte toward Place St-Sulpice, Caroline tries to tell me something about Aaron Burr having lived here in terrible poverty after he killed Alexander Hamilton and how he had gotten himself involved in the quest for Mexican independence. But owing to the champagne and feeling less antsy overall, all I can do is giggle at how so very *sophistiquée* I feel.

A Paris Romance

S O, HERE WE ARE IN PARIS, said to be the romantic capital of the world. *Moi,* with the mood I'm in these days (the boys and Rome notwithstanding), I'm not only beginning to think this is true, I have decided in my infinite wisdom that I am one of the few who understands why. I've been mulling on this unceasingly during this week, of course, not only for me but also (or so I tell myself) for my book. But somewhat out of character, so far I haven't talked it over with anyone, not to Caroline or even Sandra. So, this is just me, on the day of the evening that I will prove what I think, or not.

Here is what I suppose, at least today. The great French writer and lover Honoré de Balzac wrote, "To speak of love is to make love." So, when we say those words, and no matter how casually we toss them off—about how enchanted we are by the beauty and charm of Paris with its ancient buildings in narrow streets, its aromas and tastes, its flowing river and beckoning bridges—I suspect we are making love, experiencing in all our five senses how Paris makes us feel, how it makes us feel about ourselves and our own lives. It makes us feel romantic, whether there is an adorable silver-haired man in sight, or not. As Victor Hugo said, "He who looks into the depths of Paris grows giddy." Perhaps this is what is going on with me.

I really do believe that somehow it is Paris itself that evokes this romance. If, as Caroline reminded me, Paris is a beautifully adorned and enticing older woman, then she demands (as such a woman would) that we keep up with her, that we bring to her everything we have, just as she brings so much of herself to us. After all, doesn't she—in each of those streets and with all those aromas and tastes—bombard us continually with her romantic *souvenirs*?

Who here needs to be reminded of the city's greatest love tragedy of all time, that of the tutor Abélard and his student Héloïse? For Paris, a thousand years ago was like last week to us. Héloïse so young, Abélard older and in love, she pregnant, he castrated, separated for the rest of their lives, but resting finally in their joint tomb at the famous cemetery of Pére Lachaise, their bones together for eternity. Some consolation, I suppose.

As to my own *souvenirs* of romance—ranging from fine to so-so to best forgotten—they are fortunately being replaced today by the one to come. I am ready for whatever Paris has on its plate.

So, at least for this evening, we will forget Hemingway's blather about Paris not being so young and all that. At this age, as I have said, I still love Paris and—at least this week—how it makes me feel about myself, which I think is the point of it all. It is true that so far here, I have been making love only to Paris (except for that American businessman in my advanced French class last year, but he doesn't count). And this no doubt is about to change. All my five senses are at the ready. I am confident that Joël, *Monsieur* Himself, would agree with the sixteenth-century writer Montaigne, who said about Paris, "I love her tenderly, even her warts and stains"—if he has, indeed, ever read Montaigne. And Miss Stein—that expert on everything about Paris—wrote that, "Frenchmen love older women, that is women who have already done more living, and that has something to do with civilization." (But she preferred her mustaches on women, so how could she have known?) Well, let us hope that she is right and that with Joël this has to do both with Paris and with me.

I have been waiting for tonight for so long that I am already on the cusp between excitement and utter fatigue. Joël says he will arrive somewhere around *22h*30. I have done everything any woman would do in preparation for a new lover (losing weight, waxing legs, streaking hair). I cleaned house, changed the linens, and put out a bar of Gardenia Passion perfumed soap. It amuses me to think that whether or not this evening is a success (whatever that means), my apartment, for a change, passes muster. Perhaps I should always have a romance in mind.

And ever the optimist, I also practice, off and on all afternoon, my opening gambit. "So, *Zho-elle*," I say, ever so softly to the empty room. "Have you ever learned to make love in English?" That's really good. But what will I do if he says, "Yes"? I must have an alternative plan.

I expect him to be late, and he is, but only slightly. Yet, having dozed and then showered in the late afternoon, I am wide-awake. Anticipation alone, however, would have done the trick. Anticipation, nesting in every nuance of my soul. I have also arranged the lights so as to make me more attractive no matter where he stands. It helps if you believe these things.

I press the button to let him in downstairs, and I do not wait for him to climb the thirty-four steps. I stand at the open door. As he rounds the last corner to my landing, I smile, both in welcome and relief. *Mon cher ami* is looking *très beau,* as always, wearing a tan cabled pullover and pressed khaki pants, his hair slightly damp as though he had just combed it, which I suppose he has. *This man is seriously gorgeous*, I think, but I say nothing, hoping only he is thinking the same about me.

In one hand he has a bag with two bottles of wine, and in the other a bouquet of colorful flowers. Once inside my door, we say our hellos with the usual French-style *bisous* (but slightly shyly for both of us, I realize), and motioning him to follow me into the kitchen, I say how pleased I am by the flowers. I run some water and arrange them in a polished silver vase that I had handy, just in case.

"Shall we open the wine, *Frahn-zess, ma belle?*" Joël asks, and, nodding, I hand him the corkscrew that, along with two of my best wine glasses, has been sitting on the counter. He pours a few drops (swirling and sniffing and doing whatever it is these people do to show they know about wine), and then he pours and gives me a glass. He opens the refrigerator, and he puts the second bottle inside. Just the casual way he has taken over makes my knees weak.

"This is the Menetou-Salon I was telling you about," he says, and as his eyes blink I notice his eyelashes for the first time. How did I miss them before? "Pinot noir. I think you will like it."

"Mmm, very much," I say appreciatively, trying to concentrate, and with a fleeting wish I had paid more attention to the wine expert Richard all the times he has tried to tell me about wines. Then I might have had something more wine-y to say. "Fine color," I venture, hoping I am not making a complete ass of myself.

He seems not to notice, for he is sipping and looking around. This is a good sign. "The flowers look *jolie* in your vase," he says and standing closely by me, his arm grazing mine, he helps move them a bit, adjusting them just so. He glances around the kitchen as we make a move toward my *salon*. He admires the wildly expensive cabinet I splurged on at Conran's that is tucked into an alcove by the door. It is one of my better purchases. It pleases me that Himself strokes the rich wood admiringly, which, frankly, makes me want to speed things up. He seems to find nothing wanting. Let us hope this continues.

In the living room we sit down on the couch, the two of us again close to each other, slightly turned so we face each other. "Your living room is charming," he says, looking at the family photos on the mantel, at the pictures on the wall, the little silver family nick-knacks here and there. And then he says in a slightly lower voice, "It's just like you, *Frahn-zess.*"

"Thank you," I say, even though I know that the French don't usually say "thank you" for a compliment. If you say "thank you," they say, "Why do you thank me? It's true." I wish I knew how to respond. "That's kind of you to say?" That is more insipid than I would ever want to be. "That's kind of you to say," I add, nonetheless, my principles at bay.

Now the sweet talk begins. I notice that his knee is touching mine, but again I say nothing. I just know it is there. We talk about Paris, about cobbletoned rue Servandoni, and he asks about me and my life, about why I live here, and we talk about my work. He actually listens, though how I can talk and he can listen with our knees just so is beyond me. "You're writing a new book for Americans moving to Paris?" he asks and touches my arm. "Are there other Americans in Paris besides you?" By now I am his slave.

"Would you like to see the rest of the apartment?" I ask after we have almost finished that first bottle and I am certainly not interested in going on to the second. It is time to stop jockeying about. I stand up (feeling keenly the loss of his knee next to mine) and make a sweeping move of my arm to usher him toward the back. He stands immediately.

The grand tour, of course, takes only a few minutes. First, I explain who all the people are in the family pictures. In the entryway, he looks briefly at my desk and computer, and he scans the bookcases and says that sometime he would like to look at the American cookbooks I have brought with me. *"Bien sûr,"* I say.

Then he sees a little snapshot that I have propped onto a bookcase shelf, one that I had put there a few years ago to see if any of my French visitors would notice, but until now no one has. "That's you! You knew Jacques Cousteau?" he asks, surprised. The photo is of me sitting on a couch with Costeau at a meeting, laughing sort of coyly, saying no to something he has just suggested. (I could say I don't remember what, but that wouldn't be the truth.)

"Yes, I did," I say and say nothing more, for although I had hoped someone sometime would notice the photo, this was not the person or the time. I wish that in my cleaning, I had thought to put it away.

"You are ever more surprising," Joël says, replacing the photo on the shelf.

As we walk down the hall toward my bedroom, where the little bedside light is already on low, he puts his hand on my shoulder. Lightly but definitely, and so I decide that before I cannot, I will take my chance. I turn to him, but he goes for it first. A kiss. A very nice one, too. Worth the lunch, the wine, and all those trips down rue Guisarde. It reminds me of Guy de Maupassant's story *The Kiss,* in which he says that one's true power comes "from kissing, from kissing alone." But for a change, I have the sense to keep quiet, just to enjoy the kiss, to relish Maupassant's "prelude, a charming introduction more delectable than the work itself." And I know that now it is my turn.

"Tell me, *Zho-elle,*" I say, turning more toward him, but in a way that makes sure his hand stays just where it is. "Have you ever learned to make love in English?" It comes out exactly as I practiced it. I almost hold my breath, waiting for his answer.

"Non, chérie," he says, thank heavens (so I don't have to go to Plan B). *"Non,* not yet." At least internally, I sigh with relief, or perhaps it is just desire. *C'est parti.*

"J'ai envie de vous caresser," he whispers into my ear, and by now I am more than ready to be caressed.

Even if I could describe graphically every touch, every move, every look, I probably wouldn't. But one sensation moves to another both too slowly and too quickly to be remembered, and I am concentrating elsewhere, besides. I can say, though, that when bodies meld tangibly, sometimes intangible souls come along for the ride. And tonight, for this I am grateful, as all those fantasies, the imaginings, the inventions of my mind come true.

I speak those words in English that I promised, and they come to my tongue with hardly a thought. And somewhere in my diminished mental capacity, I hear some French. At one point, though, I have to try hard—but I do succeed—to not burst out laughing when he compares my breasts to a perfectly cooked *crème brûlée*—"*souple mais ferme.*" That makes me come to, so to speak, but not for long. I return to where I had been a moment before, relieved in every fiber to be back. And there I stay. Hallelujah. Sometimes life does meet one's expectations. One should never give up hope.

Afterward, we do not speak for a while. "*Tu es rayonnante,*" he says, finally, and I have to admit that I am feeling as radiant as he says. I also notice happily that he has moved to addressing me in the familiar *tu*.

"*Et toi,*" I respond in French, figuring that this first English lesson has gone far enough. "*Tu es très poétique.*"

What he is thinking, I don't know. As for me, the mental processes beginning to awaken once again, I wonder whether he is intending to stay all night, and then I wonder also if I want him to. Actually, no. (Does this say something about me?) But would I get a moment's sleep with Himself warmly at my side? Would I be able to relive every moment, which is more important than sleep? Would I be able to dredge up into consciousness those French words I had so dimly heard, so I could use them the next time? (Or put them into the glossary for my book?)

Yet, as before, he is faster than I. He shifts slightly so he can nuzzle my face and my neck. I begin to reconsider this business about sleeping alone. "*Frahn-zess, ma chère, ma belle*, I do not want to leave, not at all, not ever, yet I must. The movers are coming early in the morning to pack my apartment."

I sit straight up, pulling the sheet around my supple yet firm breasts. For once in this life that I lead, I am astounded. "You're moving?" Perhaps my voice is a bit shrill. I can hear it myself. I can also feel tears prickling somewhere behind my eyes.

"*Oui,*" he says, and I can see by the look on his face that he has blurted out something he wishes he hadn't. There is a silence. I look at him steadily, somehow keeping my composure. He does not look at me. Finally, he says, "*Oui, ma chère*, my wife and I decided last week to see if we can make our marriage work, once again."

"*Comment?* You're moving back in with your wife tomorrow, and you're here with me, tonight?"

He looks even more lame than before. "Well," he says, sort of sheepishly and with a shrug, "*après tout,* it might not work."

This time I do laugh, although the tears are still in place. I can see that the poor guy is so miserable that, for a moment, I actually feel sorrier for him than I do for me. I say nothing as he sits on the side of the bed. Then, after a few silent minutes, I shrug and reach for my shirt. I take a breath, which is all I can do. This is just the way it is, and I must get myself through to the end. So, somehow, I force myself to summon up what made me laugh, that he's a man and he's just hedging his bets. And after all, not believing this is really happening, I try to convince myself, if there's a fault in this, it's mine. I was the one who did the inviting, the receiving, and the opening gambit, not he. I did know he was married, did I not?

"*Je comprends,*" I do finally get myself to say. And surprisingly, the truth is that I can understand, no matter how it makes me feel. So, perhaps there is at least one advantage to experience, after all. (What would Paris have done? Well, this may not have ever happened to her.)

But after he leaves, with some strained apologies on his side and no response on mine, and I have made sure he has heard how quickly I have shut the door behind him, I sit down on the couch. I pour into my glass the remaining few drops from the open bottle of wine. I sip. It was better before. I sip anyway. I still sit. I don't know exactly how long I stay like this, but eventually I start to take stock. Tonight, I have my permission to let myself go.

First, I consider why I am more nonplussed than bummed out, despite that feeling of imminent tears. Sexual contentment may be part of the answer. That counts for a lot. I wanted an adventure, a Paris adventure, and I had one, after all. And having been single for such long periods in my life, it certainly isn't the first time I've been on the short list but not come up a winner. It's just that the winner hasn't ever been announced at such breakneck speed. But anger takes so much energy, and my energy at this moment has been numbed. Yet, I also know somewhere that despite this shakiness, this is not a tragedy on the Abélard and Héloïse scale. I wonder when I will be able to feel what I know.

So, I rev myself up. What did I really know about this guy, when it comes down to it? Had I thought any further than this evening? Had I been ready to introduce him to my family or to take him to my high school reunion? Had I thought of throwing his small things into the washer with mine? Did I think he had actually read Montaigne? Did I think he was "the one?" Again no, we had not gotten very far into this now-thwarted romance. So, being stern with myself as Caroline will surely be in our morning call, I tell myself it's better that he should go back to his wife at this point than three months from now, when I might actually be considering these things. Then I do burst into tears for a moment, but when the image of *crème brûlée* comes to mind, I can only laugh. I know myself. If I can laugh, I'm going to be okay.

Even this slight change lets me go on to the unambiguous and positive sides, of which I am capable of conjuring up a few. Finally, I have been able to form an opinion of French men, which is good, both for me and for my work. Perhaps—if I were the smarmy type—I could say I have absorbed Paris herself within me for the first time this evening, maybe even a bit of her eternal ability to charm. But more practically, having said nothing scathing or vicious, I do not have forever to avoid rue Guisarde. And who knows, it just might not work out with his wife. *On ne sais jamais.* One never knows. Do I hope it will, or not? How noble must I be in the middle of the night?

Finally, I figure that I gave it a shot, and I had a lovely evening, both sensual and romantic, starting with wine, red wine, as a Parisian interlude would. And although discomfort keeps me from considering the answer, I do ask myself whether I had actually had any idea what that shot was aiming for when I started those trips down rue Guisarde. Taking stock has to stop somewhere, even if it's short of the mark. Then I laugh aloud again. A one-night stand after all these years!

I rise to get myself ready for bed (again), and all of a sudden, I have a different question, one that Paris, that lady, must sometime answer for me. Is she fickle or is she faithful? Perhaps I should already know, having been both in my own life, at one time or another. Maybe I could learn something from her here, perhaps how always to keep people guessing. Or maybe not. Well, it's late, and I no longer have the energy for this.

Thus, at about 2:30 a.m. (having washed the glasses and put away the corkscrew), I shake my head at the folly of the world, or perhaps just my own, and then, after finally turning out my little bedside light, I actually get a good night's sleep.

So much for romance.

Moving On Again

O R MAYBE NOT. AS THE DAYS roll on, I find that although I can sometimes actually put Joël and his renewed conjugal relations out of my mind, my equilibrium fluctuates greatly. I am not working well, which, when I have the energy to think about it, worries me. I can hardly look at my Plan of Attack. I shuffle papers; I open a file on the computer and after a few minutes close it right back up. I haven't gone up to the newly trendy rue Oberkampf, which had been next on my list. I haven't toured the refurbished Musée de la Chasse et de la Nature (about hunting and nature) over in the Marais, although the thought of a falafel on a pita afterward almost touches my soul. I am behind on my email. And sometimes, I even leave dishes in the sink.

But what is this about? That there's yet again a new notch on the belt of relationships gone bad? That I put so much hope into a project gone south? Am I once again coping with that need to escape? Whatever it is, I am clearly not my Paris self. I try not to let it show, but I am not good at this. I am back on the Oreo track.

I have enough sense not to burden my daughter with it in my morning emails (I never talk with my son about such things), so my friends here in Paris must bear the brunt. Caroline and the boys are concerned about me. Klaus berates himself dramatically, but for what I do not know. But because Paul is so obviously sad for me, I reassure him that I just have to pull myself together, and I think that's true. Besides, such kindness from the three of them makes me feel guilty about being such a baby. Thus, by the middle of this following week (when sulking annoys even me), I tell myself that it's time for Paris to coax me out of my funk. If all that I have been claiming about Paris is true, then it's time to let the dear old girl do her job.

"Remember we were going to go to a film?" Caroline reminds me Wednesday morning, the day the new films open each week. She has found in today's edition of *Pariscope* a *reprise* of Burt Lancaster films, and I agree to go. "To all three days," she says. "No excuses, no backing out." Why would I? Even the way I feel? I do realize that it's a festival of Burt Lancaster films!

So, just after dinner, we meet at a little arty cinema near the Latin Quarter for the first film. It's *The Leopard*, which is one of my favorites. And the next afternoon Caroline can hardly contain herself over *Birdman of Alcatraz*. Her pleasure makes me smile. We get a *croque monsieur* (gooey ham and cheese sandwich, eaten with a knife and fork) at a nearby café and go right back for *Judgment at Nuremburg*. This has us musing and reflecting and everything else (or almost), all the way home.

And although the French generally do not start up conversations with strangers of any sort, there are more smiles all around on Friday, the last evening, when *Local Hero* is shown. Hearing Caroline and me speaking in English, one elderly gentleman does come over to us on his way out the door and says, "*Bravo.*" We assume that today, for a change, we are representatives of Hollywood and not the henchwomen of Cheney or Bush, and that we will not be trapped into a political discussion of either country or their politics. So, we just say, "*Merci,*" and move on.

"You know I had dinner with Burt Lancaster on my fiftieth birthday," I interrupt Caroline as we are walking back along boulevard St-Germain. I have been forgetting to mention this for days. She has been making suggestions about where we should stop for a drink, catering (in her kindly way) to my (rather surly) insistence that we plop ourselves somewhere different, for a change, and not always head for our usual haunts. Couldn't we just do something different for a change? Do we have to be in a rut?

"You didn't!"

"*Mais oui*. Husband Number Two and I sat next to him and his party when we went to a fancy restaurant in New York for my birthday dinner. And I said to him as we were being seated and he was looking my way, 'It's my birthday.'" And he said, 'Well, then, madam, happy birthday to you,' and he raised his glass."

"Yes, that counts as having dinner with him," Caroline nods. "You really do talk to everyone, don't you?" As we start to pass Horse's Tavern, in rue de l'Odéon, she points to an empty table. We like the terrace of Horse's, but in winter it's too cold and in summer it's taken over by tourists. So, we grab the table, we sit—she sticking to Badoit and I with a kir—and we talk about the films and my friend Burt. She refuses my offer to treat, and so we go Dutch.

And somehow, I manage not to harp on thoughts of silver-haired men when the boys and I spend Saturday afternoon together. Nor do I whine about their going to Rome. How I do this, I don't know. But it is clear they are relieved, and, frankly, I am, too. They suggest a lunch at the Bouillon Racine. We haven't been there in six months, not since I ordered the ill-fated pinkish berry beer.

"This time, I'll order for you, my dear," says Paul, as we are looking at the menu. He had looked at me sharply when we sat down, but I seem to have passed muster, for a change. I must look like I'm not going to make any kind of fuss. "Last time, you left half your beverage." He consults the list of beers, looks at me again to see whether I will object (I don't), and he orders me an amber beer.

"How is the book coming, little darling?" Klaus asks.

"I'm sure I'll meet my deadline," I hedge, not admitting that I haven't worked effectively in almost two weeks. It's preying more and more on my mind. But at least my dishes are done, now (perhaps thanks to Burt). Maybe it's time I try to start again. Monday would be good.

After lunch, we cross the boulevard and take in the Museum of the Middle Ages, one of the places that always throws me into a reverie about the Parisian past. First, we browse the upper floors. The famous Roman ruins underneath, though, are never easy for me to grasp, seeming—like the crypt in front of Notre Dame—just a bunch of bleached-out rocks and slabs. (I do know they're important and will write it so.) But later, as we look at them, I can feel the funk rising, as though from those bleached-out rocks. Yet, I peer intently, as though I had never seen rubble before. I remind myself about Caroline's observation that I am always dwelling too much. So, now, I instruct myself severely that I had better get started for real. I pull myself together. At the *acceuil* (welcome desk) on the way out, I take the museum's brochure that lists its opening hours and prices, and I put it in my purse. I can almost convince myself I'm back on form.

On my way home, I run into Mitzi. "Can you stop for a coffee?" she asks.

"I'd love to, but I can't," I respond. Neither part of the sentence is accurate, but what should I say? Bar mitzvah talk does not thrill me? "But I'm really looking forward to the bar mitzvah," I go on, which I realize with some surprise is actually true. Maybe I am snapping back.

So, on Monday afternoon, after the official reopening of my life, I decide to go when Alice suggests I come with them to the Musée Henri Cernuschi to see the Asian art, where I haven't been in a decade, I don't know why. It's off the track for first-time tourists, who need the Louvre and the Musée d'Orsay, but it's certainly worth a visit for those who want to dig deeper. Nearby is the Musée Nissam de Camondo, another one worth a trip, but not today, for after the Cernuschi we are all cultured out. Instead, Findlay suggests we stroll through the Parc Monceau, and although by now I'm pretty much ready to go back home and organize my life, again I stuff brochures into my purse, and I go. And as is the obvious purpose of Parc Monceau, I am stunned by its beauty, which has been waiting here for me all spring, without my even knowing. Am I wrong to think that it isn't the beauty of Paris that keeps people here? Is this something I have to rethink as well? Both my work and my soul need attention.

So, later on, after I have gone home, tossed the flyers on my desk, and taken a little doze in my comfortable chair, I make a few notes—museum, park, offbeat suggestions. Then, I pack up the books I borrowed from Findlay, and I go over to the Lovells' for an impromptu dinner, just the three of us, although when I arrive the French landlord is there drinking a glass of Findlay's Brouilly. Soon he says, *"Non, merci,"* to the offer of another, looks around the apartment to see if there's any little thing that needs to be done, and after kissing all our cheeks (even mine), he disappears. I'm relieved. I'd probably wind up asking him something inappropriate about French middle-aged men. So, while Findlay is in the kitchen with Alice for a few minutes, I reshelve the books I borrowed, but I'm not ready to borrow more. There are one or two, however, that do catch my eye for some future date, which I hope comes soon.

For Findlay, the dinner is a chance, once again, to relive his Embassy triumph. For me, slightly tired and definitely noble, I let him do so. Without being obvious, I try to pace myself somewhat with his Brouilly, but not at all with Alice's *hachis parmentier,* a casserole of mashed potatoes with chopped beef, which all Parisian children—and I—love.

Toward the end of the main course, when Findlay has, of course, been eyeing the cheeses on the sideboard, he turns to me and says, "I'm thinking of writing my memoirs, Fran. What do you think?"

"You mean starting when you got here to Paris?" I ask, thinking that I deserve a little cheese. I see (definitely smell) an

Epoisses, an aged Gruyere, and some kind of goat cheese. I hold out my plate.

"You always like my Paris stories," he says in a sort of response.

And he's right, I do. So, I say I think it would be a good idea, that I would look forward to reading his book and hope he will sign it for me, and that Odile Hellier will sell thousands of copies at the Village Voice, that he will have fame and fortune at last, and that he must not forget the little people, his old friends. Findlay seems gratified, while I am wondering if I have not paced myself quite enough with the wine. So, after we sit around in their comfortable living room while Alice smokes a cigarette that I wish she wouldn't, I say it's time I left. It's been a good day, I admit with some relief as I walk home, avoiding the other end of the Guisarde. I realize that I am feeling more certain about something, although I don't know what.

And so, I go on. I work again, at least sort of. I organize the informational faxes that have come in, vowing to look at them carefully later. I go back and review what I've written, editing and tightening, backing and filling, and fiddling here or there. I think about some of the eateries I've been to in the last few months, deciding which to include or not. I make the beginnings of a list. I am good at lists.

Richard, whom I've heard has been busy for weeks with some financial deal and who also knows nothing of my recent frame of mind, happens to call this next morning to invite me for an early afternoon swim at the Ritz. I swim with Richard occasionally, and fortunately, I have never again seen the odious guard who once wouldn't let me in. I would be ready to take him now, if I did. Anyway, ready for anything different, I go. Richard doesn't seem to notice that I am not in bathing suit form (I'm still wearing that old *maillot* that minimizes my hips), and being pampered as only the pompous Ritz can do—unlike my underground public pool at St-Germain—makes me both appreciate it and laugh. (I lift only a few of their perfumed towelettes.) Richard has to rush off after his swim, so as he heads toward the Île de la Cité, we kiss, and I thank him and say I'll call soon. And before I get on the bus to go home, I go over to W.H. Smith and make sure my books are in stock and where they should be. There's a new person at the desk *caisse* (cash register), who doesn't flinch as I walk by. Things are looking up.

So, Paris is doing her best for me. And she is not yet ready to ease up. Finally, two things happen that serve to snap me completely back into shape, two things totally different from each other, and one has to do with Paris, and the other has to do just with me. And they both happen on the same day.

The first thing I find is that there's nothing like being pissed off to focus my mind. I mean, whatever happened to San Francisco John? Hadn't I invited him and the little woman over for a glass of champagne? And didn't he say he'd get back to me? But there hasn't been a word, and this is not right. I am not in the mood for impolite. So, one morning at my desk, I dredge up John's email address (and reread his message saying how delighted he was to see me and how he was looking forward to seeing me again), and I shoot him a note—brief and to the point—reminding him that there is a bottle of champagne in the *frigo* waiting for him and for Rose.

About twenty minutes later, I get a call. "We should have called you," he says. I don't know what it is, but I'm not much liking his tone of voice. "I'm sorry that we didn't."

"Yeah, I've been wondering what happened to you."

"It's like this," he says. "I talked to Rose, and she's not interested."

"She's not interested in what?"

"In coming to your house for champagne."

"I've invited you over, and you're saying that your wife won't set foot in my house?"

"Aw, Fran, don't be like that. She gets like that. I don't know why. But she doesn't want to come."

I don't know what to say. (The word "pussy-whipped" comes to mind, but I don't say it.) So, I say something like, "Oh, give me a break," and I hang up.

And this necessitates a call to Sandy. "Would you like to go out for a lunch, today?"

"I can't," she says but elaborates no further. "But what's up?"

I laugh. There's no one like Sandra to get right to the point. She's uncanny that way. I lay out the story, starting those decades ago in San Francisco. "But what's it about?" I persist. "She doesn't even know me and she hates me."

"Don't be silly. John raved about you, that's all. You're smart. You're a writer. You look great, and even worse, you're single. She's just insecure about her hubby still knowing you."

"And probably rightly so," I say, for it is making me feel better having a grievance to bear. And I have not missed those kind (but obviously true) words about me. "Well," I finally say somewhat grudgingly, "you've probably not heard the end of this."

"Forget about it. Listen, J-P's secretary faxed the kids a newspaper review of the best sushi bars in Paris. Did she send it to you, too?"

"Oh yes, she did," I say, having in my blues forgotten that it was sitting in that pile of faxes I had promised myself I would look at if I were ever ready to work again.

"So, go have sushi. Try that place over in rue de Passy, the one that has the conveyer belt that brings the sushi plates to you. See if you agree with the list. Let me know if you like it."

And being a docile sort, I do as I am told. I don't even call anyone to go with me. Just like that, I put my computer on Standby, I close up shop, and I walk over to the *métro* at Mabillon. Not caring much today, I just keep on my work jeans, a sweatshirt, and the scuffed sneakers that I wear to take down the trash. But not being totally unwise, I have run a brush through my hair and looked in the mirror to make sure my mascara is on right. I mean, after all. I change trains at La Motte Piquet, and I get off in the tony neighborhood of Passy. I walk across the avenue to Matsuri, a sushi bar near where Ben Franklin had lived. Perhaps I should have ditched the sneakers and put on better shoes.

So, the second thing I find out on this one day that actually completes the snapping-back process—and this is even more important in the overall scheme of life than being pissed off—is that Paris comes up with things I never could imagine. Unexpected, unrehearsed. And perhaps this is why I'm still here, and why everyone else should hop on a plane and come.

I am just about finished eating my sushi, thinking that maybe I will research the upscale boutiques on rue de Passy (despite looking so ratty) but hoping that just one more plate of *amaebi* (raw shrimp) will come along the turntable, when a well-dressed businessman is seated beside me. I do not stare. I'm above all that. But without moving the slightest eye muscle, I know immediately that he is attractive, with slightly graying salt-and-pepper hair. That he loosens his tie (yellow, with a blue design), that he takes his Nokia phone out of the breast pocket of his jacket and puts it on the counter in front of him, and that he puts his sunglasses into that pocket, now empty, using a hand that is wearing a wedding ring. I continue to sit. I look straight ahead. I have not formally looked at him. Then without moving my head, I manage to sneak a little peek at him. Oops. He is looking at me.

"*Bon appetit,*" he says to me.

"*Merci, monsieur. À vous aussi,*" I say. It would be rude of me not to respond. I venture a *petit* smile.

"You look like you're ready to leave," he says, motioning to the empty plates stacked in front of me.

"No, I'm waiting for the shrimp to come by," I say. ("*Pas de tout. J'attends les crevettes.*")

"*Bon*," he says and looks at me steadily. "It's always disappointing to sit next to an attractive woman and have her leave just a few minutes later."

Now, I do stare at him. I say nothing. He says, "You have lovely eyes."

Oh, my God. Is this big, or what? He's a *drageur*, a man who picks up women, something I've always heard about in Paris, and now I am being picked up. It couldn't have come at a better time. *Moi!* I am being picked up. (Or have I already said this?)

Although I know better, I say, "Thank you."

And he makes the standard response. "Why do you thank me? It's true."

Fortunately, the shrimp plates do not come right away. I hope they never come. This is just too big. I take a plate of salmon sashimi, and he takes one, too. We talk. He tries out his English. (I do not laugh.) He loves the national parks in *Amérique,* he says. He has been to *Yo-seh-mite*. I tell him how it is pronounced, and we smile together. He takes a plate of tuna and a California roll. Have I ever seen the parks of France? He talks about the Alps. Where do I live and what do I do? Am I married? Do I have a *partenaire*? All alluring women should have a partner. He takes a salmon and avocado roll. What kind of books do I write?

Then it's my turn, except I don't ask about the married stuff. (Why waste time?) He's a businessman. In *informatique* (computers). He works a few streets away. He goes camping in the summer. Which national parks in France does he think I should see? Les Écrins, up in the Alps. His kids are grown and live in Arras, where he comes from. I've been to Arras. He loves sushi. He takes another plate of tuna. He comes here a lot.

The *amaebi* finally arrive, and I eat them as slowly as one can eat two pieces of sushi without making a complete jerk of oneself. And then I see nothing to do but make as to leave. I smile and shrug, signal for the bill, and put my own sunglasses on.

"Don't put your glasses on," he says. "They hide your eyes." I whip them off.

"Would you like to go around the corner to a café and have a cup of coffee?" he asks, and then looking intently into my eyes, he says, "I have no appointments for the rest of this afternoon."

"But you haven't eaten enough sushi," I say, stalling for time. What do I do? Do I go to the café? Then I think, why not? I am going home alone no matter what, so why not? I have no appointments this afternoon, either, and window shopping in Passy can wait. I can play this 'til the end.

"No, I've eaten enough," he says. I smile again, at a loss as to what to say now, and just wait for him to get his bill and to collect his Nokia phone, and then we each pay and head together to the door.

So, finally, with the passing of a couple of weeks, and with decreasing episodes of peevishness, and also with the *mobile* number of an attractive and smart *drageur* entered into my Palm (at least until it stops amusing me and I press delete), I find that I've actually moved on. Snapped back. In form. Ready to go.

And now, one morning at the end of May, when I surprise myself by awakening brightly, with that old anticipation of what Paris will bring, ready to see what's new and what isn't, I think I hear the whole city sighing with relief. Me, too. I am lucky to be where I am, and I know it. Spring in Paris can make anyone weep, but solely for joy. One of these days, I will get myself ready to dream up another project, when one comes waltzing by. That I know. But not now, not when June is almost in sight, when Paris is so vividly colored and warm, when I am taken over by that sense of gratitude that I can almost define, but not quite. In any case, Paris and I are back together. We have made up.

Caroline says she is proud of my maturity in this regard. "Yes," she says, "perhaps 'moving on' doesn't mean leaving, anymore. Maybe it means staying put."

"Oh, please!" I say with an exasperation that I instantly regret. She is not Ida. She can try and understand me all she wants. It's just that I've had enough of taking stock for a while.

Finally, the fine weather wins out. Daylight arrives earlier each morning, and now on the cusp of June I enjoy waking with the sun. I work at my desk and then go out to explore. I stroll through the famous cemetery at Montparnasse and also look at most of the six million bones in the Catacombs, an underground warren used by the Resistance in World War II. At the café Le Zeyer at *métro* Alesia, where it is said that Henry Miller and Samuel Beckett ate, I sit for a while over a dish of Berthillon *caramel beurre salé* ice cream. And then, before heading home, I buy a Camembert at Findlay's cheese store Boursault across the street. (I am clearly going wild.) I mark in my *planning* a meeting of the Democrats over near boulevard Raspail. I send out a reminder that book club is *chez moi* at the end of the month. I open the regular mail when there is any, and when the invitation to the bar mitzvah arrives—almost a book in itself with silk bows on the engraved cream vellum, an r.s.v.p. envelope, and mapped directions to the various celebratory sites—I am relieved to see in the invitation that no presents are called for, only a donation to a charity specified by the bar mitzvah boy.

Edie asks me to a concert at UNESCO on Saturday night. If Edie suggests it, it's got to be good. So, it turns out we are to hear an Asian orchestra play—among its other offerings—the "Blue Danube Waltz" on instruments made of bamboo. (Click-click-click-click-click! Click-click! Click-click!) We sit in the balcony, to the side. When the musicians come out on the stage, I whisper to Edie, "Are they going to flagellate themselves with all that bamboo?" And again it comes to me that if I can laugh so hard, I'm okay.

As we later file out with the crowd, after being enormously entertained (one way or another), I look ahead and see that new woman Anna walking with a man I assume to be her husband. I do not get to say hello, for we are too far behind, but I can hear a pretty woman in a sari pressing close behind the assumed-husband raving how wonderful the evening was. I tell Edie how wonderful the evening was.

So, I walk again through the *quartier* as usual (although so far not in rue Guisarde), even late into the evenings, relishing the rhythm of the lengthening days. And now that I no longer regularly carry an umbrella against the wind and rain, I can hear the side streets calling softly to me—despite the tourists who call loudly to each other—and in the Luxembourg, the green metal chairs begin to mention my name. Maybe it's just the breeze. Henry Miller's version of this was, "When spring comes to Paris the humblest mortal alive must feel that he dwells in Paradise."

I leave the number of the *drageur* in my Palm for the time being, for it still amuses me to know it's there. I go to the Grande Mosquée and have a cup of tea in their tearoom, and I wander around the Latin Quarter for a while. And on this last Wednesday in May, I go down to the Parc Brassens, taking with me a book on Blacks in Paris that Margot loaned me (last year), so I can check out the park while getting some tan. I lift my sun-creamed face to the sun, and I think of scathing remarks to say to John the next time I see him on the street. But although I enjoy the practice—on this altogether lovely day—I remember Sandy's advice and hope that I will put it behind me. This will take some doing on my part, for as I have said, I am not one to let things go. But I will try, for what I really think is that I owe them all and Paris my thanks.

Waiting for the Jays

PASSOVER AND EASTER HAVE COME AND gone, and I have stocked up on both matzos and chocolate chickens. The national holidays of May Day, Victory Day, and Ascension Day have also passed, and Whit Monday (*Pentecote*) is soon to come. Since Ascension Day falls on a Thursday, many people make *le pont*, a bridge to the weekend, giving them four days to go away. The beauty of Paris becomes even more evident on quiet holiday weekends, and if these days, like Victor Hugo, I can again be made giddy by the city, I'm trying to learn to keep it to myself.

So, I am catching up contentedly on my hithers and thithers, making up for those weeks given over to sulking. Now that the weather is warmer and her knee doesn't seem to be bothering her, Caroline is somewhat susceptible to distraction, and she sometimes goes along on my treks. Afterward, we refresh ourselves at a café, and I insist on treating, saying I can take it off my expenses, which is pretty much true. And even without Edie, one Sunday afternoon I pop in at a free organ concert at St-Sulpice and afterward sit on the terrace of the Café de la Mairie, feeling pleasure in the sun and my neighborhood. Perhaps I'm not as readily social as I usually am—I hope others in the gang haven't noticed—but in its way, life is approaching something I recognize once again. Normal, whatever that means.

This season in Paris has always tickled me, anyway, and it does so now, even without a male project in mind. I'm glad I'm back on form so I don't lose out on one of my favorite springtime activities, which is to search out faces I have seen a couple of times before, new people who are showing up in the *quartier*. Clearly not tourists, these strangers also walk with their grocery bags and their *baguettes*, speaking English to each other. From hearing their accents (or from seeing the men in gold-buttoned blazers and with the emblem of their golf club emblazoned to the left of their hearts), it is clear that they are Americans here for perhaps a few weeks or a month. If I see the same people often enough, I might nod or find a way to say hello and to hear just how Paris is fitting into their lives. This is not nosiness. This is research.

Research, of course, must have methodology. So, here it starts with a little smile, then the striking up of a conversation about whatever it is that binds us together—waiting at the bus stop, sitting adjacent at a casual eatery—to see where it leads. Sometimes I'm dead wrong. But often it turns out as I had imagined, that the newcomers are fulfilling a dream after once having spent a short time in Paris doing all the standard tourist things. Now back again, along with their in-depth guides (perhaps even one of my earlier books) that allow them to scout out the offbeat, they have perhaps also brought with them brochures about language courses or even sketch pads or paints.

One morning, not too early or too late, I call Edie. "Have two people from Miami Beach started your cooking classes?" I ask.

"How did you know?" she asks with surprise. Then she says, "Oh, you've talked with someone new on the street, haven't you?"

"Well, yes," I admit. "They seem nice. Lots of money, of course. They're staying three months."

"Good," Edie says. "If they stay long enough, they can learn the difference between a *béchamel* and a white sauce." I wonder what that is, myself, but not enough to ask, for I don't want to stay on the phone all morning.

But to say the least, coming to Paris in this fashion—staying for a short term for whatever reason—is nothing new. One afternoon on one of those treks, when Caroline and I—having whisked through the Jacquemart-André museum—are finally sitting in its lovely tearoom, she quizzes me. "Name just about any American politician, writer, artist, or composer of the last 150 years," she says, "and I bet you'll find their paths have brought them here, one way or another."

Forget the obvious (if the obvious will let us) and take Mark Twain, for example, who spent three months here, complaining about the incessant rain but who brought his wife and daughter over anyway to spend six months in an apartment in rue de l'Université, over in the 7th *arrondissement*. And to name a few others, there were Richard Wright, who found a haven here, and James Baldwin, whom my friend Margot actually met. (I must call her.) Also Henry James, Emerson the poet, James Whistler (*le petit Vist-laire* to the women he chased), Harry Houdini for a ten-week stand, and P.T. Barnum, who lined his pockets by exhibiting General Tom Thumb. And lo! William Faulkner, who apparently stayed for months in rue Servandoni, which I always consider *my* street.

"So, what else have you learned from your latest research?" she asks me as we are thinking of leaving the café to take the bus back home. So, I tell her of the amount the Miami Beach couple is paying for their short-term apartment. "Don't you think that they are getting totally fleeced?" I ask.

"Sounds like they can afford the fleecing," Caroline says.

"But it is a moral affront."

"Certainly. You know, I admire your openness to those 'research' conversations. You're so much more adventurous than I am."

Since she hadn't said "nosy" or even "restless," I hardly bridle. "How else would I learn things? Anyway, it's too late for me to change."

"Why would you want to?" she asks, practically, taking a last bite of the chocolate *gâteau* she had ordered. She is in one of her "a few more pounds won't hurt" spins. And since I am no longer in full diet mode, I have finished my own slice with no remorse.

But her comment reassures me, and I am also gratified to realize that I have no crushing need to parse the word "romance," either in the past or future tense. It could be the *gâteau,* but I don't think so, for one piece of cake only lasts so long.

Now, the rental of short-term, furnished *appartements* is big business in Paris—to tourists for weeks, students for semesters, and sometimes corporation employees for a year or more, like Anna and her husband, I suppose. All my friends who can do so rent their apartments when they are away. Parisians do, too, when they are going to the country for the summer, to the south for the winter, or just for the income the rent provides. And I get in on it for the month or so in the winter when I'm not here, usually renting to friends of friends. My trip to the States gets paid for this way. I always think about all of this when the Jays are about to arrive, but I also know I have to think about it for myself—six months in advance is not too soon to start.

Generally, I rent to Americans so I can specify that mine is a "no-smoking" apartment. The French would think me *folle* if I said anything like that to them. Mad! Not smoke at home? Now that they can't smoke in restaurants or cafés? Isn't it a God-given right, like letting your dog foul the sidewalk, which is also *interdit*? I used to argue with Sandra about this, but now if I run into her on the street when she is walking Julien, I just call breathlessly, "Hi," give a little wave, and move on quickly to indicate that I'm hurrying somewhere (far away). Otherwise, we do stop to gossip, but I won't stand by while she lets Julien dirty *le trottoir*. "You've gone native," I once accused her, when she proclaimed that she could let her dog do his doody wherever he wanted, despite it being against the law. The law must be working, though, for it's been a long time since I've seen those little green vacuum cleaner vehicles that used to suck up what the French so delicately call *déjections canines.*

I have to get home early this afternoon, because this is the evening for our book club, and this month, it's *chez moi*. There are ten women in the club, and with a few months off at summer and Christmas, we each have to put on the dog (pardon me, Sandy) only once each year. The hostess provides a light dinner and a few bottles of wine, and everyone brings something, as well. I even look forward to it when it's my turn, for it's nice to be at a party and not have to go home later on. So, tonight, we will snack on *crudités, foie gras de canard, jambon de bayonne,* a *baguette* or two, a large *quiche* that I will heat up just before the time, two different kinds of olives that I got at the *marché*, some *fromage bien fait* (perfectly ripe), and, of course, drinking *beaucoup de vin rouge*. I will stop at Mulot on the way home and pick up some *brohnees,* in my opinion, the best in town. Let others bring their homemade cookies, their casseroles of this and that. I will not feel guilty about keeping Mulot afloat.

A few years ago, the first time the ladies came over to this apartment I had just moved into, of course, they all looked around carefully, as people here do. I could see the mental checklist at work. Big windows and enough light. Parquet floors. Decorative ceiling moldings. Work space in the kitchen. Bedroom facing the quiet court in back. A few women commented enviously on the row of closets in the hall, so rare in French apartments, and others about the pictures on the walls. Small as it is, my flat passed muster, and I was relieved. One woman—surprising to me— said she also had a print from the Dali zodiac collection (mine is Taurus), but nobody noticed the photo of Cousteau (prominently placed just for them).

Yet, aside from the spring tourists making me think about "apt. info" for my book, another reason is that I will remind my ladies this evening that I will be looking for a renter in December, for when I am in the States. Word of mouth is the way I do it (haranguing my friends). And yet another reason is that my friends

Jack and Jennifer are due to arrive for their regular three-month summer stay, and I'm looking forward to having them back.

Both in their early fifties, Jack and Jennifer are a mixed marriage in their own way, he being Irish and she American. They live in New York, next to Central Park, where Jennifer jogs. They started their regular Paris summer adventure about five years ago, after having come here off and on for years. Jack, who translates non-fiction books from the French, is the dreamer of the couple, while Jenny, a gymnastic coach for would-be Olympians, is so practical and organized that sometimes, as Klaus says, "she squeaks." In fact, we all know the Jays (as Alice started us calling them) because one year Klaus took the "body sculpting" class Jennifer gives—totally illegal, of course, and only for cash—when she is here. By now she has a following, but still she tapes up flyers that Jack has written in French on lamp posts and puts them into mailboxes all around the *quartier* where they are staying that summer. And this was how Klaus had happened to see Jennifer's sign, on one of his neighborhood strolls.

(Mailboxes in Paris, by the way, are always stuffed full of ads—especially for locksmiths, it seems, and being superstitious, I keep one of these in the bottom of my purse. Such mailbox reminders are frequent, so I can only assume that the French, despite being so logical and precise, have some innate need to lock themselves out.)

Klaus introduced the Jays into the group by inviting a few of us over to avenue Marceau for *kir royal* and *hors d'oeuvres*. That first year, Jack and Jennifer were staying in the 8th, having swapped their apartment on West Seventy-third Street for three months for one up by the Augustine church. The Jays used to swear by the Internet apartment exchanges, since the apartments didn't cost them a *centime*. Most often they lucked out, but once they wound up in a flat with only one pillowcase and no chairs, just cushions on the floor. So, they bought an extra pillowcase and even took it back to New York when they left. "Why should I furnish their bloody flat?" Jack asked.

When they arrived at avenue Marceau that early evening four years ago, both Jack and Jennifer were obviously excited. Of course, I assumed it was because they were meeting our little in-the-know crew, *mais non*. At least not entirely. It turned out that, as they were coming down rue d'Anjou, they had seen a historical plaque on a building they passed. We all love these plaques, indicating where *un français* lived or died or was a hero at some time. (On my way to the *supermarché,* I see one that commemorates the Cincinnati Society, which one day I might remember to look up.) Many of the plaques are memorials to young patriots who died fighting the Nazis in the streets in August 1944.

I went with Findlay and Alice to the American Embassy the day in 1997 when the two plaques about the Marshall Plan—in both French and English—were dedicated. At the exit to the *métro* on rue du Rivoli, where the Lovells and I crossed the wide street, there are ten such plaques in a row, recalling a spot where a group of resistants died battling the Nazis. We stopped to pay our respects and then just made the green light across.

Yet, the large plaque the Jays described was one I had never seen. Jack had copied the text and translated it for us, not knowing that we all would have understood the French. (Richard had not yet appeared on the scene.) "General Lafayette, defender of Liberty in America, one of the founders of Liberty in France, born the 6th of September 1757 at the Château of Chavagnac in Auverge, died in this house on the 20th of May 1834."

"Born September 1757?" Paul exclaimed. "You mean he was only nineteen years old when he came to the Colonies to help fight in our revolution?"

"Yes, nineteen years old!" said Jennifer, darting an amused look at her husband. "Jack has sweaters older than that."

"Now, there's a man I would have liked to have known," Caroline said, surprisingly. "Did you know that when the Bastille fell, he was there and he took away the key to the prison? He gave it to Thomas Paine to take back to George Washington, whom he called his 'adoptive father.'"

"That's right!" Paul exclaimed and looked at Klaus. "Remember when we went to Mt. Vernon years ago and we saw the key to the Bastille?" Did Klaus remember? I'm not sure, but he said (rather archly, I thought at the time), "Certainly, I do," and he went back to pouring the drinks.

Now, the Jays are part of our ever-fluid group, so Caroline and I have been talking about the welcome luncheon for weeks. The weather has been cooperating nicely, so we plan an afternoon on the *balcon*. The lunch will be cold—poached salmon, artichokes *à la vapeur*, the vinaigrette on the side. Since I only bring desserts I like, I will go to Picard and get

some of that *caramel beurre salé* ice cream that I am now addicted to, although Ben and Jerry's Phish Food is closing in. Perhaps I'll pick up some *éclairs* as well, knowing they will defrost in time for dessert. Richard's job, without fail, is to bring the wine. *Et voilà.*

As much as I'm looking forward to the lunch, I am actually more interested in finding out which apartment Jennifer has chosen for this year. Caroline and I always offer to go and inspect a place or two before the Jays make their decision, for we don't want them to make a mistake—and besides, we get to look at a new apartment, *n'importe où* (it doesn't matter where). Everyone plays the apartment game; it's a Parisian sport. How much are

Jack and Jennifer paying this year, for how much space, and in which *quartier*? And how did they find it this time?

This is what Jennifer does. She keeps her antennae up in the States throughout the winter, sending regular emails to Alice, Caroline, and me to keep our eyes out. She looks at alumni magazines, *The New York Review of Books,* and *FUSAC,* and if nothing turns up even then, which is unlikely, she places a two-line ad there, herself. "American couple seeks comfortable Left Bank two-room apartment for summer months."

This year, it quickly turns out, the Jays will be renting an apartment on the top floor of a walk-up building in rue des Canettes. It's just around the corner from the Lovells in rue Guisarde (and ex-Joël's restaurant, of course), and in fact, it was found by Alice, who called me immediately to tell me the news. It belongs to some people whom she met one spring at the *marché*, people who are big into sailboats and summers in Maine. "The apartment is perfect for the Jays," Alice says as we are getting ready to hang up, and after we have talked about their upcoming trip to see their sons at St-Malo. "Maybe they can rent it each year."

"Do you know what they're paying?" I ask, shamelessly.

"I suspect it's about twenty-five hundred euros a month, which is fab for a one-bedroom, furnished, short-term. Even when you translate it in dollars, it's almost reasonable."

Fab? I think. *Fab?* But what I say is, "I can't wait to give it the once over," and Alice says she'll let me know when. So, before we hang up, and being a good friend and a noble sort, I offer (meaning the climb of the ninety-five steps) to water their plants while they are away, but Alice says their landlord would be disappointed if he couldn't help them out. I am off the hook.

In the days before apartments were so readily available, short-term residents stayed in inexpensive hotels. This is how William Faulkner came to stay in rue Servandoni, or so Caroline informs me over a cup of Twining's Chocolate Mint Tea *chez moi* on the morning after book club, the Friday after Alice's call.

The evening went well, meaning I have some leftover snacks (lemon squares homemade by Colette, the only French woman in the group). The book talk was great, since everyone, for a change, had read the book. People talked all at once (even while passing plates and pouring wine), interrupting each other, carrying on, and taking sides. Even Anna, whom Mitzi brought along, pitched in with the rest. (Does her coming count as us getting together?) I loved it all. So, participating in the literary mayhem and noshing on this or that, I did not fidget. Nonetheless, now that it is over, I am as glad that I don't have to do it again for another year as having hosted the club.

So, this next morning Caroline stops by on her way to the *marché*. I make the tea and put out the leftover lemon squares. After we have finished dissecting the evening, Caroline says, "Did you know that Faulkner lived in your street during the summer of 1925? In a hotel on the corner. It was where that fancy new one is now."

"Faulkner! Really!" So, somebody famous lived in my street, after all. Then it hits me that my 1001 nights may pretty soon be up. "Are you up to Faulkner already? I thought you were only up to Aaron Burr and how Talleyrand thought Burr in the duel with Hamilton had killed the greatest American statesman, and how Burr frequented the ladies of the night—*les filles de joie*."

"You were listening?" Caroline laughs. "I thought that champagne had done you in." Then she reassures me. "*Ne t'inquiéte pas.* Don't worry. I'm just up to Robert Fulton trying to persuade Napoleon to fund his steamboat. But, of course, after the fiasco with Fulton's submarine, Napoleon said *non!* Anyway, Fulton lived here with his friend Joel Barlow. Do you remember what I told you about Barlow? He was the minister plenipotentiary after..."

How could I not remember Barlow, how on a mission to Poland to negotiate with Napoleon, he wrote to his wife, "I love my darling, first begotten, long-beloved wife better & more & harder & softer & longer & stronger than all the Poles between the south pole and the north pole." Poor, adoring Barlow. Retreating with Napoleon's army, he got sick and died. Paul and Klaus are right; it doesn't do to take a chill.

"Fulton invented a submarine?" I interrupt.

"Yes, the *Nautilus*. Napoleon tried it, but the British had heard about it already and put out to sea too far for the submarine. As far as Napoleon was concerned, that was that."

"But what about Faulkner?"

"Just listen." She drags out her tote bag and pulls out a paperback book. "Here's what he wrote about your street. 'I have a nice room just around the corner from the Luxembourg gardens, where I sit and write and watch the children.' That sounds as though it could be you."

"Almost, except for the hotel part—and the talent part," I say, while Caroline shakes her head. Yet, it wasn't surprising for someone like Faulkner to spend three months in a hotel, for in those days apartments were more expensive than hotels. Impecunious artists did their writing in cafés.

"By the way," Caroline interrupts, "I found a Mary McCarthy quote that you'll like. I'll email it to you." She pauses. "And speaking of home," she goes on, "I almost forgot. Alice called to say she's going over to the Jays' apartment tonight after dinner to get it ready for them. She said to let you know."

"You almost forgot?" I can't believe this. "Of course, I'm coming." Smiling, Caroline stands and shoulders her tote bag, to go on her way to the *marché*. "Wait, I'll go down with you," I say, and I pick up my purse and my sunglasses. "I have an appointment with my banker to talk about opening accounts, what's available for expats, you know, all that stuff. Do you want to come?"

"No, thanks," she says, as we walk down the stairs. "I'm starting a new diet, so I'm going to load up on leafy green vegetables. Besides, I'm going to talk to Richard about money. He's offered to give me some advice, dollar-wise."

"Leafy green vegetables?" I laugh. "You sound like an advertisement. But good luck with the diet." Out on the street we arrange to meet in rue des Canettes just at *21h30,* and then we kiss as she walks off to the *marché.* I walk to the bank and get more information from my banker than I ever thought I would, given how harried she always seems. But then at the end, when I am walking out the door, she smiles and says, "Be sure and inform your readers about our bank. We can always use new customers." Working on commission, I suppose. No wonder she was so nice.

> ## QUOTE FROM JEAN-PAUL SARTRE
>
> "'As I was a teacher and hadn't much money I lived in a hotel; and like all people who live in hotels I spent most of the day in cafés. In 1940, the 'regulars' of the Dôme began to go elsewhere, for two reasons: the Métro station 'Vavin' was closed, and we had to make our way to the Dôme in the evenings in complete darkness and on foot from the Gare de Montparnasse. Besides, the Dôme was overrun with Germans....
>
> "Simone de Beauvoir and I more or less set up house in the Flore. We worked from nine until noon, when we went out to lunch. At two, we came back and talked with our friends till four, when we got down to work again till eight. And after dinner people came to see us by appointment. It may seem strange, all this, but the Flore was like home to us...."

Thinking about the apartment the Jays have so far not even seen, though, reminds me of my own first short-term apartment that I had also taken sight unseen. I was about to arrive to write that first Paris book, so long ago. The apartment was advertised in *FUSAC* as an elegant one-bedroom apartment on the third floor of a seventeenth-century *hôtel particulier.* After the landlady assured me that there would be a cable connection for my modem and a bathtub, plus a microwave and toaster (my cooking implements of choice), I called to ask J-P's secretary to look it over. That afternoon she called me back to say, "Take it, *Frahn, c'est charmant*." I did. Its price was reasonable, and it was on rue Christine, just where I wanted to be, midway between the Latin Quarter and the heart of St-Germain.

After a stop-and-go cab ride into the city on the *périphérique*, during which I insisted the driver speak to me in French—little of which I understood—the car could not enter rue Christine. A rather decrepit Renault was blocking the narrow street. I jumped out and ran to the large wooden *portes* of the building. I was about to punch in the code I had been given to open the door when an elderly bird-like woman with atrocious red hair came swooping out. "You will be *Madame Gend-ah-lahn,*" she said with a tight little smile. "I have been waiting since the hour. You said to be here by ten."

Obviously preoccupied, my landlady handed me a heavy ring of keys. "You must be secured and use all three keys when you go out," she said. "And here," she said handing me a scrap of paper, "is my phone number in the country. But do not give him to anyone, not even someone who says to be my friend. *Jamais!* And tell *personne* that I am away. *Personne*. I hope you achieve the work you have come to do. Now, I must go, before the traffic on the *autoroute* becomes *impossible*." And she shook my hand, walked over to the Renault, got in, revved the motor, and took off down the narrow street. I never saw her again. When I left Paris four months later, I threw the keys through the slot in the mailbox, and that was that.

You have to get used to European keys, for they are of sizes and shapes no American could imagine. My indoctrination came in Rome, so I wasn't surprised by the cylindrical key with irregularly placed prongs that looked like a medieval instrument of torture, or even the flat thick key that had just one deep triangular serration. Most front doors seem to have two or three locks, each requiring a different one of these oddly shaped keys.

Moi, perhaps I'm naive (an understatement in some regards), but admonitions from French landlords notwithstanding, I close the door behind me when I go out and give the key one simple turn when I come back. My current door is heavy wood with a metal jamb, and I turn my thick cylindrical key, double locking the door with the key that looks like a mace, only when I am going out of town.

That first apartment was just as advertised, with high ceilings, silk walls, and an unusually deep bathtub with gold-looking faucets in the shape of dolphins. The tub took so long to fill on the first night that I blew the fuse for the hot water heater, but the downstairs neighbor—whom I later found out was the famous French chef Jacques Cagna—was kind enough to help me out. I had looked up in the dictionary the words for "pilot light," "heater," and "desperate," so when I had made myself understood, he came upstairs, pushed a button I hadn't seen, and *voilà,* I was saved. (When I checked out his starred restaurant shortly afterward, he came out from the kitchen and shook my hand. Of course, the place went straight into my book. Now, though, I eat more often at his fish restaurant around the corner, l'Espadon Bleu.)

But after that first year—and before I found my nest in rue Servandoni—I decided only to rent anonymous apartments in buildings managed by rental agencies, not by *particuliers,* as individuals are known (and which is why private homes were called *hôtels particuliers).* I really have no interest in living among someone's souvenirs of a honeymoon in the Porcorolles or with a refrigerator containing half-full jars of *cornichons.*

Jack and Jennifer say that the more personal the apartment, the happier they are. They love looking at how the French really live, and they always find books on the shelves they want to read. They also finish those *cornichon*s, I'm sure. They make friends with their landlords; they visit them at the seashore; they correspond when back in the States; and they feel they are living life deeply

French. Of course, I want to make new friends among the French, and I do my best. It's just that I prefer to have more in common with people than just having used their towels.

It was in rue Christine that first year, however, that I met Edouard and Jane. In fact, it was there that they met each other, too, under what they imagined was my watchful eye. Beautiful Jane, a college girl from Scotland, working in Paris to improve her French. She was a trainee hostess—a *stagiaire*—in the restaurant downstairs. With my own minimal French, it took me a while to realize that she wasn't *Parisienne*. Once I did, we switched to English, to my relief.

The young man was the *sommelier* in a restaurant on the corner. He had to speak some English, for he poured wine to tourists who thought they knew much more than he, but the day we met, we spoke in French. He did, anyway. That day, when I was about to exit through the massive *portes,* there was the *sommelier* I had often nodded to as he was coming up from the *cave* with bottles of wine. Now, he was holding a little bird. *"Bonjour, madame,"* he said, which I understood. Then he said: *"Oiseau... tombé...mourir...peur."* Or something like that. But even I could get that the bird had fallen from a nest. There was, after all, a big tree right there.

I clucked sympathetically, and said, *"Tiens, tiens, tiens."* (By then I had learned one of Caroline's pet phrases, which means "you don't say" or "my, my.")

From then on, after the bird had recovered and flown away, Edouard, as he told me his name was (my name was *Madame* for another year) and I *bonjoured* each other, and Jane and I chatted and smiled, as well. Then one day just before the end of my stay, Jane stopped me as I was going out and said, "Guess who I'm dating! Edouard!"

"Oh, là là," I tried out, by then confident enough to use the standard phrase. (Sometimes, if really worked up, the French

might say *Oh, là là là là là là là là*.) And later that same day, Edouard called out to me, *"Madame…rendezvous…Jane…heureux…."* Again, I didn't worry about understanding, for his meaning was clear.

Now, we see each other when I drop in at the wine bar Ed has recently bought, or if I meet Jane alone for a lunch in the cafeteria at UNESCO, where she works. (I wonder if she knows Anna's husband, a high mucky-muck, it turns out.) I once was invited to the little apartment they now share down in the 13th, and Ed's wine loosened my tongue too much, of course. But they were tolerant, which my friends need to be. And over these years, Ed's English has improved, and so has my French, so our conversations go back and forth in *franglais*, which I'm sure that professor who disliked the language of *impérialistes* would deplore. I've often wished I would run into him again, now that my French is good enough for snappy comebacks.

This evening, though, at *21h20,* I head out into the evening air to meet Alice and Caroline. I have been feeling pretty satisfied all day, having perhaps written a true sentence or two and then in the afternoon even stirring myself to go to the pool. So, on the spur of the moment—and testing my mettle—I go out of my path to walk through rue Guisarde. I've only glimpsed Joël a couple of times since that evening, and that was fine, for then. But I've been thinking, over the weeks, how to handle the situation, so whether or not I feel "normal" about it, I have decided that, that is how I will act.

When I get to the restaurant I peek my head in, and Joël sees me. I wave, and he smiles and calls out, *"Bonsoir, ma grande,"* which I think means something like "Good evening, my pal," and I suppose that is what I am. Well, "normal" isn't the option I would have chosen, had I had the choice.

"You're late," says Caroline at the corner, realizing the direction from which I had come (and probably looking at my face). "Did you just happen to walk through rue Guisarde?"

"Oh, *laisse moi du mou*," I say. "Give me a break. I'm only thirty seconds late."

Alice looks at us curiously. "Why would you walk through the Guisarde?" she asks me. Caroline shrugs, and I laugh, but we don't answer. Instead, we take two grocery bags from Alice, and we walk into rue des Canettes.

"Jack will love this street," I say to the ladies, as I glance in at the gleaming copper vats in the window of O'Neil. "They'll be right above an Irish pub."

"He does love his lager, doesn't he?" Caroline agrees. "How anyone can drink so much beer and not put on weight is beyond me!" Actually, luckily for Jack, one thing Paris does not lack is pubs. There are Irish, Australian, Canadian, British, and Scottish pubs sometimes with kilted bagpipers making themselves heard. And most also have large television screens for watching sports.

But now is the time to admit without shame that I like watching some sports—although I don't like talking about them forever (as Husband Number Two seemed to do). Once during the World Cup of *football* (soccer), I took myself alone to a pub near boulevard St-Germain, and with a bunch of demented French men watched the *foot,* the match being won by *la France.* The men (at least those who noticed) were amused by the *américaine* who had infiltrated their stronghold and were eager to bestow on me those Frenchy-type kisses when France prevailed. All those boozy men left to me, their wives having wisely sent them out of the house. I had thought of going back again, but I didn't.

And now at the end of May, I have every intention of taking the *métro* by myself out to the Roland Garros tennis stadium and buying a ticket to the French Open from the scalpers outside. (How do they get tickets, when I can't?) Why none of my friends will go with me, I cannot begin to grasp. How could they miss such a Paris event? But I do not bring it up anymore, certainly not with the Lovells or Edie, but not even with Caroline, who last time looked at me as though I had possibly gone mad, but said in her kindly way, "Thanks, but I think I'll pass."

As to the boys, I feel silly that their Rome trip is so preying on my mind. But I do know that sporting events are not ticked off on their weekly list of cultural illuminations, so I don't call them, making me feel even worse. Something has to change, and I know it. I'm acting like a child.

"Do you think Jack will change his allegiance from Connolly's Corner?" Caroline says, as she peers in the window of O'Neil. "It looks pretty friendly here."

"I thought he was devoted to O'Brien's," I say, but Caroline just rolls her eyes, indicating that I am way (way) behind the times.

At the building just past O'Neil, Alice punches in the *code* and then lets us into the second door with one of the keys her absent friends have left with her. She ushers us across a sweetly landscaped courtyard and finally pushes the *minuterie* to light the stairwell so we can start the climb. Alice herself pauses a few times on the way up, but Caroline and I forge up the narrow winding stairs until we come out on top. We wait while Alice catches up and then a bit longer as she uses two other keys to open locks positioned vertically along the door.

We enter directly into one large room with a couch and several chairs at one end, a dining table, desk, bookcases, and a console with radio and *télé*. Two windows look out over a court, and opposite there is another window in the small kitchen, so on hot August days, there should be a breeze. The desk will be good for Jack to work on, we figure, and facing on the courtyard, the apartment will be quiet. And being on the highest floors, it will also be bright. We open all the cupboards in the kitchen, of course, to put away the groceries, and in the doing we inspect every closet and drawer. This is nosiness, not research.

Behind the couch is a stairwell, and the three of us climb up to a little *mezzanine* to see the bedroom and bathroom perched directly under the mansard roof. In both rooms, the ceilings angle so precipitously that only in about half of each room could any adult stand up, Tom Thumb notwithstanding. But dressers are built-in, as is a small closet, so all told, with the large bed and nightstand, it seems pretty comfortable, at least for two or three months. Up here, there are no windows, but there are three skylights that are still letting in enough of the mid-evening light so that we can see.

"This looks really nice," I begin to say, and then I realize that I am shouting, and we all laugh like mad. Through the skylights the bell tower of the church of St-Sulpice is in plain view, and the church bells, pealing wildly—*bong-bong, bong-bong, bong-bong*—are making it impossible to hear.

"You'd hate it," Alice shouts at me. "It would, as you say, make you 'crazed.' But the Jays will think it just fine. You know their passion about churches. Well, we'll see. They'll be here in about a week."

Once at home again, after walking alone with no detours, Caroline having stopped in a café with Alice for coffee and a chat, I snap the head off a chocolate chicken and sit on the couch for a while. Imagine hearing the bells of an ancient church through your open window. Could a person be both thrilled and frantic at the same time? Is normal good or bad? Is there any way I can make myself feel that the boys must do what is good for them, and not for me? (I will work on this.) I must call Jane and see what she and Edouard are up to. And Margot, who seems to be busier than thou this year. And how nice it will be to see the Jays. Tomorrow afternoon, which promises to be sunny, I will finish my work for the day and then go to the Luxembourg, and I'll watch the children sail boats in the fountain. And I will take a book, perhaps that one about Napoleon's son, finally. And I will sit in the sun and read.

Richard and Paris USA

T HE PHONE RINGS ON A SUMMERY Wednesday morning early in June while I am slogging away at my desk with the window wide open, my back warmed by the sun. For a change I'm happy to hear the phone, for I'm slightly restless, forcing myself to do what I must despite the day that is luring me out. So, it is Richard, and he suggests an early lunch before he goes off to the Ritz for his afternoon swim. "We haven't seen each other since that time we swam together last month," he says. "You remember, that time when you were in such a weird mood? And you said you were going to call me?"

"I was in a weird mood?" I ask, ignoring the last part. But how coincidental for him to call just at this point. I have been working for about an hour on a glossary—simple French phrases for those who know not one word of French and who probably never will. So now, with some relief I swivel my chair so I can look out the window and talk. What a great day. I had been planning to pick up a sandwich somewhere and then eat lunch in that almost unknown (to Americans) park in rue de Babylone, the one where they have vines and arbors, and a little vegetable garden that I am told is planted by the nuns from the convent nearby. But lunch with the linguistically challenged Richard will do just fine. It's that Paris spontaneity again that I love—none of that looking at your agenda two weeks in advance, just for a swim. "How weird?"

"Well, pretty strange," he says and continues in a teasing voice. "And I'd be back in Sausalito for the summer before you'd remember to call. So, say yes. You can catch me up on what you've been doing."

It isn't as if Richard hasn't said anything that isn't true, and I know it. But doing? I realize with an uncomfortable shock that the year is almost half gone. I'm still behind on my book, although not much. I haven't received the updated info from the *Préfecture* about renewing permits to stay. I need to trek again to l'Hôtel de Ville and yet again to the tourist office to see what new brochures have appeared in the racks. I don't have a male project, and this void is beginning to nag. (The tennis matches were a bust in this one regard.) So, I have both too much on my plate and not enough. I happily agree to lunch, and hanging up, go over in my mind some things I've been doing that haven't bored me silly.

The Jays have finally arrived. Jenny called almost immediately after they settled in to rue des Canettes, suggesting we meet over a pint of lager at the Frog and the Princess (not O'Neil), which is across from that Vietnamese restaurant the boys like in rue Princesse. Something seemed the matter when she called, but I didn't know what. I figured if I wasn't imagining it, then I'd no doubt hear about it, so at least on the phone, I didn't ask.

When the three of us had found our table and had ordered our beers, Jenny first gave me the book I had asked her to find, one identifying the "real" Shakespeare as apart from the "Stratford man"—a subject that for some unknown reason has captured my attention. She waved away my offer to pay her for it, so I said I'd pick up the tab for the beers and snacks. I think it came out even at the end, given the state (or non-state) of the dollar these days. Even with inflation, I still have enough euros in my account to last until the end of the year, unless I do something entirely nuts.

But then it started, and unfortunately, my instinct had been right. "We're thinking of moving here permanently," Jack said after we had settled in and our beers had arrived. Immediately this made sense to me, since he works with French publishers, including sometimes Jean-Pierre, and he needs to be in the know about all the new books that will appear.

But fortunately, before I could respond, Jenny bristled. "He's thinking of it," she said with an unexpected sharpness. "Not I.

I've got all my girls in New York to take care of. The Olympics aren't too far off. No, I'm not going to call it quits." So, it stopped making sense to me.

"She could find gymnasts to train here," Jack said, not looking at his wife. A long silence, and in truth, I had nothing to add on either side. So instead of responding, I nodded slightly and turned to Jenny and said, "Oh listen, I just remembered. I'd like to grill you both about the American Church over on the quai d'Orsay, for a paragraph in my book."

"Sure," Jenny said. "Come with us on Sunday morning. Afterward we could get some lunch at that café over by Invalides." Keeping her head from Jack, she tossed me a little smile. "Then you can cross the street to commune at Napoleon's tomb." So, everybody seems to know about *mon ami* Nap. In any case, last Sunday morning, hoping that God would not permit a morning of squabbles, I did go with them to the rather non-denominational Protestant church (thinking mostly of the upcoming bar mitzvah of Mitzi's boy). I said hello to more people I knew than I expected—from book club, the library, or Democrats Abroad—none of whom seemed at all surprised that I was there.

As planned, we lunched on the restaurant terrace of the Café des Esplanades. (Being out of control, I ate an entire mound of those thin matchstick fries called *allumettes* that came with my club sandwich.) No mention of moving was made, and I was relieved. But, although this made me think of the boys and Rome, I managed not to bring it up. After lunch we all crossed over to Invalides. The Jays, of course, being collectors of churches, opted for the ornate chapel built by the king. And I, as we all knew I would, descended to Napoleon's eternal headquarters, with his accomplishments etched on the surrounds for all to see. When I saw his son's tomb nestled nearby, that ill-fated "King of Rome," I reminded myself that I still had a book about half-read.

Caroline, of course, (planning the welcome celebration) also had seen the Jays, taking tea with them over at Café les Editeurs, at Odéon. They had said the same things to her as to me. "Sounds like a not too good summer for them," she said, shaking her head. "Maybe I should have a dinner, trappings and all, and not a lunch." So, since she's now all in a lather about what to serve, we made several exploratory browses through Mulot and the Grande Épicerie, the food hall of the stylish department store Bon Marché. I made a mental note to come back and browse to see what might be available during the end-of-June sales, when Sandy and I will no doubt make one of our forays. After one of those visits to Bon Marché, though, I walked over to the Musée Maillot and checked out its hours and schedules, and looked at an exhibit by the artist Botero—the one who paints those charming fat women. Given Caroline's always fluctuating weight, I was just as glad she hadn't come. But the next afternoon, I went to the pool and swam like a maniac.

And Klaus and Paul have taken the Eurostar train to London for a week or so to go to the ballet. Unable to stand myself being such a selfish cow, I finally called one morning, and it turned out to be just a few hours before they were leaving. So, when Paul asked if I'd accompany them to the train station, I picked up and went. I didn't even change my clothes or check my *planning*, that's how important I knew this was. It wasn't that I was needed in any way, and we all knew that. But in this case, even with nothing explicitly said, "normal" was something we did want to accomplish, and given all the uncertainties, maybe we did. This is probably what Paul had in mind when he asked me to come, the clever old dear.

So, at the Gare de Nord we all hugged, and I wished them a wonderful time, and they hugged me again before taking the escalator up to the waiting room. I watched Klaus, with his wildly colored, *kilim*-covered carpetbag, and Paul, dignified as ever, pulling a discrete black leather case, and my heart was back being overcome by love. Of course, I was still secretly hoping that even this brief trip would deflect their thoughts from Rome. And if they secretly hoped something as they both looked back for an instant to wave, they didn't let on.

I love train stations in Paris, where the open-air waiting areas are adjacent to the tracks, where you can see the trains coming in and leaving. I sat for a while with a cup of mango sorbet (from the Häagen Dazs stand) simply to watch the travelers bustling about. I felt a fleeting urge to go somewhere, too, anywhere, to jump on one of these trains just to see where it might take me, to talk with whomever would sit next to me, to gaze out the window and picture myself in the life that would whiz by. But then, without even so much as a shrug, I got up and walked up the steps to the No. 42 bus. This, I took to Concorde to change to the No. 84, and then after getting off in rue du Four, I took myself over to the square, and then to my street. Sure, I could have taken the No. 4 *métro*, gotten off at St-Germain, and then been home lickety-split, but I was definitely in a kind of bus and look-out-the-window mode.

Once upstairs, I finally checked my *planning*. Democrats Abroad, totally forgotten! So, still of a mood, I spiffied up a bit and walked over to boulevard Raspail, working myself up to get into it all: Iraq and Iran, the sad state of the dollar, French and American health care. The candidates for the upcoming primaries. Whatever it was, I was sure to be ready. I found a chair just inside the door. But I wasn't ready at all. The subject was how each religion had voted in the last election, but it was all statistics and charts and documents being waved about. I tried, but I couldn't bring myself to care. I felt trapped. So, I sidled out at the beginning of the question period, which always seems an excuse for tedious speeches from the audience. I think I went to begin with hoping Richard would show up, but being smarter than I, he didn't. On the way home I peeked in at the Flore to see if anyone familiar was around, but no luck there either, so in the pleasant evening air I moseyed down rue de Rennes, cut over to rue St-Sulpice, and finally was content to be *chez moi*.

As to Richard, he also has his spiel—the offbeat places he's discovered on his walks, some café or other he's just tried in an outlandish part of town. (Some I mark down, some I don't.) A concert he went to that I've missed or a book he'll lend me next time. He always wonders where to take his daughter on her visit when, no matter what, they will go wine tasting. He says what he and Freifeld have cooked up to do over near the Marais, or something about the Rotary luncheons he goes to at La Coupole. Occasionally he talks about financial stuff, at least until he sees my blue eyes glaze. And, although he doesn't often turn up for the Democrats, he can on occasion be rabid about the politics in the States, as any unreconstructed lefty would be.

Yet, Richard makes no apologies for having made a bundle in his lifetime, and to his credit he is generous both of spirit and purse. For one thing, he almost always picks up the check when we go out. He especially delights in taking people to eateries he has heard about as being popular in the outlying *quartiers*. In me, as one might suspect, Richard often has a willing companion on his ventures into the unknown. One evening in February (which I forgot to mention before), he convinced me to take the *métro* (No. 11) to Place des Fêtes, and then to walk four blocks in one of those cold drizzles Paris is famous for, just because some English-speaking taxi driver had told him about a Vietnamese restaurant there that specialized in *phö*. It was, in fact, excellent, but I doubt whether I'd go all that way again just for soup. Of course, I took a menu home and put it in the file labeled "Menus—iffy."

Today, however, Richard gives me some restaurants to choose from. "Let's go someplace nice," he says. "I haven't seen you in so long."

So, since I'm still in a train station mode, I choose Le Train Bleu, the classy old restaurant up the stairs in the Gare de Lyon. The ornately decorated ceilings, the Old World elegance. Good food, and worth every *centime*—even if Richard is paying. Usually we just grab a sandwich at our favorite *sandwicherie* in rue de Seine (Così) or a pizza at Vesuvio in rue Gozlan, but like today, occasionally he springs for Old-World French, if there is a particular place he wants to try or if he wants to linger a while.

No matter where we go, however, Richard excuses himself from the table for a few minutes after *le dessert* and before *le café*. "Be right back," he says. "Don't budge." Later, when we are ready to leave, *voilà*, the bill has already been paid. At first when he did this, I thought he was heading for *les toilettes, mais non*. I usually offer to leave a few extra euros on the table for the waiter, but that has been taken care of, too. With some people this generosity would be awkward, but somehow Richard manages to pull it off. Findlay, as he would, grumbles that it's Richard's "doggone radicalism" that makes him share the wealth.

Yet, the question of how much extra to leave on the table has no clear answer. And that's the truth. Most everyone knows that the bill includes a 12-15 percent service charge, but that they should leave a little more in cash. But how much should that be? And do the waiters get any of that 12 percent or, as the rumors flow, does the *patron* keep it for himself? When I was researching this, I asked around. Edouard the wine guy just shrugged, so at that point I was no further ahead. J-P said that Americans leave *trop*. I've watched my *aristo* friend; he puts down about three euros in a bistro and perhaps five or so in a restaurant that's a step up. As to the starred restaurants, I didn't ask. As to Richard, he just said he hates a cheap tipper and that even if he leaves a euro or so more than a Parisian would do, it means more to the *serveur* than it does to him. For the Parisians, though, it's a matter of principle, I think, and not of the dough. But I finally decided to strike a middle ground, and now I will recommend that—if the service is good—people might leave about 5 percent more. Nothing, if the service is *mauvais*.

Richard's way of living in Paris is unique, but it follows the Paris rule. If it seems little different from his old routine at home, it's still exciting enough for him. Starting at about *15h* every weekday afternoon, he glues himself to his computer, for this is when the New York Stock Exchange is in full high gear. He tunes the TV to CNBC, which shows stock trades as they are made. Richard has satellite TV. My own building is *câblé*, so I use *noos*, the cable monopoly that J-P says are *"ghang-stairs."*

So, all afternoon Richard monitors his portfolio and makes trades, his laptop varying between bloomberg.com and whatever else, I don't know. My email is aol.com on *noos—ghang-stairs* or not. Caroline uses the French provider wanadoo.fr, whose name I think is cute but which is unfortunately morphing into Orange, or so I'm told. And Findlay uses yahoo.com, but he is becoming forgetful of these little details, and when I asked for his address, he said it was "wahoo."

Until Richard's dinner time around *21h30,* he is adding to his coffers. Richard says that it is primarily the Internet that makes it possible for him to live here so easily, and he feels, as he says, that he's "fallen into the *schmaltz* pot," borrowing from Freifeld a Yiddish phrase that seems to mean having fallen into a pot of happiness, i.e. chicken fat. The *schmaltz* pot? I hope Richard got it right, given his non-existent facility with languages.

Yiddish sounds strange on Richard's lips, but the few times he tried to speak French, it sounded stranger yet. Who could forget the one time he volunteered at Edie's cooking school, chopping vegetables and setting up the equipment for her evening class? When the students arrived—all adults who had paid considerably for this course—he decided to go totally French and said, or he thought he did, *salut*, which means "hi." What he actually pronounced, unfortunately, was *salaud* which means "bastard," more or less. The audience thought it hilarious, but Edie went ballistic, and that was the end of that. We heard about it from Edie for weeks.

Richard, I suspect, hoped to learn French the way Paul Jones quickly did, through intimate conversations with a lover. Jones had followed Ben Franklin's advice and acquired a "sleeping dictionary" from various French women who were glad to oblige. (And— sigh—what of my own new dictionary?) As to Richard, his moves toward Edie ended abruptly at that point. She saw to that. No amount of flowers would change her mind. Also unfortunate, Richard's tolerance for the ups and downs of the stock market didn't extend to learning a language. So far as I know, he's never tried to master French again.

Now, the language of money is another kettle of fish. Richard seems to have straightened Caroline out, at least as far as maximizing the minimum that she has.

THOSE PESKY ACCENTS

É/é (accent aigu): The letter *e* is pronounced as in "way."

È/è (accent grave): The letter *e* is pronounced as in "left."

Ç/ç (cédille): The letter *c* is pronounced as "seem," not "clean."

¨ over a vowel (le tréma): The vowel is pronounced separately from the one directly before. Thus, the word *laïc* is pronounced "lah-eek." ~~Or like Joël~~.

R is pronounced in the back of the throat. Try to say *r* by lowering your tongue in front and raising it in back.

N after a vowel is not pronounced. Instead, the preceding vowel is nasalized. Also, if there is an *n* after a *g*, as in the word *agneau* (lamb), the combination is pronounced "nya" like "anyau."

EU/OE: Words such as *peu*, *jeux* and *coeur* are pronounced like the English interjection "er" but without the *r*. Form your mouth as though you were going to blow a bubble, and then say "er" in the middle of your mouth.

She has just opened a dual currency account and will move dollars into euros only when the exchange rate is advantageous.

"And when will that be?" she asked, sighing, but at least she seems more organized and less worried, and that's good. I know that she and Richard have been conferring almost daily now, what with inflation and all, but when asked she just says tersely, "There's nothing new." I could have explained this all to her myself, given my research and the talk I had with my own banker, but I knew she'd pay more attention to Richard, and well she should.

Richard opened his own bank account at Banque Transatlantique, the bank up in rue Franklin D. Roosevelt that caters to expats, the one where tellers speaks English, the one that caters to anyone with big bucks.

"I just love the way the French do things," Richard told the gang at his first appearance at Caroline's lunch, a few years ago, when she introduced him to us. "I went to the bank to open the account but didn't have an appointment, so I had to come back. When I finally filled out the papers, they couldn't tell me the number of my account, so I had to go back later that same afternoon. And then a few days after my funds were wired from the States, I went back again to pick up my checkbook. It took another two weeks to get my *carte bleue*. Life here is never dull, now, is it?"

Paul agreed. "And then when you run out of checks and order new ones, they may not follow consecutively from the last one that you just used up. So, after you use check number 199, for instance, your next checkbook may start with number 301."

Richard nodded with relief. "So, that's what it is. I just thought I had made yet another mistake."

So, now in his Parisian routine, Richard begins his mornings with the newspapers. Along with the *Wall Street Journal* and the *Financial Times* he also reads *The International Herald Tribune*, which he, like the rest of us, has delivered to his mailbox.

Considering—as most of us do, anyway—that Richard is still in his Paris training period, when he has time to read, he reads about Paris. About a year ago, I think it was, he learned that the *Tribune* had been founded as a result of a New York socialite supposedly having peed into a fireplace at his engagement party. This amused him (as it does everyone upon learning it). So, one Sunday evening shortly after that, when he had asked Caroline and me to the cinema to meet a visiting friend, he told us all the story over a glass of wine at a café on boulevard St-Germain. A friend of Richard's? What kind of friend?

So, we listened to the story that we already knew, for of course the stylishly thin, totally put-together woman—a neighbor of Richard's from Sausalito—hadn't heard it before, the way she laughed (a little forced, if you ask me) at everything he said. "Super!" she kept saying. "Super!" Actually, Caroline and I enjoyed the story again, for Richard waxed so enthusiastically about what he had learned. After the fireplace incident, when he was presumably dumped by his fiancée, James Gordon Bennett, Jr. settled in Paris, and in 1887 he started the *New York Herald, European Edition,* an offshoot of the New York paper his daddy owned. Even here, for a while, he was called "the crazy American." How many readers noticed that he published the same Letter to the Editor every day from 1899 to 1918, the year he died. Signed "Old Philadelphia Lady" the letter concerned how to convert temperatures from Fahrenheit to Centigrade. Now, the paper is the *International Herald Tribune* (called by locals "*The Trib*"), and is owned by the *New York Times. Moi,* I've got a temperature converter on my Internet favorites list.

"Okay, I can see you already knew all that about Bennett," said Richard to us, while his friend was still chuckling through her beautifully capped teeth and starting to stand up. "But did you hear that it was he who sent Henry Stanley to Africa in search of Dr. Livingston?"

"No, we didn't," admitted Caroline, looking at me while I was shaking my head. I was silent, for I had been caught in the act of mind wandering, wondering what there was between Richard and this attractive woman who was clearly on the make for him, and who was now excusing herself to "freshen up." Would he take up with someone whose turquoise-colored handbag matched her shoes?

"And no, before you ask," Richard said to us when Stefanie had disappeared toward the *toilettes,* "I enjoy her in Sausalito, but she's not my type. No doubts about anything. Too perfect. So, I'm glad she's here, but I'm just showing her around. And," he laughed, "maybe that's why I asked you along—for protection!"

As to Richard's mornings, after his coffee, a large bowl of fresh fruit and perhaps a *croissant* or *brioche*, he is eager to go out and about, to see how Paris is that day. He says that Alice B. Toklas' own remark (not that of her friend Gert) that "Paris is the American dream" was meant for him.

Almost every morning, he browses one fresh-air market or another. He goes early enough to have to compete with those fierce old French women pushing their way with their sturdy canes in front, wheeling their plaid shopping carts behind. He says he thinks they're sweet. I, on the other hand, go much later, having once been knocked flat by one of the old dears, who swung her cart directly in front of me and then stopped dead. *"Pardon,"* she said, hardly glancing down at me as she moved on to greener stalls.

At whichever market he goes to that day, Richard combines pointing to what he wants with one of the words he knows is the same in French and in English. There are many, including most of the words that end in "tion"—but not all, for *déception*, for instance, means "disappointment," not what an American would expect. Fortunately for Richard, the word *kilo* is the same. But a kilo is 2.2 pounds, so he tends to buy a lot of fruit. Most of us buy less than that at one time, for food in France has few additives and, being *non-traité*, tends to spoil fairly quickly. A *demi kilo* would do, or even *une livre*, which is a pound. Pronunciation is important here, too, for if you ask for *un livre* you're asking for a book. Merchants are used to Americans, however, and I've seen tourists at the fruit market in rue du Seine ask for a book of cherries and wind up with about a pound.

At the supermarket, however, Richard does better. Most of us use Monoprix, a mid-priced national chain. Sometimes Alice and I shop together at the one in rue de Rennes, giving us a chance to sit in their café and chat. Findlay and Alice refer to Monoprix as "the dime store," but if it was that in Findlay's "good old days," it certainly isn't anymore. It's a modern supermarket with other items like cashmere sweaters for winter and tee shirts for summer, all with their "designer" label, *autre-ton*. I get lots of stuff there.

But Richard walks all the way down to Sèvres-Babylone to La Grande Épicerie. Richard, whose wife died some five years ago, says he has learned to cook since then, and he has come to enjoy shopping for food, comparing prices and items here and there.

"I know that the Grande Épicerie is more expensive than Monoprix," Richard said one afternoon soon after that great Edie debacle, when I had run into him at the checkout counter. "But they've got such good stuff!" He waited while I checked out and was gathering up my bags. He looked at what I had bought. "Marshmallow Fluff? Nestlé's Chocolate Morsels?" He couldn't stop laughing.

"Well, I can't get these things at Monoprix," I said rather defensively, even though Richard's tolerant laugh was one I knew so well. And then I changed the subject. "Would you like to go across the street and get a cold drink?" So, we went across rue de Babylone to a *bar/tabac*, where Richard ordered a Gini lemon soda that is the rage, and I, for a change, *thé glacé à la pêche* (peach-flavored ice tea).

"Look, Richard," I said, when he was saying how disappointed he was about mispronunciations in French. "Not everyone has an ear for language, that's all. Don't sweat it. You get along just fine here, and that's what counts." It's true that lots of other Americans here can't speak French, either (and almost as true as I made out). But fortunately, Richard didn't say anything about Edie, so after about fifteen minutes of sitting in the sunshine at the sidewalk table, we got up, kissed the both-cheeks kisses, sorted out our grocery bags, which wasn't hard since Richard didn't have Fluff, and left.

I think that no guidebook except mine tells new shoppers—French speakers or not—that checking out in a Paris supermarket is not for the faint of heart. *Moi,* I love the whole thing. First, the cashiers invariably claim they have no change. *"Je n'ai pas de la monnaie,"* they say, meaning they have no coins. If you don't have the exact amount in *centimes*, the calculations go directly into high finance. *"Avez vous deux euros et onze centimes?"* they ask. And if you do have the two euros and eleven centimes, or whatever they want, you may get back a one euro coin, or one for fifty centimes and some bills, as well. Sometimes when the calculations are too intricate, I just take out a handful of change, stick it in front of the cashier and let her pick out what she wants. If she's so smart, let her do it.

Now, the situation escalates. In those supermarkets that still provide plastic bags, the cashier does not bag your groceries but thrusts one or two at you from a stash that she is perhaps hoarding on her lap. These you must manage to pull open at the same time you are trying to find the desired change and organize the groceries that are being pushed your way willy-nilly, so they will be balanced to carry home. And just as you are starting to load the bags, one hand has to go out to receive the return bills and coins and receipt, which you must put back into the different compartments in your *portefeuille*. At this point, of course, the cashier, who has finished with you, is sitting impassively waiting for you to take your stuff so she can start checking out the next person in the long line of Parisians who have been looking at you silently, waiting for you to be done. I no longer panic at any of this, for I've learned from the French. Nothing fazes them. So, now, I calmly deal with the money first, taking out and putting away. Only then do I start with the bags. Richard, of course, no matter how bad his French, is a whiz at high finance, so just by looking at the total on the register he can produce the most bizarre combination of coins at any time, beating the cashier to the punch.

Richard rarely mentions his late wife, and I have had to do some pretty subtle maneuvering to find out even the little I know. Caroline only knows a bit more, although years ago she was his daughter's American History professor at a university in upstate New York. This is how Richard came to be part of our group: when he arrived, he looked up Caroline, and welcoming as always, she took him in. Not that Richard inspires pity in any way. He may be oblivious to many things French, but he is certainly shrewd in the ways of life. Tall, with a full head of graying hair, tortoise shell glasses, and an unlined, open face, he looks to be in his late fifties, maybe just a little older. His wife, who had been involved somehow in art galleries in San Francisco, died in an accident, a collision head on. No wonder he wanted to start over. Although it won't be Edie, I'm sure he'll find someone again, perhaps a chic *Parisienne* who wants to improve her English in bed.

The daughter's name is Phyllis, which if you ask me is as bad as Frances, although I minded my name less in Rome, when those men trilled my name *Francesca,* or in France with *Françoise,* or even the *Frahn-zess* that Joël now calls me again with ease. (Good for him.) Yet, names in French are hard to fathom. For instance, how can the names Claude and Dominique be either feminine or masculine, and why do parents name their girls Marie-Pierre?

And their boys Pierre-Marie? *Mademoiselle* Stein herself had something to say about that (naturally), which was that it hallows a male name to add a female name to it. I could probably believe that if I knew what it meant. Richard calls his daughter Philly, which reminds me of cream cheese and which makes me yearn for good lox.

I've met Phyllis a couple of times here, but I'd know her fairly well even if she'd never come, for we all hear about each other's families—when there's news to impart from the home front, when someone has received new photos, or when some incident sparks a memory that wants to be shared. We ask about families or friends as though we knew them, and in a way we do. Phyllis (I refuse to call her Philly) seems to take after her father. Smart, affable, independent (and rich). That's not at all bad.

If Richard doesn't have a *rendez-vous* for lunch, he might grab a sandwich at Così (where the ever-shifting staff all speak some English) on rue du Seine, before he goes to the pool. He waits for the hot bread to come right out of the oven and then chooses the fillings to put in it. After lunch, if the pool or museum exhibits are not in the cards, he might go to an English-language film at one of the cinemas at Place de l'Odéon. Shortly after he arrived in Paris, Richard by chance sat next to Alice and Findlay at a movie, and they struck up a "small world" conversation, after it was determined that he knew Caroline. Americans do tend to greet other Americans seated near them, or perhaps I'm just guilty as charged. But the French could learn something here, *n'est-ce pas?*

It's hard for Americans to understand that the French don't usually make small talk in an elevator with someone they don't know, even though they are aware that the person has lived in their building for years. Intrude on your privacy? Even in an elevator? *Jamais!* Never! They will respond politely, however, if you say *Bonjour, monsieur* or *madame*. Stop right there. If you ask them how they are (or even what their name is), you might be going too far.

Yet, Americans tend to know their Parisian neighbors more than the Parisians themselves do, precisely because the French are too polite to tell us that they think we've gone too far.

Moi? I never seem to learn. Not even today. On the way to lunch with Richard, and since it's Wednesday, I stop by my neighborhood kiosk to pick up the new *Pariscope*. Perhaps because it is such a pleasant, sunny day, and perhaps because I have dressed up a little to match the occasion (silk shell under the blue blazer, just before I put it away for the summer), the vendor actually asks me how I am. *"Ça va?"* he asks. Just like that, after three years of nodding and saying *Bonjour, madame*. But do I simply answer *Oui, ça va bien, merci* and leave it at that? No, I have to tell him that everything is fine, that my work is going well, that I am going to Le Train Bleu for lunch, that an old friend from Chicago emailed me this morning to say she is coming to Paris, and that all in all, everything is swell. Then I look at the vendor's face, and my heart sinks. Once again, I have gone too far.

When at lunch Richard hears about this, he almost chokes with laughter. Uncomfortable as I am at having been such a dolt, this same *moi* who must soon write a chapter telling other people how to adapt to Parisian culture, I have to laugh, too. Also at Richard's obvious pleasure that for a change it's not he who has been the idiot. The attentive waiter speaks English as, of course, he would in such an international place, and is gracious in welcoming Richard back. He suggests the price-fixed lunch menu, and so the lunch is a huge success, with excellent food and conversation in an exquisite setting, and with service worthy of Richard's pleasantness and bucks. But, after having eaten more than usual, including sharing a *tarte tatin* (the same kind of upside-down apple whatsis that Alice made, and I will not say which was better), I am considering the word "diet" again. (Is there not the bar mitzvah and the possibility of a new project?) We do not linger long, for Richard says it's time for him to take the *métro* to the pool. Although some place or other should be checked out so I can convince myself I'm being productive, I'd rather go home to my couch and the mystery of the real Shakespeare. If the writer Shakespeare really was the "Stratford man," why did he leave no books or folios in his will? How could his children have been illiterate? Why would a writer so talented sign his name with so many different spellings? I love books like this. I mean, some people really care.

Anyway, as the week progresses, I make a plan. To be cool. So, on the Wednesday of Caroline's dinner for the Jays, I stop at the newsstand again, and hoping the vendor won't cut me dead, I just smile, quickly say, *"Bonjour, monsieur,"* ask for *le Pariscope*, pay the forty centimes and move on. I do notice, however, that he hasn't taken a chance by asking again, *Ça va?*

And I confess all at the dinner. "Well, I did it again," I say in a rare moment of silence, a long while after we all kissed and settled ourselves at the table outside under the awning to shield us from the lowering evening sun. We had started by making our welcoming toast to the Jays with Richard's wine, and then Jack started in.

"This summer we're going to buy an apartment," he announced, not looking at Jenny.

Immediately Jenny countered with, "Jack is. I'm not." There was (deadly) silence for a moment.

Then Caroline, in her kind way, said, "But looking at apartments here is so much fun. It doesn't mean you have to buy right away."

"Just so long as he knows I'm not leaving my girls," Jenny answered sharply.

Then Paul and Klaus—just back and having called to tell me they'd see me at lunch—heroically stepped into the breach to report on London and the ballet. The National Portrait Gallery, the Tate Modern, the lunch at Fortnum and Mason—and only a couple of hours away by train. I looked at Klaus. Was what I saw in Klaus's eyes a rueful longing for days gone by? Was he missing those days of stardom, of Rudi, of adventure? I am certainly one to understand that. Maybe a move would be good for him, I thought, and then I am astounded by this unusual objectivity rising in me. Could I be learning new tricks?

THE PROBLEM WITH FRENCH WINE

Unfortunately, when it comes to French wines, you can get too much of a good thing. Simply put, there's too much wine being produced for a global market that is changing. Domestic wine consumption is also declining—it fell some 11 percent between 2001 and 2005. But the major problem—shared by many Old World vintners—concerns outdated regulations at home and savvy marketing from New World producers: America and others such as Chile, Australia, South Africa, and Argentina.

To give an idea of the numbers involved, think of Bordeaux, the largest wine-producing area in France. Here, some 9,000 wineries produce 700 million bottles of wine annually, using the grapes of 13,000 growers. Yet, also think of the neighboring Bergerac, which has only about 2,000 winemakers, competing with each other (and Bordeaux) but also with the growing market for New World wines.

The general difference between Old World wines (aged longer, subtle and refined, with the name of the château on the label) and New World wines (bold, fruity, and usually consumed younger, with the name of the grape on the label) is more than just taste. Drinking wines that peak sooner means that consumers don't have to wait years for a wine to be ready to drink. And New World wines—at least many of them—cost much less.

Thus, sales of New World wines are increasing in Europe by some 10 percent each year. In China, France has lost half its market share. And in the U.S., soon to overtake France as the world's leading wine consumer, sales are markedly growing, but largely of domestic wines.

Recognizing the need for reform, the EU struggles with regulatory changes—for countries that have long subsidized an industry that has as much to do with tradition as profit. Nonetheless, in 2007 the EU decreed that some 430,000 acres of vines be removed; unsuccessful growers will eventually fail, and successful producers will be allowed over time to increase their vines. Many subsidies will end by 2012. And perhaps just as important, the grape variety may be featured on the label of many wines, allowing consumers to know more easily just which grapes they prefer. In France itself, the Ministry of Agriculture has relaxed some regulations and has increased loans to producers, but they still can't match the marketing budget of the wine producers in just the state of California.

But now, having opened my mouth, everyone looks at me expectantly (even Richard who has already heard my tale of humiliation), for they know me, and they are eager to hear my latest transgression against the reserved sensibilities of the French.

After hearing all the dramatic details, Sandy laughs. "One thing I've learned here is that when people ask how you are, you say, *La vie est dure.* Life is hard. On days when it's not so bad, you can say, *La vie est moins dure aujourd'hui.* Not so hard, today."

"That's not Fran's style," Paul smiles at me fondly. (Could he sense that unusual objectivity?) "First, she'd never say life was hard, and if she did, she'd probably then keep you there for a while, explaining why." Smiling back (I hope), I wonder if this is true. Am I this generation's Gertrude Stein?

"At least Fran's reestablished her newsstand relationship at par," Richard says, and he is right. I haven't had to change newsstands, so all is well.

The dinner works out just as Caroline planned: the cold whole salmon—perfectly poached at the fish store in rue du Bac—a variety of salads and cheeses and a crunchy *baguette*, and eight friends crowded together on the balcony late into the evening. Not drunk, but not exactly sober, either, I have to say, Richard having outdone himself with the wines. In addition to Jack and Jennifer, who finally rave about their summer apartment, although never mentioning the church bells, there is Sandy (who might—or might not—be between men, I wish I knew), plus the boys and me, and Richard. No Anna this time, nor Mitzi, who is frazzled with last-minute doings for the biggest day in the history of the world. No Edie or Margot, who are both working. And Caroline, of course, invited the Lovells, but they have extended their stay with their sons at St-Malo. So, we make a cozy group of old friends, and what with one thing or another, the evening stretches on, and none of us is particularly eager to go home.

Finally, around *23h,* we all leave, except for the Jays, who stay to help Caroline clear. Klaus hugs me fervently, and Paul for a change kisses me on the forehead. "I'll walk you home," Richard offers, which although unnecessary is nice.

"Want to do something tomorrow?" I ask Sandy, as we are all going out the door. "Scout out in advance of the sales?"

"Can't," she says. "I've invited someone over to dinner, and I've got to get ready."

"Someone new?" I ask, hoping she will elucidate, but at least my question has been answered.

"Sort of," she shrugs. "But let's go soon." And because my head is a bit fuzzy, I do not ask whatever happened to the young guy from Antoine's department in the ministry. Richard makes sure I get home, and then he takes off to Place Dauphine.

Richard, though, does mention his non-gang friends, although except for his neighbor, he hasn't so far brought them into our group. Like the rest of us, he wants to know Parisians, and he does the best he can, given his difficulties with learning French. Wednesday lunch is with the Rotary at La Coupole in Montparnasse, and Friday with his wine club. And although I've never seen this when I've been with him, he says he chats with other swimmers, the (literally) ritzy Americans at the pool (although he wasn't yet in Paris when Ambassador Pamela Harriman died there during her swim). I haven't heard about any women of his type showing up, but I suppose I would, if one did.

But wine, in fact, is the reason Richard came on his first long visit to France and one reason why, I think, he came back to stay. He is *passionné* about California wines and apparently has an extensive cellar at his Sausalito home. Like most of the gang, he goes back to the States each year to see family and friends, but for Richard it's usually toward the end of the summer, so he can also keep track of the harvest in Napa for that year. Actually, Sandy goes back every summer with the kids; Edie visits her family in Sacramento (will her brother's twins ever be toilet trained?); Findlay and Alice rarely go back, for their own kids are here; Caroline goes every few years; and I go every Christmas. Margot, though, the rather reclusive (and moody) artist, who's always outraged by whatever there is currently to be outraged about in political America, just looked at me as though I were nuts when I asked.

So, in Paris, Richard immediately took several English-language wine courses, and now he haunts the wine museum over in square Charles-Dickens. He's a regular at some prestigious *caves*—Les Caves Taillevant and Les Caves Augé. And since he met Edouard, he gets to talk about wines in English whenever he wants. I once heard them talk (in tedious detail) about the amount of alcohol in a French Bordeaux (less) as opposed to a California cabernet (more), which, according to me, is pretty much more than anyone really has to know.

But Richard now has the beginnings of a collection of French wines. When he's with the gang, he invariably brings a bottle or two. There's a myth that the French wouldn't like this, taking it as a criticism of their ability to choose the perfect wine of their own, but I'm not sure this is true. And when Phyllis is here, despite Richard's usual uncertainty about what they should do, they always take some wine-tasting weekends away. Caroline goes along, and early last summer—before she went down near Marseille to the beach and before I left to visit my British cousins—even I piled with the rest into a rented Renault Laguna that could seat five people (plus an ample trunk for cartons of wine) and was pleased to have been asked. My publisher was already talking about a new contract, and I had started my getting-ready mode. I enjoyed the ride down to the Loire as much as learning about the wines, and I'd go again, just for that. But the trip had some effect: Now, in order to be at least somewhat winely suave, when I am forced to be the one ordering wine, I sometimes can forestall the *sommelier* by ordering a Quincy (pronounced *can-see*). Perhaps owing to John *can-see* Adams, I manage to remember its name. But I do need to say something wise in my book.

And in the fall, the book contract having finally been signed, I went with Richard and Edouard and Jane up to the Clos Montmartre Winery, where I had read that vineyards on the hill had been producing for more than five hundred years. Needing to see for myself, I went for the annual grape harvesting (picking) to which the public is invited to help (for free).

"Sounds like painting Tom Sawyer's fence to me," I said.

Edouard said, *"Comment?"*

And Jane, being Scottish, asked, "What?"

But Richard said, "It's fun. You'll see." And he was right.

As to La Coupole, that Richard sets foot in at all makes Findlay completely go off his wig. "Why on earth would anyone go there?" he grumbles on a drizzly evening (yes, rain even in summer, even though it stays light until well past 22h30), with just Alice, son Howard, and me as an audience. I had dropped in to say hello to Howard and for a bit of curmudgeonly chat (to restore my esteem on a day when I couldn't manage anything right) and managed to stay until dinner time, when we decided, on the spur of the moment, to go down the street to the Mâchon d'Henri, crowding four people into the little back alcove for privacy (otherwise known as claustrophobia).

"La Coupole?" Findlay went on. "It's part of a chain. The food is brought in from a central kitchen, and the room is hideous. You should have seen it before they ruined it. When all those 1920s writers hung out." After thinking about it, I've decided (with no evidence at all) that Findlay is miffed because he thinks Richard looks down on his cheap wine. Not that Richard would ever say a word.

Of course, Findlay is known for thinking that nothing is what it used to be, but as an American he sees it as a personal affront, not like the French as a philosophical stance. I'm sure he would sue someone if he could. All in all, he seems touchiest about Montparnassse, even though *les années folles*—the crazy years— were two decades before he arrived on the scene. This was when all those American writers and artists—established, aspiring, or just hangers-on—transformed the cafés of Montparnasse (Le Select, Le Dôme, La Rotonde, all still going strong) into the heart of Odéonia.

"But Hemingway never hung out at the Coupole," I remind Findlay, taking my life in my hands. But the truth is that—the old days belonging only to Findlay notwithstanding—La Couple opened only in 1927, when Hemingway was about to go back to the States. Actually, Hem liked the Closerie de Lilas, and occasionally I think of changing to it from Procope for my tourist sagas, but stories about Franklin as a randy old man are better told than those about Hemingway in his youth.

But for corned beef and cabbage, the American crowd in Montparnasse went to The Dingo, run by the Englishman Jimmie Charters—who, in the spirit of the times, wrote his memoirs (of course). Not enough gossip for me, except for Hem's Introduction, an attack on his former buddy Stein. *La* Stein had already attacked him in *The Autobiography of Alice B. Toklas*, after Hemingway had gotten fed up with her pretensions and quit her salon.

Perhaps the feud really started with Miss Genius's review of Hemingway's first book. "Three stories and ten poems is very pleasantly said," she wrote. "So far so good, further than that, and as far as that, I may say of Ernest Hemingway that as he sticks to poetry and intelligence it is both poetry and intelligent."

"No one understands that Findlay considers himself the true keeper of the Parisian flame," Alice remarks when her husband, having ignored my comment and continued to demolish La Coupole, moves on with his "everything is *pourri*" tirade. "They should name an *arc de Lovell* somewhere after him."

"Or a statue like the one Rodin did of Balzac supposedly holding his private parts, that one over on boulevard Raspail," son Howard suggests with a straight face.

"They're not as good as they used to be either," Alice laughs, and even Findlay has to smile.

About the Coupole, Findlay does know his stuff (although being so jammed into the alcove at the Mâchon may not be the place for comparisons). Yet, La Coupole is popular with business people, tourists, a few *habitués,* and even with me, sometimes, when I consider their curry of lamb, despite it having no relation to anything Indian. I do not mention this to Findlay. Let Richard take the heat.

In the evenings, after having added a zillion or two to his fortune, Richard will go out to dinner, or he may stay home and watch some English-language TV or read. Like most of the people I know, if he has lingered over a large lunch, he'll eat less at dinner, with just a glass or two of some wine or other. On a night when he thinks Edouard might have a moment to chat, he'll go over to the *sommelier's* bar. Or if Ed isn't there, he might find another *bar à vin* to sample wines and have a snack.

(Edie's rule for *le snack:* You can snack or eat meals, but you can't do both on the same day. With this rule, she manages not to gain weight, although on her it is hard to tell. "Rubenesque," Richard called her, with admiration. His *chic* neighbor from Sausalito never stood a chance.)

Yet, if he is up for one of his true exploratory gastronomical jaunts, alone or with someone else, Richard will head out just after *21h.* I have occasionally ventured out on my own if nothing in the larder suits or if crankiness is afoot, but always earlier than Richard, during *l'heure américaine*, just when the restaurants open, around *19h30.* Waiters are always considerate to a woman alone.

On weekends, after he has checked his email to see what his broker, Phyllis, or his California cronies have to say, Richard sets out into Paris, often with some buddy he has met. With his wine club friends he'll stop in at La Dernière Goutte, the *cave* off rue du Buci that is run by Juan Sanchez, a young American who knows his wines. At the weekend *dégustations* (tastings) experienced vintners discuss the wines (every single detail). Being astute, I guess, Richard hasn't asked me along.

I, too, stop in at La Dernière Goutte, usually on the way home from a sushi lunch in rue Dauphine. (For the time being avoiding the sushi bar in rue de Passy, leaving the *drageur* to chat up someone else.) Of course, I do taste a wine or two (although not hanging around to analyze them endlessly), buy a bottle if necessary, and, if he has a minute, chat with Juan. It was he who took me the first time for a sandwich at Così to introduce the owner, the New Zealander Drew Harré. Devouring the delicious sandwich, I told him that the hot bread (that Richard loves, too) reminded me of a favorite sandwich shop in Rome.

Drew grinned. "Was it at Fratelli Palladini?" I'm sure my mouth dropped a mile. "That's where I learned to bake my bread," Drew laughed. Another thing to love about Paris. Connections to everywhere else. *Quel* small world. The Palladini brothers, after all these years. But right now, remembering the pleasures of Rome does not fill me with joy.

So, back to Richard and his jaunts! The last time I went with him on one of his exploratory excursions was that one wintertime sodden trudge up to the 19th for Vietnamese soup. So, it's time to go again. I like it especially that after walking we generally pause, usually at a café with a view of the river or a beautiful square. He likes the experience of the café, and I like to look at all the people around. (I do not talk to strangers when with anyone else. Research is a solitary job.) If Richard likes the place, he'll take the business card as he leaves. By now he has hundreds of these cards stacked in a drawer, arranged, I think, by *arrondissement,* or maybe it's by type of cuisine, each pile held together by rubber bands.

"There's so much to do in Paris, even if it looks like you're doing nothing at all," I say to him while we are sitting down (thank goodness) on a lovely Thursday afternoon the week after Caroline's dinner, when he has decided to take the afternoon off from high finance. He came at *13h30* to pick me up in rue Servandoni. First, we skirted the fountain in the Luxembourg, admiring the (yet again) newly planted flowers. Then, having flowed with the crowd up boulevard St-Michel, we browsed the *bouquinistes* (booksellers) along the *quai*. That was where we saw Jennifer taking her daily jog. She waved at us but didn't stop. After crossing the footbridge to the Right Bank, we strolled first along the rue de Rivoli and then back, and wound up having a massive window-shopping venture through the Carrousel du Louvre (my choice), the shopping mall that is open on Sunday. And when my feet gave out, we came to the Café Marly, which is always fun, despite it being oh-so-trendy.

"I didn't know we were doing anything," Richard says, sipping his *déca*. "Does sitting here count?" I just smile and nod my head. Has the man learned nothing at all?

I'm going to go back to the States in a few weeks," Richard remembers to tell me as we are about to leave. The *pamplemousse pressé* (fresh-squeezed grapefruit juice) I have drunk has given me strength. We decide to walk back across Pont Neuf, at the tip of Île de la Cité. Richard will turn into Place Dauphine, and I will head up rue Dauphine on my own. "I'm going to stop off at my old university for a reunion of the political group I belonged to. I've convinced Freifeld to go, too."

"Oh yes, I heard you mention it. It sounds like fun," I say, which isn't completely true. Then I say, "I'll miss you," which is.

Richard smiles happily. "Have an early lunch with me tomorrow," he suggests, "and then we'll take one last swim together before I leave."

Now heavy into the pre-bar mitzvah diet and at least thinking about exercise, I ask, "Where do you want to have lunch? Surely not by the pool."

"Too fancy and too slow," he says. "Let's meet at that Chinese *traiteur* in rue du Buci. It's fast and not too bad."

Alone a little later, I limp, suddenly crankily, up the narrow sidewalk on busy rue Dauphine, sure I'm getting a blister from having walked too much. Occasionally I have to step down off the curb to pass unruly tourists blocking the *trottoir*. I make sure to look both ways, for I have heard that Pierre Curie was trampled by a horse and wagon in this same street in 1906. Was he distracted, as the rumor goes, by thinking of his wife's supposed infidelity? Whatever, and suddenly feeling keenly the lack of a male distraction, I dodge the cars at the *carrefour* and pass Procope, thinking less of Franklin, for a change, than my feet and my change of mood.

I see Jenny again (showered and nattily dressed in an appallingly short skirt and tight tee shirt, which further deflates me), although she doesn't see me. She is coming out of a real estate agent's office near the corner of rue de Buci. She has some papers in hand. I keep my head down and walk on. She doesn't need a crabby opinion, and at this point that is all that I have, although I'm not sure why. To cheer myself, I stop for an instant at the Village Voice and pick up a new book about Paris. And I am revived later on, though, with a nap and the fact that I am now making great progress with the Shakespeare (or not-Shakespeare) book, and I skim the first pages of the book I bought at the Village Voice. It doesn't compete with mine in any way. Perhaps I'll finally get back to Napoleon's son.

So, on this pleasant next day after our trek, Richard and I meet at the Chinese *traiteur*, where I insist on paying for lunch. This is my offering to God for my not having rubbed a blister, after all, and for having my good humor restored. Richard accepts graciously, for a cheap Chinese lunch isn't going to break my bank. And then we wend our way to the Ritz, taking the bus to Concorde and walking from there. We swim about a half hour and then shower, drying ourselves with warm, soft towels. Again, as I did in the spring, I lift just a few packets of perfumed towelettes. Actually, I feel quite smug.

"Are you looking forward to *la fête de la musique?*" I ask, as we walk back to Place de la Concorde, he to descend into the *métro,* and I to take the bus.

Richard seems surprised by my question. "Why, of course, I am. June 21 is my favorite day of the year! Free concerts all around town? Music all night? I can't wait. Freifeld has found a kosher sushi place over in the Marais, so we'll eat and make our travel plans, and then we're going to hang out near the Bastille and listen to whatever music is around there. What are you going to do?"

"Same as always," I say. "The Luxembourg."

I do know some people who don't pay attention to the *fête de la musique,* and I never can understand why. The streets are just filled with music everywhere you go. Caroline always hangs out with the Lovell geezers near the Guisarde, and the boys are usually at some chamber concert or other, so when Edie closes up early, the two of us usually wander around St-Germain well into the early morning, standing on street corners, listening to little groups—of varying proficiency.

But first, in the late afternoon and all alone, every year I cross rue de Vaugirard to the Palais de Luxembourg, for it's the one day a year I can imagine first-hand the life of Marie de Médicis. Along with the crowds, I wait in line. I enter the palace through the massive *portes,* swoop up the marble staircase as gracefully as Marie might have done if she hadn't been so grossly fat, and I claim a chair in one of the brilliantly gilded rooms to wait for the music to begin. I picture the nobility that might also have sat there and dream about what those days must have been like. It is true that last year, lost in my reveries, I missed almost entirely hearing the young people's choir from a town down south that had come to Paris to perform. I clapped enthusiastically at the end, nonetheless. Afterward, though, I made a vow to do better this year, and I have not forgotten it.

"Pretending you're Marie de Médicis?" Richard smiles. "Like my daughter. Philly always played dress up when she was a kid."

"Phyllis isn't coming at all, this year?" I wonder if Richard is disappointed.

"No," says Richard. "I'll see her in New York in just a few weeks, so there's no real point in her taking off from work. Oh yes, when we talked yesterday, she said to say hello to you."

"She did?" I ask, surprised. "That's really nice of her."

"Next year I'll have to make sure she comes. Maybe we could do some wine trips again. But right now, I'm going to as many concerts as I can. Tomorrow evening I'm going with my Rotary friend Nicolas and his wife out to the Bois de Boulogne for the beginning of the Chopin Festival."

"You do get around, don't you?" I ask. I mean it. For a change, I'm not being snide.

He nods. "By the way, I've found a great place I'd like to take you to, Favela Chic. Do you know it?"

"The Brazilian place?" I can't think of anything I'd rather do less. I went once years ago to check it out, and that was enough. But I try to sound gracious, being pleased that he asked me. "Oh Richard, I know it's fun, but it's a bit too frenetic for me. Let's talk about it again when you get back from the States."

"Well, if you don't want to, that's okay. I'll call you next week," he says, as we kiss our kisses. "Oh yeah," he says. "Have a good time at the bar mitzvah tomorrow morning."

"No, I'll call you," I say. "I really will." But at that he laughs and disappears down the *métro* steps. I like Richard and think

I've got him figured out. It seems only to take a bit of wine and food with friends, lots of music, and exploring Paris to keep him content—as long as his finances are under control. Maybe he'll find an old lefty girl friend at the reunion to stir his radical, rich-man's heart.

So, the next morning, not even having to think for a moment about tourists and French vocabulary, I get up early and get myself dressed. It's a short blue skirt and multicolored silk overblouse kind of day, and I am ready for whatever it brings my way. I am patient and calm. A bar mitzvah should do my soul a good turn. I am almost glad to be out the door and on my way.

Yet, decades-old experience kicks in, and I know not to arrive on time, for even without being in the long ceremony, any boy there would have time enough to become a man. But having strolled to the *métro* and then changed at Châtelet (and then put on my high heels just outside the synagogue door), I still get there early enough to see how joyous everyone is and to feel touched. I do not feel impatient or trapped.

This is the American synagogue, and the service is in English and French, as well as Hebrew, of course. It could sound like the Tower of Babel, but the American rabbi clearly is making it work. The French husband (Gentile, it turns out) wears a *yarmulke*, and he speaks in French to congratulate his son. The American Jewish mother (Mitzi) cries, as do her parents, who have come all the way from Westchester County. The other American relatives keep turning around to ask their neighbors which page they should be on, and the French contingent talk incessantly, paying little attention to the goings on.. People walk in and out. As for me, I think all the *tumult* is great.

But as usual in this kind of event, no matter how I tell myself to stay with the plot, one thing that doesn't change is my attention span. Now, for the first time in years, I recall going to the synagogue with my grandmother when I was a girl, and the songs we used to sing. I loved my grandmother, and not only because I always beat her at gin rummy. So, during this service, when I hear a melody that calls to me from those Saturday mornings, I belt it out with the rest. I do not feel out of place. I'm glad I'm here.

Later, after the blessing of the wine, I kiss Mitzi, remark on the lovely service, and slip her the envelope with the check I have written to some group that supports bar mitzvahs for handicapped Jewish children in Russia. Then I walk out the door, wondering if I can now escape but knowing I can't. (Skepticism is back in force.) But right away I see Anna, arm in arm with the man who must be the UNESCO mucky-muck husband. I go over to say hello and to be introduced. His name is Avi, he's Israeli, and he read my first Paris book when they moved here, he says. This and the fact that Anna seems so glad to see me make me feel guilty, for I haven't thought of her since that book club meeting at my house. So, I stick like glue to them while a huge *autocar* rolls up, and the three of us together board the bus that will take us to the Bois de Boulogne and the lunch.

And the luncheon signals a *petit* change in my life. Not the food, which, given that there are some eight tables of ten people each and it's a three-course lunch and kosher-friendly, is surprisingly good. Nor is it that Avi to my left asks me too quietly—with his foot rubbing slowly on mine, until I jerk it away, almost kicking Anna to my right—if I'd like to have a drink with him sometime so we can talk about books, while Anna goes on more openly about what a wonderful man her husband is. Nor is it that the klezmer band that Mitzi hired after hearing it back in the spring still has that handsome saxophone player, and I wonder how I can go up to him and say hello. (I don't.) And although I have worked out in my head what to write about this park (and only slightly wishing I were anywhere else), it isn't that.

No, it's that *reb* Tom, as everyone calls their rabbi, comes over to me, kisses me on both cheeks, and says he's glad to see me, that he had seen my name on the list, and was hoping I would come.

"And why is that?" I ask. I try not to raise my eyebrow in suspicion.

"Because I want to ask you a favor."

"Oh, oh," I say. But I say it with a smile (I hope).

"Here's what it is. Our little community needs an editor for its quarterly newsletter, and I was hoping you would take it on. You being a writer, and all. The next one isn't due out until late in September, so you have time to think it over."

I look at him. I say nothing. And he says nothing more. He just smiles a little angelic smile that I think must be designed to rope me in, hands me his card, kisses me on each cheek, and then turns to greet someone else.

A Good Day

NOW THIS COULD SEEM A DIGRESSION from the matter at hand, but believe me, it is not. Early on Thursday morning of this week after the bar mitzvah, I am, as usual, slogging away and planning an afternoon ride on the new tramway (T3) that traverses the southern half of the city (with maybe a Vietnamese *bo bun* in a restaurant in the Asian *quartier* in the 13th), when the telephone rings. It is Jean-Pierre calling me himself (with no secretary intervening) to invite me to accompany him to the Sénat on Sunday afternoon, for there will be a tribute to the great French philosopher Paul Ricoeur who died not long ago.

"I remembered that you knew him when he taught at *Chi-ca-go, Frahn*," J-P says, "and so I thought you might like to come. I may have to say a few words," he chuckles just a little, that way he does to let me know he thinks he's being modest or witty, or whatever else. "But at least the rest will be interesting."

Good grief. Of course, I'll go. Not that I actually knew Ricoeur, although we did meet once. Mainly, after shaking hands and saying *Bonjour* the best I could, I managed the sense to keep quiet, while he and my neighbor Bellow walked from the Chicago campus (where I had run into them) and talked about something or other that didn't interest me much. Having worked all day and with two kids waiting for dinner, I didn't have much patience left for philosophy as I wended my own way home. But every once in a while they would toss me a verbal bone, such as Ricoeur's telling me how beautiful Paris could be in the summer, which is when this walk was taking place. I haven't thought of this in years, but perhaps now's my chance to let him know how right he was.

So, on Sunday afternoon I meet J-P at the gate to the Sénat, which, after all, is almost across from rue Servandoni in rue de

Vaugirard. I am wearing a skirt and satin blouse with a flowered silk scarf tucked around the collar (so very French), and because the walk is only four minutes, I have foregone the sensible shoes and dolled myself up with high spiky heels. J-P is waiting for me; we kiss; he looks at me appraisingly and comments on my *très bonne mine* (meaning I look very good); and we go inside.

Immediately upon J-P's mentioning his name at the welcome desk, we are ushered by a polite, almost deferential, young French man up the elegant staircase, down one beautiful palace corridor after another, and finally through exquisitely gilded rooms to the great Sénat chamber itself, the *hémicycle*. I remember that rather blasé young usher at the American Embassy in the spring who seemed so bored by it all. Too bad he couldn't see this kind of *politesse*.

The *hémicycle* is almost filled when we enter, but there are two seats with J-P's name on place cards affixed. We sit down. In front of each seat is a tiny desk with a drawer (locked, which I find out when I try to peek inside) and the name of the senator whose place it is. The seats are of a red plush material, and they are none too comfortable, perhaps to keep the senators awake.

I look around. The podium has several imposing official-looking chairs for the dignitaries, and hovering on ledges above are statues of clearly important French people from the past. The room takes my breath away, it is so impressive. What did Marie de Médicis do here before her son kicked her out of Paris for good? Did Thomas Paine ever walk through here on the way to his cell? And what about Napoleon and Josephine? Anyway, now here I am, which I am finding hard to grasp.

J-P says that the *hommage* is being transmitted *en direct* (live) on one of the national *chaines*, and I understand even more clearly how important this event is. Cameramen and technicians are bustling about, adjusting lights and twisting dials for the sound, and waiting for it all to begin is a television *présentateur* from the evening national news. I suppose this might all have happened when Sartre died in 1980, too, and I wonder for an instant whether any such intellectual in the States would get this kind of nationwide attention on a Sunday summer afternoon when baseball games compete.

The dignitaries enter, and they all shake hands before mounting to the podium. Every seat in the hall is taken, and even those in the observers' gallery above are filled. People are standing quietly by the doors, and others have seated themselves along the steep steps that form the aisles. This is big.

The president of the *Sénat* introduces the notables on the stage, whose names I do not catch, hoping I will remember to ask J-P later on. Then the speeches begin, recalling Ricoeur's life, his thoughts, his contribution to humanistic philosophy, the dignity of man, and stuff like that. I get that much, but not all, for some of the gentlemen—with ribbons in their lapels or medals of some sort—speak clearly, but not all do. Nonetheless, my mind does not wander (at least not much), and I strain to understand just as much as possible. I know a historic moment when I see one.

After four or five people have spoken and the applause dies down, it is the turn of ordinary people who knew Ricoeur in one way or another. The *micro* is passed around to the rows in front, where I am sitting with J-P. Not that any of these people are ordinary in any way. Each one recalls something that Ricoeur did or said, including a quite elderly man (more ribbons and medals) who describes the five years they were interned in the same German prison camp and the study sessions Ricoeur set up.

After another speaker or two (when, I admit I am still thinking—quite moved—about what the elderly man had said), a middle-aged woman with rather unruly red hair and a jumble of papers in her hand stands, and the *micro* is passed to her. Did she say she had been a student of Ricoeur? I'm not sure. And when I hear the words *phénoménologie* and *herméneutiques,* I just let go and give over to my own thoughts. But how can I help comparing this life I'm leading now with what was left behind in the States? I recall that life of sameness, of agreeable days that held no promise of anything new. For a change I manage not to dwell as I listen again to the woman, who is on her last page.

But I have lost the thread (if I ever had it). So, I sneak a look at my old friend J-P, who is looking down at his notes, for it is clear he will be next, and I think that—historic events aside—I don't see him enough. I know his life has changed, that he is now responsible for a major international publishing consortium, as well as being the father of two teenagers, and I think that I must make the effort to call him sometimes, and not be such a slug, waiting for his call. I applaud with the rest as the shock of red hair sits down.

The bright lights of the television cameras now focus on the composed J-P, and with *micro* in hand, he stands. He hesitates not at all. He speaks with assurance and depth about Ricoeur's books, about *Freud and Philosophy* and *Time and the Narrative*, and about the humanist tradition. And he speaks with knowledge about the responsibilities and rewards of publishing great and lasting works. In all this, however, he is brief (he has just one page of notes in his hand), and he sits down to respectful and appreciative applause.

A few more people get up to speak, but I'm ready for it to be done. At least until the question and answer period, when several ancient people who had not been on the program sweetly reminisce about knowing Ricoeur. Now I could stay forever. (I wish Findlay were here.) When the applause finally ebbs and the camera lights die down, people immediately stand up and start to file out. J-P actually introduces me to some of the people who come up to him *(quelle surprise)*. I shake hands with dignitaries and even with the woman with the unruly red hair (who kisses J-P three times, not just two). I smile and nod a little, saying *monsieur* or *madame* in acknowledgement, listening quietly to the few words they exchange with J-P. Then the two of us make our way with the crowds back through those glittering rooms and corridors, down the marble stairs, and out the large door.

Jean-Pierre takes my arm to steer me into the gardens. "I have time for a cup of coffee, *ma chère,*" he says, "if you do." *Absolument,* even if it means another hundred yards (and then back) in spiky heels. So, we sit under the plane trees near one of the refreshment kiosks with the warm late afternoon sun filtering through, he with his coffee and I with a can of cold Perrier. We go over the afternoon; I ask about Henriette and Vic; and he says it was hard to get them to study this year, but that they had done well and were soon going off to their *grandparents américains.* We compare the state of French and American publishing, and I report on the progress of my new guide. Finally, J-P looks at his watch and says he has to leave, that he has to be home. "We must get together more often, *Frahn,*" he says, echoing my earlier thought, as we stand and turn to leave.

We walk back together toward the park gate, near where J-P has left his car. I turn down an offer of a ride the few streets to rue Servandoni. "Oh no, it's just a few blocks," I say, knowing it is my mouth talking and not my feet. So, we kiss, and then I wave as he takes off to the 7th *arrondissement* and, I assume, dinner with the kids. He is a good man.

My, my, I think, walking those few streets, *here we are again with one of those memorable moments of adventure—unexpected and unrehearsed—that wind up touching my soul.* Right now, on my mental list, it's even above flying to Lapland and the kiss of the KGB.

The minute I am inside my door, I kick off my shoes, and one by one I separate my toes that by now seem glued together. And for the second time this day, I am glad that I have such a *très bonne mine.*

Sandy and I Hit the Sales

IT MAY WELL BE THAT THE most elegant *Parisiennes* shop only for the *nouveautés* (the new collections). I doubt it, but that's as far as it goes. But I do know that almost everyone shops the semi-annual sales. For three weeks in January and from now into August, *la France* waves its governmental wand and decrees *les soldes* to begin, yet another example of the French liking order in all things.

Even the shop windows have a consistent approach, many sporting nude mannequins with big-lettered banners across their pinkish torsos, proclaiming the *soldes*. With this, Paris explodes. Lines around the block near famous shops are staggering, sometimes literally. Markdowns and then more markdowns. This is big business, "I should hope to tell you," as Klaus says. Certainly, during the rest of the year *promos* (promotions) offer special deals, and, once in a while, there might appear a sign saying *prix exceptionnel*. But now at the end of June, the official summer *soldes* have begun. So, this afternoon I will hit the shops with Sandy, who understands *le shopping* better than anyone I know.

And the morning, too, started well, although it didn't continue so. I did my stretches while watching the news and *météo* on Télématin, the early show on TF2. I drank my tea and ate a fat-free vanilla yogurt, still adhering to the famous Bar Mitzvah Diet, knowing the sales were not far behind. And *comme d'habitude* (as usual), I checked the email before starting to work.

My old Chicago friend Lenore will definitely stop by Paris on her way to Provence. She'll stay at the Hotel Bonaparte, which I recommended, not far from me. I can't wait. Jane and Edouard are off to Scotland for a long weekend to see her folks (whom I met years ago in rue Christine), and Jane will call when they are back. I haven't seen them even once, this year. And Edie asks me to brunch on a Sunday soon at her apartment over near Place Maubert. Unfortunately, there was nothing from my kids. Perhaps it was seeing all the kids at the Bois de Boulogne last week that made me miss my own, but whatever, yesterday I shot off a note inviting them for Thanksgiving, and I hope to have an answer soon. My son's wife has never been to Paris, of which I reminded him pointedly, so maybe they will really come.

But that's as far as the starting-well went. For, just like that, the entire image on the computer screen turned sideways. Sideways? What had I done? Unbelievable! I stood up and craned my head sideways. No explanations. Staying craned, I managed to click on the "shut down" icon. I turned off the wretched monster and rebooted. Sideways again. This was more than my soul could bear. Still stretched sideways, I got the address book open and called Michel, my computer guru. I left a message, asking Thomas, who speaks English, to call me *tout de suite*. Right away, if not sooner. I had clearly done something incredibly stupid, but I wanted to get the full brunt of it in English rather than in French. What had I wrought?

Still pressing buttons to no avail, I answered the phone about ten minutes later, and hoping the *âllo* sounded less frustrated than I felt, I also hoped (against hope) it was Thomas. But it was Jenny, asking whether I would like to have lunch today. I could see she wanted to talk, but I wanted to hang up a.s.a.p., so we agreed to have a glass of wine over at the Deux Magots late in the afternoon (when the tourists are at their hotels, soaking their feet). Then, believe it or not, the phone rang again, and it still wasn't Thomas. It was Colette, the one French woman in the book club, who surprised me by saying that she saw me at the *hommage* as the TV camera panned the audience, and how she wished she could have been there, how important Ricoeur was to all of *la France*.

I explained about my friend J-P, which also impressed her, I realized with a smugness that picked me up somewhat.

"Would you like to get together for a coffee or a film, sometime soon?" she asked. Immediately, I said *"Volontiers!"* Wowee and *Oh, là là!* A French acquaintance making an offer to move up into the category of friend? So, I wrote down her phone number in permanent ink, and we agreed to talk in the next week or so. We hung up quickly, and I returned to my computer *angst*. Actually, there was nothing to do but wait, which is certainly not easy for me, so eventually I forced my mind to *les soldes*.

Sandy considers the *soldes* a military operation. The first tactic is to identify the field of battle. The second is reconnaissance. Next is sighting the target. And only last comes the strategic deployment of *la carte de crédit*. Today, on this initial sortie, we have decided to concentrate in our own area. The shopping maven has suggested meeting for lunch at the Café du Métro on rue du Vieux Colombier, our first line of attack. After lunch, we will start in the good shopping streets of rue de Grenelle and rue de Sèvres, and then scout Bon Marché, off boulevard Raspail. We will walk back on rue du Cherche Midi and cut across rue du Vieux Colombier to rue St-Sulpice.

People who have scoped out the merchandise before the *soldes* even begin have a distinct military edge. And smart tacticians understand that when the first round has been snapped up, another round begins. The tension heats. Suddenly again, the store windows sport signs saying *deuxième démarque*, meaning that merchandise has been marked down a second time. And after that, the warning *dernière démarque* will mean that it's the last (the dregs). This may or may not be true, for occasionally after *la France* decrees the *soldes* to wind down, a store might put a sign in the window, *soldes à l'intèrieure*, meaning there are still some marked-down goods remaining inside.

Shopping in Paris is just another one of those things to keep foreigners on our toes, although most guidebooks don't go into this. Why do signs say there are *soldes* inside? Where else would they be? Of course, they mean "in the back," but why don't they say it straight out? And why do store windows say *entrée libre*? Why would they keep customers out—except when Louis Vuitton shops limit the number of Japanese girls allowed in at one time? And what about those stores that say on their doors *"ouvert tous les jours (tlj),"* meaning they are open every day, but on the next line down say *"sauf le dimanche et lundi matin,"* indicating they are closed on Sunday plus Monday morning, or some 20 percent of the week? This inclues my own dry cleaner, who closes for lunch and all weekend just when people might want to come. Customer service? An oxymoron? So, following Paul's advice, I tell my own readers "Get used to it. It's just the way it is."

Late morning, having changed out of my jeans and tried once again at the computer with no luck, I glance (yet again) at the clock. Thomas will call back (he always does) but when? My stomach is in knots. I decide to use my *mobile* to call Klaus. He is awake, and he tells me excitedly that they are leaving for Italy in less than two weeks. Crankiness again jumps to the fore. Does he forget that, despite those kisses at the Gare de Nord, this still fills me with angst, now compounded by computer woes? I say nothing for a second, praying it will pass. And it does, and that same objectivity that I felt for the first time at Caroline's dinner manages somewhere within me to rise again. I take advantage of this little window of sanity to go on. Computer problems are not mentioned to Klaus, since any machine at all is beyond his ken—or caring.

So, I suggest having lunch one day this week, perhaps at Lipp on boulevard St-Germain, for a change, or nearby at Leon's for mussels and french fries. And at the end of places to suggest, I even offer up the "club." But Klaus regrets, as he says, that they don't have "two minutes to rub together." I am disappointed, but there's nothing else to do. I am, after all, doing my best. I'll call them once more before they leave. So as not to be able to claim even to myself that I forgot, I mark their departure down in my Palm.

Now, finally, it is time to go, and having tidied myself up, I call and leave a message for Thomas that I am leaving for lunch and will be back around *16h*. I walk out into the Paris sunshine, knowing there's nothing more I can do for the moment. I take a deep breath. It's shopping time! At the square I slow down to a crawl as I browse the fair booths at the *Foire St-Germain,* which installs itself there each June. This is the week for the displays of antiques, and browsing along the stalls of furniture and the glass cases of jewelry, I wonder about the long-dead Parisians who loved all these things and what they would think of them being sold off like this. *Moi,* I wonder who on earth would love my rather ratty (but beloved) old stuff. I get to the café exactly at *13h.*

Sandy is already at the café, seated at a table with three chairs. I am astounded (so silly of me) to see Julien perched on the third chair. Will I never be done grousing about dogs? I can hardly sit down, for the *serveur,* who has waited on me before, brushes past me saying only, *"Bonjour, madame, installez-vous."* Then he sweetly puts down on the floor a bowl of water and a little plate of goodies for Julien, saying in a tone of voice that I have never heard him use before, *"Bonjour, cher Julien, j'ai quelque chose de nouveau pour toi."* He has something new for the dog? Now, I know why Sandy suggested this café, although I'm sure Julien is known in cafés all around the *quartier. Je te jure!* Dogs and computers in one day? This really is too much!

"Pay no attention to Julien," Sandy says, as the dog jumps down and settles himself on my left foot. "I just couldn't leave him at home on such a nice day." Of course, she couldn't. Would any sane person expect Sandy to leave her poor little mutt at home while she went on an all-afternoon shopping excursion with a friend? Actually, it was dog lover Gertrude Stein who had at least an answer to this one question. "If the children are spoiled," she wrote (almost coherently) in *Paris France*, "one's future is spoilt but dogs one can spoil without any thought of the future and that is a great pleasure." With Julien, though—and unlike the computer—there's really nothing to do but give in. "Hi, Sandy," I say, and, *"Bonjour, Julien,"* since he's a French dog. And I vow that as of this minute I will give up thinking about the French and their dogs.

Sandy was a piano student in New York when she met Jean-Pierre, who was getting an MBA at Columbia. My own belief is that the young J-P, away from France on his own for the first time, was so aroused at a party one night by Sandy's rendition of Maurice Ravel's *Pavane pour une Infante defunte* that he immediately installed her in his bed. Love at first sight. *Le coup de foudre.* The thunderbolt. He didn't think at the time that he wasn't the first, and it took him a long time—too long—to realize that he wasn't the last. Knowing them as well as I do, I'm relieved that both their marriage and divorce are over. Having to be constantly sympathetic to both sides of the same little spat was wearying to my soul. But as with dogs today, I vowed a long time ago to give up thinking about Sandy and J-P. Yet, as most marriages do (even mine), it seemed to start out so well

When Sandy moved to Paris to marry J-P, she went into a Parisian frenzy, as most of us do, one way or another. As to the new bride, she had wanted to "redecorate" the apartment—one of several that the family owns in the 7th. But how, when the antique pieces J-P's aristocratic old family relinquished were more beautiful than anything she had ever seen in her life? Instead, it was Paris she took on.

Armed with brochures from the Paris Office du Tourisme, she visited museums, churches, public gardens, waterways, and parks, and the city's oldest streets. She took notes. She learned the histories of all thirty-five bridges and then crossed them, and she walked around just about every *arrondissement*. She studied French and read the books J-P brought home from his publishing house. And she took a course in French cooking, which is how she met Edie and how Edie met us all, and then—no doubt from exhaustion—she got pregnant and stayed home.

For a while she seemed content taking care of the kids. I can't imagine that it was J-P who kept her from her piano career—it must have been *Grandpère* or maybe even that staid brother Antoine. But at least in my opinion, if she had played the piano, she might not have played around. And now that the marriage is over and done with, and the kids almost on their own, Sandy is playing the piano again and—I hope to worm it out of her—God knows what else.

Sandy used to mention the men she was seeing from time to time, and it bothered me sometimes, but recently she has seemed sort of reticent, I don't know why. Maybe I'm just imagining it. But now that it seems my romantic antennae may be searching for signals once again, I will see if this afternoon she will talk about French (or any other) men. But I am patient up to a point, and I know that first, Sandy will edify me about what is currently on her musical mind. I feel so completely computer-frustrated at the moment that I probably won't admit to doing what I did, not that I have the foggiest what it was.

Recently Sandy's topic has turned to Maurice Ravel, and I know that I will hear something about *le scandale* during lunch. But before we get into *l'affaire Ravel,* I will ask about the kids, and I hope it doesn't cause a diatribe against J-P. I can understand that it remains a sore point with her that they chose to remain on weekdays with him in the 7th, rather than move in fulltime with her. But it makes sense to me that they would want to live close to their bilingual schools, and they do camp most weekends at their mother's apartment on boulevard Raspail. I like Henriette and Victor, not that I see them much anymore, now that they are teenagers—and they realize I am not.

"So, how are Vic and Henriette?" I ask right off. I am actually interested. I'm sure Victor could have dealt with my computer mess. All kids, it seems to me, are technology whizzes, although not Henriette, who seems, instead, to know everything there is to know about nail polish. "I haven't seen them at all this year."

"They did pretty well in school this year," Sandy says (not admitting that it was J-P who cracked the French whip down). "Now, they're about to go to the States for the summer, to stay with my folks. That's good. We all need the break. Oh yes, they both said to say hello. We'll have you over to dinner in the fall. You'll be surprised at how grown up they are."

So, pleased to have a dinner invitation already in hand for the fall, I say, "So, what else is new?" knowing that we will next talk about Maurice Ravel, who has been dead some seventy years.

"Did you know that *Boléro* is played about once every fifteen minutes every day of the year, around the whole world?" she begins.

"Does this count elevators?" I ask, not looking at her face to see her reaction. I break off just a little piece from a chunk of bread, since it is obviously the truth that taking one small bit at a time reduces the number of calories consumed.

"Don't be so smart," she says and then goes on after we have ordered our salads. "What it means is that every year Ravel's estate earns somewhere around two million euros. And do you know who gets them?" This is a rhetorical question, so I give her my best Gallic shrug, raising one eyebrow at the same time, a gesture I have been working on for several years.

"First, it was his brother Edouard, who, after some time, along with his wife, was in a car accident on their way to Lourdes."

"On their way to Lourdes?" I ask, trying not to laugh. "How ironic. Was God giving them something to pray for?"

"You should go to Lourdes yourself," Sandy snaps. "To cure your cynicism. You could hang it up with all the crutches." Then, undaunted, she resumes. "Anyway, enter a nurse and her husband, who took care of them until Edouard's wife died. When Edouard recovered, he made his will in favor of *madame* the nurse. To make a long story short, he dies, and then so does the nurse, and she leaves Ravel's estate to her husband."

"So, *Boléro* was then beating to the tune of the widower of the nurse of Ravel's brother?"

"*Oui,* and then the guy remarried."

"Wow. Great story," I say, thinking it is over, starting to work on the salad that has been put in front of me, and wondering if Sandy will ever broach the subject of Men. *Mais non.* But I don't really mind, for if old American gossip had gotten boring, the French still entertains.

"Wait, I'm not finished. Sacem, the musician's society, had gotten involved back in the Fifties, and again, *en bref,* the man's widow—I forget just when he died—signed over all the rights to one of the lawyers who worked on the case! Can you believe it? So, now, it seems that no one who had even the slightest connection to Ravel is getting a *sou.*"

"Can't anything be done about it?"

"It is all according to law, nothing illegal about it. Everyone down to the least law clerk has checked."

Laws are laws, of course, and the French seem to know when every pertinent law was passed. Think of all the buildings around the city that have black lettering that proclaims *"defense d'afficher, loi du 29 juillet 1881,"* meaning that you may not put up any signs or posters, according to the law of July 29, 1881. Laws concerning foreigners in France are equally clear, but, unlike the law of July 29, these are often disregarded, or in some way gotten around.

Sometimes those tourists I chat with on the street ask me about permits to stay here, about regulations and laws. I tell them the truth, that it "all depends." Staying legally depends on who you are, what you want, where you come from and what you can afford. As to my friends, though, this is what's what. Sandy has dual citizenship, thanks to her marriage to J-P. Caroline, as she would, has played the bureaucracy game, doing exactly what was required. Richard pays no attention to these things, the way rich people don't. The Jays don't need to worry about it. Yet. Margot, who has her reasons (and whom I have not yet called, of course), is so bitter about America that I have never brought it up, but Edie, who, like Caroline, has the ten-year *carte de résident* and has been talking about citizenship, hasn't yet made up her mind. As to Klaus and Paul, they've worked out something having to do with Klaus's father having been born in Austria, an EU country, and perhaps PACS—the French version of domestic partners—or whatever else, I don't know. *Et moi*, even before I got my *carte de séjour*, I felt that with all my traveling in and out of France, I pretty much fit into whatever laws applied at the time. I did not inquire as to whether *la France* agreed.

Of course, none of this is as easy as I make it sound, although I will certainly be temperate in my book. Arranging to stay here legally actually reminds me of what John Foster Dulles, the secretary of state at the beginning of the Cold War, called "brinksmanship." I often feel that *la France* keeps travel writers on the edge of the abyss. What new regulations have been promulgated that we don't know about until our books are already in print? How long does it really take to renew *cartes,* and how long will the line be at the *Préfecture* when it's finally time to go? Do retired Americans have to file taxes here if their *carte* is labeled *visiteur*? (There are two points of view on this: yes and no.) On some of these I have answers, and on some I don't and never will.

In my view, Edie really should take out citizenship, since her life is more French than any of the other Americans I know, even the Lovells, who have been here so long. (And who, like

Caroline, renew their cards every ten years.) After Edie finished her cooking and pastry courses, and after she had done all the *stages* (apprenticeships) she could manage, she either had to leave or find some legal way to stay. So, she opened her school.

"I need to make up my mind about this citizen business," she said at one of our Tuileries lunches a few weeks ago, when we had unwrapped our sandwiches and were starting to eat. "And soon. I'm tired of not feeling either American or French." She opened her sandwich to inspect the bread. "You know," she said with some testiness, "I just wish they would use fresh mayonnaise in these sandwiches instead of canned."

So, Edie was having uncertainties, too. I was surprised. But I could add nothing, having so many of my own. "I can understand your not wanting to make the sandwiches yourself," I said instead, wondering if I would be able to taste the difference. "But they'd surely be much better."

"Too much trouble," Edie answered. "And too busy. I've got some new recipes in mind."

Today, though, before the computer went berserk, I responded to Edie's email *avec plaisir*, for her brunches—for the most part— are not to be missed, capitalizing delicately on only what is at the height of its season. One winter she served scrambled eggs for six people. Scrambled eggs for a party? Yes, but eggs that only God's chickens could have laid. Truffles, cream, God knows what else. I raved (with my mouth full) while her chef friends analyzed the particularities of the "black diamond" truffles (from Périgord) and the Fleur de Sel (coarse, hand-harvested sea salt from Guérande up in Brittany). What kind of Parmesan cheese she had grated. And even her grater, for heaven's sake. Yet, I was happy, shoveling in the eggs and listening to this decidedly Parisian talk. But what made me finally put my fork down was when I heard—and this had to be repeated, in case I had misunderstood—how much these truffles cost (2000€ a kilo). One of the chefs (the cute one) was wearing a wedding ring with a big diamond in it, so maybe he could afford a truffle or two.

(Perhaps her *sanglier*—wild boar—dinner in the fall is cheaper, but I wouldn't know, for the thought of all those bristles and tusks...well....)

Yet, today, "in season" are the operative words, which is another reason (aside from the diet) I have ordered this salad, instead of my usual *omelette fines herbes* with *frites*. But imagine an egg carton in the States informing buyers when its eggs were *pondu* (laid), a second date indicating the last date those eggs might be eaten raw, and then a third saying the last day that the eggs should be *conservé*.

And imagine a package of smoked salmon in an American supermarket carrying a sticker as to when the fish was *peché* (caught) and *emballé* (packed), as well as its expiration date. Fortunately, I learned early on that asking a waiter if anything on the menu is frozen would have marked me as an American, at best, a Philistine at worst.

SCRAMBLED EGGS WITH TRUFFLES (SERVES 6)

18 eggs
30 grams of black truffles
(tuberus melanosporum)
Fresh ground pepper to taste
Butter
180 cl of cream (whipped)

White bread, no crusts
Salt to taste

Sea salt
Parmesan cheese

Cut the bread into cubes. Toss them in butter until browned. Sprinkle croutons with Parmesan cheese and set aside. Sprinkle lightly also with the sea salt.

Beat the eggs. Add salt and pepper to taste. Add sliced truffles.

In a frying pan, sauté the eggs in butter over low heat, stirring gently and frequently with a wooden spatula. When the eggs are cooked but still soft, fold in the cream, making sure the eggs stay well aerated. Remove the eggs onto a serving platter. Top with the Parmesan cheese croutons.

Having finished our salads and also with Ravel for today, Sandy asks, "Do you remember how you were always asking Jean-Pierre to introduce you to some of his men friends?"

I suddenly come to attention. "Always asking! I only asked once," I say, trying not to lose my cool. This is not the way I remember it. "Or maybe twice, but no more."

"No matter," says Sandy, which does not mollify me at all. "Calm down. I've met a man for you. I entertained at a gathering at one of the embassies a few weeks ago, and a man came over and listened to me play and talked to me. He's attractive. He likes French music. He speaks both French and English," and I note her voice lowering a little, "as well as Arabic. And he's single. So, I thought of you."

"What do you mean, 'as well as Arabic'?" I ask, picking up on the important phrase.

"He's a diplomat, attached to an embassy from one of the Arab states...."

"And?"

"Well, now, don't get yourself into a sweat. He was beautifully dressed in clearly a hand-tailored suit, and he was quite fashionable. And he was interesting. I liked him."

"Excuse me, Sandy. Are you utterly out of your mind?" (My version of "Thank you for thinking of me.")

"So, the answer is no, I take it," says Sandy, unfazed. "Well, don't say I didn't try."

"If he's so great, why don't you want him for yourself?"

"He's too old," she says, which does not, in any way, make me feel better, even though I realize that Sandy is younger than I. And that in addition to French piano music, her specialty is younger men. "And besides, I'm otherwise occupied at the moment."

"You are?" I ask, hoping that, finally, the man-talk has finally come.

"Yes," she says flatly, and that's all. "Well, let's go shopping, okay?"

I am more than ready to think about shopping instead of too old Arab diplomats. And just what is "too old," anyway? I decide not to find out. So, since today is not a day for dessert, and neither of us wants coffee, Sandy signals the waiter for *l'addition*. "Did you know that Paul and Klaus are going to Italy for six weeks?" she asks.

"Yes, I spoke to Klaus this morning," I say but say nothing about abandonment and objectivity seemingly able to go hand in hand. "They're leaving soon after the Gay Pride March. They're going to watch it from the windows of some friends who live near the Opéra Bastille."

"I asked them to take care of Julien next week while I'm getting ready for my trip," Sandy shakes her head, "but Klaus said, or I think he did, that he would be 'busy squared.'"

At least in this regard Sandy has the sense not to ask me. Julien, by the way, must have known we were about to leave, for he has jumped into a quilted basket that Sandy has propped against her chair, with just his head sticking out. We pay our bill, leave the one and a half euros change on the table for the *serveur* (this being just a café), and, well fortified, we start our first strike. I am glad to be moving on, gearing myself back up toward the afternoon's plan.

This is how it goes. First, we try to get into Longchamp, the upscale leather-goods shop in rue du Vieux Colombier. It's a zoo, so we move on. In rue de Grenelle we look in the window of Prada, spend a few minutes in Yves St-Laurent, which is crowded but manageable, and almost fifteen minutes in Sonia Rykiel, where Sandy tries on a striped tee shirt that could just about cover my left arm. While she is doing so, I whip out my mobile and check the messages on my landline. None. So, I pay attention to Sandy again, who says she likes the tee, but not enough to buy it—yet. Ferragamo, just one of the many shoe shops in the *quartier,* calls to us, but although there are a couple of styles for narrow feet (for Japanese girls, I think), the price in euros is steep and when converted to dollars, I just pass. Luckily, I don't need (need?) any shoes.

I drag Sandy into Chakok, my favorite store in rue de Grenelle, where the clothes look good on tall people, for a change. I fall in love with a crazy dress, bright red with yellow flamingos on it, that I would never have occasion to wear, since I do not hang out on cruise ships or with men wearing plaid shorts. Besides, it has a wraparound skirt, and I remembered the fiasco the one time I bought a wraparound skirt. And unlike a bicycle, once you fall off, it is my opinion that with a wraparound skirt you should never get back on.

That other wraparound, I loved with all my heart, from the moment I tried it on in a New York store one afternoon until I wore it that same night. That same night, having drinks with the writer Ralph Ellison and his wife, I wished the whole time I had been his *Invisible Man*. I couldn't keep the skirt closed. Not when I moved even an inch. I sat like a statue. It still came apart. I wished I could sink through the floor. But unlike the skirt, the floor didn't open up. And the Ellisons didn't say a word. Instead, the word inscribed on their faces spelled out *b-i-m-b-o* loud and clear. And afterward, after having minced out while holding my skirt with my left hand and shaking their hands with my right, I wished I had just confessed, "Look, guys, I'm just not good with this kind of thing." And then (with an understanding smile) Mrs. E. would have brought me a safety pin. Instead, this memory is toward the bottom of my unexpected-and-unrehearsed list.

So, empty-handed, we take a shortcut down rue des St-Pères and to look into Paco Rabane, and then we are on the west side of rue de Sèvres. It has a few nice shops, but we accelerate our steps, feeling the call of our euros from the chic Bon Marché.

After whizzing by makeup, slowing at scarves, and coming to a full stop at handbags, we take the escalator up to the designer boutiques on the first floor. We could spend days here, even if the prices are still too high, but we make ourselves move on. Sandy insists we go look at *soutien-gorges* (which are bras, the word literally meaning "support the throat"). Of course, she does, with her cute little figure. She could really be French. Slim hips and waist, small breasts. Obviously, bras do not figure into my shopping here. I do not want to buy something in size 95, which is too large around and too small in front.

I never hesitate to make this opinion known. But Alice says that since World War II, better nutrition has made the French woman taller and her hips fuller than before. (But not fat, of course.) "The couturiers will probably change their sizing in order to avoid their *grandes dames* having to go up a notch on the chart," Alice predicted. So far, however, with the more general sizes 1, 2, 3, and S, M, L, one doesn't often have to face the humiliation of asking for a blouse sized 40, which doesn't fill a middle-aged American woman used to a size 8 or 10 with great confidence.

While Sandy drapes bra after bra over her one arm (her other holding the basket with Julien) before trying them on, I look at slips, known in French as *joupons* for the half slip (and sometimes *sous-jupes)* and *combinaison* for the full length. If you asked for a *slip*, which many women tourists do, you'd be asking for men's briefs (women's are called *culottes*). I buy a black and flowered *joupon*, size 40. I overlook this depressing fact when it turns out the price has been reduced a second time, by another 20 percent. With the math done, I buy the slip. It will no doubt sit in a drawer, for I haven't worn this kind of slip in years.

Sandy buys no bras, so we cross over rue de Sevres, stopping in at Weill (pronounced *Vey*), where I am made totally breathless by a dress. It's beautiful. It's light blue and white. It has no flamingos. It's not a wraparound. I try it on. It makes me look sexy. It makes me look like I'm sure I did years ago, whether I ever did or not.

It's even almost within my budget. *Mais calme-toi, Frahn.* When and where would I wear it? And might there not be something equally seductive but cheaper in another shop later on? Sandy urges, "Buy it! Buy it! Snap it up!" But I don't.

As we walk north and turn toward rue St-Sulpice, close by the Hotel Bonaparte, I find myself also thinking about the upcoming visit of Lenore. I know she's been here several times, so I don't have to suggest doing the usual tourist things that would make my bored mind stray into avenues (projects) I'd rather not tread right now. What would she like to do? What would I like to do?

I admit that by the time Sandy and I have walked down rue St-Sulpice, I have had enough. I suggest that we get a cool drink at the Café de la Mairie, so we head back, finding a table on the terrace overlooking the square. The waiter smiles at Julien but doesn't make a fuss.

"Excuse me one minute," I say to Sandy, "but I've got to make a call. My computer is giving me fits, and I hope the technician has called." I dial my landline, and lo! There's a message from Thomas, telling me where to go in the Control Panel to put my screen back straight; I had put it in Tablet mode. Tablet mode? Tablet mode? Whatever, I am flooded with a huge relief.

Putting my *mobile* in my pocket, I turn to Sandy again. "Would you like to go next week up to Printemps and then scout out rue du Faubourg-St-Honoré?" By now we have been served our drinks, and I am beginning to feel refreshed. Not that I would ever buy anything on Faubourg St-Honoré, with its prices rubbing the stratosphere, *soldes* or not, but it needs scouting out.

"I can't," she says flatly, so that's that. "I'm getting ready for New York by then, and as Klaus says, 'I'm busy squared.' But I think you should go back and get that dress," she admonishes me. "And don't think about it too long, or it will be gone."

"I'll think about it until tomorrow, how's that?" I lie. "So, when will you be back from the States?"

"Beginning of September, probably, depending. The kids are going to stay all summer with my folks in the Hamptons, but they'll come back in time for school."

I don't ask depending on what. But I can say, "It's been a great afternoon, Sandy. It was really fun." Being diplomatic, myself, I do not mention the Arab diplomat, and neither does she.

"Yes," she agrees. "We moved in and sighted our targets, and although we didn't take any prisoners except for your *joupon*, we didn't leave much collateral damage on our *cartes de crédit*. C'mon, let's go home."

I certainly won't describe shopping that way in my book (or maybe I will), but I love the way my friends think. Quirky or not, they all fit in, one way or another, to Paris life—better, perhaps, than some well-known Americans did in the past.

This occurs to me just now because Sandy's route home takes her around the Luxembourg gates to rue Guynemer, and then a brief cut through rue de Fleurus, past the infamous number 27. Not only home to the Gert & Alice Show but also, for short a while, to Raymond Duncan, eccentric brother to the famous dancer Isadora, who, I gather, was himself a piece of work.

"What are you smiling at?" Sandy asks.

"Raymond Duncan," I say. "Can you imagine walking around the streets of Paris in a Greek toga and sandals, with a laurel wreath around your head?"

"Yeah, and his sister and her weird dancing, too. Nuts, both of them," Sandy says.

"How can you possibly judge her?" I ask, with some surprise. "Think of her life. First, amazing the Frenchies by dancing barefoot and in only some kind of gauze. Some American evangelist claimed she didn't wear enough clothes to 'pad a crutch.' Don't you just love that?"

"Yeah, so?"

"So, both her kids drowned when the car they were in rolled into the Seine. Her lovers disappeared. Her husband killed himself. Her dancing schools went broke. And finally, when she got into a convertible to leave the Riviera where Paris Singer—I think he was the father of her kids—had promised her support, she called out, *"Adieu, mes amis, je vais à la gloire."* I embellish this with a dramatic wave of my hand, but this seems not to impress Sandy at all. "Anyway, one of her friends there yelled, "Your shawl, your shawl, pick it up; it's dragging on the ground." But it was wrapped around Isadora's neck, and it got caught in the spokes of the wheel. Dead. Totally *morte*."

"Well, okay, she went to glory sooner than she thought. But nuts, anyway," Sandy persists. "She was a Communist, too. I mean, really."

"Oh Sandy, so what?" I ask. Give her a break." Suddenly I am struck again how French we are getting—arguing about somebody who has been dead eighty years.

Sandy ignores my plea, but she does moves on. "Were you here when the Democrats Abroad held that candlelight demonstration at the Flamme de la Liberté just when George Bush was being inaugurated?"

"No, I was in New York, at that point," I say, as we stand and get ourselves ready to leave. But suddenly I remember how that very day I was pining to be back in Paris, and I ask, "Don't you miss Paris when you're not here?"

"Moveable feast, my dear, moveable feast," Sandy says. We exchange kisses, and I pat Julien (making good on my pledge). Sandy says she will call when she is back, and she and her mutt walk away. All in all, a splendid Paris day. Well, I suppose Sandy tried, in my regard. One day I will thank her, at least enough to encourage her to try again.

My mailbox is as bountiful this afternoon as my email was this morning. Amid the flyers, there is a postcard from a cousin in New York just saying hello, and there is this month's issue of *à Paris,* informing Parisians of current goings on. Something about my health insurance that I must decipher. And at the bottom, there is a cream-colored envelope with J-P's address embossed on the back. I open it right away, not able to contain myself until I get up the stairs, as the French would surely do.

It's an invitation! I'm invited to *"assister au diner du Quatorze Juillet,"* meaning that I'm to come to a dinner *chez lui* on Bastille Day, although the French never call it that. At the bottom of the invitation, it says in smaller writing that after dinner we will watch the *feux d'artifice* (fireworks) from the roof terrace. Who would have expected any less? And what about that dress at Weill? I must call the boys.

But first, I listen again to Thomas' message twice, writing down what he says, step by step. I do it. *Et voilà!* I'm back in business. And just a few minutes later—as I'm playing a celebratory game of computer backgammon—Caroline calls with an idea to go down to the 13th *arrondissement* to the Tang Frères Asian supermarket and then to grab some *dim sum* at Tricotin. This, thank God, reminds me of Jenny, whom I had completely forgotten, so I quickly tell Caroline to get over to the Deux Magots, and then we can go down to the 13th from there. I rush to get myself ready and once again head out the door.

Promptly at five forty-five I am at the Deux Magots. When Jenny turns up a few minutes later, I have already captured a table outside, having swooped down just as a couple of tourists stood up. I do not mention having seen her that other day, coming out of the real estate agent's office. Nor do I say that she looks rather strained. I wait to see what she has to say. First, though, from the waiter who materializes even before we've had a chance to settle ourselves, Jenny orders a glass of the house white, and I order a *kir royal*. And then Jenny lets me have it.

"What did you do when you had a real problem with your husband?" she asks.

Clearly, I am not the right person for this conversation. "Which one?" I ask back.

"Oh, I forgot you had two." A short silence. " Well, either one," she says.

I ignore this utter silliness and ask her directly, "So, is it the idea of living here permanently?"

"He just won't listen. He has it in his head that this is what we're going to do," she says miserably.

This sounds too familiar. "Don't get divorced," I say, which may seem to Jenny a total *non sequitur*, but the tribulations of Sandra and J-P that at first seemed so minor (to me) are ringing a big bell. I couldn't go through this again.

"Divorced?" she says, astounded. "I'd sooner kill him." She starts to say more, but then looks up from the table. "Oh, hi, Caroline," she says. I smile with some relief, getting me off the hook from this train of thought. I take my purse off the chair that I have been guarding from two rapacious tourists who are also expecting someone. And when Caroline sits down, Jenny asks the same question. But Caroline, of course, has an answer.

"Compromise," she answers. "Like I said before, it won't hurt you to look. Raise the bar on what you're willing to look at. Tell him what each apartment will cost in your dollars, since you have to add more than 30 percent to the euro price. Who knows? Maybe one of you will give an inch."

Jenny is clearly paying attention to Caroline, as anyone with any sense would. Caroline hesitates when the waiter approaches and looks at my *kir royal,* but then sighs and orders a bottle of Badoit. "I keep thinking of Maynard Keynes saying that the only thing he regretted in life was not having drunk more champagne." I am glad that I'm not suffering the fate of Keynes. But I think, too, that I must find a way to pay for our dinner later down in the Asian district, since my euros are still somewhat intact.

A bit later, just before we are about to leave, the heavens open up for one of those brief summer evening storms that make you wish you could flag down Noah's Ark. So, after it starts to let up and after kissing Jenny goodbye as she dashes over to rue des Canettes, Caroline and I walk quickly to the *métro,* trying to hug the walls along with everyone else.

"Your advice was so good," I say, feeling totally inadequate.

"Maybe," she says. "They just need to talk without each one getting defensive."

As we walk in the lessening rain, I wonder how I can give people such sage advice about places when I am not attached to any place myself, but not about life when I spend so much of my own in mulling-over baths. But I put this out of my mind and tell her about Tablet mode, eliciting only one of her *"Tiens, tiens."* My, my. But she is definitely interested in talking about shopping with Sandy and the invitation from J-P. So, I do tell all to Caroline and about the dress I might indeed snap up. We natter on about what I might do with Lenore when she comes. Caroline mentions that she's at a stopping point in her writing, and will read and edit, getting ready for a new surge in the fall. And later, having made it to tang Frères just before it closed, and while eating *dim sum* at Tricotin, Caroline can hardly contain her laughter, saying wouldn't it have been a "gas" for me to go out with the Arab diplomat, after all.

When I get home, I put into my kitchen cabinet the little jar of crystallized ginger I got at Tang, and I transfer a bag of Japanese rice crackers into a humidity-proof container. Then I sit down at the computer and gingerly boot it up. No problem. Yet, I have suddenly thought of Findlay's evening at the Embassy and my wondering how I might express my gratitude for whatever it was I was feeling at that moment. So, I dig out the card of the rabbi and email him that I will be pleased to do the community's newsletter and to call me after the summer vacation or whenever suits him best.

Jean–Pierre Celebrates

YOU MIGHT THINK I'VE BEEN TO J-P's home many times, considering how long we've been friends. I might have thought so, too, at one time, until I discovered that it isn't so automatic getting invited into the homes of the French. (It's that wretched privacy thing, again.) In fact, although I've been to receptions and *vernissages* with J-P, to his *bureau* in the 7th, to restaurants for lunch and dinner, to films from time to time, plus, of course, our recent visit to the Sénat, I've only been to his Paris apartment three times since he and Sandy split, and never, not even for one *petit* weekend, to his family's *manoir* near the ancient, arcaded seaport of La Rochelle.

It is true, though, that the only times Jean-Pierre was in my own little nest in rue Servandoni were when he agreed to look it over before the lease was signed, and then when we met with the landlord before I moved in, to inspect it for damages they could later on—if I decided to decamp—not claim were my fault. We agreed on what we saw and signed some lengthy document, although naturally I later found things to add, but it was too late.

"*C'est adorable,*" J-P said that first time, it having taken him a while to check every closet hinge and to locate every electric outlet and to snap every cabinet shut, things that I would never have thought of. Since I also thought the apartment was cute, I rented it right away. (Now, having seen his eight-room duplex in the 7th, I wonder whether he wasn't being just a tad condescending, but I think he really meant it.) As we left rue Servandoni that day, J-P suggested we walk for a while around the *quartier. Quelle belle surprise.* Jean-Pierre didn't take off much time on weekdays even then, and he wasn't even *président directeur général* at that point.

I remember well that afternoon, for it was one of those marvelous days when real life and that lovely Paris woman were one. The air was warm, the sky cloudless. Leaves above were of a heartbreak green. First, we sat for a while on a bench at Place St-Sulpice, while J-P lit a cigar. (That wasn't the lovely part.) Even J-P chuckled at the dogs splashing in the fountain, and since he seemed to be feeling no pressure of work, we just sat and talked—about how I'd love the neighborhood, about my new life in Paris, about my kids and his—and it took him a while to motion me on.

Across the street we stopped in at the exclusive *parfumerie* Annick Goutal so he could buy a couple of (wildly expensive) boxes of L'Eau d'Hadrien, his traditional scented soap, and for a new apartment gift he generously bought me a box of my own favorite, Gardenia Passion. Walking along, I suggested having a cup of tea at Le Parloir, the austere Christian tearoom in rue du Vieux Colombier, where they like to talk to you about Jesus but leave you alone if it's not your thing. *Mais non.* Instead, I looked in the window of that fancy handbag store Longchamp while J-P glanced in the windows of two men's shops. "Do you want to go in?" I asked, knowing the answer all along.

Of course, he didn't want to stop in, he who has his shirts tailored at Charvet and his shoes fitted at Berlutti. "But they last forever, *chérie,*" he explained to me when I once commented that three pair of his shoes cost more than a month's rent for me. "You must become more French and buy only the highest quality." On this occasion, however, J-P just shook his head and took my arm, guiding me on.

Still arm in arm, we crossed the Carrefour de la Croix Rouge and entered rue du Dragon, where I then was renting a short-term flat and which is just yet another of the city's charming streets. We paused at a shop that sold American-style muffins and brownies but didn't go in. J-P then looked into the courtyard of the Académie Julien, the famous art institute, while, fortunately, I didn't see any shoes I just had to have in the Arche shop window nearby. J-P did go into the card shop to buy a birthday card for Henriette; we passed the cheap Korean Barbecue and, finally, we turned left into boulevard St-Germain, where (was this already in the works?) we came to a halt at the upscale Casa del Habano, so J-P could see what might be new in the world of cigars. (Now, the shop is a sushi bar. Does J-P know?)

"American muffins!" J-P mused, as we sat over a mineral water at the *comptoir*. "*Imaginez* that there are American muffins right in rue du Dragon."

Shortly after our cigar outing, invited to dine *chez lui* with him and the kids and his brother Antoine, whose wife had gone (yet again) up to the Lovell boys' spa at St-Malo for some seawater cure or other, I brought with me a variety of muffins. *What a clever gift*, I thought (and still do). Nonetheless, the only way I can describe J-P's face when he opened the polished wooden doors of his apartment and saw me holding out the little sack (that had gotten a bit wrinkled on the bus) is to say he looked the same as Tom Hanks did the first time he ate a raw minnow in the film *Castaway*.

But he said not a word. He just held up the crumpled bag I thrust at him, that look of distressed incomprehension on his face. "Muffins, from that place you liked in rue du Dragon?" I almost stammered. "Remember? We passed it when you came over to see my apartment?"

Then the light dawned. He never said, however, whether he liked the muffins or not, or whether he even took them out of the bag. Since the French are so polite, however, I assume that he tried them and hated them, or he just didn't grasp the muffin concept or how muffins fit into his world of *pain au chocolat* and *brioche*. Naturally, he would never have wanted to hurt my feelings, since

I was so kind to bring him a present in the first place. So ended the muffin caper.

Let's get something straight. Jean-Pierre isn't rude. He's just French. This means that along with being logical and precise, he is meticulously polite. His parents, I'm sure, as most French parents are, were loving yet strict, so their expectations for proper behavior were invariably met. One day recently when I actually stirred myself to go to the pool, a little girl plowed right into me. *"Pardon, madame,"* she said, coming up for air, *"ça va?"* I almost drowned with astonishment, having never heard an American kid say, "I beg your pardon, ma'am. Are you okay?"

QUOTE FROM GERTRUDE STEIN

"All Frenchmen know that you have to become civilized between eighteen and twenty-three and that civilization comes upon you by contact with an older woman, by revolution, by army discipline... and then you are civilized and life goes on normally in a Latin way, life is then peaceful and exciting, life is then civilized, logical and fashionable in short life is life."

In fact, when American tourists claim that the French are so rude, I just purse my lips, for what could I say? The French are reserved in ways Americans are not, and their upbringing neglected to inform them that Americans expect everyone to grin and chat. Casual intimacy and sentimentality are just not in the cards. This, I am sure, is what Paul means about not expecting the French to be like Americans, although one could wish occasionally that the French wouldn't expect us to be like them every second of the day. Of course, some people are rude anywhere, sometimes. One woman at a *traiteur* near Sèvres-Babylone has been rude to me for years. I consider our interactions a Paris game, so waiting for a day when I'm willing to play, I go in. I wait my turn, noting how friendly she is to "regulars," smiling, shaking hands, and saying, *"Au revoir, madame, à bientôt,"* when they leave. When she turns to me, however, a stolid look comes over her (piggy little) face and she stands pat, waiting for me to speak. But I do not, for according to *politesse*, it is up to her to start the ball rolling by saying *Bonjour, madame* or even *Je vous écoute,* meaning she is listening to me. Then I should say *Bonjour, madame* back and place my order. But no, I stare back until she gives in and greets me as she should. Sometimes we stare what seems like weeks, but lately she has been fairly fast to give in.

I have to admit that I brought her attitude on myself, that summer of the apartment in rue Christine, when everything new had to be conquered, and everything was new. One day, I questioned her choice of a slice of veal that she had selected for me, and that was it. (The frustration in my voice was—for a change—aimed at my own deficiencies in French, but Edie asked how *Mlle* Piggy was to know?) The veal was as tough as I thought it might be, and I suspect that had I understood then that the French respond greatly to form, and had I been able to say something like *Excuse me, Madame, I don't want to bother you, but if you don't mind, perhaps I might have that little piece just to the side instead, please, oh, thank you, you are so kind,* I would have had better luck.

But J-P wasn't rude during the muffin caper, nor was he rude during the salmon event. Having been to Seattle one January before returning to Paris, I brought J-P a package of Northwest-style smoked salmon. Thinking I had learned from the fiasco of the year before (never make the same mistake twice, right?), I explained clearly at a welcome-back lunch, before handing it over, that this was not like any smoked salmon he had ever had before, that it was only so he could taste something new, that he shouldn't compare it with Scottish or Irish salmon, but that it was interesting for it was smoked in the traditional Native American style, over alder wood. "*Merci, chérie,*" he said and—first making sure it was securely wrapped—put it in his briefcase under the table. That would have been the last mention of it if I hadn't (in my brassy American way) decided several months later to ask him about it.

"Remember that smoked salmon I brought you from Seattle?" I asked. "Did you like it?"

There was only a fraction of an instant's pause and my smooth French friend smiled his gorgeous smile. "Well, *Frahn*," he nodded. "It was quite interesting. It had a very particular taste." And that was the end of that. But at that moment I decided that presents for J-P were beyond my American ken. (He does get signed copies of my books.) Now for *le 14 juillet* there are no expectations I will bring anything, and I won't. There are no presents on the Fourth of July.

Americans here look forward to our own Independence Day. The American ambassador hosts a garden party to which the *crème de la crème* are invited. Being only skim milk, Caroline, Edie, Richard, and I once went all the way over to the far 16th to the Auberge du Mouton Blanc, where Edie acknowledged that she "appreciated" the hamburgers. But last year—without Edie—the three of us just ate the definitely okay burgers in rue Princesse at the Café Parisien (asking for extra raw onions and more ketchup) and then, when Richard went off for his swim, Caroline and I browsed for books at the Village Voice, hoping no one would smell our breath.

I think it was two years before (having somehow again been overlooked by the Embassy) that Edie and I took the bus up to the Théâtre des Champs-Elysées to hear a jazz concert by Quincy Jones. I had expected to see lots of American tourists wearing red, white, and blue to mark July 4, but, strangely, the audience was predominantly French. Where were all the Americans? *Chez l'ambassadeur?* Nonetheless, Edie and I felt it was an American evening, and I wished I had worn my baseball cap with the American flag on it, even though Edie had said flatly that if I did, she wouldn't go. She brought me an olive *fougasse*—a delicious rustic bread—left over from her afternoon class, so how could I complain?

And one time, humoring Caroline as she humors me, we trudged (my word, not hers) on the Fourth of July to the Cimetière de Picpus and paid our respects to the Marquis de Lafayette. We weren't the first, of course. On July 4, 1917, for instance, American troops coming to aid the French were led by General Pershing past cheering Parisians to the Cimetière, and at Lafayette's tomb were spoken the famous words, "Lafayette, we have come." The next July 4, by the way, the Great War having ended, the American troops were cheered again at Place de la Concorde as they marched alongside French soldiers carrying the banners of the French regiments that had been sent by Louis XVI to help *les États-unis* throw the British out. Caroline took some photos at the cemetery to put in her book. And one of me with my pink sunglasses, both of us laughing later when it seemed she had her finger in front of the lens.

In turn, some Americans have noticed *le 14 juillet*, including Thomas Jefferson, of course, who was here for the big one and who was in the thick of the revolutionary maneuvering (in diplomatic terms, "statecraft") with his buddy Lafayette.

Moi? One of those years when I was still staying in that flat in rue du Dragon, the *propriétaire* invited me on *le 14 juillet* to watch the *défilé* (parade) from his office windows overlooking the Champs-Elysées. What an event. Thousands of uniformed men and women marching by. Horses and tanks. Missiles on their launchers. War planes swooping low over the Arc de Triomphe. Champagne that kept flowing *chez le propriétaire*. So, a bit overcome by watching the awesome might unfolding before my eyes, I decided then and there that I, myself, would never mess with the French. *Le president,* cabinet ministers, and visiting dignitaries reviewed the troops at Place de la Concorde, and as far as I know, no heads rolled.

I think J-P is genuinely pleased that he is not one of those dignitaries and that it is his older brother Antoine who has climbed so deliberately up the government ladder, and who is about to become a cabinet minister himself, depending on the next elections, or so J-P says. But J-P prefers hanging out with writers and artists who, he says, are less *stoof-y*. I suppose Jean-Pierre could be known as *la gauche caviare*, meaning the left-wing wealthy, or *bo-bo*, short for *bohème-bourgeois*, somewhat like Richard, in his way—just more French.

Both brothers are, of course, *énarques*, meaning they are part of the French elite that has graduated from l'École Nationale d'Administration, on their way up to high governmental or corporate success. Yet, J-P opted out of government service, and he finally got the agreement of *Grandpère* to go to the States to get an MBA at Columbia, where he improved his English and met the *adorable* American *pianiste* Sandra.

Taking up with Sandy was one thing, but marrying her? I know he had to defy *Grandpère* and probably even the *stoof-y* Antoine. I would never call Antoine "Tony" (at least not to his face), but Jean-Pierre thinks it cute that I and my friends call him J-P. His names run something like Jean Pierre Philippe Henri. For me this is a close second to the great Lafayette, whose given names were Marie Joseph Paul Yves Roch Gilbert du Motier. Does J-P have a Marie in there somewhere? I could ask him about this at the dinner. I think that talking about names is acceptable dinner conversation for the French.

In this regard, just a few minutes after I opened the invitation from Jean-Pierre, having rushed up the stairs and shown my computer who was boss, I called my own aristocratic friends (the queens) for the second time in one day. They were up from their naps and were pleased to have my call. I was so excited, I couldn't even focus on their Rome trip. Besides, I realized I was ready for them to go and to decide, once and for all. And to be done with suspense.

"Going to get yourself all tarted up?" Klaus asked with enthusiasm, so I described the dress I like at Weill. He approved and instructed me about appropriate shoes. "You'll have to remember every detail of the dinner, darling," he said at last, satisfied that I would not be a total disgrace, "because we're leaving for Italy soon. *Non vedo l'ora*," he said, having switched into his Italian mode. "I just can't wait." I had no answer for that. Fortunately, Paul came on the line.

As soon as I heard Paul's voice, I started to tell him all over again about the dinner, but he interrupted. "I've heard," he said, with that avuncular tone he takes with me every once in a while (and which I love). "Now tell me, please, what are the rules? Repeat them to me, if you will, one by one."

I will not talk about anything unpleasant, such as a friend or family member who is sick (illness is out), anything dirty (*déjection canine*) or concerning bugs, nor I will mention money in any shape or form. I will not ask too many questions and none that could be seen as personal. I may, however, dissect minutely everything I dislike about George Bush (either one); I may talk about a sexual affair of someone I know if there is something amusing or scandalous about it (except Sandy, of course); and I may rail against the Pope, although why I would, I don't know. I will not criticize the French; I will say nothing that puts Paris in a negative light, nor will I agree if other guests do so. I will not ask how anyone ever voted or intends to vote in any election ever— not even J-P. And I will not get sucked into comparing—even objectively—America with France.

The most important rule, though, is not to let these people think that I imagine in any way that I am Parisian, for even had I lived here twenty years I would still be an American who lives in Paris. Frankly, since this is exactly what I want to be, it's okay with me.

"Yes?" Paul prodded. "And what else?"

"Oh, the smile," I remembered. "Only that enigmatic French smile and never the broad American grin." As the conversation ended, I managed to say in Italian and mean it, *"Buon viaggio caro, buona vacanza."*

And then Paul said something that rocked my figurative boat. "And think of going away yourself for a while, my dear. I think you could use it."

Paul's comment brought me up short. After all, with so much work to do, I hadn't once stepped foot out of Paris since January. Not like me at all. But with Paul's gentle prodding, I realized that a rut was definitely corrupting my soul. It wasn't Paris, I knew, just me. (Hello? Any new projects out there?) That old craving for something new, anywhere, anyhow. Clearly, it was time to take myself in hand. So, after hanging up, I immediately dialed my English cousins and left a message on their voice mail. "Where are you? On your boat?" I asked. "May I come? Please?"

Now, about ten days before the dinner, I go into high gear. Fortunately, the dress, since it was so pricey, has gone quickly into *deuxième démarque*. I have shoes that will do just fine, Klaus notwithstanding. I think about a little purse to carry. And last, I *prends rendez-vous* to get my hair cut the day before Lenore is to arrive, for the sides have reached the length where I am fast approaching that cocker-spaniel look I get.

The process of finding a good hairdresser or barber in Paris is as fraught with danger as it is anywhere else. There are good *coiffeurs* and those you'd like to send to *la veuve*. And as anywhere else, you just have to find someone who suits. You can ask among your friends, *bien sûr*, when they sport a haircut you like. But only among people you know.

About two years ago, the Jays and I were eating *bo bun* (that Vietnamese one-dish meal of beef, salad, and noodles) at Phö 88 down in the 13th after an expedition to Tang, and a woman came in whose haircut I admired. "Go ask her who her *coiffeur* is," Jack urged me. *Penses-tu!* You don't go up to a French woman you don't know and ask where she got her haircut, no matter how American—or Irish—you are. "Go on," Jack insisted, but Jenny and I both put down our *baguettes* (chopsticks—same word as bread) and just looked at him. He got the point.

Anyway, I've been going to Michel ever since my French hairdresser in the States recommended him to me. I don't always like my haircuts, but I don't experiment with other *coiffeurs,* partly out of inertia and partly because I know that the odds are it could very well get worse.

Michel knows a few words of English from working on a cruise ship years ago. So, when I first started going to him, he told me he thought that some "hair" words were better in English than in French. Once we settled on the fact that I only wanted a *treem* and that I liked my hair *floo-fee*, we got along fine.

This time, when I call the salon, I say that in addition to the *coupe*, I would like my hair highlighted *(les mèches)*. Both for Lenore's visit and J-P's *soirée,* I want to look as though I were spending my weekends at the beach.

For Lenore's visit, just a few days later, I am more than ready. I can't wait to bum around with my old pal. But where? How can I be so bored with the Louvre? With the parks? With restaurants that I'd usually love to try? With checking out the *quartiers* and fantasizing about neighborhood lives? Maybe I can snap out of this with Lenore.

So, on the first day (after my thanking her for the licorice Jelly Bellies she surprises me with), Lenore humors me by going over to the canal by the Bastille and boarding a boat. We sit on the deck all morning, taking a ride up the Canal St-Martin, cruising through the many locks to the museum, park, and cinema complex of La Villette (built on the site of the former *abattoir* of Paris) and admiring the charming quays. She says she forgives me. It is one of those experiences that is totally fascinating and fatally boring at the same time...all those locks...all those quays. But she regales me with Chicago gossip during the ride, which makes it all worthwhile. And she tells me that her nephew and wife had loved Procope and my stories of Ben. "Are you just saying that?" I ask with some disbelief, but Lenore assures me that it's true. So, at the end of the boat ride, I make a note to suggest the boat to the tourists. One never knows what tourists will like or think they liked in retrospect. It wouldn't be right to warn them off just because I can't sit still.

After descending from the boat (as the French say), I convince her to wander around the science museum for an hour or so—which I actually like—and then we watch a nature film on the huge screen at La Geode. Last, after a walk through the park, which she enjoys most of all, we head back to the *métro* and separate for a few hours, she going to her hotel for a jet-lag siesta and me first stopping off at Monoprix to pick up a few things on the way home.

Standing in line at the *caisse*, having browsed the snacks aisle and tossed a few boxes of this and that in my cart, along with the tomatoes and melons I have come to get, I am contentedly beginning the cashier, bag-in-the-lap, change-in-the-wallet procedure. Then I look up. And who is coming down the aisle but San Francisco John, and with him this time is the little woman. This ruins my mood in a flash. Making it worse is that they see me.

"Fran! How are you?" John exclaims with an enthusiasm that I can only hope is guilt.

"Just fine," I say shortly, bagging my pretzels and Skippy Peanut Butter, hoping he hadn't seen them.

"You look sunburned," he says, which I suppose is what sitting on the boat deck for all those hours did, although I hadn't noticed, what with the desperation being held at bay only by gossip. "But you look great," he goes on as if to say more, but then suddenly stops. He must have seen my face.

"I took a canal ride today," I say, rearranging the bag to put the tomatoes on top and to make sure the marshmallows do not show, and all the while wondering if now is when I get to say something scathing, to reflect how I feel.

"Yes," says Mrs. John. "You do look good. I like your haircut," she goes on. "I've been looking for a hairdresser. Where do you go?"

Now is my chance. Here it is. I'm sure I'll do it, for once. I'll spit it out. I'll get it off my chest. My hurt will be avenged. I'll get even, just once in my life. But no, of course not. All I do is think *Really, madam? You don't want to step foot in my house, but you want me to tell you about Michel? My Michel? Don't press your luck.* And as I always do, I let the opportunity pass.

So, wimpish as usual, I just say, "Oh, nobody in particular. There are lots of salons around here." Then I take my bags, making a grimace that they probably take as a smile, and I say, "Well, goodbye." I head for the escalator and escape.

Does this mean I have let my grievance go, I who can be as unforgiving as a plane crash? Not at all. But maybe it's best just to let John have it the next time I see him alone on the street. I'll be ready then, more ready than now. Yes, that's what I'll do. But it also reminds me to delete from my Palm the number of the *drageur* I met at the sushi bar. Even with no project in sight, it's time to move on.

When I get home, I decide to lie down and watch a film on the television, hoping I will fall asleep. So, I turn on the TV and tune the cable to TCM, which broadcasts old American films in English. I am startled to find that it doesn't come on. The screen stays black. I press both remotes to turn it all off and start again. My TV is fine, the other channels appear, but TCM is *mort*. Totally dead.

Annoyed and ready for a fight, even in French, I pick up the phone to call the *ghang-stairs* at *noos,* sure that nothing good will come out of it. *Noos* is not known for making things easy for their customers to watch TV. But again, Paris surprises me.

"Would you like to talk with an English-speaker in our office?" the operator asks me when I have explained my problem. I have done the best I can—terse, aggrieved, ready to threaten them with…with what? That I'll cancel the cable? I am not a fool.

So, *"Mais oui, merci,"* I say, astonished. This has never happened to me before. *"C'est très gentil."* I do not forget my manners. Besides, maybe they will get me an answer to my problem.

In just a moment, a man's voice says to me, *"Bonjour, madame,* perhaps I am of service?"

And this is the astounding part: Not only does he grasp the problem, he tells me which buttons to push and how to reconfigure my subscription to TCM right on the screen. And it works immediately. I thank him from the bottom of my sincere and overwhelmed heart. "Ahv a nize dey, my lady," he says, and then we say goodbye. I hang up, totally in shock. Nonetheless, TCM puts me to sleep as I had planned, and when I wake up, I am refreshed.

By early evening I am ready for the next round. I consider Procope, but being wise, Lenore declines. So, I suggest strolling over to rue de Sèvres to Le Petit Lutetia, where I don't go very often, for their delicious *confit de canard,* which is a duck leg conserved in its own fat. *Confit de canard* is another one of those mysteries about France. How could they invent this dish that sounds so horrible but is actually so good? (We will not think about the exquisite *foie gras*, which is made by actually torturing—force feeding—the bird.)

When I call to reserve, having found the number in *Zagat's*, I'm pleased that they have a table free. I think Lenore will like the atmosphere, and after a day of playing tourist, I'm dying for a glass of champagne—that nothing is tortured to make.

Finding a number in the phone book itself, however, is not always as easy as *Ah-Bay-Cey*. A restaurant might be listed in the *Pages Blanches* under its article (l'Huitrier, La Coupole, Le Christine) or even under its category (Restaurant Garnier, Chez Clement, Café Beauborg). The listings in the *Pages Jaunes* are by *arrondissement*, so in order to find out where a place is, you already have to know where it is. (Good work, France Télécom!) And where in the Yellow Pages are airlines to be found? Under the letter *T*, in the category of *Transports aériens*.

The next day, there's naught to forgive. Looking over some of the brochures I have pulled from my files, Lenore herself suggests taking the train to Melun and then a little shuttle bus to the Château Vaux-le-Vicomte, built by Louis XIV's Finance Minister Fouquet. This for me almost counts as being away! I don't even wake up the computer, and I don't check my email. I'm going out of town! We look out the train window, and we yak all the way.

First, we spend more than an hour touring the exquisite palace, and then we barrel around the formal gardens in a rental golf cart, laughing hysterically at ourselves. And we pedal around the little lake in one of those boats that look like swans. Lenore, whose Chicago garden is the envy of her neighbors (even me, in my time), looks around and says, "Hmmm, fountains."

"Melun is known for its Brie cheese?" asks Lenore on the shuttle bus back to the town, showing she has read the brochures. We are going to find a café terrace and get some lunch.

"Yeah, but, as I recall, it's a little saltier than the more famous Brie from Meaux. I don't like it as much."

"You can taste the difference?" she asks with surprise.

"Of course," I say, realizing with some surprise that I can. Could I learn the same for wine? Writing a few paragraphs about the problems of French vintners for a guidebook may be enough for the tourists, but maybe my own education could stand a course or two. I must make a list.

Late in the afternoon, once back in Paris and on the *métro*, Lenore floats an idea of coming next year and staying a month in order to look at all the gardens around Paris. "What about one of those short-term residences?" she asks.

"Sure," I say, hoping I am taking the idea of a month-long visit in stride. I love Lenore, but *a whole month?* "But those residences are usually more costly than the furnished flats people rent out, you know, like my friends the Jays rent."

"Still, I think I'd rather try one of those residences you used to stay in, where they change your linens and clean your apartment."

I nod. "There's one of those places down on the *quai,* just at the end of rue Dauphine. Citadines, it's called."

"We don't have to look at another *quai*, do we?" she asks with a sly smile, and we laugh. We agree to walk after dinner to check it out.

"I also could study French. I've always wanted to study French," she says. "I could take one of those courses for foreigners, and the rest of the time I could concentrate on the gardens. If I don't do it soon, I never will."

Having met my need for champagne and duck the night before, I am tonight thinking of a plate of Frenchified curried lamb. I suggest eating at La Coupole, but Lenore says she's heard it's gone downhill. (Does she know Findlay?)

Instead, we walk to Chez Claude Sainlouis, over in rue du Dragon, where Caroline and I went for our birthdays, where it is so typically French that Lenore almost swoons. As soon as she walks in and sees the red walls, she loves it. And being a regular, I like it that both the owner and waiter shake my hand and ask how I am. I say only, *"Très bien, merci,"* and leave it at that.

We take our time this evening, Lenore ordering a three-course *menu*, and I only two. Later, after I have mopped up the beefy sauce of my *daube à l'ancienne*—without Caroline to roll her eyes—and Lenore has polished off the fish *du jour* (even managing to bone it herself), she allows me to share her *profiteroles* for dessert. For our post-prandial stroll, we head up to the quay to Citadines and get its brochure.

Winding up back at the Hotel Bonaparte, we kiss at the door and exchange vows to keep better in touch. And I mean it, for old friends are hard to come by and sad to lose. As I walk back to rue Servandoni, I realize how good it was to have been out of my routine, even for just a few days. And running into John yesterday didn't spoil my afternoon, a clear sign of something mature, I am sure. But a visitor for a month? Even Lenore? I can just hear it now: *Don't worry, I won't get in your way—I'll just do my own thing,* which I know is not a lie at the moment it's said.

One early afternoon about a week before the big event, as I am entering my apartment after having gone to the pool for a water aerobics class and feeling quite triumphant that I have actually done so, my telephone rings. It is my British cousins finally returning my call, suggesting I join them on their barge in mid-August, to cruise up into Belgium, and, as usual, I can stay as long as I like. (Do they know what they're saying?) With great relief, I agree that I'll call them toward the end of the month to figure out a riverside town where I can join them by train. "Perfectamondo," I say, and I feel I am saved.

And just as I have hung up, the phone rings again. J-P's secretary asks me to hold the line. Could the party be off? It would break my heart. *"Bonjour, Frahn, c'est Jhee-Pay,"* says *Monsieur le PDG* when he comes on the line, and I can hear from his voice that nothing is wrong. We exchange pleasantries. I tell him about the barge trip, and he asks me about the progress on my work. This pleases me, and we talk about agents and deadlines for a few moments, and then I also tell him (even more briefly) that I have a new dress. And no doubt breaking one of Paul's rules, I nonetheless ask him—my antennae suddenly shooting up, project-wise—who else is coming to the dinner.

"You know that most *Parisiens* will be away *pendant le long weekend,"* J-P says. "And Henriette and Victor are in the Hamptons. But Antoine and a few of our friends have to be on the reviewing stand for the parade at Place de la Concorde, and some others like myself seem to find ourselves in town, chained to our desks. *C'est cette maudite mondialisation,"* he jokes (I think). "And I have invited Findlay Lovell and his charming wife, so you won't be the only American."

It is true that Paris—cursed globalization or not—is fast emptying itself of Parisians. If Paris were a sea, July and August would be a constant low tide. Most small establishments close, often for an entire month. Some restaurants might close an extra day a week or not serve on weekends. Some people make a fuss, but I think, *Who cares?* Department stores and supermarkets are open; most of the *marchés* appear on schedule, although with fewer stalls; there's always a bakery open in each *quartier;* and it's a pleasure to navigate the streets when all those Parisians drivers are gone (an *impérialiste* joke).

Antoine, J-P informs me, will be coming alone, his wife already having left for La Rochelle. (Why am I not surprised?) And Antoine, himself, will leave for a month just after *le quatorze juillet.* All French salaried employees, no matter how high—or low—the position, are entitled to a minimum of five weeks' *congé.* And they take a big batch at one time, which is why the city empties out as it does and why so many families find their way to country homes—although perhaps not on the scale of a *manoir* in Charente Maritime.

Even Jane and Edouard are decamping for the whole of August. "How can he afford it?" I asked Jane shamelessly when she called to set up a lunch before they take off.

"Why shouldn't Ed have the same vacation salaried workers get?" she asked, expecting no answer and getting none. So, they will head for the mountains, where they have found a cottage to rent through a friend of a friend. (How French can you get?) But, she explained further—and this makes more sense—with the *habitués* away it isn't economically worthwhile for the wine bar to stay open. So, we made a date for lunch at the UNESCO cafeteria at the beginning of August, just before she and Ed leave.

Edie, too, hangs up her potholders in mid-July. Fortunately for me, though, her Sunday brunch pots served up a frothy *cappuccino de melon*, a crisp *salade de fruits de mer* that was studded with *capucines* (nasturtiums) of all things, and which—not surprisingly—tasted great, a *poulet de Bresse* which, quite pleased with herself, Edie showed her guests had been poached in a pig's bladder. It was certainly the best chicken I had ever eaten. I even accepted her offer for more, promising myself next time not to look at it first. And finally, she brought out a pyramid of homemade seasonal-fruit *sorbets* layered with slivers of perfectly ripened matching fruits. Wines to go with each course and coffee for those who cared. Some of the same chefs from her winter brunch were there (even the cute one with the gaudy wedding ring), and at the pig's bladder, of course, they didn't blink one eye. I enjoyed their culinary conversation, but cute chef or not, I have sworn off *restaurateurs* who can talk only about *cassoulet*.

"Is there anything you'd like me to bring you back?" Edie asked as I was about to leave, by then late in the afternoon.

It wasn't as though I hadn't thought of this. I took my life in my hands. "Well, a box of low-fat microwave popcorn, if you don't mind? I'm just about out."

There was a long pause, and then Edie laughed, "Sure, but I won't be back until the beginning of September." I assured her I was in no hurry. We kissed; I walked out into the sunshine, and I waddled back along boulevard St-Germain.

Caroline was sitting at her desk by the window as I made a detour through rue de Tournon, and she waved me up. "What do you want to do on *le quatorze*?" she asked as I walked in, and then she offered me a cold drink.

"Did you forget I'm going to J-P's?" I asked, waving away the idea of a drink. "But let's see what's up on the thirteenth at one of those Firemen's Balls."

"Sounds good to me. Come outside. I have found someone new I want to tell you about." So, we sat awhile on her balcony, where on her table in the shade were her computer, notebook, and a library book with variously colored Post-its sticking out. She had found an old biography of an American dentist, Thomas Evans, she told me, who in the 1850s became wealthy by introducing anesthesia to European ruling classes, Napoleon III among them. He also saved the Empress Eugénie's life, spiriting her out of France during the war in 1870, when her husband was held captive and the Republic finally declared.

"Do you think Richard and Freifeld would save a queen, no matter how many medals and honors they were given?"

"No, probably not," I said. "Klaus used to know some of those royal highness types when he was dancing, and he says they're mostly 'imbesotic' jerks. On the other hand, I would."

Caroline smiled at this. "You know what Evans did for them—Napoleon III, the Prince of Wales, and the Romanoffs? Gave them nitrous oxide. Laughing gas? No wonder they loved him. Listen," she said, "I'm going to go down to La Ciotat for a couple of weeks at the beginning of August. You could always come, too, if you want. I'm sure my friends would be pleased to have you."

"Thanks," I said. "But don't worry. I'm going barging up north again with my cousins. If it doesn't work out, I may well come down." It was true that I hadn't been to Marseille in years, and the beach at La Ciotat would be fun. But intruding on Caroline and her friends from her professor days wouldn't do. And not work out? What was I saying?

Today on the phone, though, I hear J-P say, *"Frahn,"* and I grasp immediately from his tone that this is the reason he has called, "I just wanted to let you know that I have invited a woman friend to the party, one you haven't met before. I think I mentioned Marie-Claude to you when we were at the Sénat for the *hommage*, when I had to go home for dinner so quickly. I want you to like each other."

No you did not, you didn't say one word, I think but keep my mouth shut. *And what do you mean, we should like each other*, a statement that could be the kiss of death. "She doesn't live in Paris," J-P goes on. "She's going to campaign for *maire* in the town near my country home. She has a good chance of success. And I think it is only the beginning for her in French politics. She could go on to be *conseiller général* in her *département* or even a *députée* in the *Assemblée nationale*."

"I'll look forward to meeting her, J-P," I say, which is sort of true. As to whether I hope it works out for them, I'm reserving judgment. "I'll try not to be too American," I say.

"Chérie, vous êtes tout de même très mignonne," J-P assures me. Just before we hang up he tells me that because it will be a late evening, he has asked a friend to drive me home. I thank him, for although I think central Paris is generally safe, going home alone after midnight anywhere does not fill me with joy. And who is this friend? But what did he say? I'm cute despite being American? Is that what he meant?

So, Marie-Claude is a woman politician on her way up. Women in France didn't even get to vote until 1945. Despite the idea of rights for women, after the Revolution it was assumed that they would vote for royalists as their priests would instruct them to do. At the turn of this millennium, however—at least according to my research—France still ranked at the bottom of the European charts when it came to women elected to its national legislature. Even Italy ranked above. That same Italy that during the Nineties tried to decree that a woman wearing jeans couldn't claim rape, for jeans—being so tight—couldn't be removed without the woman's help. Good old Italy. How can you help but love it?

Le 14 juillet officially begins the night before. The evening of the thirteenth, *le tout Paris* dances in the streets. The city's firehouses put on those *bals des pompiers*, and fortunately, ours in rue du Vieux Colombier is known for being one of the liveliest (loud). Caroline and I, having decided to take ourselves to the Korean Barbeque for a quick and cheap dinner, wander afterward toward the festivities to see what's up. It's only *21h45* and it stays light until almost *23h*—as it did the night of the *Fête de la musique* in June—when my vow to pay better attention to the music in the Palais de Luxembourg bit the dust. Tonight, the streets are crowded and noisy, and the chaos hasn't even yet begun.

We weave around the groups of people, resuming our conversation about the dentist Evans, who also treated the teeth of Baron Haussmann, who was then in the midst of his public works. Is it a surprise that Evans speculated in real estate and made a fortune? In any case, Caroline and I are still chewing over all of this, when we hear a voice calling, "Caroline! Caroline!"

It's Ida! Ida, dressed in what in the Seventies would have been called a peasant outfit—a white, ruffled, embroidered, off-the-shoulder blouse and a multicolored, flowered kind of twirly skirt. She is also wearing heavy, dangling, silvery hoop earrings, which if she wears often will, I am sure, pull her earlobes down in later life. Her high-heel sandals have open toes, and her toenails are painted a purple with glittery stars sparkling on each one.

"Ida!" Caroline and I exclaim at the same time. And then Caroline (who is so nice) says, "You look wonderful! Are you here to dance?"

"Oh yes! I live just around the corner, you know, and I've gotten to know the *pompiers*, and they've all promised me a dance! Are you going to stick around for the dancing, Caroline?"

"No, I don't think so, not with my tricky knee," answers Caroline, while I just shake my head, for I have noticed that Ida hasn't addressed me directly. Yet, at this moment, I can't think of anything I'd rather do less than watch Ida dance with French firemen. And how does one come to know the firemen? But as we walk away I try to be like Caroline, for once, and on our way back across the square I say not a mumbling word.

The next night, although it is against every American instinct, I obey one of Paul's instructions and do not leave my apartment until five minutes after the time specified for arrival. I am not to arrive at Jean-Pierre's until at least a half-hour late. So, gussied up as I am—short-sleeved linen dress with a silk-patterned little jacket, and wearing my open-toed summer slings—I still head to the *métro*, which fortunately runs on holidays, although less frequently. It is broad daylight and will be for another three hours, and the night is quite warm. This means it is stifling in the *métro*, and the smell of the unwashed assaults me, even over the Gardenia Passion fragrance that I have dabbed on. French women never go out without having applied their scent, and tonight I must not let the American side down.

Coming up for air in the 7th, and after strolling several blocks alongside the families heading toward the Champ de Mars to *pique-niquer* until the fireworks, I finally ring the bell at J-P's. It takes several minutes for the polished doors to open, and when they do, I am thunderstruck to see Julien the dog in Jean-Pierre's arms. True to at least this particular vow, I say not a word.

Alice and I agree that we may be able to wring "dining-out conversation" about this *14 juillet* for years. For me, this is how it might go. "Well, the deputy minister says my French is *impeccable*," I could say if I have made some humiliating error. Or at book club, "But I've already read that book about Napoleon in exile on St-Helena. The author sat to my right at Jean-Pierre's dinner, didn't I tell you?" Or, if someone at the swimming pool expresses surprise at seeing me: "I'm taking the cure! You can't imagine how much Philipponnat champagne I drank on *le quartorze juillet*. Which vintage? Oh, I think it was the 1998." And modestly, "Of course, I saw the *feux d'artifice* from the rooftop terrace of a friend whose apartment overlooks the Champ de Mars. Weren't they splendid?"

To Caroline I might say, "Yes, Findlay drank too much and held forth on Paris and old-time Parisians until Alice put a stop to it." To Klaus I might proudly boast that I did not disgrace myself, and to Paul that I obeyed all the rules. To Edie I could say, "There were eleven at table, and yes, I remember every dish: *salade tiède de poisson, pintades rôtis, pommes de terres nantes, haricots verts*, and after the *fromages*—a Roquefort, a gooey St-Marcelin, a plain old Emmental that wasn't plain-old at all and some chèvre—there were wonderful Berthillon ice creams and sorbets and some little homemade *petit fours* and hand-dipped chocolates, too." To Richard, were he here, I would have to admit that I had made a point of noticing that the white wine was Muscadet, but that the heavenly red wine had been decanted and, my wine knowledge being what it is, I didn't have the foggiest. I must really start that list.

To J-P himself, I would first thank him for a marvelous evening, and then I would be dying to ask—but would refrain—just why Antoine didn't turn up, as there was clearly a setting laid for him at the table. (There's something strange going on there, I'm sure of it.) And last to Sandy, except that, of course, I actually wouldn't mention the party at all, "Music? *Bien sûr*, there was a man in a *smoking* playing J-P's beautiful Bechstein piano in the open gallery above the living room before dinner, but no, he didn't play anything by Ravel."

To anyone who asks, I could say simply, "Yes, I had a great time." But to no one will I say how hung over I was the next day, how drained I felt in every muscle and joint, and how I spent the entire day on my couch unable to move, dozing off and on. I barely turned on the computer. I checked my email and then put it (and me) back to sleep.

As to Marie-Claude, I like her, at least well enough to satisfy J-P, I think. Tall and willowy, her naturally streaked blonde hair attests that she really does spend her life near the beach. She looks to be in her late forties, but as with all those French women who have not an ounce of fat to spare or a wrinkle on their face and who look like it all came about without a moment's care, how can you know?

Marie-Claude's family's background, or so I gather, is upper-crust, much like J-P's. She's witty, as the French are, not funny in the American way, and, although she is not at all pushy, she clearly commands attention. How could she not win the mayoral race?

For a while after dinner the two of us sat on a deep leather couch in J-P's library, sipping at our *digestifs* and talking (in her perfect and charmingly accented English) about women in politics and the law passed in 2000 that required the ballot to put forth 50 percent women candidates. "It did not do as much good as we had hoped," Marie-Claude shook her head. "In the next legislative elections, only 20 percent of the candidates were women. And some women I know were turned down in favor of men who were not as well established."

"Plus ça change," I said in French, meaning in this case, "so what else is new?" I accompanied this little *mot* with Edouard's best Gallic shrug, or at least I tried. Perhaps I will leave shrugging to the Gauls.

But one of my million-dollar ideas suddenly striking me, I did ask Marie-Claude if she would like me to volunteer for her mayoral campaign when she is ready to run. Immediately, I saw that same Tom Hanks-*Castaway*-raw-minnow-look wash over her face, although officially all she did was smile and say, *"Merci, Frahn, c'est très gentil."* Perhaps she really is right for Jean-Pierre.

Much later, though, after the fireworks and fruit juice had been substituted for Cognac and Muscat, she and J-P saw me to the door, along with an elderly (decrepit) ambassador to OECD (Organization for Economic Cooperation and Development), whose driver had been waiting below and would be taking us both home. (Did J-P think this was introducing me around?) At the door, I did not miss that J-P's hand was placed possessively on Marie-Claude's shoulder or that she was happily holding Julien in her arms. After J-P and I kissed and said, *"Bonne nuit, à très bientôt,"* Marie-Claude shook my hand and suggested with that tight little smile the French often have (and which I am determined to learn), that we get together just the two of us, "...sometime." Does that mean in this lifetime or what?

Margot Finally Turns Up

"YOU KNOW, SWEETIE," CAROLINE CONTINUES AS she is packing her valise to go down to La Ciotat. I am keeping her company while she gets ready. She has been stuffing and talking, and I have been (unusually) quiet, although I'm not sure she's noticed. "Sometimes, I think that if God had been French, Genesis would have said that He rested on the seventh day and all of August." She stops for a moment to take a sip of the Pommery champagne she has uncorked without spilling a drop.

It's hot, and I'm feeling dull-witted, relieved just to sit and sip. This bottle is one of the last of the case she brought back from a trip with Richard and Phyllis up to Reims a few years ago. I am getting quite used to this champagne-at-all-hours business. What if I left here? What if the dollar falls even more, tourists stop coming and don't buy guides? Could I go back to the States? And what about Caroline's increasing problems with money? And her knee? And just why am I in this doomsday mode? This is what I am wondering as Caroline continues, taking advantage of my rare silence.

"Even some churches are closed," she goes on. "So, I suppose the faithful—at least those left in Paris—will just have to rely on faith, for a while."

Paying more attention, I still continue to watch quietly, as she now sits on the suitcase to close it. Then she affixes it to a wheeled luggage cart next to the ever-present tote bag that today is showing books, an umbrella, a bottle of water, and a little sack of chocolate-covered orange-peel candies for the train. Her suitcase, needless to say, is an aged Louis Vuitton that she got for a bargain out at the *puces*. "Will we ever understand this country? Catholic holidays in a country that reveres its separation of religion and state? Robespierre would be turning over in his grave."

It is true that since the Revolution, when Robespierre and his *acolytes* destroyed churches, killed as many clergy as they could, and renamed Notre Dame the Palace of Reason, France has steadily defended its 1905 official separation between religion and state. Except for holidays, when they decide to forget about it. And the French do love those national holidays—Easter Monday, Ascension Day, Pentecost, All Saints Day, of course, Christmas, and coming up pretty soon on August 15, Assumption Day. There is no street here named Robespierre.

"Yes, I suppose," I finally say, forcing myself into some energy, for I have been thinking how much I can't wait to get away. Maybe I'll stretch the barge trip to two weeks. Or three years. This will never do. I must pull myself together.

Even Joël, I have found out, has closed his restaurant for the entire month. I haven't seen him often, for I don't make my detour through rue Guisarde anymore. But for some reason, he called to tell me that he was heading for *La Manche* (The English Channel, to me) to spend the month on Jersey. I did notice that he didn't invoke the cosmic "we," but I managed not to ask anything officially forward. He said he hoped I would have a good month, and I said the same to him. He asked what I was doing, and I mentioned the barge trip with my cousins. Why on earth did he call? Again hedging his bets? Well, I am weary of trying to fathom hidden meanings. I've done it too often in my life. I am ready for someone more straightforward. Something will unfold. But his being gone means I can walk through the Guisarde at will.

J-P also has called to say he is in La Rochelle, having left Paris despite his protestations of having to work. "Is Antoine there, too?" I asked, this time not refraining from showing some curiosity, and hoping I would find out why his brother didn't show up for the dinner.

"No," he said, slowly. "It seems that Antoine has decided to join a government delegation doing a tour of the United States. And he didn't even tell the family he was going. Not even his wife."

"That doesn't sound like Antoine."

"No, it doesn't, *chérie*. Perhaps it is what you call a mid-life crisis. We are all very worried." After that, although I was dying to say something pointed about the almost non-existent wife getting some of her own back, we moved on to talk of beaches and heat, and how the kids were doing in the States. And J-P hasn't called me since. In years past he would have called me several times while away, but so far this month I haven't heard another word. Given the Marie-Claude situation, I do not wonder why.

So, here I am in Paris, pretty much on my own. Abandoned by one and (almost) all. Work nags at me, so being almost ready to scream with antsiness, it's good to have something I can at least pretend I'm doing. I decide I must have a fresh Plan of Attack. I make a new chart and redo the checkmarks: culture, shopping, history, lodgings, the city plant, and—since the material arrived from the Prefecture—formalities for staying. Not restaurants, for trying new ones will go on to the end, and besides, some are now closed. The dearth of checkmarks means there's much more to go, but with the chart looking so neat and clean, I tape it to the wall above the desk and don't even glance at it again. In this heat, my energy level for making forays out into the unknown is zilch. I give in. I stay close to home, fiddling with editing, organizing, and just rewriting paragraphs that I can't believe anyone in their right mind could have written.

That the weather is so scorching means, of course, that my swimming pool has closed for a week of cleaning. Since I refuse to take the sweltering *métro* to another pool, I go to every film in sight, walk across the road to the Luxembourg, and sit under a shady plane tree, trying to concentrate on one of my library books, or I watch the men playing *pétanque*, otherwise known as *boules*. (*Boules* is how French wives get their men out of the house.) I sip from a frosty can of Nestlé *thé glacé à la peche,* or get a *sorbet* from one of the refreshment kiosks. I keep a few euros in my pocket, in case I need to use the *toilettes*, and ignoring the commotion around me, I often have a doze. And sometimes, I watch the French kids sailing the little rental boats in the large round fountain in front of the Sénat.

But do not think I am alone. On the Monday after Caroline leaves, Jane calls to remind me of our lunch, which I had not forgotten. "Let's have a picnic on the Champ de Mars," she says, which is fine with me. The UNESCO cafeteria is fun, but if Anna's husband, Avi, turned up, I'd feel guilty again about being so remiss in getting together with the wife.

So, on this day to meet Jane, I first stop at the cell phone shop, for I'm not always getting my calls. I get messages, but the phone hasn't rung. I wait my turn, and when I finally get to explain, they say I need a new phone. I say this is already my second new phone. Finally convinced, the salesman admits that, just maybe, I need a new *sim* chip, and, just maybe, they will provide it for free. For free, in Paris? I effuse about how grateful I am, which is true. So, a call is made to the headquarters to assure the cell phone powers that this phone I have in my hand really belongs to the hand that holds it. I am asked my name, and I give it. I give my address and number of my landline. Then I am asked my age. My age? I give the month and day.

"And the year, *madame?*" the voice on the line insists.

"Listen, mister (*"Ecoutez, monsieur"*), you have my name and address, and you know the day and month of my birth. And if you're looking at my records, you know my birth year as well as I do. There's a shop full of people here, and this is all I'm going to say."

Mister on the other end of the phone laughs and agrees to give me the chip for free. This whole episode is both satisfactory—

having gotten what I need for free—and slightly depressing, all that age business. Why did they need to know? And why do I care?

A little later, I come out of the *métro* and see Jane waiting at the corner of avenue de la Motte-Piquet and avenue de Suffren. We pick up sandwiches and drinks at a storefront shop. Then we look for a bench on the Champ de Mars.

I love this park, almost as much as my own. It starts on the south at l'Ecole Militare, the military academy built by Louis XV to make soldiers out of gentlemen too poor to do anything else. And it ends north at the Eiffel Tower, apparently built for tourists craving tacky souvenirs. But in between, there's the park. Today people are sitting in groups on the grass—families and couples, perhaps coworkers from the offices nearby—talking and laughing over their lunch. Military men (with short-sleeved shirts and tanned arms) are walking on their way somewhere important, I'm sure. Little kids are squealing as they pedal the go-karts, sometimes careening into the plastic barriers, so their parents have to come and straighten them out. Ponies are waiting in the shade for the tiny riders that look solemn with awe as they are led around the path. Neighborhood widows are knitting furiously on benches. And all around the sides, there are leaves, flowers, bushes, and trees.

Jane and I claim a bench that has come empty, and since she is wearing a light-colored summer suit, as a professional woman would, she puts the plastic bag under her skirt to sit on, so it doesn't get mussed. As we unwrap our sandwiches and begin to eat, I say, "You know, these sandwiches would be much better if they used fresh mayonnaise, not canned." Jane looks at me as though I have said something wise.

"It's hard to believe we've known each other ten years," I say, remembering how we met in rue Christine. We have caught up on our daily lives, talked about Richard (who, Jane told

AN AFTERNOON IN THE PARK

Boules (also called *petanque*) may well be the most popular sport in France. Buy a set of *boules,* and the rest is free. You can play it on any level stretch of hard-packed dirt (at least 15 meters in length) where a ball can roll—and then stop. Although there are rules for play and strategies for winning, the object of the game often seems to be to have a good time with your buddies on an afternoon in the park.

To play, first draw a line (or a circle) from which to throw the *boules*. From here you throw the little *cochonnet* (or *but*) some six to 10 meters down the stretch. And then the teams throw their *boules* in turn, trying to get closest to the *cochonnet*, both directly and also by knocking the other team's *boules* out of the way. When all *boules* have been played, the winning team scores a point for each *boule* that is nearer to the jack than the opposing team's. The winner starts the next round, from a new circle where the *cochonnet* ended up in the last game. A game is usually played to thirteen points.

Basically, the ball is thrown with the palm of the hand down, with an arched backspin—allowing the thrower to control where the ball stops. When pointing the hand toward the jack, players might use *"la portée"* (high lob), *"la demi portée"* (half lob), or *"la roulette"* (a sort of rolling throw). No matter the names of the throws, however, if you get your *boule* closest to the *cochonnet*, you win. And you can treat for the glass of pastis that will signal the end of a pleasant afternoon.

me, has been emailing Ed something about the upcoming California grape harvest) and how the year is more than half gone. "And that you're no longer that college girl struggling to learn French."

"Yes, life is great, but I'm still not exactly sure what the future holds," she says. "I'm thinking it's time I worked that out."

"Don't rush it," I advise, thinking of how often I have rushed things. "It comes upon you whether you've helped it along or not." Then I look at her. "Everything's all right, isn't it? You and Ed are okay? You're here for good?"

"Oh yes. Really. In fact, I think that's getting even more clear. And you?"

"Where else would I go?" I ask, and I am unnerved by my equivocal answer. So, I backtrack to say what I think is true. "Yes, I'm here. Life here suits me, even when it's hot and I'm crawling with boredom." We're both quiet for a moment, and then we resume our usual subjects. Ed and closing up the wine bar. My book and the deadline. Working at UNESCO. Remembering rue Christine. No projects in my life. It's so hot. Ed's mother will take care of the cat. I can't wait to go on the boat. She can't wait to be in the mountains.

Later, as we are starting to clean up the remains of the picnic, we throw some crusts of bread and a few potato chips to the pigeons clustering around our feet. Two little girls, dressed in blue and white pinafores and dusty sandals that must have been white just a short time ago, approach us (scattering the birds for the moment), and we give them the rest of our leftovers so they can take over for us with what Findlay calls "the winged rats." Usually, I love it when the parks are noisy with the bustle of children, but now, I don't know why, I seem to be turning gloomy.

In fact, as much as I had looked forward to being with Jane, the entire lunch has made me somewhat sad. I am surprised at this. I am not ready for it. I am determined to shake it off. I am almost relieved (adding guilt to the rest) when Jane says she has to go back to work. We do the usual kisses goodbye and make a vow to get together in September. And despite all the movement around me, I stand in the middle of the path watching Jane as she turns to walk south toward UNESCO, and I continue looking after her until she turns the corner, out of sight.

Moi, a walk might do me some good. It's a smidgen cooler, as some clouds are appearing in the sky. I could stand a thunderstorm right now. So, I walk, sticking to the shady sides of the streets, allowing myself, now that I am alone, to wonder just what is going on with me. Is it that conversation at the phone shop? Is time slipping by? Am I not used to this by now, for heaven's sakes? Am I nostalgic for those old days in rue Christine, when everything was so new? Could it be because the boys haven't called from Rome? Just when will my kids tell when they're arriving for Thanksgiving, since they both agreed to come? And what about that unexpected phone call from Joël? Desperately, I turn my thoughts to packing for the barge: emergency Oreos, my Blackberry, and the Eluage neck cream that I bought and that I am sure will start to take effect any day now. And probably some shorts and tee shirts, to round it out.

As I am walking past the Luxembourg gate and almost home, I see Jenny trotting toward me in her running shoes, her shorts sticking to her thighs and her tee shirt plastered to her chest. She is dripping sweat. I wait until she reaches me, and when she sees me she slows. She takes a swig from a water bottle, which without doubt is keeping her from utter collapse.

"Everything all right?" I ask, kicking myself for not having called her.

"Better," she pants. "We're doing better. Looking at apartments. Caroline was right. Can't afford the ones Jack likes." She wipes sweat from her eyes. "We only have a short time left," she pants. "Got to make the most of it."

"Well, it won't help if you're dead," I say, for just looking at her makes me think that a cool shower might help my funk.

"Do you want to get together?" she asks, jumping up and down the way runners do, trying to keep their heart rates up while waiting for a traffic light to change. (And letting you know how fit they are and that you are not.) I am getting dizzy from all this display of exertion.

"Sure," I say, and then a brilliant idea hits me. "Why don't I put together a lunch for anyone who's still in town?"

"Great," she says and nods. "Let me know when." She leans toward me to give me the *bisous*, but wisely I just smile and push her clammy face away. "Kiss me when I have the lunch," I say.

Just a few seconds later, while turning into rue Servandoni, I suddenly wonder just who that was who volunteered me to give a luncheon. Whoever she was, she does not get my vote of thanks.

When I get back to the cobblestones of rue Servandoni, I look at the shuttered windows of the buildings and am relieved to be home on my tranquil street. My one phone message is Colette, saying she is going to Britain for the rest of the summer (and I don't blame her), and we'll get together when she is back. Then I shed my clothes and take a shower. Still damp, I lie down on the bed and promptly fall asleep. I awaken about an hour later, slightly disoriented, but then I look around and I think *rue Servandoni*. And my rather blue mood begins to lift. I listen to the thunderstorm that has blown up and am relieved, for a change, to stay home alone the rest of the day. Perhaps the lunch is a good idea, after all. I spread a few Ritz Crackers with low-fat p.b. and Fluff. And I get out a piece of paper to begin the list.

The next morning, after having at least spent some time at my desk (although by now I can't even pretend I'm working) with a glass of Nestlé's peach-flavored iced tea at my side, I call Alice. I alert her to the luncheon and say that I fully expect Findlay to come. She suggests an outing this afternoon to the Nissim de Camondo Museum, near the Henri Cernuschi where we had been back in May.

"Will Findlay come with us?" I ask.

"Are you coming, too?" Alice shouts to Findlay.

"No, you girls go," I can hear him say in the background. I think that's sweet.

"But tell her I'll come to her lunch," I hear him growl to Alice after she has told him the people I hope to invite. "Tell her it sounds good." What he means, I think, is that he approves of the guests, and he has me pegged (correctly) as the world's biggest sucker for his Paris stories.

Findlay, Alice tells me later, on our way over to rue du Four, is staying home to write an article about the charms of the *bar/ tabac*. These are those ubiquitous holes-in-the-wall where you can get a coffee and a drink anytime, plus cigarettes, lottery tickets, telephone cards—and according to Findlay, good, inexpensive meals that are often cooked by the wife of the *patron*. I do not find those bars as charming as he, I think it is fair to say, and home cooking by some sour old *Parisienne* who has cooked the same meals every day for fifty years is iffy to say the least.

When Alice and I get to St-Germain, the boulevard is completely blocked. Cars backed up on the side streets with horns honking uselessly. There is a *manifestation*. Not a parade but a real protest, with shouting and banners and stragglers. Clearly it's a solidarity march, an exhortation for something that I can't, for the life of me, figure out. The banners that the marchers are holding are being waved about in a way that I can't see what's written. And in addition to the car horns, two men are shouting something decidedly inspirational into megaphones, and I see hundreds of people talking to each other and occasionally yelling something that escapes me. How can I show my solidarity, if I have absolutely no idea what to shout? It's a mess. Alice says she doesn't want to descend into the *métro*, and who could argue, what with the stairs and that delicate summer perfume of sweat. We turn around and see a cab. I run for it, flailing my arms wildly until the driver nods and Alice catches up. "Wow! Good girl," she says and laughs. Then the driver mumbles something that I take to mean that he will have to take us all around to hell and gone to bypass the marchers, so—as he whips into a u-turn and takes off—Alice says that's fine, and we hold on.

The two of us are as content to be on our own at the museum this afternoon as Findlay is to stay home. This former mansion of the Camondo family is not on the regular tourist route, so it is not crowded and we can take our time in each room, looking at the artifacts of the Camondos' life—and death. After having been culturally virtuous for an hour or so, and I am feeling quite relieved that I have done at least one thing productive, we rest and chat outside a *bar/tabac* and have a cold drink. Alice, despite lighting up a cigarette, has looked better since spending those weeks up on *la Manche* at St-Malo.

"Everyone knows that the Camondo family was completely exterminated by the Nazis, despite having converted from Judaism to Catholicism," Alice muses. "You know, when we got here a few years after the war, people who had known them still talked about it. Now, it's simply history in a museum. Strange, about life, isn't it?"

I do not respond, for it is hot and I don't want to risk another day when Life gets in the way of living it. I just nod. Then I say, "Right. Are you ready? Let's go home. I want to stretch out with a book." We walk until we find a cabstand. The march will certainly be over, but I have had enough of coping and am ready just to be whisked home. Maybe I will hear about it on the *20h* news. Alice, of course, invites me over to "din," as she calls it, but for a change (am I sick?), I pass. It's too hot to hear stories about how hot it was way back when.

Fortunately, Paris in August gives me time to read. So, the books I have borrowed from the library include one on the l'Oréal scandal of the early Nineties, when the company's old links to the Nazi cause were made public. I have a new history of the Jews in Paris, getting me ready for the newsletter, I guess. I have Olivia de Havilland's memoir, *Every Frenchman Has One* (which could be an example, perhaps, of what I call "rich-person-comes-to-Paris-after-the-War-and-has-a-hard-time-finding-domestics" books). I have a biography of Carson McCullers, who lived in Paris for a while. And I have a hugely long novel about a Sikh detective in India that I will take with me to the boat. So, I stay home to read, and at nine p.m. when I wake with the book having fallen to the floor, I realize I've missed the news.

As to the trip to see my cousins on their *péniche*, it can't come too soon. I've checked the *TGV* (high-speed train) schedules on the *SNCF* website, and I've reserved a seat for the end of next week to go to Douai up in the *Department du nord*—about an hour north of here. We'll be barging north, with a stop at Lille, which pleases me, for I've never been there and I hear that the old part of the city is truly picturesque.

I had no problems with the TGV. It's reliable, and the *horaires* (time tables) are easy to decipher, no matter your level of French. From the Gare du Nord, the trains go north. From the Gare de l'Est, they go east. From the Gare de Lyon, the trains go in that direction. And the Eurostar goes north, under the Channel from Paris Nord to London Waterloo. I mean, even the names of the train stations in Paris are logical. Would you expect anything less?

Another gaffe I won't forget—although I got away with it, for a change—was when I took the Eurostar to see my cousins in London for the first time. My ticket said I was assigned to *voiture No.1*. So, when I saw on the side of a car the large number "1," I climbed on and found my seat. Of course, I had made just *un petit erreur*, but since tickets on the Eurostar are validated before boarding, no one threw me out of *Première Classe*. I did figure it out, however, when I was served a free lunch with wine.

For other trains, however, I have learned the drill. You must *composter* (punch) the ticket in the yellow machines along the quays before boarding. Not doing so seems a major calamity all around. I learned this first in Italy, having boarded a train without knowing about the machines and being soundly berated by a conductor who had little patience with a rather befuddled tourist who didn't know the rules.

And speaking of rules, who knows them better than Klaus and Paul (or at least Paul)? Anyway, as I knew he would, Klaus finally calls. Of course, I've been dreading the *finale* to this little drama, but I've also been wanting to have it settled, one way or the other. To be done. And it turns out, as Caroline has known all along, that all my fuss was for nothing, or sort of. For the call floods me with at least temporary relief.

"Rome is out, by the by," Klaus says, just after he asks about me and tells me that they are now sunning on the beach up at Viareggio. "It's deader than a doorpost. No longer in our minds."

"Really out?" I ask, to be absolutely sure. "You're not going to frighten me anymore?"

"No, darling. It's so far out, you can't even see it from here."

"And you're going to stay in Paris?" I persevere, flogging what I hope is a totally dead horse.

"Well, that I don't know," he says. "But for now, the summer sunshine is reviving our old bones."

So, I take in those equivocal words, but somehow I don't react. It's just too hot.

In any case, Klaus brings me up to date and gives me their current phone number, in case I need anything. (Like what?) Although they're extending their stay, Klaus reminds me that they will be back before I am, so I promise to call as soon as I open my front door. I wish him a good time, say to send my love to Paul, and I mean it.

And Richard, of course, took off for California on schedule, but not—it turned out—before he went to Favela Chic, as he told me when he called to say goodbye (not *au revoir*), and with Ida, of all people.

"Did you know she was posted in Brazil before she came to the Embassy here?" Richard all but gushed to me on the phone just before he left. "She loves Brazilian music."

"Super!" I said brightly, the way his Sausalito neighbor had, and I immediately called Sandy.

"Look," she explained patiently, "neither you nor Caroline would go with him. He wouldn't ask his Rotary friends. It's not comrade Freifeld's style. And forget about the queens. So, what did you expect?" Sandy asked. She was right, and we hung up making plans for those summer sales that we a few weeks later took in.

So, with Caroline, Richard, and the boys away, Edie in Sacramento, Sandy in the Hamptons (I think), and Jane and Edouard by now up in the Alps, and even Mitzi recovering from the bar mitzvah at her house in Burgundy, this leaves the Jays, the Lovells, Margot—if she's free, for a change—and me. The luncheon will certainly be good for my funk. Everyone responds positively to my calls, and I feel quite pleased with myself that I remember to include Anna, who, after consulting her datebook, says she will be delighted. Avi is working through lunch these days, she says with what I think may be some annoyance in her voice, but I am relieved that she will come alone.

Margot, who has a late-morning *rendez-vous* at the Church of St-Sulpice, will come over early, she says, so we can have time to chat. Not that talking with Margot can ever really be called a chat, she being the most fervent person in our group.

Margot is one of the more striking women I know. A bit older than I, in her mid-sixties, she's thin and quite tall, with good cheekbones and only a few wrinkles. She's let her hair, which she wears curly and almost cropped to her scalp, go completely white, which contrasts dramatically with her unblemished, unlined, dark brown face. Haven't I said before that Margot is Black? She's too old to call herself African American, she says. And on occasion she asks (rhetorically) why it hasn't occurred to African Americans to leave the States, as she has done. "And where would they go," she asked rhetorically, "these people who have never seen Africa?" Margot herself, whose talent has brought her acclaim, at least over here, has made a life here and has never looked back.

It took sitting next to this beautiful woman at a concert of American gospel singers at a church on the Île St-Louis some years ago for me to realize that I had no people of color as friends in Paris and that I hardly even saw any on my usual rounds that I could—in my way—accost. But having spent much of my life in

Chicago and New York, I suddenly saw—to my discomfort—how homogeneous my life had become. So, hearing this woman speak English with someone to her other side, I butted in.

Margot is the only person I know who considers herself in exile, continuing, as she says, the tradition of Blacks coming to Paris to escape the racism in the United States. "Sally Hemings, that slave of Jefferson, doesn't count," she informed me. "She was free here, but being pregnant by yon Tom, she decided to go back, even back to being a slave."

Margot, herself, whose Creole family came from the same Ward in New Orleans as that of the jazz great Bechet, has been collecting materials for a book about Blacks in Paris that an agent has asked her to write. And I know what I know because she has started emailing me tidbits (now that she finally has a computer and email), hoping that I'll be her reader along the way. I suppose this fits in with our running theme of "Who-has-had-it-worse, the Blacks or the Jews," but I'm not sure that I have the stamina to take Margot on. She's pretty intense about whatever is on her mind.

Actually, Margot does know her stuff, for she arrived as a teenager and never looked back. She has already told me how the State Department denied Richard Wright—who wrote *Native Son*—a passport, given how outspoken he was about racism in the States. But Gertrude, famous (or infamous) by then, came through, asking the French government to help. And Wright finally got out. Gert said to him, "You'll find prejudice here, Dick, but you won't have a problem."

Wright did go back to the States but returned for good after being turned down on a house in New England because the owner wouldn't sell "to a Negro." Here, Wright found an apartment of *cinq pièces* in rue Monsieur le Prince, and there he stayed. A five-room apartment in what is now the *très chic* 6th? Tell me that again?

Wright had just died when Margot settled here, but not James Baldwin, who had come here in 1948. "My flight," Baldwin wrote in *No Name in the Street*, "had been dictated by my hope that I could find myself in a place where I would be treated more humanely than my society had treated me at home….And Paris had done this for me by leaving me completely alone."

"Most of the Americans of color here now are professionals or artists or writers—people who play by those rules you and Paul are always harping on," Margot said when I called to invite her to the luncheon. She was continuing the pressure about my helping her out with her book. Actually, talks about Blacks and Jews are pretty much a cornerstone of our friendship.

"You really think it's so much better here for Blacks than in the States?"

"Don't get me wrong," she instructed me. "Race relations are problematic anywhere. But France officially instituted equal rights in 1792, and when did Blacks in the United States get to drink out of "Whites-Only" drinking fountains? Not for another hundred and sixty years. *Ne me fais pas rire,* as you would say. Don't make me laugh."

"But did they get equal rights then? The Jews didn't really, although they did become citizens like everyone else."

"I know, you've already told me that. And you also told me about that bigwig duke during the Revolution who said that France should refuse everything to the nation of Jews, but grant everything to the individual Jew."

"I did?" Who was it, I tried to remember. Clermont-Tonnerre?

"Yes, but in America, it's the opposite. It created official equality for Blacks, but when it comes to a Black person walking down the street at night, it refuses everything." To this, I had nothing to say.

"So, are you coming to lunch?" I asked, finally.

"Of course. I wouldn't miss it." I put Margot at the top of the list.

JAZZY PARISIANS

When toward the end of World War I the all-Black 369th Regiment of the United States Army disembarked at Brest, and the French heard James Europe's forty-four-piece jazz band, for them it was *le coup de foudre* (the thunderbolt). And for the "colored" soldiers' part, if they could do only menial jobs for their country, if they were not allowed to march alongside American White soldiers on Bastille Day, if they couldn't return home on "Whites-Only" ships, and if a return to America meant eternal subservience, they could only realize that to the French they represented this wonderful sound called jazz. The French loved jazz then, and they love it now.

Today's jazz lovers may crowd the city's clubs and flock to the summer jazz festival out at the Parc Vincennes, but by now, almost a century after their great-grandparents discovered jazz, they've probably never heard of those early bands—The International Five, The Seven Spades, the Southern Syncopated Orchestra (of which the famous alto saxophonist/clarinetist Sidney Bechet was a member)—or of the American people of color who established themselves up in tolerant Montmartre. But you can imagine, as writer Maya Angelou later did, those Black actors and musicians speaking their version of French, their sentences being mixed with "Yeah, man's" and "Oo la la's."

It was here in "Mo'Mart" that Sidney Bechet left his most enduring legacy. Although Duke Ellington said of Bechet, "I honestly think he was the most unique man ever to be in this music," Louis Armstrong surpassed Bechet's fame in America, but not in France at that time, where Bechet returned to perform at the Paris Jazz Festival in 1949 and moved permanently in 1951. Although he was deported for a while after a gunfight, he returned some years later, maintaining a ménage with wife and mistress, buying an estate outside Paris. Bechet lived here and performed to acclaim until his death in 1959.

On one steamship voyage over, in 1925, Bechet had an affair with the young Josephine Baker, who wound up living most of her own life in France. ~~Bechet took her under his wing, so to speak~~. Baker first wowed the natives by dancing with only a string of bananas around her waist, but later earned a different respect by joining the Resistance during World War II. She was awarded the Legion of Honor and, when she died in 1975, thousands paid her homage. Her most well known song was *J'ai deux Amours, Paris et mon Pays* (I Have Two Loves, Paris and my Country). Parisians also have two countries: *la France* and jazz.

But just what about the Jews of France? So-called *egalité* didn't mean that as late as 1894 the Jewish Colonel Albert Dreyfus wouldn't be convicted twice of conspiring with the Prussians, despite the "evidence" having already been proved to be forged. It took until 1906 for him to be reinstated. To many, it's still yesterday, and I began to grasp this French compressing of time when I went to see his tomb in the cemetery at Montparnasse and listened to the guide tell the story to a rapt French group. And like many Parisians, I know where anyone-who-was-ever-anyone is buried.

Up in the 20th *arrondissement,* the cemetery of Père Lachaise is, as Henry Wadsworth Longfellow said, "the Westminster Abbey of Paris." Parisians promenade there, putting flowers on the tombs of the famous and others who have somehow managed to get in (not just being dead). Maybe the French have a right to complain about this *mondialization*, though, for the most visited grave, or so I've been told, is that of Jim Morrison of The Doors, who died here in 1971 at the age of twenty-seven. *Moi*, I like to go and see the tomb of Abélard and Héloïse.

The first time I went to Père Lachaise—when researching my first Paris book, years ago—it was for a guided lecture tour, *une conférence*. Had Lenore been along, there would have been nothing to forgive. All those tombs, all those stories, were better than all those quays. After passing the grave of the idolized French singer Edith Piaf, we saw the memorials to the French who had been deported, to resistance fighters, to others who were never accounted for, and to the memory of victims of Auschwitz. Having stopped to catch my breath and wipe my eyes, I hurried to catch up with the group at the graves of the Misses Stein and Toklas and their dog Basket. And then we moved on.

Now, despite not a word being written, work does nag. What should I write about Jews in France, when (if) I ever get to the section about religion? Could I summarize it like this? When *les juifs* fled to Gaul in the fourth century, as Roman Christians began persecuting them, did they think they would have a moment's peace in the next sixteen hundred years? *Ne me fais pas rire.* (Okay, so I do say that a lot.) In the seventh century, the Frankish King

Dagobert said convert or leave. In the eighth century, Charlemagne said stay. In 1182 Philip Augustus said leave but changed his mind in 1198 and said come back and bring your money with you. By 1269, Louis IX, the future holy saint, said Jews must wear an identifying badge, and in 1306 his grandson Philippe le Bel threw them out entirely. This lasted until 1315, when Louis X said come back—but only for twelve years. By the time of the Inquisition, they had been thrown out, supposedly for good.

But having straggled back when they were given equality during the Revolution, Robespierre & Co.'s anti-religion stands included synagogues, of course. But Dreyfus aside, was it not the French police who rounded up the Parisian Jews in 1942 on orders from the government in Vichy? As to this, I'm not sure I agree with Alice that it's just history now. I think the French Jews would side with me.

One night a few years ago, I was invited to a Passover seder at the home of some Parisians who had once sat next to me at the opera, and whom I convinced to talk with me, with my bad French and all. *Madame* was wearing a Star of David pendant, and so (naturally) one thing led to another, and *voilà*, I was invited to Passover *chez eux*, up in the 19th *arrondissement* near Place des Fêtes. Unfortunately for me, these people soon after retired to their country home (to which I have not been invited), so that was the end of that.

In any case, I arrived at their door early, as I often do, and I knew enough not to ring the bell. I decided to pass some time in the *bar/tabac* around the corner, waiting until—if not late in the French fashion—I would at least be not too close to the time specified. *"Bonne fête,"* the *patron* said to me, admiring the flowers I had placed on the bar (my not yet knowing to send flowers before or after, but not the night of an occasion). An old drunk at the end of the bar said to no one in particular, "It's all the fault of the Jews." The *patron* raised his eyebrows at me, and I said nothing. What was there to say?

On the day of my luncheon, I am out of the house early with my shopping list in one hand and dragging my shopping cart with the other. I go only to the Grande Épicerie, since although I'm now actually looking forward to the afternoon, my desire to traipse around any neighborhood is at a low. It's too hot to think of reheating anything, so after I put a one-euro coin into the *caddie* slot to dislodge the shopping cart from its mates, I head to the salad counter. I choose the *asperges en saumon, oeufs en gelée* (jellied eggs), a *salade de pommes de terre* (potato salad), and the pastry layers *millefeuille au crabe*. I choose enough to have a leftover or two. I select some cheeses and a buy a *baguette*. Finally, I reattach the shopping cart, and pop out and then pocket the coin, which is why I'm always finding coins and even bills in my clothes. And which, I remember now, annoyed Husband Number Two no end, when I'd exclaim, "Look what I found! A five-dollar bill!"

I already have several bottles of Badoit chilling in the *frigo*. Next to them are a few bottles of the same Menetou-Salon that Joël brought over (how many months ago?) and which I know Findlay will like. I set out the cheeses to *chambrer* (bring to room temperature). On my desk—my table is too small for everything—I have put away all the papers and turned off the computer, and now it is festive with a bowl of colorful, ripe fruit (*pêches, abricots, nectarines*) from the *marché* in rue de Buci. It's not yet the season for the tiny, yellow, plummy *mirabelles*.

On the table, I also have a vase of bright summer flowers. When I was asked by the *fleuriste* whether they were *pour offrir*— that is to be offered as a gift—I spared myself insanity and said that they were *pour la maison*, which was true. Who can have the patience to wait while a florist first deliberately trims every stem and slowly discards each unsightly leaf, then carefully lays down one single flower after another amid just the right green sprays that she has selected, and then arranges them ever so artistically in a plastic cover, of course, not forgetting to attach the company's own sticker at just the spot where she has reflected it will best be seen? Nothing is simple in France.

Just at the moment when I think everything is ready, the *interphone* rings. Margot has arrived.

After the kisses, Margot hands me a slightly crumpled bag, which unlike J-P does not faze me, and which is from Mulot. I know what must be inside, brownies, and I'm right. I thank her, while putting them on a plate to offer as another dessert—along with some *sorbet*. Margot immediately installs herself on the couch (not noticing how nicely I had fluffed up the cushions). "I had a splendid Paris morning," she says (without commenting on the flowers). "But I'm going to wait until the others come to tell you about it."

"So, tell me instead what you've got in mind for your book," I start right in. "Can you really say something new?" (Am I worried about her book or mine? I put this out of my head.)

"Well, how about Eldridge Cleaver and his wife living here, and I mean legally, in the mid-Seventies?"

"I thought he lived in Algiers."

"You see? It was afterward. I was here when they arrived." Margot smiles. "Did you know that Eldridge designed some men's clothing that would show to advantage men's nether regions? Codpiece trousers, I think he called them...."

"The return of the codpiece?" I burst out laughing. "Yes, you better write a book about this." She starts to say something about Eartha Kitt living here when she was young, but the buzz of the interphone at this point interrupts her, and I jump to answer the door.

The Jays announce themselves on the interphone, saying that Anna is with them, so I push the button to unlatch the door. I am relieved they have arrived together and I don't have to introduce them, for once again I've forgotten Anna's last name. But in just a minute they are up the stairs, Anna carrying a bouquet of flowers, and I wonder where on earth I will put them. The Jays, on the other hand, hand me a paper sack, which turns out to be filled with a large *courgette* (zucchini), several raw beets, and a few dusty-looking pears.

"Thank you, I think," I say, as we kiss all around. "And why am I being so honored with these delights?" In the kitchen, I manage to fill a vase with water and stuff the flowers in. Then I put them on the coffee table, stowing my library books underneath on the floor. The vegetables stay in the kitchen, but I rinse the dust off the pears and put them in the bowl with the fruit.

Jack explains, "Since we're leaving at the end of next week, we thought we'd have a last outing. So yesterday afternoon we took the *RER* out to Versailles. We spent about two hours out there, visiting the Royal Chapel and then just wandering around."

"They sell beets in the gift shop?"

"No, not at the château," says Jenny. "We also went to Louis XIV's vegetable garden, the *Potager du Roi*. You should see it! It's laid out just like it was in 1690, and now the national horticultural school operates it. So, the beets are from the boutique."

Actually, I am pleased to have the pears in the bowl. And this—meaning the train trip to Versailles—will (in hostess terms) give another topic for discussion during lunch. The *RER* (pronounced *air-er-air*) is the commuter rail network, stopping at major Paris *métro* stations and at its own in the suburbs. And for just slightly more than the price of a *ticket de métro*, you can go to Versailles, either *aéroport*, the stadium at St-Denis, the château at St-Germain-en-Laye, and even Napoleon's home at Malmaison, which he gave to Josephine upon leaving her and where he continued to address sweet letters to her even after that. (Was his last word really "Josephine"?)

By now it's *13h30,* and we are all wondering where the Lovells could be. "Call them," Jack says. I do. There's no answer. "Could they have forgotten?" I ask. "Should we be worried?"

"Not yet," says Margot firmly, although it is clear that we are all concerned. "Let me tell you about my morning." We turn our attention to her. "There's this elderly sculptor I know, who is known for carving only angels and saints," she says. "Muriel. That's her name. Today I met her to visit her *atelier* in the church of St-Sulpice. She took out some rusty old keys and opened a wooden door behind the Mary Chapel. We went in, and I followed her up a spiral staircase inside. Let me tell you, we trudged round and round up those stone steps, with only a rope against the wall to hold on to, and nothing on the other side. I'm sure if I had looked down, which I didn't, I'd have fainted dead out. And that old gal, Muriel, she kept talking all the way up, when I could hardly breathe. She says she's climbed those stairs twice almost every day for thirty years.

"Then at the top, she opened another one of those big old doors, and we went out onto a wide parapet. And right there, there was a little house. I couldn't believe it. A real, two-story house, with window boxes, an herb garden in clay pots, a dish drainer just behind the kitchen window. A cute little house hidden away on top of a church!"

"We've been in St-Sulpice so often and never even suspected such a thing!" Jack exclaims. "Was that the studio?"

"No. But someone does live there. I don't know who. Anyway, Muriel took another key and opened yet another weird door that opened into a paint-peeling hall and then finally into her *atelier*. Amazing. It must have been the *salon* in an elegant apartment a century ago. High ceilings, walls covered in faded silk, and there's a marble fireplace with a gold-framed mirror. Of course, the whole room now is cluttered with angels of all sizes and materials. And dust. She made me coffee on a little electric hotplate, and we talked about work as though we were anyplace in the world."

"What a great story," Anna says. "You know, I'm sure that no matter how long you've been in Paris, it seems there will always be something new to discover."

"Exactly," says Jenny, while we are all nodding our heads in agreement. "And tomorrow, Fran can discover beets."

"Speaking of eating," I say, picking up the phone to try the Lovells, again. Still no answer. "I hope they've just forgotten and that nothing is wrong." I am thinking the worst and know that everyone else must be, too. "But why don't we eat? I don't see what else we can do."

With everyone seated and making noises of appreciation as they pass around the serving plates, I take on my duties as hostess for real. "And you, Anna, what have you been discovering?"

"Just the French," says Anna, but it is clear she has been waiting to tell us her story, too. "You know I live over in the 7th. Well, last week, I noticed in rue Lourmel a locksmith claiming to be open on Saturday. So, on Saturday I went to have some keys made. Closed! Then late on Monday morning, I tried again. I was informed, though, by a young woman who refused to get off her *mobile* that I would have to come back at *15h*. So, I walked toward home, to the other side of the Champ de Mars, and found another locksmith. Okay, so by now it was 12:20, and the chap insisted I leave my keys and come back after *15h*. I said I couldn't do that because I wouldn't be able to get back into my apartment. Finally, he made the keys, and, of course, it took him no time at all. And it cost me sixty euros for four of those weird keys they have here."

"Be glad the keys worked," Margot says. "Sometimes the stories are a lot worse than that."

"But here's the good part. As I was walking across the Champ de Mars, I saw some sparrows splashing in a puddle, left over from that thunderstorm, remember? They were flapping around, and a few people had stopped to watch them." Anna nods. "Everyone was smiling and commenting, and it was so much fun."

"That's it!" I exclaim, realizing that I am still in my figuring-out-Paris mode (despite officially being a sloth, work-wise).

Miss S. would be so proud. "This is what I love so much here. Everything is an event. An amazing house on the top of a church or just watching birds in the park. How could anyone ever get bored?" Or restless, I wonder to myself.

Now the current event begins in earnest. Jack (almost immediately taking a second helping of the salmon-wrapped asparagus stalks) talks about a visit he and Jenny made over to the onion-domed Alexander Nevsky Cathedral in the 8th and the beautiful Russian icons they saw. Anna (taking a piece of bread and—*mon Dieu!*—putting it on her plate, not to the side) describes some of the concerts she's been going to as part of the city-wide summer festival. Jenny has seen Catherine Deneuve crossing rue Bonaparte, and this, of course, stops us in our tracks, bringing about a discussion of plastic surgery, as well as films we've seen (while Jack pours us all more wine). Margot (concentrating mostly on the jellied eggs) says how much she is enjoying Paris in August, now that the Marais is *tranquil*. And *moi*, content that the lunch isn't showing up any deficiencies in my hostessing, I pitch in about my upcoming barge trip and about how I'm counting the minutes until I can get away.

"I was thinking about that during Margot's story," Jenny says. "Last year, remember how we took one of those Jet Tour weekends and went to Barcelona, just to get away? To see the Sagrada Familia Cathedral? Well, Jack made it to the top of those winding stairs, but I finally had to slither back down. This year, though, we were so busy that we only did that one-day trip to Auvers-sur-Oise to visit the church Van Gogh painted and his grave."

Enough about churches. "Did you eat in the great restaurant there?"

"The Hostellerie du Nord?" Jack asks. "No, it's a little pricey for us these days, what with the low dollar and all."

"Yes, I know what you mean," I say, thinking that Jenny might be one of the few people I know actually benefiting from the dollar's decline. But I say nothing, of course, neither about apartments or politics. I do not want to spoil the lunch. Luckily, Jack finishes by saying, "But we had a great day, anyway, and I got to sleep in my own bed." He laughs. "Being serenaded by those blankety-blank church bells. I can't wait until we have our own apartment, here."

Jenny shoots me a glance but says nothing. "How's the hunt going?" I ask Jack brightly, not looking back at his wife.

"We're still looking," he says, happily. "We can't afford what we want this year, but I'm sure we'll find something next time." Jenny still says nothing, and neither do I. She stands to help me clear the plates.

The ripe cheeses (made extremely aromatic by the heat) are downed easily with the rest of the *baguette*, along with the fruit, which we all peel and eat with a knife and fork, even Anna, who may actually have learned something in the months she's been here.

Margot's brownies are a hit, and I am pleased to see there are a couple left for later on. Not being a coffee drinker, I have forgotten about buying any to serve after the dessert. Among the French, this could be a major *gaffe*, but today—all of us American—everyone is kind, and a chorus of "It's too hot for coffee, anyway" reassures me.

We sit around until just past *15h30*, when most people stand up to go. I am relieved they don't offer to help clean up, as they might in the States. My kitchen is too small for a crowd.

"Are you sorry to be leaving?" I ask Jenny, thinking about throwing away the *courgette* before I leave.

"Always," she says, and then looking at Jack, she amends it, "At least a little. But leaving always means we can have the anticipation of coming back." I get what she is saying, but Jack, looking at my bookshelves in the hallway, seems not to notice.

"Yes," Anna chimes in, "as Abigail Adams said, 'Nobody ever leaves Paris but with a degree of *tristeness*.'"

Jack comes back from the bookcase and says, "*Tristeness!* What a great word."

"That's right!" I say. "I remember that, too." I must use that somewhere.

"You've been talking to Caroline," Margot accuses Anna. "The trick is not to leave Paris, at all. And I think we're all hooked. Even Fran, although she'd never say so."

Before I can react, Anna says, "Yes, Caroline. She loaned me a book about the Embassy when she was giving me a tour around Place de la Concorde." Caroline gave Anna a tour? And she didn't tell me? Being in a generous frame of mind (two glasses of the Menetou-Salon will do that), I decide that she just forgot. I will email her that I forgive her.

We complete our kisses routine, and I give the Jays each a longer hug, since I won't see them again until I'm in New York at Christmas. I remember to mention that I am starting to look for a renter for my apartment in December and to keep me in mind if they hear of anyone looking.

As he walks out the door, Jack asks me to call right away when I hear from the Lovells, and I tell him I'll first try them again, and if there's no answer, I'll walk over to rue Guisarde and ring their bell. "If no one is home, I'll look for their landlord and see if he knows where they might be." So, last, with Anna blowing another kiss behind her, everyone but Margot leaves.

"Great afternoon," Margot says, as she picks up some dishes and walks the few steps into the kitchen. She looks around at the mess, puts the dishes down, and quickly backs toward the door. "You do the dishes," she says," and I'll entertain you with a joke I just heard."

"Shoot," I say. Margot loves jokes, but still being fairly new to email, she's entranced by jokes that most of us heard years ago.

"So, George Bush is studying the menu in a French restaurant in Washington. He considers every dish. When the buxom waitress comes over, she says, 'What would you like this evening,

Mr. President?" And George W. looks up and says, 'Well, miss, I'd like the quickie.' Whereupon his aide quickly whispers, 'Mr. President, that's pronounced *quiche.*'"

"Very good," I laugh, not telling her I had heard the same story years ago, then told about Bill Clinton. Caroline would be proud of my tact. But it does remind me to tell the joke to J-P (if he ever calls), for it would appeal to the French, one version being linked to the peccadilloes of an American president, about which the French would be quite tolerant, and the other about a president's intellectual inadequacies, about which they would never be. The French love wit, especially when it's at some politician's expense.

"So, let's talk about your book," I say to Margot, as I arrange the plates in the dishwasher. She is picking up her things and seems ready to go. "How will it be different from *Paris Noir*?" I ask, relieved that I had remembered to put it by the door to return it to her on her way out. When she loaned me her book, I had at that same time loaned her the diary of a Jewish hairdresser who hid in a maid's room in Paris while the Nazis had him on their deportation rolls. Margot said she had finished it, just as I said I had read every word of *Paris Noir*. (When she returned my book, I loaned it to hairdresser Michel, who seems now to be lending it to every other *coiffeur* in town. I'll probably never see it again.)

"What I have in mind is short, with chatty anecdotes, mentions of the streets and buildings where people lived, their dates, lots of their quotes about Paris. And with my own opinions." (Of course.) "Listen," she says. "Give me that *courgette* and the beets. I know you're not going to cook them, and I will."

"Oh to be so predictable," I say, gratefully handing her the sack. "Now, here's another question," I start, but then the phone rings. Even while picking it up, I know it's the call I've been dreading all afternoon. I am right. It's Alice. She is calling from the Pitié-Salpêtrière hospital to say that Findlay has had a stroke, and that he is out of the emergency room and in his own room in the neurology ward. And that she's sorry she didn't ring before.

Findlay on My Mind

"**F**INDLAY? A STROKE?" I ASK SOMEWHAT dumbly, for although I had been dreading the worst all afternoon, I am surprised. It has always been Alice who has seemed so frail. "What happened? How is he?"

"It was mild, and he'll be fine," Alice reassures me quickly. "This morning, while we were making breakfast, he got dizzy, said his legs wouldn't work. Ida was here for coffee, and she dialed 18 for the *pompiers* to come. I wanted to go to the American Hospital, but Ida knew the firemen who came, and they said Pitié-Salpêtrière was the best for strokes. But he was stable and already complaining on the way to the hospital. Hold on," she says, and I can hear Findlay's voice in the background.

"Findlay says to tell you that he's sorry he missed your lunch."

I mouth to Margot that Findlay has had a stroke but that he's okay, although gentlemanly apologies on his part do not sound normal to me. Margot whispers something back to me. "Margot's here," I say to Alice, "and she sends her best. Are you sure he's okay? Should I come over?" I ask, putting thoughts of Ida and firemen out of my mind, at least for the moment.

"Not today, thanks. I'm going home now, myself. But come tomorrow, maybe late morning, if you would. Visiting hours are then. I've called the kids, and they'll be here tomorrow, too. Perhaps you could bring a book and some magazines, and maybe a portable radio? You know how Findlay is about TV." I hear him say something in the background again, but this time Alice doesn't transmit.

"Of course I will," I say. "And I'll do whatever I can. And call me anytime if you need something."

As I hang up, my mind races. How best to get to the hospital from here? The No. 6 *métro*, the 87 bus? Will I be too laden down and have to fork up the euros for a cab? Do I call Caroline and the boys right away or wait until I've seen Findlay for myself? How long can Howard and Mark stay, given that this is their busy season at the spa? I hope I won't feel that I'll have to cancel my trip with the cousins, since just about everyone else in the gang who could help is out of town. This decision can wait until I size up the situation. Besides, there's always Ida.

"Luckily, it was mild," I say to Margot, recounting the story. "I'll go over to the hospital tomorrow."

"Do you think you'll have to postpone your trip?" Margot asks, as she opens the door to go out, we having kissed once again.

"Oh, I hadn't thought about that," I say with feigned surprise. "But now that you mention it, it doesn't look as though I'll have to, with Ida and their sons here. And I don't think I'll call Caroline until after I've been to the hospital." Margot nods in agreement, and she is out the door. I leave messages for the Jays and even Anna right away, for they are not yet home. And then I do turn on the radio, and listen to part of a drama on BBC 4, while I finish with the dishes and cleaning up.

The next morning, I do not pretend to work for long. I get myself ready to go. I put a paperback mystery—what Findlay calls a "penny dreadful"—and the radio into a tote bag, along with the two *brohnees* that I have decided to sacrifice to the cause. I do not mind lending Findlay the radio. I've always got the TV. And Findlay, as he would, hates TV.

Not I, at least not in France, where they don't ruin your concentration with commercials every few minutes, where people actually converse instead of showing car chases, where the quiz programs give books and pride as prizes, not zillions of bucks. And what about the prime-time documentaries that everyone watches, even I (until I fall asleep)? When I told J-P about my pleasant experience with *noos,* he said only that I must have been having a *look-y dey.*

I decide to buy a flowering plant for Findlay's room at the hospital, one light enough to take on the bus. But as I am rushing out the door, I run into a man I have never seen before standing right there on my landing. Immediate panic! But I quickly recover, for the middle-aged man, whose facial expression shows that he, too, is in a panic, says in Italian-accented French, "*Bonjour, signora.* It seems I have left my keys inside my apartment. I have just moved here, to the apartment above you. I do not know what to do."

Calm now, I ask, "Isn't there someone you can call?" This seems to me a reasonable question.

"My friend who owns the apartment, he is in Miami, and his *numero di telefono* is inside the apartment. And so is my *telefonino.*" His expression is now one of being hopelessly lost.

"And no one else has a set of keys?" I ask, already knowing the answer.

"No, I do not know anyone," he responds, and I give up ideas of the *fleuriste* for the moment.

The man, who is of an indefinite age (but certainly within shooting range), says he is Italian (as though I hadn't guessed), a businessman, and that he has come to Paris to try and put together some international deal. But in addition to being quite attractive and looking trim and fit, he looks decent—although, how would I know?—so, I tell him to come in while I look for the number of the *serrurier* (locksmith). I leave the door open, in case of what I do not know.

"Your *mobile* is in the apartment?"

"*Sì, signora,*" he says. "On charging. I was only going to be gone two minutes."

So, I pick up the phone to call. I could have given the guy the card with the locksmith number, but something tells me that the hapless fellow wouldn't know how to make a call. And that, given the Italian lunacy about cell phones, he also wouldn't have a *télécarte* to use in a phone booth.

In any case, the locksmith says he can arrive within the hour and will charge a minimum of seventy euros, depending on the lock. I inform the Italian. He winces. The locksmith is pressing, "*Oui ou non?*"

I ask, "*Oui* or *non?*"

Finally, *l'italien* says, "*Oui,*" and I say, "*Oui,*" so the *serrurier* says he is on his way. After I hang up, my neighbor says he only has with him a few euros and that he had been on his way to a *distributeur*. So, now, I also know that I am going to lend this stranger—who has with him no keys, no emergency number to call, and no money—seventy euros so he can get back home.

We make conversation at the door for a few minutes, in a combination of Italian, English, and French, which I find fun. Yet, striking as he is—tall, with curly gray hair, bright blue eyes, and that charming sheepish smile—I wonder how any grownup could let himself be so unprepared in a new city. Just as I am wondering that, however, Luca (as he tells me his name is) says, "I think I must leave an extra key with you, from now on." Perhaps he's not so feckless after all. I nod and then say I have to leave, and he says he will wait downstairs for the locksmith. We walk down the stairs together, and Luca says, "*Mille grazie, signora.*" I say he's welcome, and I am out the door. I do not ask him if he is single. I can—at least from time to time—show restraint.

As I stroll across the over to the bus stop for the No. 87, my bag is heavy with the radio and the penny dreadful. With only a "*Bonjour, monsieur,*" I pick up *l'Express* (the weekly French news magazine) and the European edition of *Time* at my *marchand de journaux*. I am also carrying an *hortensia* (hydrangea) from the florist. I am eager to help, but I'm already thinking of sitting in the shade in the park later on. I have brought some manuscript pages with me to review, meaning if I can stay awake.

I enjoy the bus ride as we turn onto boulevard St-Germain and then cross the river at the end of the Île St-Louis. Through part of the Marais and past the Place de la Bastille and the boat basin. I wonder about *Zho-elle* for a moment, remembering that he likes to look at the boats here. But he doesn't stay long in my mind, I notice, for we are nearing the terminus at the Gare d'Austerlitz and the Pitiè-Salpêtrière. Besides, I can't keep from wondering if a new project could be knocking at my door.

It will be interesting for me actually to go inside the hospital, which, of course, I researched for my original Paris book. It got top marks then, despite the fact that this is where Princess Diana died, but no one blames the hospital for that. *Moi,* I might once have gone straight to the American Hospital, where most of my doctors practice, for when I was setting myself up in Paris, my French could best handle groceries and ordering *mousse au chocolat*. But now, I've learned the vocabulary of ultrasound, chest x-rays, blood tests, and mammograms, and if I had to, I could handle telling in French where it hurts and how much, on a scale of one to ten. Nonetheless, on the bus, I think of what I wrote about the American Hospital in a previous book, and I wonder if it will still do.

Findlay is sitting up in bed when I enter the sun-filled room. He has a semi-private room, but there's no one in the other bed, which I suspect is better for everyone concerned. He looks a bit pale, a great contrast to how flushed his face has seemed in the past few months. "Did you bring the radio?" is the first thing he says to me, and his words are clear. Alice is here, sitting on a straight chair, eating a *croissant* and watching TV without the sound. I quickly dig out the radio and pass it over. Findlay smiles and uses the remote to turn off the TV. Alice shoots him a look. What this means to me is that the Lovells will be back to normal pretty soon. The barge trip is on, the calls to Caroline and the boys will be reassuring, and I don't have to think about Ida, not yet.

Sitting on the empty bed next to Findlay's, I tell the Lovells about my Italian neighbor and the keys, and I can tell that Findlay is off his form, for he does not counter about Italians having been better in the old days. This gives me a pang. In fact, after a while he waves us away so he can rest. Alice and I leave, crossing boulevard Vincent Auriol to sit at a sidewalk table outside a café and get a bite to eat. Here she lights up a Marlboro. Given the circumstances, I do not even give her a dirty look. Just as we are standing up to go, after each having happily consumed a half dozen extremely garlicky snails, a crunchy *baguette,* and split a half bottle of Chablis, we see her elder son, Mark, exit from the *métro*. We both call, "Mark! Mark!" He comes over and gives his mother a huge hug and me the normal *bisous.* So, I leave, promising to come back in the morning.

The bus ride back is just as quick, and I make a beeline for the Luxembourg. But finding not an empty chair near the fountain, and unwilling to share a bench with two drunks who, being gentlemen, have scooted over to offer me a place, I go home.

Before I can even peek upstairs to see if the lock on my Italian neighbor's door has been changed, I see leaning up against my own door a bouquet of flowers with an envelope tucked in. With admirable restraint, I wait until I am inside to read the card and to take out a fifty-euro note and a twenty that are tucked in. The card thanks me once again and includes Luca's telephone number, inviting me for a cup of coffee or an *apéritif*.

Another bouquet of flowers. I have no more vases. I put them in a pitcher. On the kitchen counter. They look nice there. And having studied the note twice for hidden meanings (none), I call Luca right away. It's only polite.

Luca immediately answers *"Pronto,"* in the Italian way. He sounds pleased to hear from me. We arrange to meet for a drink the next evening. He suggests going to Indiana on boulevard St-Germain, for he has discovered piña coladas there, and he says it is hard to find these exotic drinks in Bologna, his beautiful city in *Italia*. I had automatically been thinking of a *kir royal* but being a flexible sort (sometimes), I agree and that Luca should knock on my door at 7:00 p.m. I'll certainly be back from the hospital in time to doll myself up.

I settle in with the phone. Margot has left a message asking for an update on Findlay. I call back. "Did you take him the brownies?" she asks. Nobly, I say that I have. Jenny has also phoned, saying she will go to the hospital with me tomorrow if I am going. I call her back, and we agree to meet at the bus stop at Place St-Sulpice at *13h* to take the 87. "Let's not stay long," she says. "I've still got to finish my packing." Finally, I call Caroline, who

THE AMERICAN HOSPITAL OF PARIS

American Hospital of Paris: 63, boulevard Victor-Hugo 92202 Neuilly-sur-Seine (tel: 01.46.41.25.25; www. American-hospital.org; Bus No. 82). Full-service, private, not-for-profit hospital with multi-lingual personnel, accredited both in the United States and France. 24-hour emergency room, also equipped for dental emergencies. More expensive than Parisian hospitals but accepts Blue Cross insurance for inpatient services and provides forms for outpatient reimbursement of insurance. Credit cards accepted for some services. For people with French health insurance, it is *agréé* but *non-conventionné*, meaning that services such as lab work are covered by French insurance to some extent, but that the hospital itself is not part of the *Securité Sociale*.

The American Hospital was founded more than a century ago by two American doctors who wanted to offer tourists, students, and American residents the best medical care possible—from doctors who had trained in the States. During World War I, it established an ambulance service, and it provided care to some ten thousand soldiers. Expanding as its excellence became known, in World War II, under the Red Cross, it again provided care to wounded Allied soldiers. In recognition of its services during the War, France awarded the hospital the *Ordre de l'Armée* and *Croix de Guerre*.

Today the American Hospital is a thriving international center, with 200 beds and the most up-to-date equipment, continuing its mission to provide the best health care in both the American and French traditions. The hospital is well-maintained; there's an excellent restaurant and casual café, a gift shop, and even a quiet tea room for those times when you have to wait.

immediately gets worried when I say, "Don't worry, everything's fine." I bring her up to date, even telling her about Ida. I say nothing about Luca. Yet.

On the other hand, a few minutes later, I do tell Klaus in Viareggio that I've met an interesting Italian who has moved in upstairs from me. "Do nothing until we're back in ten days," he urges. "I know Italian men better than you." I remind him of my barge trip, and he is reassured.

My email has notes from both kids about Thanksgiving. My daughter says she can't come after all, so "Why don't you come to Toronto for Christmas?" she asks. But my son says they'll arrive early Wednesday and leave late on Sunday. I write back that I'll make reservations at a hotel in the neighborhood. The Recamier? The Bonaparte? The St-Germain? I'll work on it. I write my daughter back, confirming Christmas in Canada. My publisher briefly wishes me a good vacation. (What does this mean? Is she worried I won't make my deadline at the end of November?)

Then I glance at a note from my cousin, saying they can't wait to see me (more than I can't wait to see them?) plus a joke she got from her grandson. This one makes me laugh. *What does the zero say to the eight? Nice belt!* I delete a chain letter from a sort-of friend (but who won't be much longer if she keeps sending junk). And Jane—who has her laptop with her in the Alps—asks me to hold a date in mid-September because she and Edouard will have a party, *chez eux*. I mark it down in my *planning*. Lenore says she is back home now, taking French lessons, and is eager to come back. *Didn't she just leave?* When I answer her, I'll mention the *Potager du Roi* but not the dusty beets.

The next morning—after having slept later than usual—on the way to meet Jenny, I stop at my local *pharmacie* to pick up a few items that Alice has asked for. Jenny, as she would be, is on time, waiting at the bus stop. And, rare for the No. 87, it comes right away. We get on and settle ourselves in, getting ready to chat during the ride. I decide not to mention my Italian neighbor, although the evening to come is certainly present in my mind.

Then as the bus takes off, I do, too. "Jack seems content with the summer," I say. "Do you think you've convinced him that moving here is not a good idea?"

"I doubt it, but I don't know."

"You haven't asked him?"

"Fran," she says, and turns from the window to look at me directly, "I'm going to be like you. I'm not going to ask questions when I don't want to know the answer. And I've got until next summer not to think about it." I get the hint. I shut up.

At the hospital, seeing that Findlay is clearly doing well, we stay only a half hour before heading back. Mark has gone back north, but Howard is now here, so I feel comfortable about leaving for my trip. At the end of our bus ride, Jenny and I walk up to the Luxembourg and get a cold drink from one of the kiosks, and we sit in the shade until she says that Jack will be waiting for her. They are going up to Sacre Coeur for one last look at the mosaics before they leave. We kiss our farewells once again, promising to see each other at Christmas when I'm in New York. I sit a few moments to people-watch. Then I walk home, noting that the gentlemanly bums from the day before are nowhere to be seen.

Luca is exactly on time, ringing my doorbell at 7:21 p.m. He is Italian, after all. His hair is wet and sort of slicked down, given all the (delightful) curls, and he is wearing a flowery short-sleeved shirt and khaki pants. Nice arms. Despite knowing the odds, my hopes for the evening and, of course, the rest of my life are at a high.

"How is your friend; he is better?" Luca asks as we walk out the door into the quiet cobblestone street, and the evening is off to its start. *C'est parti.* The evening has begun.

As we head for boulevard St-Germain and the crowded sidewalk-terrace at Indiana, I think about these American-style establishments that are so popular here, especially with the younger French and with American tourists, as well—Joe Allen, Susan's Place for Tex-Mex, and several soul food places that Margot says she likes from time to time. Yet, I've passed Indiana hundreds of times, and I've never had the desire to go in.

It isn't that I adhere to the culinary doctrine of the boys. Often I want real American food, like spaghetti, sushi, and General Tso's Chicken. And even Edie succumbs occasionally to a hamburger, such as on Independence Day. "We're only following in footsteps," Caroline rationalized during one of our burger runs. Didn't Thomas Jefferson's garden grow "American" vegetables from seeds he had sent over from home? And didn't Thomas Edison, when he was here in 1889 for the Universal Exhibition, host an American dinner for Buffalo Bill with roast beef, baked beans, peanuts, and apple pie, topped off with good old American coffee and the passing of his hip flask all around?

So, when in the course of our conversation and sipping our second piña coladas, Luca asks me if I know a good place for pizza or pasta, of course I do, and I am pleased (ecstatic) that dinner has now been added on. In between the incessant ringing of his *telefonino*, which requires him to chatter rapidly in Italian—something about a check not having deposited somewhere in time for something—we converse about Italy and New York and Paris and his late wife and his son and about my kids and what I do and how he taught economics at The University of Bologna—the oldest university in the world—for thirty years. But he skirts talking about the pending big deal, which I find just a little strange. We leave Indiana after we have downed two drinks, which, I realize when I stand up, were stronger than I am used to. I pray it doesn't show. I am having a very (very) good time.

In any case, there are two Italian eateries near boulevard St-Germain, so we decide on Vesuvio, which is closer, Luca taking my elbow to steer me across the street (and not because I am drunk). We each order our own little pizza and a salad, and we share a bottle of red wine. And, making sure I don't embarrass myself silly, I also order a bottle of San Pellegrino. The evening is a success. I wish Caroline were home.

"Let us meet again, very soon," Luca says as he leaves me at my door, and he actually kisses my hand. "Call me when you have time free. Call me anytime. My telephone is always on."

I wait two days. I call. If we're going to see each other again before I leave for Douai, it has to be today. Luca answers immediately, and says he is in a meeting, but that he will knock on my door at seven o'clock. I wish it were *19h* right now. But where will we go? While I am getting out my suitcase and organizing everything for the boat, I contemplate a walk in the Luxembourg, or a stroll along the *quai,* and then a glas of champagne, perhaps on one of those restaurant boats that are docked below in the Seine. Sunset on the river always appeals. I am in high romantic gear. As I did once in the spring, I say to myself, "Well, well, well."

By 18h30 I am ready, having packed efficiently, showered, and made myself irresistible to all men by wearing my spiky heels, a short skirt, a low-cut tee shirt, and earrings like Ida's that would pull down my ears in later life if I wore them a lot. I dust off that biography of Napoleon's son, hoping to finish it, all the while keeping an eye on the clock, at least until I realize that it is now late, even for an Italian. Just before eight o'clock I call, but there is no answer. I do not leave a message. His phone is not on, and I think he has forgotten our date. By eight, I am sure. I open the last of my low-fat microwave popcorn and snap open a Stella Artois, a lager beer. Now, especially, would have been the right time for those *brohnees*. I throw out all the flowers, which will surely die before I get back from the boat. I crunch them into the garbage bag with great force.

All evening I try to concentrate on the poor Duc de Reichstadt, all but abandoned by his mother Marie-Louise who, having had several illegitimate children, married her lover the moment she heard that Napoleon had died. And for this he dumped Josephine? Even dictators need some sympathy sometimes, I think. My phone doesn't ring.

This next morning, I am relieved to be getting out of town. I wait until I hear Luca's door open, and then, as I hear his footsteps above me, I begin to slam my suitcase step by step down the stairs. This is just what I want, because I have been practicing sarcastic comments in my head all morning. I slow down, so he can catch up.

"Oh, the charming *Francesca*," Luca says with that toothy smile that I am now prepared to hate. "You are going with your cousins today? Here, let me take your *valigia*." He lifts my suitcase but then puts it down and looks at me. "I thought we were to have a drink this evening," he says, and I can see he is puzzled and disappointed. "Perhaps my English is not so good, and I have misunderstood." All sarcastic comments go immediately out of my head. It's a good thing. I probably wouldn't have said them, anyway.

Two Weeks in September

MY COUSINS DO THEIR BEST TO persuade me to stay through the end of a second week, and I am tempted. But gliding on a boat through mysterious kingdoms (or so it seems to me), enjoying ten guilt-free days—well, they have done their trick. I may not have gone far, but I feel as though I've been away and so I am ready for Paris to beckon, as she does, once again. All the way north in Flanders, I can hear her luring me in with her siren's voice. Or perhaps it is just that with a new project realistically in mind (another kiss of the hand that last morning on the stairs was all the proof I needed), it is best to be home and get on with it. Thus, having expressed my thanks with kisses all around and having agreed on another trip next spring, I roll my suitcase behind me to the station in Courtrai (Kortrijk in Flemish), and I take the little choo-choo to Lille, where I change to the fast TGV train home.

But why in my great wisdom I have chosen to come back from these ten days away on the most crazed Sunday of the year, I cannot begin to fathom. This is the weekend of the famous *rentrée* (the re-entry after the summer). This is the last gasp of August, foretelling a new beginning, when children prepare for the new school year, when political and social life are energized to once again do whatever it is they do. This is the weekend when cars on the *autoroutes* are backed up for miles, when trains are like cattle cars, when the *métro* is a jumble of rucksacks and shopping bags, and the smells of the tired and sweaty, all returning at this last moment from their *vacances*. Fortunately, having at least over the years gained some craftiness, I have my train reservation in hand, and I have a window seat from which I can wonder about the lives I am passing by. Unfortunately, my seatmate snores all the way back, and the peaceful feeling of my week away is hard to sustain. But I do. This, after all, is the first day of the rest of my life.

Of course, even on the boat, I was distracted sometimes, practicing the Italian language in my head instead of French. This was not for naught, for as per Luca's desire, I called him on my *mobile* one afternoon, while my cousin was peeling something or other in the kitchen below deck and the captain (her husband) was passed out above on a chair under a large white awning, tight asleep. Luca twice wished me *Buona vacanza,* but he also asked twice just when I would arrive back home.

Perhaps my description of the trip would not exactly match that of my cousins, but this is my version, of course. Having hugged and kissed at the Douai train station, we got back to the boat in time (after having unhitched the lines and started moseying up the canal) for the late morning "pick-me-up," which took us into the white wine with lunch, the "drinkee" when the August sun was nowhere near the yardarm, and finally the red wine with the dinner my cousin had prepared with great attention to the placement of parsley sprigs, and which we also ate under the broad white awning spanning the deck. The dinners were hearty and the wine always red.

Actually, if we're talking facts, the days—pleasantly sunny and not too hot—were spent gliding along canals and rivers, maneuvering through locks and around swinging bridges. I always love that boat! As "Number 3" on the crew, I sometimes steered the ninety-foot boat, I put the lines to moor us in the locks and then coiled the ropes back up, and I swabbed the deck. And in the evenings I stacked the dishwasher, all without thinking that any of this was "work." I only checked my Blackberry at night, when everyone else was asleep. We moored at the edge of small towns such as Armentières, made famous in World War I by that "Franglish" song, "*Mademoiselle from Armentières, parley-vous?*" There, having fixed our lines and strolled at lunchtime to a local pub, I was touched by a memorial to the civilians shot or asphyxiated during that war, when chemical weapons meant mustard gas. As I sometimes do when I pass those sad memorial plaques in Paris, I suddenly teared up. I don't think my cousin noticed, I'm relieved to say, for she seems to feel it her duty to let me know just how peculiar she thinks Americans are—or maybe it's just me. ("Peanut butter?" she once exclaimed. "Not in my house!") At that pub meal and others, we dished about people we knew or didn't (going back a hundred years). Late into the evenings we played board games without keeping score, and at the close of each day, I slept without moving an inch.

Sometimes, standing on the foredeck, waiting for the gates to a lock to open so I could put the line to moor us once we had glided within, the uncertainties in my life would rise within me as surely as the water filling the lock. But it was always more immediate to watch the water rise to the point where I would unhitch and signal to the captain that we were free to move out, to wave thanks to the lockkeeper, to marvel with my cousin about the beautiful flowers (what on earth were they?) along the banks. And to go back into the deckhouse to help do whatever had to be done. I kept wondering why I don't go away more often. And then I considered that perhaps it's because generally—occasional restlessness notwithstanding—I find living in Paris already being constantly "away." And this is another reason why I am so glad to be back.

I can't wait to tell all to the gang. About docking in a village called Wambrechies in Flanders and the three of us walking to the jenever distillery there (offering sips of Genièvre aux 4 Fruits during the telling). That charming *port fluvial* where we had docked, the nineteenth-century tourist office, the ancient château, and best of all, that old gin distillery. The gleaming vats and pipes, the cavern-like tasting room, the tasting, (the tasting even more) and the buying, of course. The staggering back to the

boat and the delicious nap. In years past when I have gone on the
boat with my cousins, sometimes I thought I'd surely come back
to some intriguing place we explored, but so far I never have.

But now my apartment is cool and dim with the curtains
closed. I see that a note has been slipped under the door. Call
Luca. *Oui*! As soon as I throw everything down and open the
windows, I dial his *mobile,* realizing that Caroline, who has emailed
to my Blackberry that she is home, has become second on my list
of calls, the boys having slipped back to third. He answers on
the first ring. *"Finalmente!"* he exclaims. "Can we have a drink and
dinner tonight, *Francesca, per favore?*" he asks, and would I tell him
all about my trip? I should choose the restaurant where I'd like
most to go.

Thinking guiltily of Caroline, who might be assuming a dinner
with me, I nonetheless accept. *"Volontiere,"* I say in Italian, since
it worked so well with Joël in French. "Come by sometime
after seven o'clock." This time I'm sure he'll show up. This is
getting good.

I then call Caroline, who says she is on the diet to end all
diets. She enjoyed the beach and her friends but ate too much, and
now she's really serious about losing weight. (I say nothing, for
I've seen these huge blink-of-an-eye diets before.) She is working
again, reading about the American artist Man Ray, who spent
much of his life here. "Yeah, I know about Ray," I say, quickly, for
although his works—like other of the Dada artists—make me
marvel at their humor, I don't want to hear about him, now.

I am patient enough to hear about her trip, about how
beautiful France is, who's back and who isn't, that Findlay at
home has Alice climbing the walls, and that she has committed us
to taking dinner over there next week. But eventually, I need to
spit it all out.

"Listen, Caroline," I say with a bit of trepidation. She has,
after all, seen my own projects come and go in that same blink of

an eye. "I've got something big to tell you." And I blurt it all out, both about Luca in general and my dinner for tonight.

"Oh, sweetie. I'm so pleased for you," Caroline says. She is so kind. "Besides, I wasn't sure when you were coming back, and I'm having dinner with Margot tonight to talk about artists who lived here, like Ray and Alexander Calder, too."

"Wonderful," I say with relief that I hope Caroline does not pick up. So, now, I become eager to check in with Klaus and Paul and get on with my day. But we ring off in our usual manner, making arrangements to meet at the Café de la Mairie for an omelet the next afternoon. "No fries," she says. "Or maybe just one."

Actually, I do hope Caroline will tell me more about Ray, the only American to be accepted into the Dada and Surrealist movements here, for art with such whimsy gets my vote. After that walk with Richard in June, when I was limping so crankily home down rue Dauphine, I saw in the window of a gallery a small, white, wooden box. Above a bright red horizontal line were flashing colored lights, sequined spinning whirligigs, dancing red pinwheels, and pulsing polka dots. Inked at the top was the French word for woman, *femme*. Below the horizontal line, centered in a seemingly vast empty white space, was simply an on/off switch. And inked at the bottom, the word for man, *homme*. For some reason the gallery was closed, or I would have gone in, and to use Sandy's phrase, snapped it up. It would have cheered me up, but I no doubt would have been tired of it by now.

When I call the boys, Paul answers right away. I thought he might, since the library is closed on Sundays and Mondays. He had been wondering when I would call. He tells me about their time in Rome—the museums, the *gnocchi* in the *piazze* under the spreading white umbrellas, and the evening with old friends from the ballet, but he admits that both he and Klaus had been ready to come back. In his more precise way, he echoes Klaus' comment by saying, "By the way, I know Klaus informed you that Rome is no longer a possibility. But we'll still have to think about what to do over the winter. Now, please, relax. You were so tense all spring." Will I join them for lunch tomorrow, he wants to know, but I can't. I ask nothing about what "what to do over the winter" means.

"How about Tuesday?" Paul asks. "Can you meet us at Kim Lien, that Vietnamese restaurant at Place Maubert? After all that pasta, I have a hankling for Vietnamese food." Certainly, I will, already considering the bus route, although I am thinking I should walk.

"A hankling?" I ask, trying not to laugh, but not succeeding. "To whom am I speaking, here? Paul or Klaus?"

"Oh, my word," Paul sighs. "My word." We agree to meet at *13h* and, I realize, suddenly overcome, how much I've missed them, not just this summer but also during the spring, when I was being such an idiot

Finally, I reach Alice (I did call twice from the boat, helping keep guilt at bay), who tells me about the ambulance driver who carried Findlay up the five flights of stairs, although her husband grumbled the whole time that he could walk just fine. "I've walked these stairs since before you were born," he had said to the driver, who agreed pleasantly, Alice reports, but who carried him up nonetheless. "Now he is convinced both that he's fine and that he's going to die any minute, so he wants to dictate his memoirs to me all the time." Alice laughs. "I may have to call in the troops." I assure her that Caroline and I stand at the ready, which is true.

I check my voice mail. Richard in California says he has something to tell me. (He, who took Ida to Favela Chic?) My son says that he had to change the reservation and that he and his wife will arrive early Thanksgiving morning in time for the big meal, still leaving late on Sunday. My daughter first leaves a message saying she is excited I'm coming for Christmas and to drag out my woolies, and then asking where am I, anyway? Jenny says they are home and that she and Jack are looking forward to seeing me in December. (No hidden messages that I can hear.) Anna asks whether I'd like to go with her to the Musée de l'Eventail, a museum for fancy fans. (Is this for me?) Mitzi says she has a conflict, and would I host the book club *chez moi* at the end of the month? (No.) Colette says she's back and leaves her number to call. And totally flooring me, Ida herself, speak of the Devil, leaves a message saying only, "Fran, it's Ida. Call me."

I glance through the mail. I discard the flyers. A postcard from La Rochelle says J-P will be back on Friday and perhaps we could have dinner when he gets back? (Making up for neglecting me.) A notice from the library says the biography of Carson McCullers is overdue. A reminder of book club at Mitzi's toward the end of the month. There is a statement from France Télécom. I set it aside to record in my checkbook, since the amount will be deducted automatically from my bank account. A brochure from the bank suggests investing in a fund that would certainly make them a lot of money. A slick booklet from Dior almost convinces me that I will be beautiful this fall if I buy all the products therein. And the synagogue asks how many tickets I need for the High Holy Days and how many of the services I would like to come to. This requires deliberation. What is the minimum I can do and still feel somewhat spiritual? Perhaps this is not the right way to look at it.

But this reminds me that I must get busy with the newsletter, so I email the rabbi and suggest we have a lunch somewhere in the Marais, where he can get kosher food, and where I haven't been all year. I still have not forgotten that falafel that Richard and Freifeld had in May.

As I go out just after *13h* to check the market before it closes, *la rentrée* is in the air. Officially, it is *la rentrée des classes*, referring to the beginning of the school year. But most people just say *la rentrée,* as my hairdresser, Michel, did before he departed for parts unknown. (It's better that way, since he once regaled me with a description of his *vacances* in a French nudist colony.) Instead of saying *À bientôt,* he said, *"À la rentrée."* I make a mental note to *prendre rendez-vous* for a haircut, to call the *dentiste* to get my teeth cleaned, and also my *généraliste* for my yearly checkup.

As I walk and look around my lovely old *quartier,* I remember (yet again) those Steinly words that "Paris is my hometown and it is as it has come to be." The restaurants have reopened, some having been spruced up during their *congé.* The familiar stalls have reopened in the *marché St-Germain,* and shoppers are once again using their wheeled carts as weapons. The streets are deadly with cars, Sunday notwithstanding. I peek into the *gymnase* and see that the pool is open and crowded. Energy has hit Paris once again.

After trying on three different outfits, I look satisfactorily smart (sexy but demure) by the time Luca arrives at *20h.* His curly hair is wet and slicked down, and he smells like talc, so I know he, too, has gussied himself up. He is at his most attractive best. And happily for me, he thinks the same, for when I open the door, he says right away, *"Madonna!* You look lovely tonight, *Francesca."*

We have now progressed to the point where we stroll together arm in arm in the pleasant September evening over to the Place de l'Odéon and ensconce ourselves on the terrace of La Mediterranée, that fish restaurant the boys frequent after going to the theater across the square. I notice when Luca switches into Italian, which he does from time to time, that he has already started to *darmi del tu,* speaking to me in the familiar. (Leaving formality, thank heavens, to the French.) We begin by ordering champagne; we choose our *entrée* and *plat;* and Luca asks me to pick a nice French wine, he knowing only those from Italy.

"White?" I ask, grateful that we'll be eating fish so I can sound somewhat suave. I think of John *can-see* Adams and ask, "How about a Quincy?" He nods and tells the waiter what we would like. And, again, a bottle of San Pellegrino. I must avoid the giggles, if I can.

But just as I lift my glass for a toast, Luca's *mobile* rings, and he has a spirited conversation in Italian with someone he calls *Dottore*, while he shrugs sheepishly at me to indicate that he has to take this call. Upon hanging up, he dials another number and in a variety of languages says, "*Bambino!* Have you done it? *Alors*, do it, *per favore*. And call me *dopo*." This kind of cryptic conversation happens throughout the meal, which I enjoy, for the *cabillaud* is as flaky as cod should be, but which would have been better had I not been eating somewhat alone. I do still like the Quincy, and I notice that Luca is managing to down his share in between bites of fish and imprecations on the phone.

All this notwithstanding, we linger after dessert almost until the restaurant closes, he drinking his *expresso* and then a cognac, and I drinking a Mandarine Napoléon orange liqueur. His phone no longer rings, so we talk as though we had to start from Adam and Eve, and we wonder about Life. (A man who takes stock? Is this karma, or what!) Finally, as we notice the restaurant emptying, Luca signals for the check, and we stand up in the warm evening air. Fortunately, his phone is still in his pocket as we stroll back home along rue du Vaugirard, again arm in arm. With his free hand, Luca covers mine.

As we enter our building and we start walking up the stairs, I consider, as I have all day, inviting him in. The truth is that while I was doing my errands and getting myself organized, I was also practicing my opening gambit in Italian. Now I am ready to try it out. As we reach my floor, he smiles at me and squeezes my arm. I take this as an advance in the situation.

As I start to open my door, however, his *telefonino* rings and, shrugging once again, he answers it and says impatiently, "*Sì, sì, Bambino*, I'm home now. Did you give it to him? *Non? Pourquoi pas?*

Give me just a moment." He smiles that same apologetic smile, says he has to go, and please would I call him tomorrow, for he'll be waiting for my call. He bends to kiss my hand, looks up at me, says only, *"Francesca,"* and then kisses the hand again. And he is gone up the stairs. Disappointed (to say the least) and with the opening gambit dying on my lips, I decide to wait a few days before I call. And why is it that he can't call me?

Nonetheless, Monday morning comes. Vacation is a thing of the past. Work starts, and I suppose I'm ready. I write my editor that I am back (to keep her calm). I am all too aware that my deadline is in just about three months. I organize my dwindling list of places to check, my chapters, my notes. But I wonder. Have I begun to understand anything deeper about Paris than the new Tramway No. 3? (Twenty-five million riders in its first year.) When I have made my visits, narrowed my choices, filled my quotas, what will I have learned? Does the 17th *arrondissement* being spruced up mean anything in the scheme of things? I put these thoughts aside and refocus my attention. There are more restaurants to try and then the winnowing them down (to a precious few). Also, I better go see that Josephine Baker swimming pool floating in the Seine down in the 13th before Paris gets cold and dark. I'll reward myself by traversing the footbridge to the park at Bercy and getting lunch at Chai, and maybe even seeing a film at the twenty-screen cinema at the end of the charming cobblestone arcade. Yes, I will go next week. Actually, it's clear to me that I can't wait for this all to be done. To edit and polish. To wrap it up. I'm ready to be thinking of something new.

As I walk over to the Café de la Mairie, I feel impatient, that old edginess of needing to get on with things, to have them settled once and for all. I will it to pass. So, I don't mention it to Caroline, as we dig into our omelets. Instead, she wants to know everything about the new project. But slightly uneasy, I just say, "He's fun. Interesting, too. We always seem to have a lot to talk about. He's a widower, and he's tall and quite good-looking. Slightly mysterious, too. He's involved with some big business deal. I'll probably see him again later in the week."

"Is your house clean, sweetie?" Caroline asks somewhat mischievously.

"Of course, it is," I laugh. "But he has yet to see it."

"Well, at least that means it's serious."

"We'll see," I say, hoping that she's right, but unwilling to admit it, not even to myself. Then I move to surer ground. Asking about Alexander Calder, Caroline then tells me he arrived in 1926 on a creaky freighter that he helped repaint.

"Did you know," Caroline asks, clearly a rhetorical question, for there's little about Calder that I know. "Did you know that he first began experimenting with wire models here and that one of his earliest works was of Josephine Baker? Margot told me that yesterday."

"Can you imagine capturing that sexy figure with just a bunch of wires?" she goes on, and then laughs as she picks up a *frite* (french fry) from my plate. "Wiry is not a word that anyone would ever use about me." I think this is the shortest diet I have ever seen Caroline take on (and I feel guilty about not telling the waiter to skip my *frites*). *Moi,* I will definitely walk to the lunch with Klaus and Paul.

At Kim Lien this next day, the gang of three orders *raviolis vietnamiens, bo bun,* and *phö*, which is as good as in the *gargote* in Belleville that Richard schlepped me to (whose card is buried in my files). I present them with a bottle of the Genièvre aux 4 Fruits, and they are pleased. But because Klaus is bursting, we first talk about Rome, which he says is now becoming more international, and that people seem to be feeling optimistic.

"Then why did you decide it was out?"

Paul smiles. "It rains there, too, you know. But perhaps we should review those reasons why Paris suits us," he says. "The total comfort. The beauty. The stimulation, even at our age. On the other hand, there's something to be said for looking for sunny days in those long, dark winters."

"Oh, not now, Paul," Klaus begs. "Let's save all that for another time. I want to talk about our trip."

So, I hear about Viareggio, its beach and the sea, and walking along the promenade alongside those Italian couples arm in arm. I hear about the restaurant da Bombetta and its seafood appetizers (which, remembering my own meal there years ago, makes my mouth water, even while eating my *bo bun*). I hear about their Italian friends and the spaghetti party on the *balcone* at midnight, what they call the *spaghettata*. But, of course, I have in the back of my mind those words about "long, dark winters." Again, I feel no particular reaction. I simply cannot take on worrying right now.

And then it is my turn. I describe my lunch for the Jays, the scare with Findlay, and, last, those enchanting days on the boat. I am also more forthcoming about Luca and his mysterious dealings on the phone than I was with Caroline. I tell all the details (barely able to contain myself, in fact). Paul looks at Klaus, who raises his eyebrows and then takes my hand. "We're reserving judgment," he says. "But if he hurts you, darling, we'll obliviate him."

The boys are clearly back in the swing. Paul says that, after lunch, they will stroll back over to the Pantheon—that great domed building built by Louis XV to thank the saints for having recovered from being ill. Many French famous *personages* (those who didn't recover?) are entombed there. I walk with them for a few minutes and then say I really should be picking up the novel for the book club meeting over at the Village Voice. It is *Waiting for the Barbarians* by Coetzee, a book I am happy to read again. Paul says to say hello to Odile; we kiss more fervently than usual; and we decide to get together on Saturday afternoon for an outing that they will suggest.

"The last time you suggested something," says Paul with a smile, "it was the apartment where Lenin had lived and that's now a museum. Remember? I think you should leave the outings to us." He's right. I'm as bad as Anna and the museum of historical fans. I must call her back. At the bookshop, Odile and I chat a few minutes, and I mention casually that I will have a new book out at the beginning of next year. She gets the point about stocking it.

So, I start to work again, in earnest. I mean, what else can I do? I let myself get absorbed again. I actually go swim in the Josephine Baker pool, and I have lunch afterward at Chai, which is so trendy that no one notices my hair is not slicked with pomade, but simply wet. I write about the Museum of Decorative Arts that has been so exquisitely restored, but also the Magic Museum for kids (which makes me laugh). And as I do each autumn, I collect the materials I need to renew my own *carte de séjour*, which expires in six weeks, and I send them off to the *Préfecture*. I am ready for whatever challenges *la France* will throw my way (except for the long line in October when I go to pick up the *carte*).

I will myself to get back into the *r.d.v.* (*rendez-vous*) swing. I bite the bullet. I get an appointment right away at the *coiffeur*; I *prends rendez-vous chez le dentiste* for mid-October to get my teeth cleaned; and my doctor's receptionist reminds me to pick up the *vaccin antigrippale* so I can get my flu shot during my annual checkup. She will also send me authorizations for blood tests and that sort of stuff. I realize with some surprise that I won't even have to report a hangnail this year. Perhaps I am doing something right, after all? Unlikely. It's probably just luck.

I also call Colette, and using my best French (I hope) we plan a lunch for next week. "I have to be near Concorde in the morning for an appointment, *Frahn*," she says (not blurting out what kind of appointment, the way I would). "So, shall we have lunch on the Champs-Elysées?"

"How about Mood?" I ask. "I love Mood."

"I ate there just last week," Colette says. "But do you also like Flora Danica? The fish is exceptional, and it's generally quiet at lunch, so we can talk."

Do I! I had forgotten about it, but now I remember how much I love the salmon there. A Danish restaurant, so I might not put it in my book, but when I do remember it, I like it a lot. Salmon in every different form possible and a *degustation* plate so you can try several at once. So, I say as usual, *"Volontiers!"* and we agree to meet there at *13h* on Thursday. To ingratiate myself a little, I tell her how much I like the lemon squares she brings to book club.

And last, during a telephone call that I knew I had to make, Ida at the embassy tells me what I already know about Findlay and Alice. Since it is the *rentrée,* I decide to rise above my cynicism and invite her to lunch. Surprisingly, she accepts and suggests that on Monday, when she won't be working, we go to the basement café of Monoprix. A week should give me time to gear myself up toward pleasantness.

In the midst of my own calls, Reb Tom calls me. We fix a date to have tea late one afternoon in the Marais, close to where he lives, since he is swamped at work, getting ready for the New Year holidays. No falafel. And just what have I taken on?

So, anticipating my annual confab at the doctor's after my test results are ready (meaning as soon as I work up the courage to have them done), I manage to swim three afternoons in a row. My route takes me easily—and without any qualms—through rue Guisarde, where I either wave to silver-haired Joël or stop for a moment to chat. Still with wife, but sounding less sure. (Officially, I do not notice.) I wait for J-P to call and for a decent interval to reach Luca. One afternoon, I finally do go to the 17th, which I admit is looking better than it used to, and afterward, I treat myself to browsing the upscale shopping center at the Porte Maillot. I buy nothing, thinking both of the low dollar and the January sales. And so it goes. "Decent interval," by the way, means just how long I can stand not making that call. I manage until Thursday but then only get to leave a message on Luca's *mobile,* saying, "It's *Francesca,*" and please call.

No call. What does this mean? But I soldier on, and on Saturday afternoon just after lunch as planned, I meet Klaus in front of the imposing church in Place St-Sulpice. Unfortunately, Paul called in the morning to say that he was under the weather with a *crise de foie* (that liver thing, again). He then made me promise—no matter where Klaus and I decided to go—not to let the dear boy buy too much.

So in the afternoon we meet on the steps of the four-hundred-year-old church. After taking a look at the Delacroix frescoes in the Angel Chapel to the right of the entrance, we take a hurried tour around, and then I suggest a brief visit to the Delacroix Museum over in Square Furstemberg. Again, no doubt because Klaus is impatient to shop, this does not take long. So, we take the *métro* back at Mabillon, getting off at La Motte-Piquet Grenelle, heading for the Village Suisse, a warren of antique stalls on avenue de Suffren. Now, Klaus is itchy as all get out. We don't visit all hundred dealers—although I am sure it's in the cards—but Klaus does buy a small, charming landscape oil painting that may well be the bargain he says it is. One painting should not put me in the doghouse with Paul.

"Let's go sit down," Klaus says, and I can see he is getting tired. So, we laze a bit on the *terrasse* of Le Suffren, a café across from École Militaire, close to UNESCO, and feeling so content, I think for a moment of that picnic with Jane when I was so blue, but whose party tomorrow I am greatly looking forward to. Klaus has a *citron pressé* and I a Badoit.

Settled in at the table, Klaus talks about French antiques, and I listen (off and on), for he knows his stuff. Then together, we muse more about Rome. One of my million-dollar ideas hits me, and I suggest planning a trip together for next summer. It's time

I saw Rome again. And maybe Bologna at the same time? (Reality at bay, including the no-response to my call, I am still totally optimistic, Luca-wise.) "Oh, little darling," he answers, "we'd be so thrilled."

We also talk about the upcoming weekend of *les Journées du Patrimoine*, the one weekend each year when *la France* opens its public palaces for the public to view. This year the guys are planning a visit to the Palais de l'Elysée, the president's residence. Because they both have *cartes prioritaires* issued to elderly residents, they never have to stand in a line. Not wait? Thinking of my own line at the *Préfecture* in late October, I say I will come, too.

I leave Klaus at the bus and dash home to check my messages. I am flooded with relief. Luca's voice, warm and intimate, says he is so sorry that he is in Lyon and will be there over the weekend and then well into the coming week. He has missed me, and he'll call me immediately upon his return. And in Italian, he says not to forget him, *Francesca, per favore*. His tone of voice tells me what I want to know. I will not need the opening gambit, after all.

So, late on Sunday, for Jane and Ed's party, I trundle down to la Butte aux Cailles (Quails Hill) in the 13th. It's another of those traditional areas that tourists rarely see, but should. If you want to see Paris as the working-class village that it once was, come and walk on the narrow cobblestone streets, see its Art Deco ambience, and sit down at one of the now-trendy cafés and just look around. When I get off the *métro* and start walking on the hilly streets with their low-rise old buildings and local shops, I am, as usual, carried away. Several *quartiers* in Paris can still sweep me into reveries of other times, whether I ever knew them or not. Paris is still Paris, here.

Do the immigrants who crowd the high-rises in the adjoining *quartier*—that of Tang Frères and *dim sum* at Tricotin—care that the river Bièvre once flowed here or that textile factories tossed so much waste into the waters that about a hundred years ago the city finally had to cover the river up? Unlike me (and Findlay, of course), they are probably not entranced by what is now trivia of the Paris past. I keep remembering Alice's phrase, that it's only history now. And frankly, it's not even important enough for more than a small mention in my book. Come here. Look around. Then go a few blocks farther for the city's best Asian food.

Most of the people at the party are Edouard's boyhood friends and wine bar *habitués*. Besides Jane and her parents who are visiting from Scotland, I am the only Anglophone around, Richard—the only other person from our group whom Edouard knows well— still being away. I sit for a while with Jane's mother, who says she is claustrophobic and never takes the *métro*, doesn't speak French, and is a vegetarian. She may also have never bought a new dress in her life. So, sitting between her and Ed's mother and aunt, both of whom I have also met before and who are actually well-dressed, but more cordial than warm, I desperately try English on one side, French on the other. But finally having nothing to say to me, the French contingent soon again starts to talk with each other. And I, having little to say to the dowdy vegetarian who also doesn't go to museums, I look at Ed and Jane. I think that, despite our age differences, I have more in common with them and their international attitudes toward Parisian life than their parents, my age. But I valiantly return to the Scottish mother, and I start to talk about vegetarian restaurants I know. She has been to several, so we finally get a conversation going.

Jane passes a platter of hot cheese puffs called *gougères*. The buffet on the dining table consists of *crudités,* country-style paté*, nems* (little Vietnamese egg-roll-type things) that Edouard had picked up at an Asian *traiteur* nearby, and a *pain surprise,* just like the one served at the Embassy in the spring, these filled sandwiches filled only with *saumon fumé.* There are cheeses and sliced *baguettes* to go with them, a variety of *petit fours*, and a bowl of fruit, including the delicious tiny yellow *mirabelles* that are, at last, in season. (I eat a handful.) The wines are excellent, as they would be, and I think of Richard, who would have had a field day monopolizing Ed with wine tedium (my word).

Nonetheless, pleased as I am to have been included, about 21*h* when it is starting to get dark, I think of going home. I am about to stand up, but just then Edouard takes a spoon and clinks it against a glass to get everyone's attention.

"Chers amis," he says, and he and Jane are standing together, holding hands, both with cat-that-ate-the-canary smiles. "Jane and I are happy all our dear friends are here together, because we want to tell you that we have become engaged and that we will be married next June. And that you must all come to the wedding."

Everyone, myself included, jumps up to congratulate them, taking the opportunity to kiss everyone in sight and to slap each other on the back. "Don't do it! Don't do it!" I want to cry out, but I don't.

Monday finally comes, as I knew it would. I dredge up my best attitude and get myself set. Perhaps this will truly be a new beginning for Ida the beanpole and me. I'm willing to give it a shot. So, I walk across Place St-Sulpice and then up rue Bonaparte toward Monoprix. Although it is still warm, it is clear that fall may soon be in the air. Along with the nights being longer, the breezes have a slight edge to them, and I am reluctantly thinking that soon I'll have to put away my summer clothes, including my new dress.

"I want to hear how your lunch with Ida goes," Caroline says in our morning chat. This is as close to being catty as she ever gets.

Ida and I arrive at Monoprix exactly at *12h30*, and we take the escalator down to the *sous-sol*. I am at least looking forward to the food. The café, which is to the front of the supermarket, is only partially filled, so we are seated quickly and even given menus. The *serveur* tells us that veal roast is the special of the day, and we each order it right away, agreeing to split a large bottle of Badoit. I settle in and I look at Ida, sitting across from me. Resolved to be positive at all costs, I admit to myself that she is looking quite nice (considering) and even happy.

After a few minutes, however, I notice that Ida keeps darting looks at various parts of my anatomy or, rather, how I am decked out on those parts. I take inventory. I'm wearing a great watch with a ratty watchband. Nothing wrong with my nice little gold bracelet. Fine nail polish color, but the coating on one nail is slightly chipped, and that nail is broken. My cable-knit, pink tee shirt (that I just had to wear one more time) is a little grimy around the inside of the collar, but can Ida know that? I look down at my wrist, where Ida is looking, and then I look back to her. "Is something wrong?" I ask as innocently as I can muster, looking back down to my wrist.

"I am not inspecting," she says vehemently, and I realize from her phrasing that other people must have accused her of this. (Which I hadn't, actually, had I?) But I also realize that this lunch will be a bust. By *13h04*, having worn out the Lovells in conversation, how crowded with tourists the *quartier* was all summer, and how the veal is good at the price, she says suddenly that she doesn't eat dessert and that she has to leave. She signals for the check, which we split; she leaves her euro change on the table for the waiter; and then, saying again that she has to be off, she departs. No kisses. I watch her take the escalator up to go God-knows-where, and I move on to pick up a few groceries in the supermarket. Having looked at my watch, the one with the ratty band, I realize that the big get-together luncheon took exactly thirty-nine minutes.

Late the next afternoon, my outing takes me to Mariage Frères—the wonderful tearoom in the Marais. The rabbi orders tea, but unable to control myself, I also order warm scones with butter. I realize this newsletter is something I can do without much fuss, or perhaps it's the butter melting on the scone that is doing the talking. I'm to put out a call for material on email, edit the articles and notices for correct English or French, decide on the order of the material, and then send everything to the woman who does the layout. A week later, there will be proofreading, and *voilà,* I will have done a good deed. The rabbi asks whether I am coming to Rosh Hashonah services, and I find it hard to say no. I pay for the tea, figuring that rabbis don't make a whole lot.

Before I head back to *métro* St-Paul, I take a chance and ring Margot from my *mobile,* just to see if she is home. Would she be interested in having a drink and then grabbing a falafel at L'As du Fallafel later, as long as I'm here? Margot can occasionally be cornered for an impromptu chat—and now she has her book to focus on, after all. Fortunately, she answers and invites me up.

When, over a glass of chilled Sancerre (which tastes mightily like Quincy, to tell the truth) I tell her why I am in the Marais, she says, "Okay, so you're being Jewish and I'm being Black. Now, you have to help me with my book."

So, I agree, since my own book will soon be finished and out. "Listen," I say. "I know you've talked with Caroline, but call Findlay, okay? He knows so much about the old days." And I think it will do him good.

Actually, I'll be pleased to see Margot more often than I have this year. But I'm disappointed that she doesn't want to go out to eat, and so, on the spur of the moment, I go to l'As du Fallafel myself. And why not? I am quickly ushered into the dive (shoved, more likely), which is already raucous at *19h.* The tiny Formica table is crammed against a side wall, but who cares? The waiter immediately comes over and expects me to order, which I do—a falafel plate and some kind of fruity Israeli nectar. And when it is dropped in front of me a few minutes later, I love it. All of it. The Jewish bustle and shouting, the food that I wolf down, the atmosphere of something almost familiar to me, whether it actually is, or not. And of course, the knowing not to linger, so the next people can have my place.

I walk out into the fall air still feeling good about the afternoon, my decision to do the newsletter, and especially the falafel. I must go to the Marais more often. I go home, thinking I will read or watch a film on TCM. I am not at all cranky at the thought.

And the next evening, because I know that Alice and Ida are friends, I say nothing about Ida (or about Luca) when Caroline and I take dinner over to the Lovells. I had, of course, filled Caroline in about the mystery lunch. She said nothing, but I think I moved up a rank on the scoreboard.

As Alice opens the door, relieved to have the "troops," as she calls us, to give support, Caroline proffers the foods we have brought from Bon Marché—a vegetarian quiche, several salads, avocado halves stuffed with crab, slices of smoked salmon and of *foie gras*, some blinis, a *baguette*, and four small *tartes au chocolat*.

"Lafayette, we have come," Caroline says to Alice, who looks exhausted. *La France* and Alice have been saved.

FURTHER READING, PART II

Benbassa, Esther: *The Jews of France: A History from Antiquity to the Present*. Princeton, Princeton University Press, 1999.

Campbell, James: *Exiled in Paris: Richard Wright, James Baldwin, Samuel Beckett, and Others on the Left Bank*. New York, Scribner, 1995.

Culberton, Judi and Randall, Tom: *Permanent Parisians*. Chelsea Vt., Chelsea Green, 1986.

Stovall, Tyler: *Paris Noir: African Americans in the City of Light*. New York, Houghton Mifflin, 1996.

Findlay, who is sitting in his chair with a blanket draped over his knees, opens a bottle of wine.

"Hi, Findlay," I say. "How are things today?'

"Any day you're on this side of the dirt," he says, picking up a glass, "is a good day." He pours wine for Caroline and me, but for himself only a few drops. Caroline and I shoot each other a glance. He passes some sliced sausage snacks, taking none for himself, and immediately he begins to talk about writing his memoirs.

"I'm going to concentrate on the people I've known and events I participated in, rather than myself," Findlay says, displaying a moment of modesty. It looks like the stroke has slowed him down somewhat, after all. But then he doesn't wait for our approval, and I am reassured. "I was remembering today how I used to spend hours over on the quai d'Orléans at Jimmy Jones' three-floor apartment. Oh, he had money all right, from *From Here to Eternity* and having worked on that film *The Longest Day*. Gawd, didn't everyone turn up there? But Jimmy never got the hang of things here, and he finally left. I wonder who has that apartment, now."

"We're thinking of giving up this apartment," Alice says, and both Caroline and I are truly shocked. "Findlay's old age target isn't so moveable anymore, I guess. We can't really navigate the stairs, and because I worked in the French system, we qualify for a public retirement home. There's one just a few streets away on boulevard Raspail, and we have an interview scheduled."

"What about going back to the States?" Caroline asks.

"We've talked about that..." Alice begins, but Findlay interrupts.

"Why would we do that?" he asks flatly, and that's the end of that. "Yes," he goes on as though he hadn't been interrupted. "I used to know 'em all. I knew 'em all."

"Were you already here when Carson McCullers and her husband lived here?" I ask, thinking that I must get to the library and return the book. Findlay shakes his head. "No," he says, clearly not happy at this interruption. "They had left in 1947, before we got here, and then when they came back, they stayed mostly out in the country. Why?"

"No reason. I just wondered." I smile, not bringing up excess drinking and strokes and paralysis, or even talent—by 1946 McCullers had already written both *The Heart Is a Lonely Hunter* and *Reflections in a Golden Eye*. In the States, were she and her husband continually stoked the way they were here? Anyway, after a stroke finally partially paralyzed the Missus, they left. An ambulance met Mrs. Mcullers at the pier in New York, and also the Mister who had had an attack of delirium tremens on the boat. This is not Paris' fault.

Fortunately, at dinner the talk turns to *quiche* and Brouilly, to the new films in *version originale* that opened on Wednesday— although Findlay isn't up to the cinema yet—and to my need for a renter for the month of December. The Lovells have switched to San Pellegrino, for Caroline—that font of dieting knowledge— has remembered that it has less sodium than Badoit. Water flows more copiously than wine. While we are eating our chocolate *tartes,* Alice mentions that the *Salon du Chocolat* will take place next month. This is obviously a highly cultural Parisian event. An afternoon's browsing (tasting) for the three of us is planned.

"I'm going to be the editor of the synagogue newsletter," I venture, toward the end of the meal.

"You are!" Alice says. "Why? Because we went to the Camondo museum, and you were so touched by their story?"

"No," I say, "I'm thinking I should get involved in the real life of the community, and not just be an American on the outside." Although this has only now occurred to me, I realize it is true. Sometimes, things come to me out of the blue.

Findlay goes back into the living room after dinner, and Caroline and I shoo Alice away while we clean up the kitchen. When we go back into the living room, both Lovells are asleep in their chairs. Caroline points to the ashtray next to Alice, and I realize it is empty. We nod. Then, closing the door behind us, we walk quietly down the stairs. I notice that we are walking even more slowly than before, but I decide to wait and let Caroline bring up her knee problem when she is ready. I am becoming a master of tact.

And so, this is life in Paris after the *rentrée*. In just a few days, vacation has become a thing of the past. My apartment stays clean, of course, waiting for Luca to come back. I listen for his footsteps above, but all is quiet. There is nothing left but for me to continue my morning work habits, which I do. I write. I delete. I write some more. I sip my tea. I talk to J-P, who has finally turned up, but Richard does not call. Edie does. She has my popcorn, and she says we'll get together when her schedule of *demonstrations* has been set. American Airlines confirms my flights for the beginning of December and the return in January, as well. Sandy is nowhere in sight, and I wonder if I can pry some dirt out of Jean-Pierre when we have dinner together on the fourteenth, which is what we have arranged. Perhaps it would be best just to ask him how Julien is and wait to see what he says.

On Thursday morning, I dress as I think a French woman would for a lunch on the Champs-Elysées, hoping I will pass inspection by Colette. This takes some time and thought (resulting in the same outfit I wore to the homage with J-P, but without the spiky high heels), so I then quickly close up shop and head out into the day. On the way to the *métro*, I stop in briefly at the Hotel St-Germain to make reservations for my son and his wife to stay three nights. And then I get to Flora Danica about ten minutes early, finding Colette already there. I do like the salmon tasting plate, and I do very much like the placid elegance and good service. But what strikes me is how I could have known this woman for so long (in years of monthly book meetings) and not known anything about her. It was, I suppose, that combination of her French reticence about personal information and my own utter distraction— toward whatever I was mulling on at any given time.

But now, I know that she teaches American Literature at Polytechnique, a major *grande école*; her husband is a producer of French films; her son is at Oxford (which is why they spent August in England); and in the summers, she makes quilts and sells them through her own company online. Not only is she interesting, we were talking so fiercely and eating everything put before us, that if she inspected, she did it in a very discreet French way.

"À propos," Colette says, "the book club will be at my apartment this time. Mitzi can't make it, after all."

"You will make your lemon squares, *n'est-ce pas?*" I ask. And Colette smiles that reserved French smile that I can only rarely achieve, and says, *"Bien sûr."* I'm glad she thinks it's "of course."

After this satisfying lunch and with goodbyes that we'll see each other in just a couple of weeks—I take my book to the Luexmbourg and read, now seeking out sun instead of shade. When I finally get back home, I muster the energy to call Anna. The voice of France Télécom announces that the number doesn't exist. I must have written it down wrong. I email Mitzi, asking for the right number, and she writes me back immediately, also saying she's "so glad" I'm doing the newsletter for the synagogue. So, I finally reach Anna and pass on the museum of fans but promise that we'll get together soon. Promise may be too strong a word, but it's still not as strong as a vow. And besides, there is—or there isn't—Luca. At least I know he's still away, for the floor above me does not squeak.

And late on Thursday morning, I take the No. 87 bus to the library to return Mrs. McCullers and pay the fine, and to borrow more books, making sure it is close enough to lunchtime to run into Paul and Klaus. When I appear beside them, they stand and we kiss, and then they go back to the periodicals before them. Paul's liver crisis is over, and I am relieved to see both men looking so well.

I look at the new guides (none about Paris) and check out a few books and then wait for the boys to be ready. I wander around, and I check the ads on the bulletin board by the ladies' room. One of them concerns somebody in Ohio who offers an apartment exchange. And lo! This reminds me, finally, to search the reference books for the Cincinnati Society, remembering that plaque near the Grande Épicerie that commemorates its meetings at Marshal Rochambeau's digs in 1783. When Louix XVI was still in command, if that's the right word.

On the back of a grocery receipt from Monoprix (writing really teeny), I take some notes: "Franco-American friendship. Hereditary society for officers of Continental Army—Hamilton, Washington, French Gnl Roch. (Yorktown)—Lafay (Valley Forge). Named for Lucius Cincinnatus—Roman consul—took control of armies in wartime and returned power to Senate after. Went home. Louis XVI: ok for French membs to wear foreign eagle emblem, although usually not. L's descendants still have Washington's Cincinnati Eagle." There's no more room on the receipt. I rummage in my purse and find another, slightly crumpled, but so what.

I continue: "Objectives: 'preserve…rights so dearly won; to promote…continuing union…and to assist members in need… widows…orphans. Now, 3500 members. Purpose: educate about founding U.S.A… Fr. *Société* commems Yrktwn, visits tomb of Lafay. 7/4; recalls role of France in the Amer. Rev. Scholarships for French to visit U.S. Exchanges—French and American families. Internships here for Americans, and also for French in U.S."

I can't wait for the boys to be ready to go. For a change, I have a great story to tell. How Rochambeau—like Lafayette a "hero of two worlds"—was sentenced by Robespierre to *la veuve.* Just as he was about to step into the overcrowded tumbrel on its way to the guillotine, the executioner

> ## QUOTE FROM THOMAS JEFFERSON
>
> On the basis of its conflict with republican values, Thomas Jefferson objected to any American society limited to former officers and based on heredity. In 1786—before the overthrow of Louix XVI—he expressed his opinion in a letter to the Cincinnati Society's first president, George Washington:
>
> "To know the mass of evil which flows from this fatal source, a person must be in France. He must see the finest soil, the finest climate, the most compact State, the most benevolent character of people, & every earthly advantage combined, insufficient to prevent this scourge from rendering existence a curse to 24 out of 25 parts of the inhabitants of this country."

waved him back. "Wait a little, old *maréchal,*" he called. "Your turn will come later on." But Robespierre's head fell first. I can hardly contain myself, telling this all to Paul and Klaus as we leave the library together. I begin to feel a little like Scheherazade myself.

Klaus carries my books as we walk over again to the No. 87, which will take us to l'Institut du Monde Arabe and its exotic tearoom for lunch. They have kindly agreed to go there (they had suggested the "club") when I claimed I needed to check it out, once again...which is more or less true. (As J-P would say, today is my *lookey-dey.*) Klaus is impressed as he looks into the book bag, for this first foray since the *rentrée* shows a renewed willingness on my part to be edified. (I hope it lasts.) On the top of the pile is a tome about Paris during the Occupation. I have a biography of Benjamin Franklin. I have Herbert Lottman's *The Left Bank*, about writers in Paris in the Thirties and Forties. I have snared *The Radetsky March* by Joseph Roth, to read again just to read something I already love. Last, although Klaus does look at me sharply for a moment, I have borrowed two videos for when there's nothing worth watching, even on TCM. I'm beginning to sound like Findlay.

We linger over our lunch and talk long about a trip to Italy next summer. At the Institute itself we spend two hours looking at an exhibit on the Golden Age of Islam, which fascinates all of us. Finally, I suggest a stroll through the nearby Jardin des Plantes— basically because I want to see the ostriches at the zoo. But the guys insist they're ready to go home, which they do, leaving me to do the zoo on my own. I skip the ostriches after all, and, having eschewed the bus on the way over, I walk back home, as well. My books don't weigh me down as I walk.

Finally, my waiting pays off. On Friday, footsteps above and the gurgle of running water above tell me that Luca has come back. I am both exhilarated and relieved that he calls right away. Life is looking up, again. He says he has an important meeting at six o'clock, but he will call me when he's finished, and is there any place we can get good Chinese food? *"Certo,"* I say in Italian, immediately picturing a nice walk at sunset down boulevard St-Michel, then slices of *canard laqué* (caramelized duck) and sides of Chinese greens and *riz cantonais* (fried rice) at Mirama in rue St-Jacques, and perhaps afterward a long stroll along the *quai*. And after that, what? The opening gambit?

By *20h00*, however, I'm getting hungry, wondering if I should have just a little snack while I'm waiting. I decide not to interrupt Luca's meeting, but to harbor resentment instead, which I am good at. Finally at *21h30*, after I have downed my last two Oreos, the rest of an open bag of pistachios, seven almost overripe *mirabelles*, and six of the remaining licorice Jelly Bellies that Lenore brought me, the doorbell rings. Although Luca looks endearingly apologetic, I am no longer hungry, and I beg off. I am, however, a forgiving type (so far). We arrange again for the next night, which I am happy to say turns out just the way I pictured it. The walk down the *quai*, the bottles of Chinese beer and the *canard laqué*, laughing together as he maneuvers his chopsticks, as though we are both old friends and new lovers, which we, much later in the evening, become.

This time it's different. All those quotes in my head, the analyses both of the kissing and the act itself never come to mind, as they are submerged into a haze of sensations that take me over, more enveloping than I would have thought. And later, I do not even wonder whether I should ask him to stay, and besides, Luca has no *mamma* waiting at home. Yes, this is different, not a project anymore. So, after we talk and doze and talk some more, we untwine ourselves, and he takes his leave as the sun is coming up. This time there are no farewells and no taking stock, just Luca saying, as usual but with a slow kiss at the door, "Call me, *Francesca, carissima.*" This time, I do not take exception, for I am in love.

Late in the morning there is a bouquet of flowers in front of my door. This makes me giggle (even totally sober). I wait only one day before I call, for I believe that if something is worth doing, it's worth doing too much. Luca answers, and we flirt for several minutes, he having now shortened *Francesca* to "*'Cesca,*" and I calling him Lou in the American way. He asks if I am free this evening, for he would like a steak, and he laughs, saying sweetly, "so that I will have the strength of ten." Certainly, I know just the place, Le Relais de l'Entrecôte, over in rue St-Benoit. I haven't been there in years. He agrees, sending me *un bacione* (big kiss), as we hang up. Of course, I am ready well before *19h30* as arranged, but this time Lou doesn't show up, at all. And he doesn't call. And I am out of cookies. I may take to drink. Yet, I still know I am in love.

I cannot tell whether this is a Luca-thing or an Italian-thing, or what. It certainly isn't French, for the French seem predictable in their peculiarities. They always arrive late for a dinner, as the host fully expects them to. If you arrive early, you must wait someplace for a while. Find the nearest café, as I did with those people for the Passover dinner years ago, order a mineral water, and wait.

As to meetings or a *rendez-vous* in a restaurant, however, if they are going to be only a moment late, they will call you on their *mobile*. They will say, "I'm just at the entrance to the restaurant. I'll be right there." In case there is a mix-up, the French never admit to being wrong, so always take the blame on yourself, asking whether perhaps you have misunderstood. They love this. But no matter what, they do not just stand you up.

Dinner with my best French friend on the next evening, however, helps takes my mind off Lou, at least sort of. J-P's choice of restaurants shows how guilty he feels about neglecting me, and that's all right with me. We meet exactly on time at *20h30* on the rue de Longchamp in the 16th at Hiramatsu, awarded one star by the Michelin guide. I have dressed myself up—although no longer in my summer fancy duds—piled on the eye shadow and blush that I have bought at the cosmetic counter at Monoprix, and I even carry my little dress-up purse instead of my everyday *sac*.

After we kiss and say our hellos, the maître d'hôtel comes over to shake Jean-Pierre's hand and, while seating us, to have a brief chat. J-P seems to be an *habitué* here, and I know we will be treated exceptionally well. While the two men are talking, I work out in my head what I want to say, and when there is a lull in the conversation, I decide to go brazen (*Jhee-Pay*-wise) and say in French, "*Pardon, monsieur*, I don't want to seem *trop américaine*, but I would like to tell you that I like your tie."

"*Bravo, Frahn!*" exclaims Jean-Pierre. "I like his tie, too, but I would never have said anything." Of course, he wouldn't have, but hey, he's French. And male.

I am right about the dinner. Jean-Pierre and I eat the most refined, most delicious, and most costly meal I have eaten since the last time J-P had reason to feel guilty, having called and awakened me to complain about something Sandra did (or did not) do. That was at Taillevent, an unforgettable dinner, the best I ever had. So, tonight I'm glad that once again I have that *très bonne mine*. (Looking good counts.) The waiter provides me with a menu *sans* prices, which I complain to J-P is condescending to women. He starts to tell me not to worry about it, but then stops himself and tells me that the *entrée* I want to order costs forty-eight euros, and that his is just about the same. For the main course (*les plats*), it's just a little more. Being also *très sophistiquée*, I do not gasp.

Or maybe I did. "Don't worry about it," J-P says with that little aristocratic chuckle that indicates he is about to say something he thinks is funny. "I get paid in euros, not dollars."

I smile, of course. But then J-P goes on. "*À propos,*" he says. "Is your friend Caroline ready to show her book to a publisher? If she is, have her call me."

I say I will definitely do that. Could her dollar problems be solved just like that? Then I wonder about the dinner again.

"Order the lobster," J-P suggests. "You won't find it better anywhere else. Or have the lobster *entrée* instead of the langoustines."

Yet, after having eaten the *entrée,* which is as exquisite as J-P said it would be—with lobster, smoked pigeon, a little poached egg, and some nutty kind of creamy sauce, I am still overwhelmed when my *plat* arrives—with its beautiful, really beautiful, pink lamb slices and its garnishes of onion compote and colorful *legumes.* And, oh yes, with truffle juice, to boot. J-P, having said he wanted "something simple," has ordered roast veal, although it looks decidedly unsimple to me. I offer J-P a taste of my lamb, hoping for a bite of his. And all I can say about every taste of every dish is that Hiramatsu knows best (which may become my culinary motto.) Tasting each other's dishes may not be a habit of the French, but J-P is used to me. He likes my American ways, or so he says. His veal needs hardly be chewed, and the sauce is one I could drink. Fortunately, I don't have to, for I have already tasted the wine. So, I go back to my own celestial dinner, eating as slowly as I can, hoping it will never be gone.

The *sommelier* had showed J-P the wine before pouring a bit for him to taste, and I could see it was a Château Margaux. "Why did you choose that wine?" I asked J-P, who had just finished that swirly-sniffing ceremony.

He chuckled as he nodded to the *sommelier*. "For two reasons. First, it is a great Bordeaux, and you'll like it. But, you see, the château is owned by a woman, which is rare, and I am having my consciousness raised by Marie-Claude. And she would agree about the menu you were given, which is why I told you the prices." He raised his glass, and we made a toast. "To good friends," he smiled. "And strong women."

So, here we are again. The two of us. Old friends, good friends, survivors. It is true that feelings of an unsettled romance continually pop into my mind, but this evening it is not so hard to remind myself that everything I am doing is a choice, and so far I haven't been too wrong, or if I have been, so far I've been pretty good at cleaning up the mess.

So, with J-P I do not mention romance, love, or confusion, and being kept on my toes. But I do talk about my ten days on the boat, about the jenever distillery, gliding past the scenery and through the locks, about my manuscript whose deadline is beginning to loom, and I even ask about Marie-Claude, for it is clear that he is content with her, the politician on her way up. Yet, I realize I am relieved that there is no particular announcement on that front.

"*Oui,* I had a good summer," J-P says, although I think he says it strangely, with kind of a sigh. "But I'm very happy to be back with Henriette and Victor."

"And do you still have Julien?" I ask as innocently as I can with a straight face.

Now there is a real silence, and a look of pain comes over J-P's face. Finally, he says. "This is difficult for me to say, *chérie. Très difficile.* It seems Sandra has been having an affair with Antoine. I do not know for how long. But it seems that when he took off for America in the summer, he went to see Sandra."

I am speechless. I cannot even lift my fork. This is big.

"But we had a family meeting at our country home when Antoine came back, and he has promised not to see her anymore. *Grandpère* made sure that Antoine understood the effect on his career and on the family. Antoine is very unhappy."

"What about his wife?" I manage to ask.

"It is too soon to know. I think they will try to see if they can get back together. But I do not know."

"And you, *mon cher,*" I ask. "What about you?"

He doesn't answer directly. "How could she ask me to take care of her dog, when she was sleeping with my brother? That, as you say in English, '*ees ze question.*' And he... *Non.* Please, *Frahn,* let us talk about something else."

So, we talk about the dinner, but not about Luca. We talk about our work, but not about Sandy or Antoine. We talk about our kids, but not about romance or betrayal, or about sadness or even confusion. Yet, these are all there both on the table and in the air around us. We eat our dinners, more quietly but comfortably, as always, each of us with our own thoughts.

"*Frahn,*" J-P says, after a few minutes of silence, during which I am secretly lamenting my emptying plate. "Marie-Claude noticed at our July dinner that *nous nous vouvoyons.* She says I'm old fashioned and that you and I should speak to each other in the familiar, to *tutoyer.* And I agree. What do you think?"

"That's lovely, J-P." I say, thinking *Oh God, another French verb tense I have to master.* "That pleases me enormously."

At what is clearly becoming the end of the meal, J-P—who doesn't have a sweet tooth—orders a selection of cheese from Aléosse (up in the 17th, one of the best, of course) and then his coffee. I skip the cheese but not the dessert, and I resist licking my dessert plate of something only an ignoramus might call rice pudding. Knowing me so well, when the *expresso* arrives, J-P automatically pushes toward me the little plate of handcrafted chocolates that generally come with. As I select the first one carefully (before I select the second one carefully), I think that this evening together is worth every one of those many thousands of *centimes* that he will pay. I know he thinks so, too—even without the snifter of cognac for J-P and the little glass of muscat the host sends over for me, and which I sip, content to stay where I am. In any case, J-P just signs *l'addition* when it comes, and not a muscle on his face twitches. It is now nearly *23h30*, and the maître d' has called us a cab, which is waiting at the curb. The men shake hands once more, and we are in the cab.

The ride is short, and we are fairly quiet on the way. I get out in rue Servandoni. Again, respecting J-P's wishes and fighting against my every instinct to hash out every detail of the Sandy and Antoine debacle, I merely thank J-P for the evening, and at the end of our goodbyes, just say, *"Bon courage, mon cher ami."*

Je descends, we do our kisses once again through the open window, and J-P says he will call soon again. He shuts the door of the cab, and I can hear him instruct the driver to head over to the 7th *arrondissement*.

But, just as the taxi is taking off, I remember something and yell as loudly as I can, "Hey, J-P!" I know this is not what a *Parisienne* would do, but it has its effect. The taxi slams on its brakes, and elegant Jean-Pierre looks out the window at me, with some amazement, I think. Nonetheless, I say with as much aplomb as I can, "Did I tell you that I'm looking for a renter for when I'm away in December?"

"Non, ma chère," he replies. "But there is an English author my company publishes who wants to spend one month here, perhaps two. I will ask, and I'll call you. *Bon soir, chère Frahn.*" The taxi again leaves, and this time I let it go.

I hurry up to my landing, and just what I had hoped for is there—another large bouquet of flowers—and this time, also a bottle of Italian wine. Luca may make me crazed, but he also makes me smile. And as I arrange the flowers and put them on my desk, I relax. My anxiety has been relieved. I am more than ready for a mulling-life-over bath and bed. I must review the French verbs once again.

Yes, life is exciting and unpredictable, I think, as I swish the water around. Isn't that what I always say I want? With Luca it seems to be everything that I could hope for, except when it isn't. I mean, this business of not showing up. Of cryptic dealings on the phone. But if I am an adventurous sort, after all, I must also be adaptable, or so I tell myself this late evening. It may not be April in Paris, but I am in love (I think).

And it is now mid-September. Although the parks are still flowery and lush, there is a sense that soon a leaf somewhere will turn yellow and fall. The streets are lively, and on late Saturday afternoon, after I've inhaled a dozen oysters at L'Huitrier up in the 17th and checked out the actual cheese store Aléosse on rue Poncelet, Caroline meets me on boulevard Haussmann, and we see the new exhibit at the Musée Jacquemart-André. We pass by the lovely tearoom without going in, perhaps a first for Caroline. The Sunday afternoon church concert with Paul and Klaus is pleasant, and the stone floor is not yet cold. Afterward, as we walk up boulevard St-Michel, I see the boys dart a glance at each other. But they do not mention Luca, and since there is nothing that I can say with any certainty, at least at this point, I say nothing at all.

As to the rest, I am waiting for Sandy to return to hear her version of the story. I'll get my popcorn from Edie; my books will get read; and this one I'm working on myself may well be finished on time. My beloved Plan of Attack is covered with checkmarks, with only a few blank boxes to go. The newsletter will get edited and sent out. Margot will turn up from time to time with her chapters, and, actually, I think that will be fun. Richard will call sooner or later, and then he'll come back. Caroline and I will do what we can for Alice, and for Findlay, of course. Rosh Hashonah will come, and I will go. And my resolutions to swim and lose weight will no doubt get submerged as they do each Rosh Hashonah into an over-arching but futile resolution to be a better person overall.

So, taking stock can go no further for this moment. All I can really say for sure, at this point, is that, for someone always on the lookout, I find I am still of the persuasion that this city is the place to be. And with or without Lou.

Another Good Day

THIS IS THE TRUTH, AND I would swear to it if asked. Early one Wednesday morning at the end of October, I realize it is time to go to the *Préfecture* to pick up my renewed *carte de séjour*. *La France* has had enough time to do whatever it is that it does in that massive building on the Île de la Cité to keep us foreigners on our toes. It is six weeks since I sent in the form, having meticulously followed every instruction. In fact, I had my picture taken three times until I was satisfied I looked more like my sister than my mother.

Picking up the *carte*, even if it is ready and waiting for you somewhere in that warren of *dossiers,* is not as easy as it sounds, not lah-di-dah by any means.

So, following the advice I have already written for foreigners sharing my plight, I leave my apartment at nine, which is something I have long managed to avoid—along with wearing suits and carrying a briefcase in one hand and my breakfast bagel in the other. Nonetheless, once a year I go to the *Préfecture*, prepared to wait for hours. If you don't get there early in the day, you are a fool. (This must be made clear.) I have in my purse my passport and my now-expired *carte*. And in my tote bag slung on my shoulder, the *Herald Tribune,* a Power Bar in case I start to die of hunger, and a small bottle of Badoit, if the same goes for thirst.

The *métro* stop is Cité. The *Préfecture* is directly across the *parvis* (forecourt). From the moment you emerge, you can see the length of the line waiting to get in. You are either disheartened or totally bummed out. Fortunately, there is an awning running along the side of the building, so that if it is raining, we foreigners will not get drenched, catch pneumonia, and stage a *manif* right then and there. Ten people are allowed into the revolving door at one time, but usually there are twelve or more, shoulder to backpack, front to butt, face to hair. And then, once inside, you are in the cubicle with the x-ray machine and the *gendarmes* (national police). Here, eight of the twelve people have forgotten to remove their *mobiles* or keys from their pockets and must go through the x-ray twice, slowing the rest of us down.

Fortunately, there are a lot of official reasons to come to the *Préfecture* and not all people go to the building that concerns itself with identity papers. This does not mean there is no line. No, there is a line to get into the room where you finally get to take a number and where there are a few chairs so that some of the people with numbers can actually sit down.

Now this is when it gets interesting, at least to me. Sometimes, I do not read my newspaper at all, as I pay attention to the dramas unfolding. Last year, for instance, there was a man who seemed unclear on the concept of identity papers. So, instead of waltzing up when his number was called, turning over his passport, and waiting just a moment for the *fonctionaire* to pull his dossier out of the cabinet, he created a scene to which, of course, every official in the room had to join in.

"I'm sorry, *monsieur*," the first functionary said to the man, whose accent, I thought, was Slavic. She handed him back his passport. "The photo on this passport isn't you. It's the picture of a woman."

"*Oui,*" said *monsieur*. "It's my wife. She's working, so I came to get her papers."

"*Non,*" said the *fonctionnaire* with admirable patience, I have to say, for this ranked pretty high on the idiot scale, if you ask me. But by this time the ears of the other workers in the room had picked up, although they had not yet joined the fray. "She has to come and pick up the papers herself and sign for them."

Then the Slav himself went on the attack. "But she can't leave work," as though the woman was out of her mind. "They would fire her. And *you,*" he pointed his finger almost in her face, "would be adding to the unemployment in France."

Murmurs of disbelief rippled through the other workers, who immediately clustered around their colleague, causing those of us waiting also to ripple with disbelief, as our own wait increased, with no one any longer helping any of us. *"Non,"* they all said, in a cacophony of sounds. "She has to come, herself. We have to see her. She has to sign for her own *carte.* Everyone does." Their shrugs were deep and long suffering. I loved every minute, I have to say. I would have laughed out loud, except no one else in the room would have joined in.

And so, he went. And so it goes. But now comes my attestation.

This year, in mid-October, I, Frances Gendlin, with all my emergency reading and foodstuffs, emerge from the *métro* and see that there is not one person outside the *Préfecture. Quel choc!* Is it Sunday? Has there been a bomb alert? Have they moved the *Préfecture* to the other side of town? Is there a new entrance? No, the awning to shield supplicants from the rain is still in place, and the door seems open. I take a chance. I walk in. By myself. I put my stuff through the x-ray machine. I walk around the corner to the right hall and, by myself, open the door to the room.

I am alone with all the *fonctionnaires.* But, as I said, it is not good to be a fool when it comes to the *Préfecture.* So, alone as I am, I take a number from the machine. As I look at it, the woman (the same one as last year) behind the counter calls out, *"Quatre-vingts."* Number 80? That's me! *Quelle surprise!* I give her the number and my passport. She takes a file from a folder, hands me the plastic card, and gives me a paper to sign. And I am out the door. In two minutes flat. Signed, sealed, and delivered.

And this is my point, and I know I've made it before. But it's important to stress, even again. For better or for worse, everything in Paris is an event.

Feeling Close to the End

S O, SEPTEMBER AND MOST OF OCTOBER come and go, and so does Lou. Here's what I know. When Luca and I are together, my mind turns to mush, and I think I am in love. But when I'm on my own, caution raises its rarely heeded head and, well, I wonder. Either way, the weeks of autumn are going by, and I find that although my life is less than *tranquille,* I am not particularly discontent. If it is true, as people say, that the years pass more quickly the older you get, experience reminds me that it is only those in which I've been distracted that vanish before I am ready. The others seem never to end. So, I realize that this year has passed so quickly, what with my new manuscript and His Royal Bolognese Elusiveness, that I am almost surprised to find my December trip needing attention. In some small part of my being that is not constantly preoccupied with the species of Italian male, I do know that it's for the best for me to have something else to ponder.

Thanks to Jean-Pierre, it worked out easily this year for me to rent my apartment. I've had several pleasant conversations with his English author, a professor who says she is writing a biography of Simone de Beauvoir (what, yet another?) and who will work all of December and January—until I reclaim my apartment—at the Bibliothèque Nationale and other archives. I told her how much I loved my little nest, and she said that J-P had already told her how *adorable* it is. She has agreed to my price, not to smoke, and not to make long distance calls on the phone. Her *mobile* works in France. We also agreed how nice J-P is, and she asked me if he is married. I said that he was not. Let her have a go at him, if she wants. That intelligent, naturally blonde, and totally French Marie-Claude will not easily give ground, of that I'm sure. So, the professor is happy, and now apartment-wise, all I have to do is arrange everything tidily and give my keys to J-P's secretary before I leave, the week after Thanksgiving.

"I will miss you, *'Cesca*," says Luca plaintively one drizzly evening during a quiet dinner *chez moi* of *gnocchi al burro e salvia* that Luca actually prepared himself in my little kitchen. (He even went to the *marché* and bought the fresh sage.) "Do you have to stay away so long?" Of course, it is tempting for me to cry out, "No, no, my dearest, I will stay here in your arms." But I don't fall into that old trap, for I know that his arms (delicious though they are) are somewhat elusive, and besides I have learned not to base my life on the whims of a man. I wonder if this is really true.

Currently, with about five weeks to go, I'm making lists of this and that, adding more items and striking some out. I don't know why I make such a fuss. All my American friends, except the intractable Margot, go back regularly for personal and business transactions, or just because it's time. I am in both groups. It's time for family and friends, most of whom I'm eager to see. I'll spend a week in Pennsylvania with my son, Christmas with my daughter in Canada, and the rest of the time with publishing friends in New York. So, I will dig in my trunks in the *cave* (basement) for boots and mittens when it's time to dust off the *valise*.

But it's also time to renew my American driver's license, to consult a financial advisor about euros and dollars, to see my agent, and to hear publishing gossip that I have sorely missed. And not at all least, American as I am, it's also time to buy shoes in narrow widths and to scarf down Hebrew National low-fat hot dogs with all the fixings. The French would probably eat them with a knife and fork.

But first, the ever-present book. Before I leave I will nudge my editor as to the publishing date, for by then the manuscript will be out of my hands and in hers. I am definitely thinking of the end game, now that the city treks are pretty well over.

Finally, the restaurants. Which to include, which not? More "further readings" still to suggest. The explanatory cover letter. The acknowledgments. The author's bio for the back page. The photo. All told, about three hundred pages of text. And sent by email, with notes to the editor highlighted in yellow. How easy this has become since I wrote the first one: no more hard copies and schlepping to the post office with a huge package and a backup diskette. No more waiting in line, paying a fortune, and then waiting again for several weeks for any comment at all—the revisions, the editing, the date to receive the proofs. Now it's almost immediate and free (so to speak). This assumes, of course, that the basic work gets done.

Thus, I am busy both in my routine and travel plans. This would be normal at this season, except that this year, of course, Luca my mercurial lover is like a computer program continually running in the background of my mind. But I toil, nonetheless, at my desk each morning (attuned always to every nuance of noise above), and I am also in the personal countdown to the end. I have switched from Earl Grey Tea to Lapsang Souchang, which I can get at Bon Marché. Cookies stay the same (although fewer). Late mornings, generally after I have opened a bottle of Orangina Light—another major change in my life—the telephone often rings, and I answer *âllo,* hoping first that it is Luca (although basically it is still "Call me, *'Cesca'*") and then that whoever it turns out to be will not ask me to adjust my brain *tout à coup* to French.

Alice complains about being trapped at home with the crotchety Findlay. Margot, having already met with Caroline, keeps me up to date on Black Americans in Paris. (Also, she has started sending jokes from her computer, which I must gently tell her to stop). Even Findlay, himself, calls once in a while, now that he remembers he has in me a ready ear for his stories. Anna has called twice to invite me to something or other, but my *planning* was *complet* each time. (This is the truth.) Edie has added an extra hands-on workshop that she'll tell me about soon, she says, when we make our date to hand over the popcorn, not just the one box I had expected but two. I suggest going out to dinner for *pot-au-feu* (a rather flavorless boiled beef stew that the French adore) at a place up in the 9th (aptly named Le Roi du Pot au Feu), for I know better than to make her a meal, but this doesn't interest her at all. (Too bad. I needed to get its card.)

"There's a chamber music concert at Sainte-Chapelle late Sunday afternoon," she says. "Let's do that instead."

"Great idea," I say. I would never have thought of this myself. But regular chamber music? No zithers? No harmonicas? Is Edie going soft?

But I am relieved when she says, "Don't fret, I'll get the tickets. I go right past the ticket agency every day. I love the Sainte-Chapelle, no matter what they play."

Mitzi rings to say how much she liked the newsletter and again that she's "just so tickled" that I'm doing it. And frankly, the task wasn't bothersome. So, I don't mind the thought of sending out the call for articles for the January edition from my Blackberry while I am in the States. And I did go to Rosh Hashonah services, where I thought of my grandmother while I sang the songs. The *gymnase* calls and says my membership is expiring and asks if I want to renew. In one of those bursts of trying to be a better person, I agree. I even sign up for yoga classes. I hope I go.

And Caroline is now in a dither about J-P and his publishing house. So, in our usual morning calls, we hash over everything again and again, about when she should call him, which chapters she should send, should it be by email or hard copy, and everything else. I keep telling her that whenever she is ready, he will be, too. But I have endless patience with Caroline, paying her back for her endless patience with me.

But there are two unusual calls, as well, and they finally end the suspense. The calls both come on the same afternoon, of course, wouldn't you know? The first is from Richard, finally ringing me again, and it is *incroyable,* as Klaus would say. At least it is unbelievable to me. Richard's friend Freifeld is leaving Paris for good. He is leaving France behind. And I gather, he is leaving his wife, most of all. By January, he will be gone. Richard wonders if I would please call Freifeld to try and get him to change his mind.

"Why me?" I ask. I mean, I hardly know the man.

"You have such great common sense," Richard answers, and I wonder if this is really me he is talking about. But he goes on to explain that at the infamous reunion in southern California of the Fair Play for Cuba Committee, Freifeld took up with a girl he had met once at a protest march during those halcyon days, and they have decided after one week's rutting (my interpretation) to live together forevermore.

"It's crazy," Richard says. "You have to do something. It's a shipboard romance. They really don't know each other. They didn't even know each other thirty years ago."

"I'll try," I agree in my best half-hearted manner. "But not this week. I'll call after I've gotten my plans set for Thanksgiving and my trip." I still have a lot to do, and this *petit* postponement will allow me at least some breathing room until I can figure out what to say.

"You're a brick," Richard says. (A brick? Is that good?) And just as I think of hanging up, Richard changes the subject. "By the way, are you going to be in New York at Christmas?"

"No, I'll be in Canada with my daughter," I said. "Why?"

"I'm going to be in Manhattan with Philly," he says, "and she suggested that we ask you over to her place, if you're there. I won't be coming back until January this year, and it's a long time not to see my Paris friends." As he hangs up, Richard says he'll call again, soon.

And just an hour later, Sandy calls. "Fran, I'm back," is all she says.

"Oh my, you sound terrible," I say. Then I own up, having wondered for weeks whether I would. "I know about you and Antoine," I add quickly. "This must be a hard time for you."

"I can't believe that 'Twan gave in to *Grandpère*," she says, and I can hear that she's on the verge of tears. With a tremor in her voice, she fills me in on the details of her summer that I both do and do not want to hear (mostly do). "They convinced him that he'd never be president if he got divorced. Which is clearly not true. Clearly. Having a mistress was okay, but leave his wife? Oh no. *Grandpère* never liked me. I thought it was 'Twan, but it was just *Grandpère*."

"Antoine, president?"

"I can't imagine what got into me, taking up with another one in that ridiculous family. I'm giving up men entirely."

It suddenly comes to me to suggest she look for that Arab diplomat that she mentioned in the summer, but I wisely refrain. I just repeat, "I know this must be a terrible time for you. But you're strong. You'll move on."

"No. Never. Now that the kids are so grown up, I'm going to devote myself entirely to Julien."

"I was afraid of that," I answer, and Sandy manages a laugh. She thinks it a joke.

"But I've also decided that I'm here to stay, no matter what. They can't drive me out. So, I'm going to fix up my home, and I'm going to do some publicity at embassies and ministries about entertaining at gatherings. You'll help me write a brochure."

I will? "Of course," I say, "and I'm glad you're going to stay." And this is true, for not only do I like Sandy, I think it's the right thing for her to do, at least until the kids are off and on their own. And I noticed she stressed the word "home." "I'm sure you'll work it all out. Besides, you could just give up on French men, not the rest." I could mention the virtues (but not the faults) of Italian men, but again I keep my mouth shut.

While Sandy goes on about the redecoration, I listen only somewhat, wishing we could somehow get back to the subject of men. All of a sudden, Antoine has become interesting, after all. But, finally, before we hang up I suggest a shopping trip in a couple of days to get started on the new redecorating plan. This perks her up, and she readily agrees. I also remind her that she promised to invite me to dinner when she was back, and she promises that, again—soon.

Late Sunday afternoon, I finally meet Edie at the fountain at Place St-Michel, and we walk in the cool air across the bridge together to Sainte-Chapelle. The river is glistening in the slanting sun. We don't have to wait long in the line, and we climb the steep, windy staircase up to one of the most beautiful chapels in the world. Fortunately, it is still bright outside, so we can see the light coming through the vividly colored stained-glass windows of this sanctuary, almost seven hundred years old. I'm glad we came.

The violins entertain us with comforting classics—Vivaldi, Strauss, and Brahms—and Edie listens rapturously, her eyes closed. Not I, for what is going on with the performers was worth the climb. Grimaces from the conductor toward one of the violinists and his finally standing directly in front of her, waving his bow in her face indicating she should play faster. And the cellist, a bearded young man whose soulful eyes remind me of a basset hound or a fifteenth-century Italian youth in love, staring only to the heavens as he plays. And the rather phlegmatic (or stoned) violist playing his part (pluck-pluck-pluck) and then standing impassively while others of the group beam and bow. This concert is one of the best!

"Let's go get a drink," I say afterward (eyeing the little sack protruding from her large purse). "My treat." We cross back over to St-Michel and sit ourselves down in a café, where she hands over the bag with the microwave popcorn, waving away my offer to pay. That's what people do—like the Jays with the Shakespeare book—and generally it evens out. I've done even more for Edie. Once, I actually brought back a heavily wrapped beef brisket in my suitcase, since the French don't cut beef the same way, and so with the popcorn she has paid her debt. Luckily, I got to eat the brisket, which she had cooked slowly with coffee, ketchup, Ginger Snaps, and onion, which sounds decidedly barf but which transported me back to the good old days of somewhere I never knew but wished I had.

So, we drink Lillet and catch up, mostly her version of Stateside news. I hear about her younger brother, the doctor who hates to fly and never comes to Europe, how he, along with other Sacramentans, talks about sightings of Arnold Schwarzenegger "the Governator" and the summer heat of the Sacramento Delta. I know her brother already, although not ever having met him, and I inquire about his kids (the twins are finally toilet trained). I am patient—at least for a while—since it's part of the Paris "family" we're part of. Or at least I try, but soon I have heard enough about Sacramento and am ready to change the subject. Yet, as often happens with my friends here, there is a surprise.

"And I've decided to apply for French citizenship," Edie says, as she is wrapping up the family saga and my eyes are beginning to glaze. This makes me snap to. "I'm going to get on it, right away. Are there any new regulations I should know?"

"I'll send you what I've written," I say. "But what tipped your decision?" This is research, not nosiness (or maybe it's both), for there's no way it was a romance thwarted that kept her guessing.

"When I was in California this time, I kept asking myself just what I had in common with life there, anymore. They eat Brie cheese—cold, right out of the fridge—before dinner as an appetizer, can you believe it? And iceberg lettuce for salad. And oh, I don't know, lots of things."

"Excuse me? You're going to become a French citizen because they serve Brie cheese with the before-dinner cocktails in Sacramento, that great bastion of international sophistication?"

Edie looks at me and shrugs. "I know that sounds silly," she sighs. "I guess what it means is that I'm too used to the way of life here. I'm not even going to go back next year."

"What will you do, instead?"

"I'm thinking of buying a little farm in Burgundy and growing my own vegetables. One of my chef friends knows of one for sale." She points her finger at me. "And it will be your job to dig up potatoes."

"Don't think I won't," I retort. I am already anticipating that summer desperation to get away, a trip on the boat and perhaps to Rome with the boys. But what about my fantasies of Bologna and Lou? Am I ready to admit that they're just fantasies, or can I hold on a little longer in my denial mode?

So, Edie moves on to the new workshop she had mentioned, which she's giving just for her French chef friends. It seems, although Brie cheese in America is off her list, that despite the exquisitely decorated *gâteaux* in France—chocolate curlicues, sculpted meringue, and glazed fruit slivers—French chefs don't do the same kind of wonderful work with frosted flowers that Americans do. "Oh, anyone can do a flower," Edie says as though it were obvious. "But you have to know how to dust them and to bring them out." And I do get it, once I have brought my mind back to the here and now. Edie is an artist, and she has decided finally to be a French artist, American frosting notwithstanding. This is just how it is.

"By the way," Edie says, as we are taking our leave, "I'm going to make *sanglier* again this fall. Is this the year you're going to try it or not? You've turned me down twice. You do realize that wild boar in season is a real delicacy."

"I know, I know," I say without committing myself, as we kiss each other's cheeks. I button up my jacket, for the air has turned slightly cool. "And thanks again for the popcorn."

"Hoard it," she says. "I won't bring you any more."

By the time Sandy and I find a day that suits us both for the shopping expedition—she busy with the kids and I with (or almost with) Lou—the afternoons are already beginning to be cool and sometimes damp. So, wearing a jacket and carrying her umbrella once again, Sandy comes over to rue de Rennes so we can take the No. 95 together. We settle ourselves in and start to chat. She does not mention Antoine, but I can see that her face is somewhat drawn. Yet, although I have steeled myself, Sandy is without Julien, so I take this as progress in some way that I cannot define. (I say nary a word, either about men or dogs.)

We pass by Brentano's, where I do not even suggest taking a peek to check on the placement of my books, and we get off the bus by Galeries Lafayette. After looking at just one department, I actually buy a navy blue cashmere *pull* (a pullover sweater) that is on *promo* and that Sandy says brings out the blue in my eyes. "Wear it with your lucky blue blazer," she says. As if I hadn't thought of that.

We look around a bit more at clothes, but I can tell Sandy is eager to get into her redecorating mode. So, we cross boulevard Haussmann to the furniture department, where she seems to brush her hand over every single item on the floor, sometimes twice. After what seems like forever, we see a large canopied bed that would do well for founding dynasties, but not being in the dynasty business (anymore), I just wish I could curl up on it and take a nap. Fortunately, at the point where I think I might disgrace myself by screaming, Sandy says we should move on.

So, we get back on the bus (the No. 42), going back over to the Village Suisse in the 15th *arrondissement*, where Klaus and I had browsed right after the *rentrée*. I help Sandy by not saying anything caustic as she enters one wildly expensive antique shop after another, inspecting French furniture, Italian tile-work, and English decorations. Clearly, the globalization that concerns her ex-husband does not enter her mind.

At the end of the afternoon, just as we are getting off the No. 82 for me to cut across the Luxembourg and Sandy to boulevard Raspail, she says, "Listen, how about coming over to dinner at the end of the week? The kids reminded me to ask you." While this is not the most gracious of invitations, I'm pleased that the kids are thinking of me. And I don't think that Sandy means it the way it came out. I am certainly one who knows how that is.

Thus, on another cool Saturday toward the end of October (when Luca is doing something or other with Dottore, or so he says), I go over to the boulevard Raspail apartment to inspect the progress being made. Henriette and Victor are there, at least until at the end of dinner they excuse themselves, politely, kiss Sandy and me on both cheeks, put on their jackets, and go out to wherever teenagers go on Saturday nights.

"*Papa* told me you had a good summer," Victor says, as we are sitting in the living room before dinner. I am struck not only that he and J-P talked about me, but that Victor has become a young man with a curiosity about people—not just those of his age—that will take him far in life. He clearly gets this from *Papa*, whom he resembles from head to toe. (And could he also not be the next *PDG?*) I wonder about Victor. Will J-P allow him to go to the States for an MBA? Will *Grandpère?* In response to his question, although he leans toward me as though he would like to hear everything I have to say, I manage to mention only my barge trip (the standard spiel about the locks, skipping the part about the gin) and how *tranquil* Paris was on the hot summer days.

"You lead such an exciting life, Fran," he says, finally. I have no idea what on earth he could mean, so I just smile and nod, and I say, "Oh, you will, too, I have no doubt about that."

Henriette, on the other hand, whose blouse does not cover her belly and whose pierced navel shows a little silver stud, stays on her *mobile* before dinner. And then she only picks at her food. When Sandy prods her to eat, she says, with teenager exasperation, "But *Maman*, I have to pay attention to *la ligne*." Pay attention to her figure? At age sixteen? No wonder French women don't get fat.

And then, finally, having only made patterns on the plate with her *gâteau au chocolat* (that Sandy paid a fortune for at Le Nôtre, I'm sure), she nudges Victor sharply and says they have to go. Yet, she is polite, as well. "It was nice to see you, Fran," she says, as she pushes back from the table. "I'm sorry we have to leave. But you remember what it's like to go out on Saturday night, *n'est-ce pas?*"

"Yes, I do," I say, but I do not take offense, for I am older than her mother, and this must seem ancient to her. I keep myself from mentioning that, actually, these days, I'm not doing too badly on Saturday nights. "Have a good time."

Later, after Sandy has had her coffee and I have tried an herbal *infusion* called Maroc (that I decide to pick up at Monoprix), she talks more about decorating. She asks me what I think of what she's done. I knew she would, so during dinner I prepared myself. I mean, I cannot be a member of the taste police. If I eliminate would-be friends lacking character or wit, I simply cannot add a lack of decorating taste to the dwindling list. I had thought to say that I always liked the apartment the way it was—with its airy look, its low cushiony chairs and couches, the Steinway concert-grand piano, oriental carpets, and filmy drapes. But I change my mind. The imposing armoire dominating the entryway and the bedroom suite with that seductive canopied bed and more heavy armoires show me that she is going traditionally French. And I see what she's doing—telling the world (or *Grandpère*) that no one is going to run her out.

So, perhaps I will get to see Sandy more often, at least so long as her celibacy lasts. As to myself, it does seem that—most Saturday nights notwithstanding—I am sometimes realistic enough to acknowledge to myself that I seem to be somewhat available, too.

So, now about Lou. Frankly, life with Lou continues to have its ups and downs. This does not always mean up to his apartment or down to mine, although that does happen—and often enough to keep me totally hooked. It basically means that sometimes he's too busy with his big deal to remember our dates, and they slip his mind. His apologies are imaginative as he is, and almost against my will, they make me smile. But they must also be costly, for they are usually accompanied by flowers or a bottle of wine, or even once with a package of tortelloni, some tomatoes, and a strand of fresh garlic—which I found wickedly funny, and which the next night we prepared together.

But apologies are wearing a bit thin, especially when I might have gone to a gallery *vernissage* with the boys and bumped into Margot, or to the *puces* with Caroline, who has decided to replace her chandelier. (Sandy, obviously, is not the type for the *puces,* just as Caroline is not for the Village Suisse.) Edie, who has developed her frosting course, invited me to help her experiment with something or other concerning sugar and egg whites, but I thought I was otherwise occupied (I wasn't), so I said no. (I also declined the *sanglier,* but for reasons other than Lou.) And I even fibbed to Colette, who suggested an outing to the Marmottan Museum to see the Monets. I feel so guilty and annoyed at myself for turning down my friends, so often for naught. And I thought I had learned? Clearly, there's work to do here.

Only Caroline has so far met Luca, when in early November the three of us have lunch at the Café de la Mairie. We eat upstairs, where it is less hectic than below. Luca is at his best, trotting out his irresistible Italian charm. It works. Caroline gives me a thumb's up and a wink when Luca's head is turned. And he, as just the two of us later walk over to Monoprix after lunch, tells me how much he likes her, how she reminds him of his older sister, who is a nun. I do not laugh. Should I tell this to Caroline, or not?

But what also interests me about this particular lunch is that when Luca and I entered the café, heading to the stairs, I saw Sandy—just a few weeks after dinner *chez elle*—sitting in the back, *tête-à-tête* with a youngish man in a business suit. They were holding hands. Not a piano colleague to be sure. Sandy did not look up, so I just left her to her friend and Luca to me. Actually, I was pleased that she was back on track, even though I knew I wouldn't be seeing her so much anymore. It had only been four weeks, perhaps a record for celibacy for Sandra. I hadn't really thought it would take her very long.

Luca and Caroline and I, however, arrange to see a film the following afternoon, and, of course, Luca doesn't show up on time. Caroline, who by now has heard (too often) about his disappearing acts, suggests sensibly, while I am craning my neck left and right, "Let's just go inside. If he comes, he can find us. We'll save him a seat." And this is what we do. I, however, am ready to have my day spoiled, and Caroline's, too. So, in a fit of snippiness, I tell her what Luca said about his sister. She says not a word.

Finally, Luca arrives when the film seems about half over, and as he slips in beside me, he immediately reaches for my hand and kisses it. Which, of course, makes me melt, at least part way. Caroline says nothing afterward, but when I get home—and Luca has gone upstairs to bring us down a bottle of Chianti Reserva from his stash—there is a message on my voice mail. All it says is, "Could you be married to someone whose sister is a nun?"

Anyway, sometimes I think I'm used to Luca and his ways, and sometimes I don't. But the bottom line is that I'm willing to try, for when Luca and I are together, I forget all the times that we're not. (This is not exactly true, but I can, during our times together, at least park the others somewhere out of reach.)

But, of course, I am in Paris, and everything is the same and it is different. I work, but I know I'm nearing the end, so I have a spurt of energy to work at the same time as being impatient for it to be done. I run into people on the street, but not Jenny or Jack. The daily *menu* in the restaurants has changed to the specialties of autumn. The boys and I are back together—the lunches, the walks, the concerts, and even my being taken in hand from time to time—the tension of last spring put on hold. My summer clothes (including the tee shirt I wore to lunch with Ida) are clean and put away. And I am wearing thigh-high stockings again, with the adorable lacy tops.

Trying the last few restaurants and taking notes. Hounding l'Hotel de Ville and the Tourist Office, and the *mairie* of my *arrondissement,* considering wearing a burka so no one can see that it's me yet again. Organizing chapters over and over again. Doing word counts. Deleting early drafts. Making the final checks on the Plan of Attack. It's just work by now. I'm used to "just work."

But, with the arrival of my son and his wife on the horizon, I am actually in a state of excitement, imagining their long weekend *à Paris.* What touristy things will they want to do? What will they think of Luca? I must tell them about him in advance. As to Lou, he says he is looking forward to meeting my *famiglia.* How will this all go? I am also thinking about the Big Meal, which I will make myself, in my fashion. And I am also in high gear in my getting-ready-to-travel mode. This latter means, for one thing, deviling American Airlines with requests for special meals, aisle seats, upgrades, and whatever else I can wangle.

International airlines have France's version of 800-numbers— although they are not always free. And often, the answering end is not in France at all but is in Ireland or someplace else where it's cheaper for them to be based. This is perfect, for then I can explain in English—in forceful detail—just why the company should accommodate my request, even though whatever it is I want is not exactly according to Hoyle. My French is improving steadily, but I have not yet mastered wheedling on the phone. (I have, however, learned that the French word *voler* means both "to steal" and "to fly." Given the price of a round-trip ticket to the States, visiting three cities and making a short hop to Toronto, this makes total sense.)

I tried going to the airline offices themselves, here, but I quickly found that dealing with French employees in person— even at American companies—gets you the French idea of service, which mainly means zilch. But once I grasped this, I also quickly accepted that this is just the way it is, and I began to figure out what the French call *le système D*. After all, I did not forget that this is one of Paul's rules. The French have their own way of doing things, so don't make a fuss. Do what they do: figure out what you need—and get it.

Le système D is a must, if you're going to understand the French way of coping with life. The French learn *le système débrouillard* at an early age, so they're clearly at an advantage over those of us who didn't. After all, they have to arrange everything else in their lives, as well as making travel plans and whatever else. So, they have their ways.

Literally, *le système D* means being resourceful on your own, getting by, muddling through. In reality, it means finagling any way you can—within acceptable legal parameters—to get what you need. This might be through *piston* (a personal connection) or otherwise, using every wile in your repertoire to convince an office clerk to bend a rule just a little—something that may not be a rule at all. For me, it's all part of the Paris game.

Moi, I watched the *le système D* at the hands of a master, Jean Pierre Philippe Henri when I first got my apartment in rue Servandoni. And this started me on my way.

My kitchen, as is normal in France, came equipped with nothing but a sink. (This is called *non équipée*.) So, having signed the lease on my apartment with J-P's help, I next had to buy all the appliances and cabinets—the works. I bought the cabinets at Ikea, taking with me a gay Australian handyman, who while I was deciding, spent the entire time picking out scented candles for his bedroom. But later, he did put together and hang the cabinets with a minimum of fuss. Also, at Conran's I splurged on that expensive artisan's cabinet that *Zho-elle* ran his hand over so lovingly that night so many eons ago. (Sigh.) And for the appliances, J-P came with me to Darty on a Saturday afternoon—or perhaps I went with him.

That J-P would come was a relief, because, in fact, in my case *le système D* was easier said than done. I think that J-P, who can maneuver anywhere in the world, enjoyed the process of making the salesman give me the whopping discount that I'm sure both men knew he would, even before starting the game.

After choosing a stove, refrigerator, freezer, and washer/dryer, I handed Jean-Pierre a paper with the model numbers written down. Now the drama began. J-P just sat there at the salesman's desk, calmly chewing on his cigar, insisting we wouldn't pay more than the amount he had written down on his notepad for all the appliances, and that the extra three-year warranties should be thrown in, to boot. (With no cigar to chew on, I was made a dishrag by suspense.) Eventually—at just the calculated moment, I'm sure—the salesman and J-P pored over the figures, and the salesman gave in. I got a better price than I could have on my own, thanks to J-P; Darty made the profit it expected all along; and the appliances were delivered and installed on time. And there's nothing I can do about the fact that my stove was built for Tom Thumb, for I hadn't noticed that all the appliances at Darty were raised off the flooring on platforms about four inches high.

But now, with my having provided lifetime income for half the airline staff by confirming my ticket, there is only the problem of gifts. Bringing charming French gifts to Americans presents a problem every year. When Ben Franklin left France and her ladies for the last time, or later Thomas Jefferson (who also found some pleasant diversions here), I'm sure they had no trouble with gifts. Jefferson, in fact, had a list of requests to fill, and upon leaving this "great and good country," he brought back books for Franklin and a bust of Paul Jones for John Jay. Our Founding Fathers may not have had indoor plumbing, but they had no trouble with gifts.

Two years ago I brought everyone a useless—but unique in its creativity—brightly painted little lead Napoleon. One fall evening while I was walking over to the Lovells in the Guisarde (before Joël was in and out of the frame), I saw *Monsieur N.* in the window of a toy soldier shop. I went in and bought the entire stock. My American friends humored me, but did they keep him? Or were they like *courgettes* and dusty pears? But last year, I handed out attractive yet practical roller-ball pens inscribed with the logo of the Sénat, its souvenir shop being just five minutes away from *chez moi*. I think I did better with these.

So, at the end of this week, which the *meteo* indicates will be cold but fair, Luca and I will have lunch in rue Dauphine and then walk up to the Money Museum on the *quai* to take a look at their gift shop. Perhaps they will have a small paperweight or a practical calendar for next year. If not, Luca has promised (promised?) he'll walk across the footbridge with me to the Carrousel du Louvre, which houses gift shops of The Louvre. When Richard and I window shopped there in June, I noticed some arty little prints and some Frenchy kind of tea towels. I need to find things that are small, unbreakable, and within my *budget* (pronounced *boo-jhay*).

But for now I have other things to do. One late morning, I back up my next-to-last chapter (finally almost finished with restaurants, just one or two more), and I ready myself to go to the doctor for the checkup and flu shot. Test results were all normal, so at least there's success on that front.

The forecast is for showers, but right now it is only grey. I walk easily up rue Servandoni and then through the square to the bus stop at Place St-Sulpice, to wait for the 87—my doctor's office is over by École Militaire. As I am about to cross rue St-Sulpice, I see Catherine Deneuve coming out of her apartment building on rue Bonaparte. Wow! She is wearing a light-colored raincoat and a colorful silk scarf that almost covers her copious blonde hair. Although the day is not bright, she is wearing enormous, dark sunglasses, as any respectable movie star would. (Mine are enormous, but pink. I must think this through.) I am sure everyone around has seen her, but no one says anything. She has a right to her privacy, does she not, and this is her neighborhood, where she lives. So, I do not jump up and down and gawk.

I am in fine fettle. Lou will pick me up after he gets home and takes a shower, he said early this morning when he left, and we will go to an Italian film he wants to see, with some actor he particularly likes—and maybe get a pizza, as we did that first time we went out. Nor do I mind waiting at the bus stop, sheltered in case the clouds decide to spit, for there is always something to look at (even when movie stars have moved on), and sometimes there is even someone new to talk to. Several buses pull up—the 63 and the 86—but not the 87 (reinforcing my claim that my own bus is the slowest and least frequent in town). So, keeping my eye peeled for the bus, I wander over to look in the window of Annick Goutal, that Parisian *parfumerie* where J-P bought me my Gardenia Passion soap. I could use a new supply. I am using it up, fast.

I spy the bus. I turn around and big as life, and as I knew would happen someday, there is John, and he is waiting for the bus. And I can see that he is alone, without the back-stabbing Rose. Aha! It's time for me to let him have it. I've been waiting all these months and here, finally, it is. And, I think, I'm ready to go.

As I board, John is standing by the driver, fishing out some coins for a ticket. I walk behind him, swipe my *carte navigo* against the electronic eye, and then I find a seat. So far, so good. Other people take their seats, for the bus is not crowded at this hour, and there is still an empty place next to mine. Now John is walking down the aisle, and he finally sees me.

"Fran!" he says, and he comes toward me.

And what do I say? Do I let loose with the comments I have stored away for this rainy day? Do I let him have the brunt of my hurt feelings, still with me after all these months? Do I? Of course not. I don't say a word. Instead, I smile and exclaim, as he did, "John! Come here, sit next to me."

"I thought you might still be mad at me," he says.

"Oh, we've been friends too long," I say. "Come sit down." And he does. Can you believe this? Can I believe this, hearing those friendly words that have come out of my mouth? Will I always be a wimp? Or have I learned something about being civilized from the French?

I stay about forty-five minutes at the doctor's, being examined, getting the flu shot, chatting about this and that, and being told (as I am every year) to exercise more. "Any questions?" he asked at the end, and I kicked myself for not having thought of anything in advance.

"Well, I've been meaning for years to ask you," I said, thinking about the duck breast at La Giberne, where I am going to lunch, perhaps the last restaurant on my list to try. "Does *magret de canard* have a lot of cholesterol? Is it okay to eat?"

A look of horror came over the doctor's face. "Oh!" he exclaimed. "I could never tell anyone not to eat *magret de canard!* It's too good!"

"And bird flu?" I continue, only because I'm not ready to leave.

"No," he says with some patience. "So far, only swans are dying, not *poulet* with *frites.*"

Yet, although I'm gratified at being healthy, as I start my walk over to the restaurant La Giberne on avenue de Suffren, disappointment with myself wells up (John-wise). Maybe I'll do better next time. Luckily, the *magret de canard*, with its green peppercorn sauce, bears out my doctor's judgment of the dish, and my humor is (somewhat) restored.

On this next afternoon, still somewhat pissed that Luca (with kisses galore and a friendly pat or two) insisted I go to the film alone because he had to wait for Bambino—I walk to visit the Lovells in rue Guisarde. (*Zho-elle* is nowhere in sight.) Hearing Alice's stressed voice on a morning call, I have decided to do a *bonne action* (good deed) and let her get out for a while, raising my self-esteem a smidge. Findlay, or so she has warned me, has decided that writing his memoirs should last him the rest of his life, and so they will take two volumes, not just one. I suggest she go to the film, for I did indeed go by myself, and it amused me (despite being bummed out about Luca and even his rotten kisses galore) to listen to the Italian and read the subtitles in French. But Alice says perhaps she will stroll over to the Musée d'Orsay and spend the afternoon with the Impressionists. I say I will come over right after my swim, which I do, wet bathing suit and towel in my *sac* and my hair still damp. The stairs seem not to bother me. This could be good news.

As she leaves to tackle the ninety-five steps down, Alice says to me softly, "Margot called. She wants to talk with Findlay about her book. He's thrilled. Did you have something to do with this?"

"Who, me?" I ask with a smile.

Alice stops for a moment with a surprised look on her face. "I had something to ask you, but I've forgotten what it is. Well, maybe it wasn't important."

"Go. Have a good time. Call me later, if you remember."

Now, in the course of my visit—after I have turned down the offer of Brouilly and Findlay drinks none himself—he tells me this idea of two volumes. Unfortunately, I raise my eyebrows and I laugh, asking, "And how many did Thomas Jefferson write?" But Findlay just snorts and begins to tell me some of his old stories. I settle in for the duration.

Findlay is now up to the late 1950s—having covered the family's arrival in Paris with two little boys, the beginning work of the Marshall Plan, and the need for modernizing the crumbling city. He is not yet up to the student rebellion of 1968, he says, but instead talks about John Kennedy coming here in 1961. The Lovells were invited to that famous State dinner given by President Charles de Gaulle, when even then everyone knew it was Jackie who stole the show.

"Did you see that exhibit a few years ago," I ask, "when they displayed the clothes she wore here?"

But with another snort, Findlay indicates this interests him not at all. "*M. le President* gave Kennedy some good advice about how to deal with Khrushchev," Findlay says, brushing aside my question and starting to tell me what it was. "He told Kennedy to be firm, that Khrushchev didn't really want war or he would have started one already."

"Give it only a few sentences," I beg, since by now, late in the afternoon in this apartment that is cozy and warm with the windows closed, I have begun to battle what seems to me a coma coming on. And I am wondering if there will be a message from Lou by my door—and if so, what it could possibly say to melt my stone cold heart. "That is, unless de Gaulle gave the advice to you, too. These are your memoirs, not theirs."

All of a sudden, Findlay begins to cough deeply, hacking and turning red. I am in a panic. What if he dies on my watch? But then he takes a long drink of water, clears his throat, and catches his breath.

"Thought I was a goner, didn't you?" he chides me.

"Of course not," I lie with some outrage, yet considering that maybe the retirement home on boulevard Raspail is a good idea, after all. "What were you saying about Kennedy?"

But a short while later, walking down the ninety-five steps, actually having been edified about Paris of a half century ago (which to Findlay is yesterday), I decide I was wrong, so I trudge back up and knock on the door to tell Findlay that. History— and Findlay's take—are important. Besides, one can take only so much of Mrs. Kennedy's clothes. And I had been only halfway down the stairs.

When I get to my door there is a Monoprix sack with a bottle of Barolo, a package of chicken breasts, some broccoli, and a *baguette*. Tired as I am after the swim and the stairs, and still annoyed at having gone alone to the film, this does not sit at all well with me. For a change, I do not smile. But then I read the note that says, "I love you, *'Cesca*. Tonight, all night?" This is the first time he has told me in words how he feels. Suddenly, once again *la vie est belle*. I immediately think of how best to make the chicken

THREE GUIDES TO PARISIAN RESTAURANTS IN ENGLISH

Zagats Survey: Paris Restaurants: Rated as to patrons' opinions.

The Michelin Guide (red): Restaurants rated with one to three stars, based on quality of food, service, décor, plus "personality" of food and overall experience. In 2007, nine Paris restaurants sported three stars.

Gault-Millau: Restaurants awarded chef's "toques" based on the food. Other aspects are rated separately. The highest possible is twenty, although few have ever achieved that high mark.

and what to wear to get myself dolled up. One must compromise when one is in love.

AND...A SMALL SAMPLING

HISTORIC

- 6e: **Closerie des Lilas**: 171 boulevard du Montparnasse (tel: 01.40.51.34.50). Hemingway's still-charming hangout. Choose among a brasserie, restaurant, or piano bar.

- 6e: **Le Procope**: 13 rue d l'ancienne Comédie (tel: 01.40.46.79.00). Oldest Paris café, now catering to tourists, but nice to know that you ate where Benjamin Franklin did. ~~Waiters seem bored.~~

- 12e: **Le Train Bleu**: Gare de Lyon (tel: 01.43.43.09.06). Lovely Belle Epoque ambience and exquisite frescoes; updated classic cuisine.

TRENDY

- 6e: **Mood**: 1 rue Washington (tel: 01.42.89.98.89). French-Asian fusion cuisine, with a well-priced lunch *menu*. Just off the Champs-Élysées.

- 12e: **Chai**: 33 Cour St-Emilion (tel: 01.53.44.01.01). In the restored Bercy Village adjacent to the charming park, a modern wine bar and restaurant.

STARRED RESTAURANTS

- 8e: **Taillevent**: 15 rue Lamennais (tel: 01.44.95.15.01). *Haute cuisine* with both a formal and intimate ambiance.

- 16e: **Hiramatsu**: 52 rue de Longchamp (tel: 01.56.81.08.80.) Imaginative, refined New French cuisine by a master Japanese chef.

FORMER COLONIES

- 6e: **Le Palanquin**: 12 rue Princesse (tel: 01.43.29.77.66). Upscale Vietnamese cuisine.

- 5e: **Kim Lien:** 33 Place Maubert (tel: 01.43.54.68.13). Try the *bo bun* with *nem* at this casual eatery—a one dish meal of meat, salad, noodles, and topped with Vietnamese dumplings. Menus have pictures of the dishes.

- 17e: **Chez Nini**: 24 rue Saussier-Leroy (tel: 01.46.22.28.93). Tunisian couscous. Appetizers to share.

SPECIALTIES

- 9e: **Le Roi du Pot-au-Feu**: 34 rue Vignon (tel: 01. 47.42.37.10). Traditional boiled beef with vegetables.

- 6e: **Relais de l'Entrecôte**: 20 bis rue St-Benoit (tel: 01.45.49.16.00).

- Choose how you want your steak cooked--the rest is up to the restaurant.
- 7e: **La Cigale Recamier**: 4 rue Recamier (tel: 01.45.48 86.58). Fluffy soufflés made with seasonal ingredients. Next to a hidden little park the locals love.

FAST and GOOD

- 4e: **L'As du Fallafel**: 34 rue des Rosiers (tel: 01.48.87.63.60). Always crowded, and no wonder—the best falafel and schwarma in town.
- 6e: **Cosi**: 54 rue du Seine (tel: 01.46.33.35.36). Sandwiches on Italian bread hot from the oven. Choose your own ingredients from those displayed.

LOCAL BISTROS

- 6e: **Le Claude Sainlouis**: 27 rue du Dragon (tel: 01.45. 01.29.68). Friendly local bistro. Varied, excellent selection—fish, steaks, frog legs, and save room for the chocolate mousse.
- 16e: **Auberge du Mouton Blanc**: 40 rue d'Auteuil (tel: 01.42.88.02.21). Great burgers, French style.

FISH

- 8e: **Flora Danica**: 142 avenue des Champs-Elysées (tel: 01.44.13.86.26). For salmon lovers, this is the place to come. Smoked, marinated, poached, or roasted—whatever you might want.
- 6e: **La Méditerranée**: 2 place de l'Odéon (tel: 01.43.26.02.30). Classic French fish dishes.
- 17e: **L'Huitrier**: 16 rue Saussier-Leroy (tel: 01.40.54.83.44). The freshest of oysters and fish.

TEA ROOMS

- 1er: **Angelina**: 226 rue de Rivoli (tel: 01.42.60.82.00). Comforting pots of hot chocolate and pastries in an "Old World" tearoom. Known for its luscious *mont blanc*.
- 4er: **Mariage Frères**: 30 rue du Bourg-Tibourg (tel: 01.42.72.28.11). Teas for sale and sampling in this elegant tearoom founded in 1854. Other addresses.

ICE CREAM

- 4e: **Berthillon**: 31 rue St-Louis-en l'Ile (tel: 01.43.54.31.61). Addictive flavors, ~~especially the caramel beurre-salé.~~ Closed part of July and all of August.

Yet, although Luca arrives on time (for him), and the dinner and the entire night together that follows rekindle my flames once more (but for what?), I am coming over the weeks to realize that I am being more often stood up. And I'm not sure why.

It isn't that we don't see each other almost every day, one way or another. We have dined in many evenings, watching the news on TV. We've been to several concerts at Châtelet and out to dinners in the *quartier*—a few not even interrupted by the ringing of his *telefonino* (which I am ready to pitch into the Seine). Caroline came over for one of Luca's *gnocchi* dinners, and after having walked her home he knocked on my door and helped with the dishes. We finished the Chianti, and then we turned in. Once, he suggested a charming restaurant he had found in rue Guisarde, but when he told me the name, I quickly suggested we stay in. No Italian man turns down homemade *pasta al ragu*.

We finally ate steak at l'Entrecote for his birthday. We did go to the Money Museum together, and I did find my gifts. We walked around the museum and looked at a few exhibits, and then walked to the *quai,* and while standing and looking at the river, we talked, Lou's arm around my shoulder. "Soon, I will show you my lovely Bologna," he said, and he kissed me. I wondered whether this meant that his mysterious deal was coming to a close. But, of course, I didn't ask. Instead, as we stood there, I pictured us in Bologna together. Just what does one wear to meet a nun?

One of the best afternoons in recent memory was on a lovely Indian summer afternoon—all slanted sunny rays and foliage at the best of its colors—when we walked the entire length of the elevated railroad turned park—the Promenade Plantée—from the Bastille to the Jardin de Reuilly. Luca's arm, for the most part, was draped over my shoulder or linked with mine. Was autumn always like this and I just hadn't noticed? We sat quietly on a bench, and Luca kissed me sweetly several times. "I'm happy with you, *'Cesca,"* he said. That was all.

And one Saturday morning, we rose at dawn and took a long ride in one of those huge *autocars* to Mont-Saint-Michel for a tour of the abbey, including a lunch in a fourteenth-century château. We were back in Paris in time for a snack at the Flore, and then, both of us exhausted, we walked home and said goodnight on the stairs. He nibbled my hand, which I never cease to find seductive, but I was too tired even to think of more. "Call me, *'Cesca"* he said as always, heading up to his apartment. And naturally, I said I would. (But why should I?)

But we have also not gone to the theater to see a play by the Italian Dario Fo, even when I had agreed to go and get tickets. (But, it being a Saturday, Edie could go, so that was good.) We have not eaten together an *osso buco* that I spent all one afternoon preparing at his request. He just didn't show up. And five days after that we did not meet at the Café Mabillon, where I waited a half hour before I gave up, drank a *kir royal* alone, and then came home. If I think that I thrive on uncertainty and change, I also currently think that Luca is testing that assumption too well.

But, as I said, I am not particularly discontent. I am who I am, and if my friends put up with me, I suppose that I can only let other people be who they are, too. If I like people who are out of the ordinary, how can I complain when they do out of the ordinary things?

Wait! Do I finally have something Parisian almost in my grasp? *Paris is tolerant, perhaps even overtly encouraging the particularities of people's lives.* For guidebook talk, that's a good start.

And I now wonder. Could this be what Miss What's-her-Stein meant? I mean, what with one thing and another, I have managed to avoid her for some time, but now she is back on my mind.

So, I stop to consider all her pretensions to genius and all her dislikes and jealousies and huffs. And in the doing, I am also forced to reflect on her insights into this city and its life. And so, it comes to me. Who could have been more encouraged in a particular life here than she?

Winding Down and a Surprise

WELL, FINALLY ON A RAINY MID-NOVEMBER afternoon, and as I recently have suspected it would, my relationship with Lou comes to an end. The other shoe drops. I hear it come down with a bang. I am, of course, watching the news at *13h* while I eat lunch, waiting for the weather report to mislead me once again. The fitful rain, which has already made a liar of Méteo France once this morning, is clearly a taste of winter to come. Lunch, however, is comforting—some kind of tender tiny chicken called a *coquelet* that I have picked up still warm at the Grand Épicerie and a salad of beets and mache. Feeling virtuous, I pour myself a glass of Evian. Feeling less so, I have put into the oven a *moelleux au chocolat,* bought frozen from Picard. I am already debating whether to swim or to nap, when I hear from the television the words *Italien* and *entrepreneur*. These words stop me in my tracks.

I almost drop my fork. It seems that a French *député* from somewhere down near Lyon (who shall remain nameless only because I didn't catch his name) might have to resign, since it is alleged that he has been taking "campaign contributions" from an Italian businessman living in Paris who has been trying to put together some kind of big business deal. That's what Bambino was doing, and Dottore? Bribing the government? For them, this was *le système D*? If there were anyone around, it would be clear that I am speechless. But there isn't, so I am left to be in shock all alone.

Astounded and almost in a daze, I toss what's left of the *coquelet*. I take the chocolate cake out of the oven. Hot as it is, I start nibbling at it on the way to the table. I am desperate. I have grasped what was behind Lou's constant preoccupation and at the same moment I have understood, too, that this bodes ill for him and me. Or maybe just me. My heart sinks. My eyes feel prickly. There's nothing to do but wait. This is not something I am good at.

Unfortunately, all too soon I am proved right. An hour or so after lunch, feeling more than cranky and imminently teary, while I am actually getting out my bathing suit and towel, thinking that a swim might distract me somewhat, I hear the sound of suitcases being dragged down the stairs from above. I fluff up my hair while rushing to the door.

"*Cesca, carissima,*" Lou says, and his face is pale. "I have an emergency at home, and I must go back to Italy right away."

"Oh no," I say, innocently. I hope my makeup isn't smeared. "I'm so sorry. I hope nobody is sick or dead."

"Not that," he says, and it is clear he is preoccupied and upset. "But I will explain the next time I see you. I will call you every day. Do not worry about me. You are in my heart forever. But right now *je suis très pressé*. I must hurry home." The last hand kiss. The last stroking of my face. "*Au revoir,*" he says, thrusting at me the keys to the flat. He disappears down the stairs. I throw the keys in a desk drawer and push them toward the back.

So, I've been dumped, or sort of. Even if that's not exactly true, it feels that way. Shock gives way to grief. Molten chocolate now sits heavy in my gut. I do not swim. I do not go out. I stay home the rest of the day. I cry. I pout. I cry some more. And unexpectedly, I recall some words Caroline had shown me written by her neighbor—couldn't Luca at least have been as gallant as Paul Jones was when he dusted off one *Mme*. Chaumont? "I shall carry with me thro life," Jones wrote, if I remember correctly, having hied himself safely to the far remove of his ship, "the most Constant and Lively sense of your polite Attentions and of your delicate and Unreserved Friendship." I loved it—at the time.

But Luca is not Paul Jones, and I am weary of thinking about Paris, about permanence and life. Is it time to move on? Will I never resolve my life? Will I never understand reality when it knocks on my door? For the next day or so, during which there are no calls from Italy, I am totally bummed out. I talk for a few minutes each morning with Caroline, who heard the same broadcast and who wants to come over, but I say no. I am not ready to be comforted. I do not call the boys. I sit on the couch. I stop crying (saving my tears for the fallen heroes of the French). I just remain low of spirit, low of energy, low of morale. In other words, zonked.

After two days of this, I try to muster up the will to take stock. I can't. This is more serious than I thought. This had turned from a project into Love. No matter that it was so unpredictable, no matter that my life was turned upside down by it, no matter that somewhere in my soul I knew that something was fishy. And I did know it, didn't I? It was never unequivocal, but when it was good, it just suited me so well, and that is what hurts. And it doesn't help that, yet again, I must add another name to that disappointing roster of relationships that came and went.

Finally, one late afternoon, Klaus calls to say they are wondering how I am, for they haven't heard from me in days. I spill it all out with, I must admit, a quite effective weep. So, he does not rub it in about Italian men. All he does is say, "Oh, little darling, oh, little darling!" Upon hearing this, Paul grabs the phone and, ever gentle, he says wise words—that I am not ready to hear.

But after a day or so, when feeling sorry for myself alone is wearing thin, I figure I should allow other people to suffer with me. And besides, as I did (long ago) in the spring, I decide to give Paris a chance to do her stuff. I call the boys back, whining, asking whether I could please come over for a while, and they immediately say I must be there by tea time. They will be waiting for me. So, I clean myself up and put on something warm and cozy (but fit for the 16th *arrondissement,* of course). And with some relief to be out and about again, no matter how surly I feel, I go.

After I get off the No. 63 and walk up avenue Marceau, I see Klaus waiting for me at his door. We climb the marble stairs, which I must say is difficult, given that he has his arms completely entwined around me, as though I needed the physical support. And after the *bisous* all around and a cup of a pale greenish tea (with antioxidants, Klaus assures me, as though I cared), Paul suggests a turn at the piano. So, Klaus puts his arms around me once again, and we sing while Paul plays. Paul does not play romantic songs.

Afterward, we have a glass of sherry, and then they suggest we walk over to the Drugstore Publicis on the Champs-Elysées for an early, light meal. It is just starting to rain as we leave the building, and I notice Paul's mouth tightening, his lips pursing as he opens his umbrella. *It is November*, I think, *and the cold rains are only just beginning.* Klaus reaches over to Paul and arranges his scarf so that his neck is entirely covered, and we begin our walk.

At The Drugstore, we are seated right away. The man at the table next to us has ordered a club sandwich, and we all do the same, although when ours come, we do not eat them with a knife and fork. I feel touched by my old friends, worried about them for a change, and not me. *I must watch out for them now,* I think, with a sudden and surprising clarity. *It's time for the balance to shift.* The sandwich is dreadful, but I say nothing. I am consumed by a startling care for these lovely—and loving—men. All too soon, I see them to their door, and the kisses later as we part are sweet.

The next afternoon I ring Caroline's bell on my way back from doing an errand in the *quartier* (replenishing my cookie stash). She is home and shouts into the interphone to come up. Once we are seated in her living room, she opens a half-bottle of champagne, and I add a few drops of cassis to mine to make a *kir royal.* Caroline does her best to console me with stories of F. Scott Fitzgerald.

The champagne has its effect, and I actually giggle about Scott asking Hemingway to look at his private parts to see if they were satisfactory. Hem said he didn't see anything wrong.

Caroline has found a used copy of *A Moveable Feast* at the San Francisco Book Company, and she gives it to me, saying I should take a look at it again. So, I put Hemingway into the bag with the Pepperidge Farm Chocolate Chunk lovelies, and decide to put the book on the nightstand, ready to read if I ever finish another I was tackling before the great *rupture*. A book about all the Americans here during the French Revolution that I no longer have the will to read.

Walking home from Caroline's along rue de Vaugirard, I see it is late enough that there is no line at the Luxembourg Museum. So, I stop in. The exhibit is of self-portraits by famous twentieth-century painters and photographers. After a few minutes of whipping through and stopping here or there, interested in how these artists saw themselves, I am blown away by seeing a photograph of a young man looking in a mirror, but also looking at me. I knew him! I did! I knew him when I was young and he was very old. Herbert Bayer, of the Berlin avant-garde art movement called the Bauhaus (before Hitler did it in). He was still so elegant when I knew him, erect, tanned, with a shock of white hair and a smile that showed teeth that almost matched his hair. And here he is, young and striking, with his hair dark. I hadn't thought of him in decades. And now he is—as Alice says—memory and history, staring at himself and me. I stand, feeling connected with my past, almost remembering who I am, again, until the crowd forces me on.

As I dart across rue de Vaugirard, I can feel some progress in my mood. Fitzgerald's private parts! Bayer's public face! Yet, I am not ready to give up misery entirely. So, in one last burst of self-pity, I continue walking down to the end of rue Servandoni, along the side of the square and up the stairs of the big church, having decided to talk it over with one of the saints. Perhaps even with St-Sulpice himself.

I take a seat at the Mary Chapel, at the back where there are some straight chairs. I mean, a good talk with a saint might take some time. I will have to start at the beginning, wherever that is. So, although people are walking about and some are lighting long tapers and putting them in sconces nearby, no one else is sitting, and I get to choose a chair in the back row all to myself. I put my jacket on the seat beside me and settle myself in. I am ready for the heart-to-heart. But just as I am about to introduce myself, a shabbily dressed, rather scruffy man comes running up to me and shouts something odious—it must be odious, otherwise why would he be shouting in church? And then, even before I can figure out what is the matter, he picks up one of the chairs and hurls it at me. Fortunately, the chair only grazes my leg, yet he is still shouting, and I still can't figure out if I have done something wrong. (One never knows, after all, with the French.)

Within a few seconds, however, all of St-Sulpice has come to my aid. The tourists with their cameras, two quite elderly women who are clearly holy (no makeup and tie-up, brown, rubber-soled shoes that would never squeak), and a priest who skillfully ushers away the man, who turns out to be just drunk, talking to him firmly, as though this was not a first offence. I, however, am being hovered over, which immediately claims my attention, making me forget about saints.

"Are you all right?" one of the holies asks with genuine concern.

"*Oui, oui, merci beaucoup,*" I sigh as pathetically as I can. "I'll... be...all right." ("*Ça... va... aller.*")

"We're so sorry you were disturbed while you were praying," the other one says. "Do you need a doctor?"

This last makes me realize that it's time to scram. "*Non, merci, ça va, ça va.*" I'm fine, just fine, I assure them both and thank them again. "I think I'll just go home and have a cup of tea." And after a few pats on my shoulder and the escort of these truly fine women all the way to the door, I walk back down the steps, ready for a good laugh, which for the last few minutes I could hardly contain. And as I said in the spring: I know myself. If I can laugh, I'll be okay.

Nonetheless, the next afternoon at Sandy's on boulevard Raspail, I wait for her to impart something wise from her experience about men. (But not about Arab diplomats.) I am drinking a cup of that Maroc tea I had liked in September but, of course, forgot to buy.

But what she says is this: "Yes, *Frahn-zess,* I knew you had a man. You thought I didn't see you when you and he were having lunch at the Café de la Mairie." She says nothing as Julien comes over and sits on my foot. (Surprisingly, at least to me, I do not move my foot away, and I only think that her imitation of Joël is amusing, not sad.) "You didn't come over and say hello, so I thought I'd just leave you be."

This makes me smile. I practice my Gallic shrug. It's getting better. "No, I was leaving you be, because I thought you were so enrapt with a new young man."

"Well, maybe, I was," she says. "But I'm not now. And don't forget that men are like buses. Another one will come along."

I am not as sure about that as I used to be, but I do know—as I did in the spring with *Zho-elle,* who is no longer on my to-do list, despite a surprising resumption recently of those old blown kisses—that if my particular bus doesn't come along, I will scout one out. After all, two projects in one year do not constitute methodological research. But that doesn't mean that right now I don't long to hear those floorboards squeak on the floor above.

"By the way, Fran," Sandy says, interrupting my thought, "I'm going to be entertaining at the Embassy again, so if you were going to invite me for Thanksgiving, I won't be able to come."

"Well, I was going to," I say quickly. "How about next year having the dinner here, sitting at your nice new dining room set?" Sandy is pleased at this, and I am gratified to have had the presence of mind to say it. In fact, her apartment does look good, in its French sort of way. Even Julien seems to fit, he being a French dog and all. I pat him on the way out. The city's law about cleaning up dog stuff seems to be having an effect. Maybe I can be over my Cold War against dogs.

Anyway, now that I am almost back on form, I decline Caroline's offer to help me with my Thanksgiving errands. So, I bundle up one late morning and—after having spent several hours thinking of some final words to write about Paris, knowing that there truly never will be one final thing to say—I start out to the shops. I think of how much my son loves Paris, and I am sure his wife will, too. In rue de Buci I stock up on a variety of the pungent cheeses I know they like and that I can have to myself after they leave. I also go to La Fnac Digitale on boulevard St-Germain and buy a new USB flash drive (blue and silver).

Thus, the final countdown begins for my dinner, for the work odds and ends left to do, and for the winding down of the year in Paris. My depression is to the side for me to deal with later, if it all. I don't have time for this, now. Impatience sometimes helps. It has done, all my life.

I start with the dinner. In addition to my son and his wife, I have invited the "family"—Caroline and Paul and Klaus. The Lovells aren't up to coming, so I will send over some leftover turkey and pecan pie. Margot also declined, and I managed to avoid hearing most of the reason why, which had to do with exploitation of Native Americans. (Do I have the stamina for this?) Edie is having a dinner for her chef pals, *chez elle*. Mitzi and her husband have invited people from the synagogue. Being noble, I call Anna, but the recording tells me that I have dialed a nonworking number. I call Mitzi again for info (gossip), and she tells me that Anna and

Avi have split for good, and Anna has gone back to Cleveland. "I'm sorry I forgot to tell you," she says.

"And what about Avi?" I ask, sure that I know the answer already.

"Avi? Oh, he's here, at least for another year or so, I think," Mitzi says, and lowers her voice, as though her house were bugged. "I saw him walking near UNESCO with some pretty woman in a sari."

Do I need feel guilty about always forgetting Anna and not going to the museum of fancy fans, I wonder, after we hang up. Did I contribute to her not having a good time here? Do I wonder at all about Avi and the woman in the sari? Do I feel sorry that their marriage is kaput? The answers are no, maybe no-maybe yes, no, and yes.

So, last for the dinner, at what would have been Luca's place, I will put some flowers and a colorful trivet. That will be festive, after all. There will be six at table, just right. I will put my son next to Klaus, who held him in his arms three days after he was born (and who never lets my son forget it). Caroline will sit next to Paul, and my son's wife will be to my right. Life is too short for boy-girl seating.

At the same counter at the Grande Épicerie where I found the ill-fated *coquelet*, I order the turkey to be stuffed and roasted and picked up by me at *18h30* on Thursday. (Bon Marché will be open Thursday, since Thanksgiving seems not to be a holiday here.) I discuss which type of stuffing would be best. This almost counts as making it myself. I will make the cranberry sauce from Ocean Spray cranberries, also from the Grande Épicerie. I will microwave the *patates douces* in advance and mash them later on. I call to order the pecan pie from The Real McCoy, the American grocery over on rue de Grenelle, and I will go over Wednesday afternoon to pick it up. Last, at La Dernière Goutte, I pick up a couple of red wines to go with the turkey, and I think I'm all set. I even remember to buy coffee and filters this time. I am on a roll.

Although I still jump whenever the phone rings, I am fully aware that there will be no calls ever again from the brother of the nun. And with this firmly implanted in my soul, I can finally take stock. Actually, it doesn't take long. It's over, that's all, and the truth is that I never did know what it really was. I didn't care so much about that when I fell for that toothy smile, but I suppose (know) I should have. And those strange disappearances that began to wear thin that now make sense. As I once thought about *Zho-elle,* I think again that I'm too old to be kept guessing. And there's always *la France* to keep me on my toes. When I get back from the States, perhaps my project energy will have been renewed. *On ne sais jamais.* One never knows.

This now leaves Freifeld, and one does what one has to do. On the Tuesday before the Big Day, I am at my desk at sunup. (Which is at 7h55, these days, so it's later than it sounds.) I update the author's bio for the back page and write the cover letter. I riffle through the manuscript one last time, looking for inconsistencies and typos, and I find a couple to fix. The spell check is done. (The grammar check in Word is so bad it makes me laugh.) I make sure there are no blanks on the Plan of Attack. I back up the manuscript to the blue and silver flash drive, and I am done. So now, I can't put it off any longer. Freifeld is next.

Reluctantly, I dial the number Richard gave me. Freifeld and I chat a few moments, he not seeming surprised by my call. Yet, he says nothing about *le scandale* until I bring it up, myself. "I hear you're deserting us," is all I say. Freifeld, however, immediately lets me have an earful, although I hear nothing (yet) about whoever she is.

Certainly, people do leave Paris forever. Corporate types get transferred elsewhere. Diplomats like Tom Jefferson get called back to help in the governing of their country. Some like Ben himself are tired, and forsaking Paris and her various charms, are ready for America, once again. Others, and I can understand this (more or less), find it too hard to live so far away from what they still think of as "home." And a few, like Freifeld, seem just to have had enough. Enough of Paris, enough of his wife, enough of his job, just enough. This, of course, took him twenty minutes to say.

"Do you want to know what the last straw was?" he asks, but wisely does not wait for my answer. "My nephew Shelley came to visit from Cleveland. He's a professor, very distinguished. I got him a room at the Hotel Mercure, over in the 15th. His meeting was at the Hilton, next door. The hotel was fine, but Shelley got some kind of stomach virus, and he and my daughter Sara went over to a pharmacy in boulevard de Grenelle."

"And?"

"And on the way back to the hotel, Shelley had an attack. They saw a small hotel, a different Mercure, so they went in, and Shelley asked in English whether he could please use the *toilettes*. The people at the desk actually said no! He showed the room key from his Mercure, but they still refused. For security reasons, they said. If they let him use the toilet, they'd have to let all the homeless people do so. *Merde*. Couldn't they tell the difference between a well-dressed sick American and a French habitual drunk? I tell you, I can't wait to get out of here. And I'm not coming back."

"Okay, that was the last straw," I acknowledge as graciously as I can, for it is true that I never understand about the paucity of French restrooms and the unwillingness of the *patrons* to let others use them. But I think to myself of my interactions with *Mlle* Piggy at the *traiteur* and how there's always someone rude, somewhere. I think it's time to get to the ditching of his wife and meeting a new Ms. Wonderful. "What else?"

But Freifeld does not yet oblige. "It's the French. *J'en ai marre.* Absolutely, 100 percent fed up. They don't look where they're going and will never adjust their direction when you're walking toward them. And they block the middle of the sidewalk when they're standing talking to each other and won't even budge. And they complain we don't speak French, but if we do they answer us back in English, which I find quite rude. No matter what, you're always an outsider, here."

"Well, I guess," I say, but what effort did he make to belong? I think, with some smugness (I admit), about my decision to do the newsletter. And I am reminded of one of Paul's comments. "After all," he once said, "if we wanted to spend our lives with people just like us, we could have stayed in the States." So for me now, none of Freifeld's reasons would be grounds for divorce. "But that can't be all?"

"No, I'm just beginning. Nothing ever goes smoothly. I'm tired of standing in line for every bureaucratic need. I'm tired of dog crap on the sidewalk. I'm tired of waiting a month for an appointment to get my teeth cleaned. I'm tired of all the rules. Rules you know, rules you learn about after you've broken them, rules you couldn't figure out if you tried. I'm tired of the yearly TV tax. I'm tired of the strikes that foul up the city, and I've always been a union supporter, believe me. And most of all, I'm tired of being married to a French woman. Period."

Of course, nothing Freifeld says has been inaccurate in itself. And he's not the only one to think so. Suddenly, I remember that quote from Mary McCarthy that Caroline emailed months ago. While Freifeld is nattering on, I click on my computer file of quotes and find this: "The bedrock Parisian trait is probably resistance to change. This trait, almost animal, explains all the others: xenophobia, rigid adherence to rules, suspicion, even stinginess."

But I have my own pet peeves. Would I not? People in the *métro* who wear backpacks, not grasping that they have added ten inches to their girth and who swing around and smack you without so much as a by-your-leave. People who call me on my *mobile* even when I'm at home working, sitting next to the landline. People who think voice mail is an opportunity to tell you in detail what they're going to tell you again when you call back. And restaurants that use the same pot for coffee that they do for hot water for tea, not caring that the aromatic oils of the coffee seep into the glass. But little of this has to do with *la France*. They're just things I hate.

So, with Freifeld, I pass over the TV tax, for it subsidizes the documentaries that I doze through. I skip the dentist, for *sans doute* he'll fare no better with appointments when he goes back. I have enough sense not to get into a discussion about how *la France* works to someone who has had enough. And I don't say how I view everything in Paris—for better or for worse—as an event. But I do say, "Oh, so it's your marriage that has precipitated all this." I have nothing to lose. "Richard said you've fallen in love with someone from your college days. Are you sure it's for real?"

I suppose that if people fall in love in romantic Paris, others might well fall out, such as Hemingway did with wife Hadley, although he seems—or so it's claimed—to have regretted that later on. But perhaps Ann Arbor, where Freifeld will live, is romantic to him, although I've been there and somehow missed its great attractions, four months of snow being among them. But having mulled on this for an instant, I realize with dismay that I have missed what Freifeld has said about this woman with whom I gather he had once shared holding a banner saying *Viva Fidelito* in a political parade. And he is now moving on to the faults of his wife.

"Tell me again. I dropped the phone and didn't hear you," I say, covering for my lapse. So, I hear about how *froide* his wife is and how warm is his new love. I hear how the one doesn't appreciate his great sense of humor and how the other one does. I hear how she keeps kosher, and that he will have a new life built around the synagogue. The new love, though, according to Freifeld, has aged considerably over these thirty years, and I wonder if he has recently looked in the mirror himself. I hear how lonely she's been since her husband died and how much, with no children or grandchildren, she needs him, but it seems to me that she is the lifeboat in his marital storm. And I hear, once again, how his wife doesn't understand him, but I do not say that I don't, either. As for the rest, my occasional "um-hmmm" seems enough for him.

At this point, I have no intention of trying to dissuade Freifeld from going, since he has his mind made up. There's no point in his spending the rest of his life being unhappy (or wasting my time). Yet, I'm sorry that he is leaving so bitterly, although I know a bad marriage can make one just that. And it's too bad that he has to take it out on Paris. I prefer to think, as Hem finally did, "There is never any ending to Paris and the memory of each person who has lived in it differs from that of any other...Paris was always worth it and you received return for whatever you brought to it."

Freifeld says he will move into his honey's home that is paid for, free and clear. Good for him that accounting and romance go hand in hand. *Moi*, I care more about Ben, who, when leaving Paris, shipped home 128 crates of Stuff. Or even Jefferson, whose "baggage" included his slave Sally Hemings—who was not a slave in France. Yet, being pregnant, she did refuse to return to America unless Jefferson promised to free her (their) children when they reached the age of twenty-one. So Jefferson promised, and so he did. Hemings chose slavery for a man? More than I would do.

As Friefeld rants, I feel a fidget coming on. I just tune out again and let Jefferson in. Sometimes, when I pass the convent on rue de Grenelle where his daughters went to school, I picture him fussing over them or spending time in his garden, and I think of him plotting over dinners with his friend Lafayette in the cause of political reform. And sometimes in my mind I can hear Jefferson say, as he did to a French gentleman who inquired whether he was replacing Benjamin Franklin, "No one can replace Doctor Franklin, Sir. I am only his successor." I wish I could think so fast. And he probably said it in French.

Finally disposing of the graceless Freifeld, however, and ready to chew it all over with my sensible friend, I call Scheherazade. She is not at home, so I leave a message suggesting a bowl of comforting dumpling soup for lunch at Mirama over on rue St-Jacques.

Caroline calls back, saying she had been in the shower and that I should walk by and ring her bell. So, just before *13h*, I go to the corner at rue de Vaugirard, walk left across from the back of the palace of Marie de Médicis, and turn into rue de Tournon, passing again the last home of the ill-fated (but always courtly) Paul Jones. I buzz Caroline, and she comes right down.

Over our soups, I relate the Freifeld story. In lurid detail and with relish. I ask, "But what can I say to Richard? I don't think Freifeld's departure is any great loss, but who will sing lefty songs with Richard? Do you want to walk down St-Germain calling out 'Solidarity'?"

"I don't know Freifeld well, but I wouldn't write him off," Caroline says in her levelheaded way. "People's lives change. Just look at yourself. And all those people we talk about—you know, like Jefferson, Mary McCarthy, James Jones—they all left, for one reason or another. So, don't be too hard on Freifeld."

Caroline is right about Freifeld, and I am immediately contrite. "Okay, I guess Freifeld just hasn't grasped *le système D*. And I suppose, I could always take Richard to the Lenin Museum."

"Sure, and to the Musée de la Monnaie at the same time," Caroline says. I laugh at this, and I notice that I feel only a slight pang that the Money Museum was the destination of my last walk with Luca, Luca the absent, Luca who hasn't once called and won't. But the sensation is fleeting. It isn't that Luca is appearing any less frequently in my mind, it's that there is a certain release in not always having to be on my toes. Of realizing something is over, done, *finis.*

"You know…" Caroline starts to say.

"You know…" I say, at the same time, and we laugh. "I know what?" I ask. "You go first."

"Well, to change the subject. I've been thinking about things left undone. With all your adventures this year, I've been thinking." She laughs sheepishly. "So, pardon my French, but I'd like just one more good fuck before I die!"

"Caroline! For heaven's sakes!"

"Well, I would. That's all there is to say about that. Now, what were you going to say?"

"Nothing so startling, I assure you. But it's been on my mind. Just that we should be grateful that another year has gone by without your knee giving out."

"Oh my," sighs Caroline, helping herself to another dumpling, "I haven't mentioned it, but it looks like a knee replacement is in order for next spring. Do you think you'll be here?"

"Of course!" I say. "No matter what, I'll be here." This sounds about right, actually.

'Good. And speaking of next year…"

"What? A good you-know-what for you? You know, it's never too late, even with a bum knee." I say this, but I'm not sure I believe it, no matter what the magazines claim.

"No, no. I doubt I'll be so lucky. Have you talked with Alice?"

"Not in the past few days. Why? Is there something I should feel guilty about?"

"Oh, no. Except for that old age moveable target they've hit, they're fine. She just wonders, when they move over to the retirement home over on Raspail, if you'd be interested in taking over their apartment."

I am dumbstruck. I do not know what to say. This must have been what Alice had wanted to ask me, but couldn't remember. I do love their apartment, so large, bright, so comfortable. Immediately, my innate need for change makes me want to scream aloud *Yes!* But could I handle those five flights of stairs? Is it too big for someone who lives alone? How would I feel about living in rue Guisarde? But a new apartment! I am quiet a moment, thinking where I would put my lovely kitchen cabinet, the one Joël admired so many months ago.

"What do you think?" I finally ask.

"You don't have to give Alice an answer now," Caroline says. "I know the landlord will save the place for you if you want it. He's said as much to Alice."

Quiet again, I consider this possibility. The French landlord? I think about how astute Caroline is, about the Lovells and their moveable target of old age, and about how much I will miss our circle, as Caroline calls it—for she would never call it a gang— while I'm away. I know, though, that I'll hear if there's anything I am missing. And on email, she'll put up both with my eagerness to hash out the possibilities for a new apartment but also my doubts about stairwells and rue Guisarde. And what about her knee? How had I not noticed that it was so bad?

It is also a comfort to realize that as soon as Thanksgiving weekend

FURTHER READING, PART III

Bizardel, Yvon (Wilson, June P. and Higginson, Cornelia, translators): *The First Expatriates: Americans in Paris During the French Revolution*. New York, Holt, Rinehart and Winston, 1972.

Gendlin, Frances: *Culture Shock! Paris*. New York, Cavendish, 2007.

Habegger, Larry & O'Reilly, Sean, Eds. *Travelers' Tales Guides: Paris*. San Francisco, James O'Reilly, Travelers' Tales, 1997.

Morton, Brian N.: *Americans in Paris: An Anecdotal Street Guide*. Ann Arbor, Olivia & Hill Press, 1984.

White, Edmund: *The Flâneur: A Stroll through the Paradoxes of Paris*. London, Bloomsbury Publishing Plc, 2001.

is over and my kid and kid-in-law head once more for the plane, I will swing into real travel mode. Lists will certainly diminish as everything gets done and I let myself feel the excitement of the adventure to come. *Give in to it,* I admonish myself. *Don't always fight everything so hard.*

But what on earth can I tell people in the States that I did this year? Exotic things they might imagine (wrongly) as Parisian? More than that I worked at my desk and drank my tea and hung out with my friends. Okay, this year I explored every inch of Paris, tried dozens of restaurants, and wrote a book. I went to French films and to weird concerts. Of course, the museums, the readings at the library and the Village Voice. And I spent much of the summer reading in the lovely Luxembourg (before and after my doze). But although I think I can make my point, in retrospect to me, it doesn't sound like a lot, but the year was too short to do more.

I could just say, though—for these would do the trick—that I barged for ten days in Flanders and went to an ancient gin distillery. That I took a day-trip to Mont-St-Michel. (Omitting mention of Lou.) I could try to convey what sitting in that great Sénat chamber with Jean-Pierre meant to me, whether they have ever heard of Paul Ricoeur or not. And I could say that I made a new French friend.

But how can I explain my own private triumphs in figuring out ever more about what, indeed, may be a new "hometown?" I may not be up to *le systeme D*, but I am making definite progress in the *ABCs*. Will they grasp that I finally enjoyed the French films I saw as much as the American ones, now that my French has moved up a notch? Or that a few streets I hadn't seen before sent me into waves of nostalgia for a life I have never known? Or how sitting in that gorgeous *jardin* under a shading plane tree can fill me with such peace and goodwill, which I so desperately need? And just how can I describe that elusive feeling of anticipation that I might burst out of my skin?

As we walk slowly back along boulevard St-Germain, Caroline thanks me for treating her to lunch, celebrating, as I claimed, the end of my work for this year. "But this is the last time," she says. "It looks like J-P will offer me an advance on my book pretty soon."

Then she sees my face. "No, no, I'm not near finished with the book. You haven't heard much about Whistler, or Henry Adams, or even Edna St. Vincent Millay." So, I am relieved. Scheherazade will keep me hooked for perhaps 1001 nights.

And," Caroline goes on, as we turn down rue de Seine, "Edith Wharton, of course."

"Of course! I forgot about her!" And it's true, for in my litany, I forgot one evening in spring when we had met the boys at the library to hear the American writer Louis Auchincloss speak about Wharton's life here. About how she was one of the founders of the library. Afterward, the four of us walked down avenue de la Bourdonnais into the back of a grocery, to a restaurant that specializes in *foie gras.* Each table has a toaster, so everyone's toast is always hot. Afterward, having parted with kisses, the boys went up to avenue Marceau, and Caroline and I took the No. 96 back to Montparnasse and then a long stroll home in the evening spring air.

So, I'm eager to get on with it, to get away, to be on the move. But it seems I'm already looking further ahead, to being back. (So much for living in the present.) And just what will the next year bring? A new apartment? A wedding in June. A newsletter to edit and maybe more trips to the synagogue (or maybe not). Proofs to read and perhaps a new project—work or otherwise—to conceive. Helping Caroline when it's time. And, of course, my old uncles Klaus and Paul, who really do need me, now. A trip to Rome with them, and perhaps a midnight spaghetti party on the beach? Definitely playing with cousins on the barge in the spring. A French friend (who makes lemon squares), perhaps. Digging potatoes on Edie's farm? No wonder the years pass so quickly in my mind. It occurs to me to stretch out my walk this afternoon and detour through rue Guisarde, but I don't.

As I am walking up the stairs, I imagine I hear the floorboards squeak above. I know it's not true, for I still have those keys Luca pressed upon me. I haven't forgotten for a moment where they are, stuffed in the back of my desk drawer. I have a pang of loneliness, of emptiness, perhaps. But I shake it off. I've had enough of this. Maybe there will be a new neighbor in the new year? But right now, I only have thirty-six hours to go.

So, the day before Thanksgiving, I spend the early morning cleaning (even without a project at hand), setting out dishes, wanting to get everything just right. I email the manuscript and make sure everything is backed up. The Plan of Attack gets taken down and put in my file. A huge sense of freedom overcomes me as I walk out the door. The No. 87 takes me to the Real McCoy for the pecan pie (and a hugely expensive box of imported Grape Nuts), and then I get back on the bus to go home.

And by evening, everything is in order. The fretting has yet to begin. I feel relaxed, with nothing to do. I go into the bedroom (which has fresh flowers on the dresser), and I pick up a book about Paris in the Twenties (before I stow it in my bookcase, for good). I sit in the chair with the footstool, and I leaf through the pages. It's almost impossible to keep up interest now that my own book is finished and gone.

But does Life ever leave me alone? (And do I actually wish it would?) After just a few minutes, I come across a quote from that same Miss Stein. Somehow, I can't imagine why, I had thought that she and I were through. But as other things have done in this rather tumultuous year, it stops me in my tracks. "There ain't no answer," she seems to have said about something or other in her genius way, I don't know what. "There ain't gonna be any answer. There never has been an answer. That's the answer."

I sit for a few minutes with the book on my knees. *Who actually cares? Haven't I done enough for one year? Do I have to be responsible for the soul of Miss* Stein? *Don't I have enough trouble with my own?* I remember what Klaus said once to Caroline, "Life is the only fulltime job." With some finality, I put the book away, and I take a shower, not a bath.

On Thursday morning, the big day itself, the phone rings at *8h.* I am wide-awake, dressed, and poised for settings, and I'm thinking of giving a last minute dust here and there. The phone must be my son ringing from the airport to tell me that they

> **ABOUT THE AUTHOR**
>
> After a career in both American magazine and book publishing, Fran Gendlin now writes travel guides to Rome, Paris, and San Francisco for the *Culture Shock!* series. She lives in Paris ~~at the moment~~, and in winter also enjoys the beaches of Mexico.

have just arrived. (It certainly isn't Luca, and what would I say if it were?) But it is Richard. At first I am surprised, but then I realize that it is only 11:00 p.m. in Sausalito, and he is calling before he goes to bed. "Happy Thanksgiving, Fran," he says, and I am pleased to hear his voice. Although I do not want to stay too long on the phone, I relay the conversation with Freifeld, adding no editorial comments of my own, thanks to Caroline's common sense.

"Thanks for trying," he says. "That's all we can do. But that's not really why I called. Listen, Fran," he says, and then stops for an instant. "I've been wondering."

"Oui?" (Even Richard understands that.)

"I've been wondering if when I'm back just after the New Year, you'd like to come with me for a long weekend to taste some wines in Burgundy? It's time you learned a thing or two about French wines. And maybe about me, if you get my drift."

After a long—too long—silence on my part, during which I am considering every ramification of this astonishing but not at all unpleasant suggestion, Richard asks again, "So, what do you think? Would you like to spend a few days with me at Château Chorey-les-Beaune? It's lovely when the weather is good, and we could rent a car and buzz around for some wine tasting? It would be nice to spend time together, just the two of us. Hello, Fran? Are you there?" Then, after another moment, and from six thousand miles away, I hear one of Richard's familiar, tolerant laughs. "Fran? You're not taking stock, are you?"

Who me? And *moi,* do I get his drift? *Oh, là là là là là là.*

Acknowledgments

THIS BOOK COULD NEVER EVEN HAVE begun to take shape without the presence in my daily life of true historical *personages* such as Benjamin Franklin and Thomas Jefferson, two of the first Americans to call Paris home—whose reasons for coming were statecraft, but whose writings showed how much they appreciated their Paris lives, even then. I bring them to mind often as I walk on streets they might also have trod, and I thank them for having made their country so welcome in this city that even two hundred years later Americans can continue to live off their legacy and still easily call Paris home.

In this regard, I am especially grateful to Gertrude Stein, who lived in Paris all her adult life, except when the Nazi occupation forced her out to the countryside. That she spent many years trying to grasp the essence of the city and wrote about her observations in *Paris France* made my own quest easier—and more fun. The same holds true for Miss Stein's sometime friend Ernest Hemingway and his book *A Moveable Feast*. From time to time within the book I question their opinions, but with no disrespect intended. Paris speaks to each person with a different voice.

I read dozens of books while writing the guidebook that is described herein, but three were of particular use in figuring out how Americans have benefited from the continuing epic that is Paris. As an American I am glad these works documented so clearly the presence of Americans here over the centuries—and as a writer that I came across them. *American Footprints in Paris,* by François Boucher, then the assistant curator of the Musée Carnavelet (translated by Frances Wilson Huard and published by the George H. Doran Company, 1921) details how Americans fit into the life of Paris from the first of our countrymen to come here through about the end of World War I, indicating the streets and buildings in which they lived. Brian N. Morton's *Americans in Paris* (Olivia and Hill Press, 1986) does the same until our current era, and is as the subtitle informs us: *An Anecdotal Street Guide*. Last of these three, Stephen Longstreet's chatty narrative *We All Went to Paris: Americans in the City of Light: 1776-1971* (Macmillian, 1972) tells stories of those same—and other—Americans but more personally, interlacing history with humor and the gossip of the day throughout.

For help in keeping me and this book grounded in this new Parisian century, I send *bisous* especially to the ever-patient Virginia Crosby, Jean Coyner, and Helen Cohn. I would like to thank my first reader Joyce Engelson for her encouragement, John Crossman, Karina Veal, and Dana Zeller-Alexis for their suggestions, and Christina Crosby, Mary Duncan, Pepi Granat, Diane Johnson, James Keough, Matt Spencer, Steven Weinstein and Maya Windholz, all of whom had questions or comments as I went along. Colette and the late Claude Samama, Newby Schweitzer, and Marietta Wheaton read parts of early drafts, as well. Thanks also to Joy Eckel for her meticulous editing, Dominic Ambrose for his patience while working on the amazing cover, Andrea Valerio for her photo of rue Servandoni, and Robert Stahman for the cover photo.

Spending several weeks writing at the peaceful Moulin d'Andé Centre Culturel in Normandy helped me to finish the book, and I am grateful to Suzanne Lipinska and Maurice Pons for their kindnesses to me while I was there.

I would also like here to remember some Paris friends, Jean and Warren Trabant, who didn't live to see themselves portrayed as Alice and Findlay Lovell, and who are greatly missed in the area around rue Guisarde. And Muriel Pulitzer who for some fifty years quietly sculpted only angels and saints in her atelier hidden at the top of the Church of St-Sulpice.

I am extremely grateful to my longtime friend Fred Hill who suggested this project to me over that glass of champagne in San Francisco, but who, I think, didn't expect me to take it in the direction that I did. Fred, I hope you're pleased. And to the late Carol Houck Smith, who for thirty years was consistently encouraging of my work and, last, of this book. I am grateful above all for her friendship.

And, of course, I think of my family whom I have perhaps neglected by moving to Paris, but who have been supportive throughout nonetheless, and who have withstood several years of a certain distraction and preoccupation with my somewhat imagined self. You have my abiding love.

Made in the USA
Lexington, KY
28 November 2010